The Collected Plays of
Edward
Albee

The Collected Plays o

Edward Albee

1966-77

A Delicate Balance
Everything in the Garden
Box and *Quotations from*
Chairman Mao Tse-Tung
All Over
Seascape
Listening
Counting the Ways
The Lady from Dubuque

OVERLOOK DUCKWORTH
New York • London

First published paperback in the United States in 2008 by
Overlook Duckworth, Peter Mayer Publishers, Inc.
New York, Woodstock, and New York

NEW YORK:
Overlook Press
141 Wooster Street
New York, NY 10012
www.overlookpress.com

LONDON:
Duckworth
90-93 Cowcross Street
London EC1M 6BF
www.ductnet.co.uk

Cataloging-in-Publication Data is available from the Library of Congress

Book design and type formatting by Bernard Schleifer
Manufactured in the United States of America
FIRST EDITION
3 5 7 9 8 6 4 2
ISBN 978-1-59020-053-7 (US)
ISBN 978-0-71563-799-9 (UK)

Contents

NOTE: The plays contained within this anthology include some changes the author has made over the years. Although he may revisit these texts again one day, he considers them to be, at this point, the definitive versions for both reading and performance.

Introduction

THIS IS VOLUME 2 OF A PROJECTED THREE-VOLUME EDITION OF MY plays so far—twenty-seven dating from 1958 to 2003. Assuming that I live forever (I am seventy-six, this being 2004), there will be Volumes 4, 5, etc.

The plays in Volume 1 could be called early plays; those in this volume early mid-period; and the ones in Volume 3 late mid-period. The late plays will have to wait until later.

In my introduction Volume 1, I devoted several paragraphs to musing about my career, its ups and downs, and why I do not talk about my methods. These paragraphs apply to *all* of my plays, but the publisher of these volumes decided not to repeat them here. They do remain available in Volume 1, however.

The eight plays collected here include one adaptation, an Americanization of a British play, *Everything in the Garden* by the late Giles Cooper. My producers—Richard Barr and Clinton Wilder—asked me to take an hour or so out of my schedule and reset the play in the United States and do whatever other minor fixing might be necessary. Several months later I finished the work, with barely a line of the source play unaltered, and with several other socio-cultural changes, leaving little more than the spine of Mr. Cooper's play intact.

I particularly enjoyed changing the name and nationality of the whore mistress from a German-Jewish refugee in Mr. Cooper's play to an upper-class British lady named Mrs. Toothe (nothing sharper than?) in celebration of British subtle anti-Semitism.

The play was quite successful commercially, largely in part due to a film sale. The film was never made, which pleased me greatly, considering who they had planned to have star in it.

Listening was commissioned by the BBC and an American radio group called Earplay, as a radio play. Taking note of Samuel Beckett's ingenious idea of writing a play that would be equally effective on the radio and on the stage (as he did with *Embers*) I wrote mine with the same duality of purpose. I prefer it on stage, where, unfortunately, it is performed infrequently, perhaps because it is a fairly dense work.

Box and *Quotations from Chairman Mao Tse Tung* are separate plays and are one play at the same time. *Box* was written first; then *Quotations from Chairman Mao Tse Tung* occurred. Each has its own identity and can be performed without the other. However, it seemed to me that combining the two (as they are printed here) more than doubled the experience of the two separately. *Box* is performed now and then by itself, and the two together no more frequently, which is a shame as I am very proud of the attempts they made to expand the boundaries of theatre—clearly my "dense" period.

Counting the Ways was composed to be done with *Listening*—before it—as a nicely varied evening. It has proved to be far more popular by itself, at least without *Listening*. It was performed most recently, in New York City, very successfully on a bill with, and following, three short plays by Beckett. Perhaps what I have written is a "curtain lowerer" rather than the curtain raiser I had supposed. It had its professional premiere in London, at the National Theatre, where, for reasons having to do with either malice or insanity, it was—all 45 minutes of it—done in the huge Olivier Theatre all by itself! It is a delicate play, for all its toughness, and did not do well. I am quite proud of it—the play, not the London experience.

The four *other* plays (*A Delicate Balance*, *All Over*, *Seascape*, and *The Lady from Dubuque*) are quite straightforward—naturalistic, one might say, except that there is no such thing as naturalism in the theatre, merely degrees of stylization.

A Delicate Balance and *Seascape* have proved to be the most popular of the four, though revival has bolstered the reputation of them all.

A Delicate Balance concerns itself with a comfortable family invaded by reality long after they are capable of dealing with the invasion.

All Over examines the dregs of a family during the deathwatch of its most important member.

The Lady From Dubuque deals with the question of whether our reality is determined by our need and is not an absolute.

Seascape wonders whether we are an evolving species or perhaps a devolving one. Two lizards; two humans.

As you can see—family plays all.

The three volumes of this collection will take you through the corpus and bring you up to date. I hope you will have as much enjoyment as I have had.

—EDWARD ALBEE
New York City
October 4, 2004

A Delicate Balance

For John Steinbeck
Affection and admiration

A DELICATE BALANCE

—A Non-reconsideration

My mind is going, I suspect; I have no idea how long I've known most of my friends; the names of most people are beyond me, and I cannot recall the emotional or physical experience of the writing of most of my plays, or how long ago the experience I cannot recall occurred.

The only senses I fully retain—and very sharply these—are picture images and sounds. Hearing two bars of almost any piece of serious music has me naming the composer, the piece, and often the date of composition and opus number—or K., or Hoboken, or whatever. Seeing a painting for a second time—in a new context, of course—has me instantly recalling on what wall it hung, in what room, in what country, when I saw it first.

But names and events . . . that's another matter. Once I looked straight at my mother and couldn't figure out who she was. (Well, I guess we've all had that one!)

So . . . is it *really* thirty years since the first production of *A Delicate Balance?* It seems like yesterday, as they say? No, certainly not . . . but thirty years?

The play has not changed; that *I* can see. I've had to rewrite only two lines—making it clear that topless bathing suits (for women, of course) are not made anymore, and changing "our dear Republicans as dull as ever" to "as brutal as ever" (that second change long overdue).

The play does not seem to have "dated"; rather, its points seem clearer now to more people than they were in its lovely first production. Now, in its lovely new production (I will not say "revival"; the thing was not dead—unseen, unheard perhaps, but lurking), it seems to me exactly the same experience. No time has passed; the characters have not aged or become strange. (The upper-upper middle-class WASP culture has *always* been just a little bizarre, of course.)

The play concerns—as it always has, in spite of early-on critical mis-understanding—the rigidity and ultimate paralysis which afflicts those who settle in too easily, waking up one day to discover that all the choices they have avoided no longer give them any freedom of choice, and that what choices they do have left are beside the point.

I have become odder with time, I suppose (my next play but one will be about a goat, for God's sake), but *A Delicate Balance,* bless it, does not seem to have changed much—aged nicely, perhaps. Could we all say the same.

—Edward Albee
Montauk, N.Y.
August 1996

A Delicate Balance opened in New York City on September 12, 1966, at the Martin Beck Theatre.

JESSICA TANDY *as* AGNES

HUME CRONYN *as* TOBIAS

ROSEMARY MURPHY *as* CLAIRE

CARMEN MATHEWS *as* EDNA

HENDERSON FORSYTHE *as* HARRY

MARIAN SELDES *as* JULIA

Directed by ALAN SCHNEIDER

The Lincoln Center Theatre production of *A Delicate Balance* opened in New York City on April 21, 1996, at the Plymouth Theatre.

ROSEMARY HARRIS *as* AGNES

GEORGE GRIZZARD *as* TOBIAS

ELAINE STRITCH *as* CLAIRE

ELIZABETH WILSON *as* EDNA

JOHN CARTER *as* HARRY

MARY BETH HURT *as* JULIA

Directed by GERALD GUTIERREZ

CHARACTERS

AGNES
A handsome woman in her late 50's

TOBIAS
Her husband, a few years older

CLAIRE
Agnes' sister, several years younger

JULIA
Agnes' and Tobias' daughter 36, angular

EDNA AND HARRY
Very much like Agnes and Tobias

THE SCENE
The living room of a large and well-appointed suburban house.
Now.

ACT ONE

(In the library-living room. AGNES *in a chair,* TOBAIS *at a shelf, looking into cordial bottles)*

AGNES

(Speaks usually softly, with a tiny hint of a smile on her face: not sardonic, not sad . . . wistful, maybe)

What I find most astonishing—aside from that belief of mine, which never ceases to surprise me by the very fact of its surprising lack of unpleasantness, the belief that I might very easily—as they say—lose my mind one day, not that I suspect I am about to, or am even . . . nearby . . .

TOBIAS

(He speaks somewhat the same way)

There is no saner woman on earth, Agnes.

(Putters at the bottles)

AGNES

. . . for I'm not that sort; merely that it is not beyond . . . happening: some gentle loosening of the moorings sending the balloon adrift—and I think that is the only outweighing thing: adrift; the . . . becoming a stranger in . . . the world, quite . . . uninvolved, for I never see it as violent, only a drifting—what are you looking for, Tobias?

TOBIAS

We will all go mad before you. The anisette.

AGNES *(A small happy laugh)*

Thank you, darling. But I could never do it—go adrift—for what would become of you? Still, what I find most astonishing, aside, as I said, from that speculation—and I wonder, too, sometimes, if I am the only one of you to admit to it: not that *I* may go mad, but that each of you wonders if each of *you* might not—why on earth do you want anisette?

TOBIAS *(Considers)*

I thought it might be nice.

AGNES *(Wrinkles her nose)*

Sticky. I will do cognac. It is supposed to be healthy—the speculation, or the assumption, I suppose, that if it occurs to you that you might be, then you are not; but I've never been much comforted by it; it follows, to my mind, that since I speculate I might, some day, or early evening I think more likely—some autumn dusk—go quite mad, then I very well might.

(Bright laugh)

Some autumn dusk: Tobias at his desk, looks up from all those awful bills, and sees his Agnes, mad as a hatter, chewing the ribbons on her dress . . .

TOBIAS *(Pouring)*

Cognac?

AGNES

Yes; Agnes Sit-by-the-fire, her mouth full of ribbons, her mind aloft, adrift; nothing to do with the poor old thing but put her in a bin somewhere, sell the house, move to Tucson, say, and pine in the good sun, and live to be a hundred and four.

(He gives her her cognac)

Thank you, darling.

TOBIAS *(Kisses her forehead)*

Cognac is sticky, too.

AGNES

Yes, but it's nicer. Sit by me, hm?

TOBIAS *(Does so; raises his glass)*

To my mad lady, ribbons dangling.

AGNES *(Smiles)*

And, of course, I haven't worn the ribbon dress since Julia's remarriage. Are you comfortable?

TOBIAS

For a little.

AGNES

What astonishes me most—aside from my theoretically healthy fear—no, not fear, how silly of me—healthy speculation that I might some day become an embarrassment to you . . . what I find most astonishing in this world, and with all my years . . . is Claire.

TOBIAS *(Curious)*

Claire? Why?

AGNES

That anyone—be they one's sister, or not—can be so . . . well, I don't want to use an unkind word, 'cause we're cozy here, aren't we?

TOBIAS (*Smiled warning*)

Maybe.

AGNES

As the saying has it, the one thing sharper than a serpent's tooth is a sister's ingratitude.

TOBIAS

(*Getting up, moving to a chair*)
The saying does not have it that way.

AGNES

Should. Why are you moving?

TOBIAS

It's getting uncomfortable.

AGNES (*Semi-serious razzing*)
Things get hot, move off, huh? Yes?

TOBIAS (*Not rising to it*)
I'm not as young as either of us once was.

AGNES (*Toasting him*)
I'm as young as the day I married you—though I'm certain I don't look it—because you're a very good husband . . . most of the time. But I was talking about Claire, or was beginning to.

TOBIAS

(*Knowing shaking of the head*)
Yes, you were.

AGNES

If I were to list the mountain of my burdens—if I had a thick pad and a month to spare—that bending my shoulders *most,* with the possible exception of Julia's trouble with marriage, would be your—it must be instinctive, I think, or *reflex,* that's more like it—your reflex defense of everything that Claire . . .

TOBIAS

(*Very nice, but there is steel underneath*)
Stop it, Agnes.

AGNES (*A little laugh*)
Are you going to throw something at me? Your glass? My goodness, I hope not . . . that awful anisette all over everything.

TOBIAS (*Patient*)

No.

AGNES (*Quietly daring him*)
What then?

TOBIAS (*Looking at his hand*)

I shall sit very quietly . . .

AGNES

. . . as always . . .

TOBIAS

. . . yes, and I shall will you to apologize to your sister for what I must in truth tell you I thought a most . . .

AGNES

Apologize! To her? To Claire? I have spent my adult life apologizing *for* her; I will not double my humiliation by apologizing *to* her.

TOBIAS (*Mocking an epigram*)

One does not apologize to those for whom one must?

AGNES (*Winking slowly*)

Neat.

TOBIAS

Succinct, but one of the rules of an aphorism . . .

AGNES

An epigram, I thought.

TOBIAS (*Small smile*)

An epigram is usually satiric, and you . . .

AGNES

. . . and I am grimly serious. Yes?

TOBIAS

I fear so.

AGNES

To revert specifically from Claire to . . . her effect, what *would* you do were I to . . . spill my marbles?

TOBIAS (*Shrugs*)

Put you in a bin somewhere, sell the house and move to Tucson. Pine in the hot sun and live forever.

AGNES (*Ponders it*)

Hmmm, I bet you would.

TOBIAS (*Friendly*)

Hurry, though.

AGNES

Oh, I'll *try*. It won't be simple paranoia, though, I know that. I've tried so hard, to . . . well, you know how little I vary; goodness, I can't even raise my voice except in the most calamitous of events, and I find that both joy and sorrow work their . . . wonders on me more . . . evenly, slowly, with*in*, than

most: a suntan rather than a scalding. There are no mountains in my life . . .
nor chasms. It is a rolling, pleasant land . . . verdant, my darling, thank you.

TOBIAS *(Cutting a cigar)*

We do what we can.

AGNES *(Little laugh)*

Our motto. If we should ever go downhill, have a crest made, join things,
we must have that put in Latin—We do what we can—on your blazers,
over the mantel; maybe we could do it on the linen, as well . . .

TOBIAS

Do you think I should go to Claire's room?

AGNES *(Silence: then stony, firm)*

No.

   (TOBIAS shrugs, lights his cigar)

Either she will be down, or not.

TOBIAS

We do what we can?

AGNES

Of course.

   (Silence)

So, it will not be simple paranoia. Schizophrenia, on the other hand, is far
more likely—even given the unlikelihood. I believe it can be chemically
induced . . .

   (Smiles)

if all else should fail; if sanity, such as it is, should become too much. There
are times when I think it would be so . . . proper, if one could take a pill—
or even inject—just . . . remove.

TOBIAS *(Fairly dry)*

You should take drugs, my dear.

AGNES

Ah, but those are temporary; even addiction is a repeated temporary . . .
stilling. I am concerned with peace . . . not mere relief. And I am not a
compulsive—like . . . like some . . . like our dear Claire, say.

TOBIAS

Be kind. Please?

AGNES

I think I should want to have it fully . . . even on the chance I could not . . .
come back. Wouldn't that be terrible, though? To have done it, induced, if
naturally looked unlikely and the hope was there?

   (Wonder in her voice)

Not be able to come back? Why did you put my cognac in the tiny glass?

TOBIAS *(Rising, going to her)*

Oh . . . I'm sorry. . . .

AGNES

(Holding her glass out to him; he takes it from her)

I'm not a sipper tonight; I'm a breather: my nose buried in the glass, all the wonder there, and very silent.

TOBIAS

(Getting her a new cognac)

I thought Claire was much better tonight. I didn't see any need for you to give her such a going-over.

AGNES *(Weary)*

Claire was *not* better tonight. Honestly, Tobias!

TOBIAS

(Clinging to his conviction)

I thought she was.

AGNES *(Putting an end to it)*

Well, she was *not*.

TOBIAS

Still . . .

AGNES

(Taking her new drink)

Thank you. I have decided, all things considered, that I shall not induce, that all the years we have put up with each other's wiles and crotchets have earned us each other's company. And I promise you as well that I shall think good thoughts—healthy ones, positive—to ward off madness, should it come by . . . uninvited.

TOBIAS *(Smiles)*

You mean I have no hope of Tucson?

AGNES

None.

TOBIAS *(Mock sadness)*

Hélas . . .

AGNES

You have hope, only, of growing even older than you are in the company of your steady wife, your alcoholic sister-in-law and occasional visits . . . from our melancholy Julia.

(A little sad)

That is what you have, my dear Tobias. Will it do?

TOBIAS

(A little sad, too, but warmth)
It will do.

AGNES *(Happy)*
I've never doubted that it would.
(Hears something, says sourly)
Hark.
(CLAIRE has entered)
Did I hear someone?

TOBIAS

(Sees CLAIRE standing, uncomfortably, away from them)
Ah, there you are. I said to Agnes just a moment ago . . .

CLAIRE

(To AGNES' back, a rehearsed speech, gone through but hated)
I must apologize, Agnes; I'm . . . very sorry.

AGNES

(Not looking at her; mock surprise)
But what are you sorry *for*, Claire?

CLAIRE

I apologize that my nature is such to bring out in you the full force of your
brutality.

TOBIAS *(To placate)*
Look, now, I think we can do without any of this sort of . . .

AGNES

(Rises from her chair, proceeds toward exiting)
If you come to the dinner table unsteady, *if* when you try to say good
evening and weren't the autumn colors lovely today you are nothing but
vowels, and *if* one smells the vodka on you from across the room—and
don't tell me again, *either* of you! that vodka leaves nothing on the breath:
if you are expecting it, if you are sadly and wearily expecting it, it *does*—*if*
these conditions exist . . . *persist* . . . then the reaction of one who is burdened by her love is not brutality—though it would be excused, believe
me!—not brutality at all, but the souring side of love. If I scold, it is
because I wish I needn't. If I am sharp, it is because I am neither less nor
more than human, and if I am to be accused once again of making too
much of things, let me remind you that it is my manner and not the matter. I apologize for being articulate. Tobias, I'm going to call Julia, I think.
Is it one or two hours' difference? . . . I can never recall.

TOBIAS *(Dry)*
Three.

AGNES

Ah, yes. Well, be kind to Claire, dear. She is . . . injured.

(*Exits. A brief silence*)

TOBIAS

Ah, well.

CLAIRE

I have never known whether to applaud or cry. Or, rather, I never know which would be the more appreciated—expected.

TOBIAS (*Rather sadly*)

You are a great damn fool.

CLAIRE (*Sadly*)

Yes. Why is she calling Julia?

TOBIAS

Do you want a quick brandy before she comes back?

CLAIRE (*Laughs some*)

Not at all; a public one. Fill the balloon half up, and I shall sip it ladylike, and when she . . . glides back in, I shall lie on the floor and balance the glass on my forehead. That will give her occasion for another paragraph, and your ineffectual stop-it-now's.

TOBIAS

(*Pouring her brandy*)

You *are* a great damn fool.

CLAIRE

Is Julia having another divorce?

TOBIAS

Hell, I don't know.

CLAIRE (*Takes the glass*)

It's only your daughter. Thank you. I should imagine—from all that I have . . . watched, that it is come-home time.

(*Offhand*)

Why don't you kill Agnes?

TOBIAS (*Very offhand*)

Oh, no, I couldn't do that.

CLAIRE

Better still, why don't you wait till Julia separates and comes back here, all sullen and confused, and take a gun and blow all our heads off? . . . Agnes first—through respect, of course, then poor Julia, and finally—if you have the kindness for it—me?

TOBIAS *(Kind, triste)*

Do you really want me to shoot you?

CLAIRE

I want you to shoot Agnes first. Then I'll think about it.

TOBIAS

But it would have to be an act of passion—out of my head, and all that. I doubt I'd stand around with the gun smoking, Julia locked in her room screaming, wait for you to decide if you wanted it or not.

CLAIRE

But unless you kill Agnes . . . how will I ever know whether I want to live?
(Incredulous)
An act of passion!?

TOBIAS *(Rather hurt)*

Well . . . yes.

CLAIRE *(Laughs)*

Oh, my; *that's* funny.

TOBIAS *(Same)*

I'm sorry.

CLAIRE *(Friendly laugh)*

Oh, my darling Tobias, *I'm* sorry, but I just don't see you in the role, that's all—outraged, maddened into action, proceeding by reflex . . . Can you see yourself, though? In front of the judge? Predictable, stolid Tobias? "It all went blank, your honor. One moment, there I was, deep in my chair, drinking my. . ." What is that?

TOBIAS

Anisette.

CLAIRE

"Anisette." Really? Anisette?

TOBIAS *(Slightly edgy)*

I *like* it.

CLAIRE *(Wrinkles her nose)*

Sticky. "There I was, your honor, one moment in my chair, sipping at my anisette . . . and the next thing I knew . . . they were all lying about, different rooms, heads blown off, the gun still in my hand. I . . . I have no recollection of it, sir." Can you imagine that, Tobias?

TOBIAS

Of course, with all of you dead, your brains lying around in the rugs, there'd be no one to say it *wasn't* an act of passion.

CLAIRE

Leave me till last. A breeze might rise and stir the ashes. . . .

TOBIAS

Who's that?

CLAIRE

No one, I think. Just sounds like it should be.

TOBIAS

Why don't you go back to your . . . thing . . . to your alcoholics thing?

CLAIRE *(Half serious)*

Because I don't like the people. . . .

TOBIAS

What is it called?

CLAIRE

Anonymous.

TOBIAS

Yes; that. Why don't you go back?

CLAIRE *(Suddenly rather ugly)*

Why don't you mind your own hooting business?

TOBIAS *(Offended)*

I'm sorry, Claire.

CLAIRE *(Kisses at him)*

Because.

TOBIAS

It was better.

CLAIRE

(Holds her glass out; he hesitates)

Be a good brother-in-law; it's only the first I'm not supposed to have.

TOBIAS *(Pouring for her)*

I thought it was better.

CLAIRE

Thank you.

(Lies on the floor, balances glass on her forehead, puts it beside her, etc.)

You mean Agnes thought it was better.

TOBIAS *(Kindly, calmly)*

No, I thought so too. That it would be.

CLAIRE

I told you: not our type; nothing in common with them. When you used to go to business—before you became a squire, parading around the ancestoral manse in jodhpurs, confusing the gardener . . .

TOBIAS (*Hurt*)

I've never done any such thing.

CLAIRE

Before all that . . .

(*Smiles, chuckles*)

sweet Tobias. . . when you used to spend all your time in town . . . with your business friends, your indistinguishable if not necessarily similar friends . . . what did you have in common with them?

TOBIAS

Well, uh . . . well, everything.

(*Maybe slightly on the defensive, but more . . . vague*)

Our business; we all mixed well, were friends away from the office, too . . . clubs, our . . . an, an environment, I guess.

CLAIRE

Unh-huh. But what did you have in common with them? Even Harry: your very best friend . . . in all the world—as far as you know; I mean, you haven't met everybody . . . are you switching from anisette?

TOBIAS (*Pouring himself brandy*)

Doesn't go for a long time. All right?

CLAIRE

Doesn't matter to *me*. Your very best friend . . . Tell me, dear Tobias; what do you have in common with him? Hm?

TOBIAS (*Softly*)

Please, Claire . . .

CLAIRE

What do you really have in common with your very best friend . . . 'cept the coincidence of having cheated on your wives in the same summer with the same woman . . . girl . . . woman? What except that? And hardly a distinction. I believe she was upended that whole July.

TOBIAS (*Rather tight-mouthed*)

If you'll forgive me, Claire, common practice is hardly . . .

CLAIRE

Poor girl, poor whatever-she-was that hot and very *wet* July.

(*Hard*)

The distinction would have been to have not: to have been the one or two of the very, very many and oh, God, similar who did not upend the poor . . . unfamiliar thing that dry and oh, so wet July.

TOBIAS

Please! Agnes!

CLAIRE *(Quieter)*

Of course, you had the wanton only once, while Harry! Good friend Harry, I have it from the horse's mouth, was on top for good and keeps twice, with a third try not so hot in the gardener's shed, with the mulch, or whatever it is, and the orange pots . . .

TOBIAS *(Quietly)*

Shut your mouth.

CLAIRE

(Stands, faces TOBIAS; *softly)*
All right.
(Down again)
What was her name?

TOBIAS *(A little sad)*

I don't remember.

CLAIRE *(Shrugs)*

No matter; she's gone.
(Brighter)
Would you give friend Harry the shirt off your back, as they say?

TOBIAS

(Relieved to be on something else)
I *suppose* I would. He *is* my best friend.

CLAIRE *(Nicely)*

How sad does that make you?

TOBIAS

(Looks at her for a moment, then)
Not much; some; not much.

CLAIRE

No one to listen to Bruckner with you; no one to tell you're sick of golf; no one to admit to that—now and then—you're suddenly frightened and you don't know why?

TOBIAS *(Mild surprise)*

Frightened? No.

CLAIRE *(Pause; smile)*

All right. Would you like to know what happened last time I climbed the stairs to the fancy alkie club, and why I've not gone back? What I have *not* in common with those people?

TOBIAS *(Not too enthusiastic)*

Sure.

CLAIRE *(Chuckle)*

Poor Tobias. "Sure." Light me a cigarette?

(TOBIAS hesitates a moment, then lights her one)

That will give me everything.

(He hands the lighted cigarette to her; she is still on the floor)

I need. A smoke, a sip and a good hard surface. Thank you.

(Laughs a bit at that)

TOBIAS *(Standing over her)*

Comfy?

CLAIRE

(Raises her two arms, one with the cigarette, the other the brandy glass; it is a casual invitation. TOBIAS looks at her for a moment, moves a little away)

Very. Do you remember the spring I moved out, the time I was *really* sick with the stuff: was drinking like the famous fish? Was a source of great embarrassment? So that you and Agnes set me up in the apartment near the station, and Agnes was *so* good about coming to see me?

(TOBIAS sighs heavily)

Sorry.

TOBIAS *(Pleading a little)*

When will it all . . . just go in the past . . . forget itself?

CLAIRE

When all the defeats are done, admitted. When memory takes over and corrects fact . . . makes it tolerable. When Agnes lies on her deathbed.

TOBIAS

Do you know that Agnes has . . . such wonderful control I haven't seen her cry in . . . for the longest time . . . no matter what?

CLAIRE

Warn me when she's coming; I'll act drunk. Pretend you're very sick, Tobias, like you were with the stomach business, but pretend you feel your insides are all green, and stink, and mixed up, and your eyes hurt and you're half deaf and your brain keeps turning off, and you've got peripheral neuritis and you can hardly walk and you hate. You hate with the same green stinking sickness you feel your bowels have turned into . . . yourself, and *everybody*. Hate, and, oh, God!! you want love, l-o-v-e, so badly—comfort and snuggling is what you really mean, of course—but you hate, and you notice—with a sort of detachment that amuses you, you think—that you're more like an animal every day . . . you snarl, and *grab* for things, and hide things and forget where you hid them like not-very-bright dogs, and you wash less, prefer to *be* washed, and once or twice you've actually soiled your bed and laid in it because you can't get up . . . pretend all that. No, you don't like that, Tobias?

TOBIAS

I don't know why you want to . . .

CLAIRE

You want to know what it's like to be an alkie, don't you, boy?

TOBIAS *(Sad)*

Sure.

CLAIRE

Pretend all that. So the guy you're spending your bottles with starts you going to the old A.A. And, you sit there at the alkie club and watch the . . . better ones—not recovered, for once an alkie, always, and you'd better remember it, or you're gone the first time you pass a saloon—you watch the better ones get up and tell their stories.

TOBIAS *(Wistful, triste)*

Once you drop . . . you can come back up part way . . . but never . . . really back again. Always . . . descent.

CLAIRE

(Gently, to a child)
Well, that's life, baby.

TOBIAS

You are a great, damn fool.

CLAIRE

But, I'm not an alcoholic. I am not now and never was.

TOBIAS *(Shaking his head)*
All the promise . . . all the chance . . .

CLAIRE

It would be so much simpler if I *were*. An alcoholic.
(She will rise and re-enact during this)
So, one night, one month, sometime, I'd had one martini—as a Test to see if I could—which, given my . . . stunning self-discipline, had become three, and I felt . . . rather daring and nicely detached and a little bigger than life and not snarling yet. So I marched, more or less straight, straight up to the front of the room, hall, and faced my peers. And I looked them over—all of them, trying so hard, grit and guilt and failing and trying again and loss . . . and I had a moment's—sweeping—pity and disgust, and I almost cried, but I didn't—like sister like sister, by God—and I heard myself say, in my little-girl voice—and there were a lot of different me's by then—"I am a alcoholic."
(Little-girl voice)
"My name is Claire, and I am a alcoholic."
(Directly to TOBIAS)
You try it.

TOBIAS

(*Rather vague, but not babytatk*)

My name is . . . My name is Claire, and I am an alcoholic.

CLAIRE

A alcoholic.

TOBIAS (*Vaguer*)

A alcoholic.

CLAIRE

"My name is Claire, and I am a . . . alcoholic." Now, I was supposed to go on, *you* know, say how bad I was, and didn't want to be, and How It Happened, and What I Wanted To Happen, and Would They Help Me Help Myself . . . but I just stood there for a . . . ten seconds maybe, and then I curtsied; I made my little-girl curtsy, and on my little-girl feet I padded back to my chair.

TOBIAS

(*After a pause; embarrassedly*)

Did they laugh at you?

CLAIRE

Well, an agnostic in the holy of holies doesn't get much camaraderie, a little patronizing, maybe. Oh, they were taken by the *vaude*ville, don't misunderstand me. But the one lady was nice. She came up to me later and said, "You've taken the first step, dear."

TOBIAS (*Hopeful*)

That was nice of her.

CLAIRE (*Amused*)

She didn't say the first step toward *what*, of course. Sanity, *in*sanity, revelation, self-deception. . . .

TOBIAS (*Not much help*)

Change . . . sometimes . . . no matter what . . .

CLAIRE (*Cheerful laugh*)

Count on you, Tobias . . . snappy phrase every time. But it *hooked* me— the applause, the stage presence . . . that beginning; no school tot had more gold stars for never missing class. I went; oh, God, I *did*.

TOBIAS

But stopped.

CLAIRE

Until I learned . . .

(AGNES *enters, unobserved by either* TOBIAS *or* CLAIRE)

. . . and being a slow student then in my young middle-age, slowly . . . that I was not, nor had ever been . . . a alcoholic . . . or an. Either. What I did not have in common with those people. That they were alcoholics, and I was not. That I was just a drunk. That they couldn't help it; I could, and wouldn't. That they were sick, and I was merely . . . willful.

AGNES

I have talked to Julia.

TOBIAS

Ah! How is she?

AGNES *(Walking by* CLAIRE*)*

My, what an odd glass to put a soft drink in. Tobias, you have a quiet sense of humor, after all.

TOBIAS

Now, Agnes . . .

CLAIRE

He has not!

AGNES *(Rather heavy-handed)*

Well, it *can't* be brandy; Tobias is a grown-up, and knows far better than to . . .

CLAIRE

(Harsh, waving her glass)

A toast to you, sweet sister; I drink your—not health; persistence—in good, hard brandy, *âge inconnu.*

AGNES

(Quiet, tight smile, ignoring CLAIRE*)*

It *would* serve you right, my dear Tobias, were I to go away, drift off. You would not have a woman left about you—only Claire and Julia . . . not even people; it would serve you right.

CLAIRE *(Great mocking)*

But I'm not an alcoholic, baby!

TOBIAS

She . . . she can drink . . . a little.

AGNES

(There is true passion here; we see under the calm a little)

I WILL NOT TOLERATE IT!! I WILL NOT HAVE YOU!

(Softer but tight-lipped)

Oh, God. I wouldn't mind for a moment if you filled your bathtub with it, lowered yourself in it, DROWNED! I rather wish you would. It would give me the peace of mind to know you could do something well, thoroughly. If you want to kill yourself—then do it *right!*

TOBIAS

Please, Agnes . . .

AGNES

What I cannot stand is the selfishness! Those of you who want to die . . . .
and take your whole lives doing it.

CLAIRE

(Lazy, but with loathing under it)

Your wife is a perfectionist; they are *very* difficult to live with, these people.

. TOBIAS

(To AGNES, *a little pleading in it)*

She isn't an alcoholic . . . she says; she can drink some.

CLAIRE

(Little-child statement, but not babytalk)

I am not a alcoholic!

AGNES

We think that's very nice. We shall all rest easier to know that it is willful;
that the vomit and the tears, the muddy mind, the falls and the absences,
the cigarettes out on the tabletops, the calls from the club to come and get
you please . . . that they are all . . . willful, that it *can* be helped.

(Scathing but softly)

If you are not an alcoholic, you are beyond forgiveness.

CLAIRE *(Ibid.)*

· Well, I've been that for a long time, haven't I, sweetheart?

AGNES

(Not looking at either of them)

If we change for the worse with drink, we are an alcoholic. It is as simple
as that.

CLAIRE

And who is to say!

AGNES

I!

CLAIRE *(A litany)*

If we are to live here, on Tobias' charity, then we are subject to the will of
his wife. If we were asked, at our father's dying . . .

AGNES *(Final)*

Those are the ground rules.

CLAIRE *(A sad smile)*

Tobias?

(Pause)

Nothing?

    (Pause)

Are those the ground rules? Nothing? Too . . . settled? Too . . . dried up? Gone?

    (Nicely)

All right.

    (Back to AGNES*)*

Very well, then, Agnes, you win. I shall be an alcoholic.

    (The smile too sweet)

What are you going to do about it?

AGNES

    (Regards CLAIRE *for a moment, then decides she—*CLAIRE*—is not in the room with them.* AGNES *will ignore* CLAIRE*'s coming comments until otherwise indicated.* TOBIAS *will do this, too, but uncomfortably, embarrassedly)*

Tobias, you will be unhappy to know it, I suppose, or of mixed emotions, certainly, but Julia is coming home.

CLAIRE *(A brief laugh)*

Naturally.

TOBIAS

Yes?

AGNES

She is leaving Douglas, which is no surprise to *me*.

TOBIAS

But, wasn't Julia happy? You didn't tell me anything about . . .

AGNES

If Julia were happy, she would not be coming home. *I* don't want her here, God knows. I mean she's welcome, of course . . .

CLAIRE

Right on schedule, once every three years . . .

AGNES

    (Closes her eyes for a moment, to keep ignoring CLAIRE*)*

. . . it *is* her home, we are her parents, the *two* of us, and we have our obligations to her, and I have reached an age, Tobias, when I wish we were always alone, you and I, without . . . hangers-on . . . or anyone.

CLAIRE *(Cheerful but firm)*

Well, I'm not going.

AGNES

. . . but if she and Doug are through—and I'm not suggesting *she* is in the right—then her place is properly here, as for some it is not.

CLAIRE

One, two, three, four, down they go.

TOBIAS

Well, I'd like to talk to Doug.

AGNES

(As if the opposite answer were expected from her)
I wish you would! If you had talked to Tom, or Charlie, yes! even Charlie, or . . . uh . . .

CLAIRE

Phil?

AGNES

(No recognition of CLAIRE *helping her)*
. . . Phil, it might have done some good. If you've decided to assert yourself, finally, too late, I imagine . . .

CLAIRE

Damned if you do, damned if you don't.

AGNES

. . . Julia might, at the very least, come to think her father cares, and that might be consolation—if not help.

TOBIAS

I'll . . . I'll talk to Doug.

CLAIRE

Why don't you invite him *here?* And while you're at it, bring the others along.

AGNES *(Some reproach)*
And you might talk to Julia, too. You don't, very much.

TOBIAS

Yes.

CLAIRE *(A mocking sing-song)*
Philip loved to gamble.
Charlie loved the boys,
Tom went after women,
Douglas . . .

AGNES *(Turning on* CLAIRE*)*
Will you stop that?

CLAIRE

Ooh, I *am* here, after all. I exist!

AGNES

Why don't you go off on a vacation, Claire, now that Julia's coming home again? Why don't you go to Kentucky, or Tennessee, and visit the distiller-

ies? Or why don't you lock yourself in your room, or find yourself a bar
with an apartment in the back. . . .

CLAIRE

Or! Agnes; why don't you die?

(AGNES *and* CLAIRE *lock eyes, stay still*)

TOBIAS

(*Not rising from his chair, talks more or less to himself*)

If I saw some point to it, I might—if I saw some reason, chance. If I
thought I might . . . break through to her, and say, "Julia . . . ," but then
what would I say? "Julia . . ." Then, nothing.

AGNES

(*Breaking eye contact with* CLAIRE, *says, not looking at either*)

If we do not love someone . . . never have loved them . . .

TOBIAS (*Soft correction*)

No; there can be silence, even having.

AGNES

(*More curious than anything*)

Do you really want me dead, Claire?

CLAIRE

Wish, yes. Want? I don't know; probably, though I might regret it if I had
it.

AGNES

Remember the serpent's tooth, Tobias.

TOBIAS (*Recollection*)

The cat that I had.

AGNES

Hm?

TOBIAS

The cat that I had . . . when I was—well, a year or so before I *met* you. She
was very old; I'd had her since I was a kid; she must have been seventeen,
or more. An alley cat. She didn't like people very much, I think; when people came . . . she'd . . . pick up and walk away. She liked *me;* or, rather,
when I was alone with her I could see she was content; she'd sit on my lap.
I don't know if she was happy, but she was content.

AGNES

Yes.

TOBIAS

And how the thing happened I don't really know. She . . . one day she . . . well,
one day I realized she no longer liked me. No, that's not right; one day I real-

ized she must have stopped liking me some time before. One evening I was alone, home, and I was suddenly aware of her absence, not just that she wasn't in the room with me, but that she hadn't been, in rooms with me, watching me shave . . . just *about* . . . for . . . and I couldn't place *how* long. She hadn't gone *away,* you understand; well, she *had,* but she hadn't run off. I knew she was *around;* I remembered I had caught sight of her—from time to time—under a chair, moving out of a room, but it was only when I realized something had happened that I could give any pattern to things that had . . . that I'd noticed. She didn't like me any more. It was that simple.

CLAIRE

Well, she was old.

TOBIAS

No, it wasn't that. She didn't like me any more. I tried to force myself on her.

AGNES

Whatever do you mean?

TOBIAS

I'd close her in a room with me; I'd pick her up, and I'd *make* her sit in my lap; I'd make her stay there when she didn't want to. But it didn't work; she'd abide it, but she'd get down when she could, go away.

CLAIRE

Maybe she was ill.

TOBIAS

No, she wasn't; I had her to the vet. She didn't like me anymore. One night—I was *fixed* on it now—I had her in the room with me, and on my lap for the . . . the what, the fifth time the same evening, and she lay there, with her back to me, and she wouldn't purr, and I *knew:* I knew she was just waiting till she could get down, and I said, "Damn you, you like me; God damn it, you stop this! I haven't *done* anything to you." And I shook her; I had my hands around her shoulders, and I shook her . . . and she bit me; hard; and she hissed at me. And so I hit her. With my open hand, I hit her, smack, right across the head. I . . . I *hated* her!

AGNES

Did you hurt her badly?

TOBIAS

Yes; well, not badly; she . . . I must have hurt her ear some; she shook her head a lot for a day or so. And . . . you see, there was no *reason.* She and I had lived together and been, well, you know, friends, and . . . there was no *reason.* And I hated her for that. I hated her, well, I suppose because I was being accused of something, of . . . failing. But, I hadn't been cruel, by design; if I'd been neglectful, well, my life was . . . I resented it. I resented having a . . . being judged. Being *betrayed.*

CLAIRE

What did you do?

TOBIAS

I had *lived* with her; I had done . . . *everything*. And . . . and if there was a, any responsibility I'd failed in . . . well . . . there was nothing I could *do*. And, and I was being accused.

CLAIRE

Yes; what did you do?

TOBIAS

(*Defiance and self-loathing*)

I had her killed.

AGNES (*Kindly correcting*)

You had her put to sleep. She was old. You had her put to sleep.

TOBIAS (*Correcting*)

I had her killed. I took her to the vet and he took her . . . he took her into the back and

(*Louder*)

he gave her an injection and killed her! I had her *killed!*

AGNES (*After a pause*)

Well, what else could you have done? There was nothing to be done; there was no . . . meeting between you.

TOBIAS

I might have tried longer. I might have gone on, as long as cats live, the same way. I might have worn a hair shirt, locked myself in the house with her, done penance. For *something*. For *what*. God knows.

CLAIRE

You probably did the right *thing*. Distasteful alternatives; the less . . . ugly choice.

TOBIAS

Was it?

(*A silence from them all*)

AGNES (*Noticing the window*)

Was that a car in the drive?

TOBIAS

"If we do not love someone . . . never have loved someone . . ."

CLAIRE (*An abrupt, brief laugh*)

Oh, stop it! "Love" is not the problem. You love Agnes and Agnes loves Julia and Julia loves me and I love you. We all love each other; yes we do. We love each other.

TOBIAS

Yes?

CLAIRE *(Something of a sneer)*

Yes; to the depths of our self-pity and our greed. What else but love?

TOBIAS

Error?

CLAIRE *(Laughs)*

Quite possibly: love and error.

(There is a knock at the door; AGNES *answers it)*

AGNES

Edna? Harry? What a surprise! Tobias, it's Harry and Edna. Come in. Why don't you take off your . . .

*(*HARRY *and* EDNA *enter. They seem somewhat ill at ease, strained for such close friends)*

TOBIAS

Edna!

EDNA

Hello, Tobias.

HARRY

(Rubbing his hands; attempt at being bluff)

Well, now!

TOBIAS

Harry!

CLAIRE *(Too much surprise)*

Edna!

(Imitates HARRY's *gruff voice)*

Hello, there, Harry!

EDNA

Hello, dear Claire!

(A little timid)

Hello, Agnes.

HARRY *(Somewhat distant)*

Evening. . . Claire.

AGNES

(Jumping in, just as a tiny silence commences)

Sit *down.* We were just having a cordial. . . .

(Curiously loud)

Have you been . . . out? Uh, to the club?

HARRY
(Is he ignoring AGNES' *question?)*
I like this room.

AGNES
To the club?

CLAIRE
(Exaggerated, but not unkind)
How's the old Harry?

HARRY *(Self-pity entering)*
Pretty well, Claire, not as good as I'd like, but . . .

EDNA
Harry's been having his shortness of breath again.

HARRY *(Generally)*
I can't breathe sometimes . . . for just a bit.

TOBIAS *(Joining them all)*
Well, two sets of tennis, you know.

EDNA
(As if she can't remember something)
What have you done to the room, Agnes?

AGNES
(Looks around with a little apprehension, then relief)
Oh, the summer *things* are off.

EDNA
Of course.

AGNES
(Persisting in it, a strained smile)
Have you been to the club?

HARRY *(To TOBIAS)*
I was talking to Edna, 'bout having our books done in leather; bound.

TOBIAS
Oh? Yes?
(Brief silence)

CLAIRE
The question—'less I'm going deaf from all the alcohol—was
(Southern accent)
"Have you-all been to the club?"

AGNES
(Nervous, apologetic covering)
I wondered!

HARRY *(Hesitant)*
Why . . . no, no.

EDNA *(Ibid.)*
Why, why, no, Agnes. . . .

AGNES
I wondered, for I thought perhaps you'd dropped by here on your way from there.

HARRY
. . . no, no . . .

AGNES
. . . or perhaps that we were having a party, and I'd lost a day. . . .

HARRY
No, we were . . . just sitting home.

EDNA *(Some condolence)*
Agnes.

HARRY *(Looking at his hands)*
Just . . . sitting home.

AGNES
(Cheerful, but lack of anything better to say)
Well.

TOBIAS
Glad you're here! Party or not!

HARRY *(Relieved)*
Good to see you, Tobias!

EDNA *(All smiles)*
How is Julia?!

CLAIRE
Wrong question.
(Lifts her glass)
May I have some brandy, Tobias?

AGNES
(A savage look to CLAIRE, *back to* EDNA*)*
She's coming home . . . I'm afraid.

EDNA *(Disappointment)*
Oh . . . not again!

TOBIAS

(Getting CLAIRE's *glass, attempted levity)*
Just can't keep that one married, I guess.

EDNA

Oh, Agnes, what a shame!

HARRY

(More embarrassed than sorry)
Gee, that's too bad.
(Silence)

CLAIRE

Why *did* you come?

AGNES

Please! Claire!
(Back, reassuring)
We're *glad* you're here; we're glad you came to surprise us!

TOBIAS *(Quickly)*
Yes!
(HARRY *and* EDNA *exchange glances)*

HARRY

(Quite sad and curious about it)
We were . . . sitting home . . . just sitting home. . . .

EDNA

Yes . . .

AGNES *(Mildly reproving)*
We're *glad* to *see* you.

CLAIRE *(Eyes narrowing)*
What happened, Harry?

AGNES *(Sharp)*
Claire! Please!

TOBIAS

(Wincing a little, shaking his head)
Claire . . .

EDNA *(Reassuring him)*
It's all right, Tobias.

AGNES

I don't see why people have to be questioned when they've come for a
friendly . . .

CLAIRE *(Small victory)*

Harry wants to tell you, Sis.

EDNA

Harry?

HARRY

We . . . well, we were sitting home . . .

TOBIAS

Can I get you a drink, Harry?

HARRY *(Shakes his head)*

. . . I . . . we thought about going to the club, but . . . it's, it's so crowded on a Friday night . . .

EDNA *(Small voice, helpful, quiet)*

. . . with the canasta party, and getting ready for the dance tomorrow . . .

HARRY

. . . we didn't want to do that, and I've . . . been tired, and we didn't want to do that . . .

EDNA

. . . Harry's been tired this whole week.

HARRY

. . . so we had dinner home, and thought we'd stay . . .

EDNA

. . . rest.

HARRY

So we were sitting, and Edna was doing that—that panel she works on . . .

EDNA *(Wistful, some loss)*

. . . my needlepoint . . .

HARRY

. . . and I was reading my French; I've got it pretty good now—not the accent, but the . . . the words.

(A brief silence)

CLAIRE *(Quietly)*

And then?

HARRY

(Looks over to her, a little dreamlike, as if he didn't know where he was)

Hmm?

CLAIRE *(Nicely)*

And then?

HARRY (*Looks at* EDNA)

I . . . I don't know quite what happened then; we . . . we were . . . it was all very quiet, and we were all alone . . .

(EDNA *begins to weep, quietly;* AGNES *notices, the others do not;* AGNES *does nothing*)

. . . and then . . . nothing happened, but . . .

(EDNA *is crying more openly now*)

. . . nothing at all happened, but . . .

EDNA (*Open weeping; loud*)

WE GOT . . . FRIGHTENED.

(*Open sobbing; no one moves*)

HARRY (*Quiet wonder, confusion*)

We got scared.

EDNA (*Through her sobbing*)

WE WERE . . . FRIGHTENED.

HARRY

There was nothing . . . but we were very scared.

(AGNES *comforts* EDNA, *who is in free sobbing anguish.* CLAIRE *lies slowly back on the floor*)

EDNA

We . . . were . . . terrified.

HARRY

We were scared.

(*Silence;* AGNES *comforting* EDNA. HARRY *stock still. Quite inno-cent, almost childlike*)

It was like being lost: very young again, with the dark, and lost. There was no . . . thing . . . to be . . . frightened of, but . . .

EDNA (*Tears, quiet hysteria*)

WE WERE FRIGHTENED . . . AND THERE WAS NOTHING.

(*Silence in the room*)

HARRY

(*Matter-of-fact, but a hint of daring under it*)

We couldn't stay there, and so we came here. You're our very best friends.

EDNA (*Crying softly now*)

In the whole world.

AGNES

(*Comforting, arms around her*)

Now, now, Edna.

HARRY (*Apologizing some*)

We couldn't go anywhere else, so we came here.

AGNES (*A deep breath, control*)

Well, we'll . . . you did the right thing . . . of course.

TOBIAS

Sure.

EDNA

Can I go to bed now? Please?

AGNES

(*Pause; then, not quite understanding*)

Bed?

HARRY

We can't go back there.

EDNA

Please?

AGNES (*Distant*)

Bed?

EDNA

I'm so . . . tired.

HARRY

You're our best friends in the world. Tobias?

TOBIAS

(*A little bewilderment; rote*)

Of course we are, Harry.

EDNA (*On her feet, moving*)

Please?

(*Cries a little again*)

AGNES

(*A million things going through her head, seeping through management*)

Of . . . of course you can. There's . . . there's Julia's room, and . . .

(*Arm around* EDNA)

Come with me, dear.

(*Reaches doorway; turns to* TOBIAS; *a question that has no answer*)

Tobias?

HARRY

(*Rises, begins to follow* EDNA, *rather automaton-like*)

Edna?

TOBIAS (*Confused*)

Harry?

HARRY (*Shaking his head*)

There was no one else we could go to.

(*Exits after* AGNES *and* EDNA. CLAIRE *sits up, watches* TOBIAS, *as he stands for a moment, looking at the floor: silence*)

CLAIRE (*A small, sad chuckle*)

I was wondering when it would begin . . . . when it would start.

TOBIAS

(*Hearing her only after a moment*)

Start?

(*Louder*)

START?

(*Pause*)

WHAT?!

CLAIRE (*Raises her glass to him*)

Don't you know yet?

(*Small chuckle*)

You will.

CURTAIN

ACT TWO

SCENE ONE

(Same set; before dinner, next evening JULIA *and* AGNES *alone.*
AGNES *sitting,* JULIA *on her feet, pacing maybe)*

JULIA
(Anger and self-pity; too loud)
Do you think I like it? Do you?

AGNES *(No pleading)*
Julia! Please!

JULIA
DO YOU!? Do you think I enjoy it?

AGNES
Julia!

JULIA
Do you think it gives me some kind of . . . martyr's pleasure? Do you?

AGNES
Will you be still?

JULIA
WELL!?

AGNES
THERE IS A HOUSE FULL OF PEOPLE!

JULIA
Yes! What *about* that! I come home: my room is full of Harry and Edna. I
have no place to put my things. . . .

AGNES *(Placating)*
They'll go to Tobias' room, he'll sleep with me. . . .

JULIA *(Muttered)*
That'll be different.

AGNES

What did you say, young lady?

JULIA

I SAID, THAT WILL BE NICE.

AGNES

You did *not* say any such thing. You said . . .

JULIA

What are they *doing* here? Don't they have a house anymore? Has the market gone bust without my knowing it? I may have been out of touch, but . . .

AGNES

Just . . . let it be.

JULIA

(Between her teeth; controlled hysteria)
Why are they here?

AGNES

(Weary; head back; calm)
They're . . . frightened. Haven't you heard of it?

JULIA *(Incredulous)*
They're . . . what!?

AGNES *(Keeping her voice down)*
They're frightened. Now, will you let it be!

JULIA *(Offended)*
What are they frightened of? Harry and *Edna?* Frightened?

AGNES

I don't . . . I don't know yet.

JULIA

Well, haven't you *talked* to them about it? I mean, for God's sake. . . .

AGNES *(Trying to stay calm)*
No. I haven't.

JULIA

What have they done: stayed up in their room all day—*my* room!—not come down? Locked in?

AGNES

Yes.

JULIA

Yes what?

AGNES

Yes, they have stayed up in their room all day.

JULIA

My room.

AGNES

Your room. Now, let it be.

JULIA

(*Almost goes on in the same tone; doesn't; very nice, now*)

No, I . . .

AGNES

Please?

JULIA

I'm sorry, Mother, sorry for screeching.

AGNES

I am too old—as I remember—to remember what it is like to be a daughter, if my poor parents, in their separate heavens, will forgive me, but I am sure it is simpler than being a mother.

JULIA (*Slight edge*)

I said I was sorry.

AGNES

(*All of this more for her own bemusement and amusement than anything else*)

I don't recall if I ever asked my poor mother that. I do wish sometimes that I had been born a man.

JULIA

(*Shakes her head; very matter-of-fact*)

Not so hot.

AGNES

Their concerns are so simple: money and death—making ends meet until they meet the end.

(*Great self-mockery and exaggeration*)

If they *knew* what it was like . . . to be a wife; a mother; a lover; a home-maker; a nurse; a hostess, an agitator, a pacifier, a truth-teller, a deceiver . . .

JULIA

(*Saws away at an invisible violin; sings*)

Da-da-dee; da-da-da.

AGNES (*Laughs softly*)

There is a book out, I believe, a new one by one of the thirty million psychiatrists practicing in this land of ours, a book which opines that the sexes are reversing, or coming to resemble each other too much, at any rate. It is a book to be read and disbelieved, for it disturbs our sense of well-being. If the book is right, and I suspect it is, then I would be no better off as a man . . . would I?

JULIA

. (*Sober, though tongue-in-cheek agreement; shaking of head*)
No. Not at all.

AGNES (*Exaggerated fret*)
Oh! There is nowhere to rest the weary head . . . or whatever.
(*Hand out; loving, though a little grand*)
How are you, my darling?

JULIA (*A little abrupt*)
What?

AGNES
(*Hand still out; somewhat strained*)
How are you, my darling?

JULIA (*Gathering energy*)
How is your darling? Well, I was trying to tell you before you shut me up with Harry and Edna hiding upstairs, and . . .

AGNES
ALL RIGHT!
(*Pause*)

JULIA (*Strained control*)
I will try to tell you, Mother—once again—before you've turned into a man. . . .

AGNES
I shall try to hear you out, but if I feel my voice changing, in the middle of your . . . rant, you will have to forgive my male prerogative, if I become uncomfortable, look at my watch, or jiggle the change in my pocket . . .
(*Sees* JULIA *marching toward the archway as* TOBIAS *enters*)
. . . where do you think you're going?

JULIA (*Head down, muttered*)
. . . you go straight to hell . . .

TOBIAS (*Attempt at cheer*)
Now, now, what's going on here?

JULIA
(*Right in front of him; force*)
Will you shut her up?

TOBIAS *(Overwhelmed)*

Will I . . . what?

AGNES

(Marching toward the archway herself)

Well, there you are, Julia; your father may safely leave the room now, I think.

(Kisses TOBIAS *on the cheek)*

Hello, my darling.

(Back to JULIA*)*

Your mother has arrived. Talk to *him!*

(To TOBIAS*)*

Your daughter is in need of consolation or a great cuffing around the ears. I don't know which to recommend.

TOBIAS *(Confused)*

Have . . . have Harry and Edna . . . ?

AGNES *(Exiting)*

No, they have not.

(Gone)

TOBIAS *(After her, vaguely)*

Well, I thought maybe . . .

(To JULIA, *rather timid)*

What was that . . . all about?

JULIA

As they say: I haven't the faintest.

TOBIAS *(Willing to let it go)*

Oh.

JULIA *(Rather brittle)*

Papers?

TOBIAS

Oh, yes; want them?

JULIA

Anything happy?

TOBIAS *(Hopefully)*

My daughter's home.

JULIA *(Not giving in)*

Any other joys?

TOBIAS

Sorry.

(Sighs)

No; small wars, large anxieties, our dear Republicans as brutal as ever, a teen-age marijuana nest not far from here. . . .
(Some wonder)
I've never had marijuana . . . in my entire life.

JULIA

Want some?

TOBIAS

Wasn't fashionable.

JULIA

What the hell do Harry and Edna want?

TOBIAS (Scratches his head)
Just let it be.

JULIA

Didn't you try to talk to them today? I mean . . .

TOBIAS

(Not embarrassed, but not comfortable either)
Well, no; they weren't down when I went off to the club, and . . .

JULIA

Good old golf?

TOBIAS (Surprisingly nasty)
Don't ride me, Julia, I warn you.

JULIA (Nervously nicer)
I've never had any marijuana, either. Aren't I a good old girl?

TOBIAS

(Thinking of something else)
Either that or lying.

JULIA

(Exploding; but anger, not hysteria)
Great Christ! What the hell did I come home to? And why? Both of you? Snotty, mean . . .

TOBIAS

LOOK!
(Silence; softer, but no nonsense)
There are some . . . times, when it all gathers up . . . too much.

JULIA (Nervously)
Sure, sure.

TOBIAS *(Not put off)*

Some *times* when it's going to be Agnes and Tobias, and not just Mother and Dad. Right? Some *times* when the allowances aren't going to be made. What are you doing, biting off your fingernails now?

JULIA *(Not giving in)*

It broke off.

TOBIAS

There are some *times* when it's all . . . too much. *I* don't know what the hell Harry and Edna are doing sitting up in that bedroom! Claire is drinking, she and Agnes are at each other like a couple of . . . of . . .

JULIA *(Softly)*

Sisters?

TOBIAS

What? The goddamn government's at me over some deductions, and you!

JULIA *(Head high, defiant)*

And me? Yes?

TOBIAS

This isn't the first time, you know. This isn't the first time you've come back with one of your goddamned marriages on the rocks. Four! Count 'em!

JULIA *(Rage)*

I know how many marriages I've gotten myself into, you . . .

TOBIAS

Four! You expect to come back here, nestle in to being fifteen and misunderstood each time!? You are thirty-six years old, for God's sake! . . .

JULIA

And you are one hundred! Easily!

TOBIAS

Thirty-six! Each time! Dragging your . . . your—I was going to say pride—your marriage with you like some Raggedy Ann doll, by the foot. You, you fill this house with your whining. . . .

JULIA *(Rage)*

I DON'T ASK TO COME BACK HERE!!

TOBIAS

YOU BELONG HERE!

(Heavy breathing from both of them, finally a little rueful giggle;
TOBIAS *speaks rather nonchalantly now)*

Well. Now that I've taken out on my only daughter the . . . disgust of my declining years, I'll mix a very good and very strong martini. Join me?

JULIA *(Rather wistful)*

When I was a very little girl—well, when I was a little girl: after I'd gotten over my two year burn at suddenly having a brother, may his soul rest, when I was still a little girl, I thought you were a marvel—saint, sage, daddy, everything. And then, as the years turned and I reached my . . . somewhat angular adolescence . . .

TOBIAS

(At the sideboard; unconcerned)

Five to one? Or more?

JULIA

And then, as the years turned—poor old man—you sank to cipher, and you've stayed there, I'm afraid—very nice but ineffectual, essential, but not-really-thought-of, gray . . . noneminence.

TOBIAS *(Mixing hardly listening)*

Unh-hunh . . .

JULIA

And now you've changed again, sea monster, ram! Nasty, violent, absolutely human man! Yes, as you make it, five to one, or better.

TOBIAS

I made it about seven, I think.

JULIA

Your transformations amaze me. How can I have changed so much? Or *is* it really you?

(He hands her a drink)

Thank you.

TOBIAS *(As they both settle)*

I told Agnes that I'd speak to Doug . . . if you think that would do any good. By golly, Dad, that's a good martini!

JULIA

Do you really want to talk to Doug? You won't get anywhere: the compulsives you can get somewhere with—or the illusion of getting—the gamblers, the fags, the lechers . . .

TOBIAS

. . . of this world . . .

JULIA

. . . yes, you can have the illusion 'cause they're after something, the jackpot, somehow: break the bank, find the boy, climb the babe . . . something.

TOBIAS

You do pick 'em.

JULIA *(Pregnant)*

Do I?

TOBIAS

Hm?

JULIA

Do I pick 'em? I thought it was fifteen hundred and six, or so, where daughter went with whatever man her parents thought would hold the fief together best, or something. "Love will come after."

TOBIAS *(Grudging)*

Well, you may have been pushed on Charlie. . . .

JULIA

Poor Charlie.

TOBIAS *(Temper rising a little)*

Well, for Christ's sake, if you miss him so much . . .

JULIA

I do not miss him! Well, yes, I do, but not that way. Because he seemed so like what Teddy would have been.

TOBIAS

(Quiet anger and sorrow)

Your brother would not have grown up to be a fag.

JULIA *(Bitter smile)*

Who is to say?

TOBIAS *(Hard look)*

I!

(Pause. CLAIRE *in the archway)*

CLAIRE

Do I breathe gin?

*(*JULIA *sees her, runs to her, arms out, both of them, they envelop each other)*

Darling!

JULIA

Oh, my sweet Claire!

CLAIRE

Julia Julia.

JULIA

(Semi-mock condemnation)

I must say the welcome-home committee was pretty skimpy, you and Daddy gone. . . .

CLAIRE

Oh, now.

(*To* TOBIAS)

I said, do I breathe gin?

TOBIAS (*Not rising*)

You do.

CLAIRE (*Appraising* JULIA)

Well, you don't look too bad for a quadruple amputee, I must say. Are you going to make me a whatever, Tobias?

(*To* JULIA)

Besides, my darling, it's getting to be rather a habit, isn't it?

JULIA (*False smile*)

Yes, I suppose so.

CLAIRE

(*Sees* TOBIAS *is not moving*)

Then I shall make my own.

TOBIAS (*Getting up; wearily*)

Sit down, Claire, I'll do it.

CLAIRE

I wouldn't want to tax you, now.

(*Generally*)

Well, I had an adventure today. Went into town, thought I'd shake 'em up a little, so I tried to find me a topless bathing suit.

JULIA (*Giggling*)

You didn't!

TOBIAS

(*At the sideboard, disapproving*)

Really, Claire.

CLAIRE

Yes, I did.

JULIA

They're not making them anymore.

CLAIRE

I know. Shhhh. I went into what's-their-names', and I went straight up to the swimwear, as they call it, department and I got me an eighteen-nineties schoolteacher type, who wondered what she could do for me,

(JULIA *giggles*)

and I felt like telling her, "Not much, sweetheart" . . .

TOBIAS

Are you sure you wouldn't rather have a . . .

CLAIRE

Very. But I said, "Hello, there, I'm in the market for a topless swimsuit." Hurry up there, Toby. "A what, Miss?" she said, which I didn't know whether to take as a compliment or not. "A topless swimsuit," I said. "I don't know what you mean," she said after a beat. "Oh, certainly you do," I said, "no top, stops at the waist, latest thing, lots of freedom." "Oh, yes," she said, looking at me like she was seeing the local madam for the first time, "those." Then a real sniff. "I'm afraid we don't carry . . . those." "Well, in that case," I told her, "do you have any separates?" "Those we carry," she said, "those we do." And she started going under the counter, and I said, "I'll just buy the bottoms of one of those."

JULIA

No! You didn't!

CLAIRE

Yes, I did. She came up from under the counter, adjusted her spectacles and said, "What did you say?"

TOBIAS

Shall I bring it, or will you come for it?

CLAIRE

You bring. I said, "I said, 'I'll buy the bottom of one of those.'" She thought for a minute, and then she said, with ice in her voice, "And what will we do with the tops?" "Well," I said, "why don't you save 'em? Màybe bottomless swimsuits'll be in *next* year."

(JULIA *laughs openly*)

Then the poor sweet thing gave me a look I couldn't tell was either a D minus, or she was going to send me home with a letter to my mother, and she said, sort of far away, "I think you need the manager." And off she walked.

TOBIAS

(*Handing* CLAIRE *her martini; mildly amused throughout*)

What were you doing buying a bathing suit in October, anyway?

JULIA

Oh, Dad!

CLAIRE

No, now; it's a man's question.

(*Sips*)

Wow, what a good martini.

TOBIAS

(*Still standing over her, rather severe*)

Truth will get you nowhere. Why?

CLAIRE

Why? Well.

(*Thinks*)

. . . maybe I'll go on a trip somewhere.

TOBIAS

That would please Agnes.

CLAIRE (*Nods*)

As few things would. What I meant was, maybe Toby'll walk in one day, trailing travel folders, rip his tie off, announce he's fed up to there with the north, the east, the suburbs, the regulated great gray life, dwindling before him—poor Toby—and has bought him an island off Paraguay . . .

TOBIAS

. . . which has no seacoast . . .

CLAIRE

. . . yes, *way* off—has bought him this island, and is taking us all to *that*, to hack through the whatever, build us an enormous lean-to, all of us. Take us away, to where it is always good and happy.

(*Watches* TOBIAS, *who looks at his drink, frowning a little*)

JULIA (*She, too*)

Would you, Dad?

TOBIAS

(*Looks up, sees them both looking at him, frowns more*)

It's . . . it's too late, or something.

(*Small silence*)

CLAIRE (*To lighten it*)

Or, maybe I simply wanted a topless bathing suit.

(*Pause*)

No? Well, then . . . maybe it's more complicated yet. I mean, Claire couldn't find herself a man if she tried, and here comes Julia, home from the wars . . .

TOBIAS (*Quiet contradiction*)

You could find a man.

CLAIRE (*Some bitterness*)

Indeed, I have found several, briefly, and none my own.

TOBIAS

(*To* JULIA; *terribly offhand*)

Julia, don't you think Auntie Claire could find herself a man?

JULIA (*Didactic*)

I *don't* like the subject.

CLAIRE

. . . and here comes Julia, home from the wars, four purple hearts . . .

JULIA

Why don't you just have another drink and stop it, Claire?

CLAIRE

(Looks at her empty glass, shrugs)

All right.

JULIA *(Rather defensive)*

I have *left* Doug. We are not *divorced.*

CLAIRE

Yet! Are you cooking a second batch, Tobias?

(Back to JULIA*)*

But you've come back home, haven't you? And didn't you—with the others?

JULIA *(Her back up)*

Where else am I supposed to go?

CLAIRE

It's a great big world, baby. There are hotels, new cities. Home is the quickest road to Reno I know of.

JULIA *(Condescending)*

You've had a lot of experience in these matters, Claire.

CLAIRE

Sidelines! Good seats, right on the fifty-yard line, objective observer.

(Texas accent, or near it)

I swar! Ef I din't love muh sister so, Ah'd say she got yuh hitched fur the pleasure uh gettin' yuh back.

JULIA	TOBIAS
ALL RIGHT!	THAT WILL DO NOW!

CLAIRE

(In the silence that follows)

Sorry. Very . . . very sorry.

*(*AGNES *appears through the archway)*

AGNES

(What she may have overheard she gives no indication of)

"They" tell me in the kitchen . . . "they" tell me we are about to dine. In a bit. Are we having a cocktail? I think one might be nice.

(Puts her arm around JULIA *as she passes her)*

It's one of those days when everything's underneath. But, we are all together . . . which is something.

JULIA

Quite a few of us.

TOBIAS

Any word from . . .
   (Points to the ceiling)
. . . up there?

AGNES

No. I dropped upstairs—well, *that* doesn't make very much sense, does
it?—I *happened* upstairs, and I knocked at Harry and Edna's *Julia's* room,
door, and after a moment I heard Harry say, "It's all right; we're all right."
I didn't have the . . . well, I felt such an odd mixture of . . . embarrassment
and irritation, and . . . apprehension, I suppose, and . . . fatigue . . . I didn't
persevere.

TOBIAS

Well, haven't they been *out?* I mean, haven't they eaten or anything?

AGNES

Will you make me a . . . thing, a martini, please? I am told—"*they*" tell me
that while we were all out, at our various whatever-they-may-be's, Edna
descended, asked them to make sandwiches, which were brought to the
closed door and handed in.

TOBIAS

Well, God, I mean . . .

AGNES *(Rather a recitation)*
There is no point in pressing it, they are our very dear friends, they will tell
us in good time.

CLAIRE
   (Looking through her glass)
I had a glimmer of it last night; thought I knew.

AGNES *(So gracious)*
That which we see in the bottom of our glass is most often dregs.

CLAIRE
   (Peers into her glass, over-curious)
Really? Truly so?

TOBIAS
   (Holding a glass out to AGNES*)*
Did you say you wanted?

AGNES
   (Her eyes still on CLAIRE*)*
Yes, I did, thank you.

CLAIRE

I have been trying, without very much success, to find out why Miss Julie here is come home.

AGNES

I would imagine Julia is home because she wishes to be, and it is where she belongs if she wants.

TOBIAS

That's logistics, isn't it?

AGNES

You too?

JULIA

He's against everything!

AGNES

Your father?

JULIA

Doug!

AGNES

You needn't make a circus of it; tell me later, when . . .

JULIA

War, marriage, money, children . . .

AGNES

You needn't!

JULIA

You! Daddy! Government! Claire—if he'd met her . . . everything!

CLAIRE

Well, I doubt he'd dislike *me;* I'm against everything too.

AGNES *(To* JULIA*)*

You're tired; we'll talk about it after . . .

JULIA *(Sick disgust)*

I've talked about it! I just talked about it!

AGNES *(Quiet boring in)*

I'm sure there's more.

JULIA

There is no more.

AGNES *(Clenched teeth)*

There is a great deal more, and I'll hear it from you later, when we're alone. You have not come to us in your fourth debacle. . . .

JULIA
HE IS OPPOSED! AND THAT IS ALL! TO EVERYTHING!

AGNES *(After a small silence)*
Perhaps after dinner.

JULIA
NO! NOT PERHAPS AFTER DINNER!

TOBIAS
ALL OF YOU! BE STILL!
  (Silence)

CLAIRE *(Flat; to* TOBIAS)
Are we having our dividend, or are we not?
  (Silence; then, a gentle mocking apology)
"All happy families are alike."
  *(*HARRY *and* EDNA *appear in the archway, coats on or over arms)*

HARRY *(A little embarrassed)*
Well.

CLAIRE *(Exaggerated bonhomie)*
Well, look who's here!

TOBIAS *(Embarrassed)*
Harry, just in time for a martini. . . .

HARRY
No, no, we're . . . Julia, there you are!

EDNA *(Affectionate commiseration)*
Oh, Julia.

JULIA *(Bravely, nicely)*
Hello there.

AGNES *(On her feet)*
There's just time for a drink before dinner, if my husband will hurry some. . . .

HARRY
No, we're . . . going home now.

AGNES
  (Relief peeking through the surprise)
Oh? Yes?

EDNA
Yes.
  (Pause)

AGNES

Well.

(*Pause*)

If we were any help at all, we . . .

HARRY

To . . . uh, to get our things.

(*Silence*)

Our clothes, and things.

EDNA

Yes.

HARRY

We'll be back in . . . well, after dinner, so don't . . .

EDNA

An hour or two. It'll take us a while.

(*Silence*)

HARRY

We'll let ourselves . . . don't bother.

(*They start out, tentatively, see that the others are merely staring at them. Exit. Silence*)

JULIA

(*Controlled, but near tears*)

I want my room back! I want my room!

AGNES

(*Composed, chilly, standing in the archway*)

I believe that dinner is served. . . .

TOBIAS (*Vacant*)

Yes?

AGNES

If any of you have the stomach for it.

CURTAIN

SCENE TWO

(Same set, after dinner, the same evening AGNES *and* TOBIAS *to one side,* AGNES *standing* TOBIAS *not;* JULIA *in another corner, not facing them)*

JULIA

(A statement, directed to neither of them)
That was, without question, the *ugliest* dinner I have ever sat through.

AGNES *(Seemingly pleased)*

What did you say?

(No answer)
Now, what can you mean? Was the ragout not to your pleasure? Did the floating island sink? Watch what you say, for your father is proud of his wines. . . .

JULIA

No! You! Sitting there! Like a combination . . . pope, and . . . "We will not discuss it"; "Claire, be still"; "No, Tobias, the table is not the proper place"; "Julia!" . . . nanny! Like a nanny!

AGNES

When we are dealing with children . . .

JULIA

I must discover, sometime, who you think you are.

AGNES *(Icy)*

You will learn . . . one day.

JULIA

No, more like a drill sergeant! *You* will do this, *you* will not say that.

AGNES

"To keep in shape." Have you heard the expression? Most people misunderstand it, assume it means alteration, when it does not. Maintenance. When we keep something in shape, we maintain its shape—whether we are proud of that shape, or not, is another matter—we keep *it* from falling apart. We do not attempt the impossible. We maintain. We hold.

JULIA

Yes? So?

AGNES *(Quietly)*

I shall . . . keep this family in shape. I shall maintain it; hold it.

JULIA *(A sneer)*

But you won't attempt the impossible.

AGNES *(A smile)*

I shall keep it in shape. If I am a drill sergeant . . . so be it. Since nobody . . .
really wants to talk about your latest . . . marital disorder, really wants to talk
around it, use it as an excuse for all sorts of horrid little revenges . . . I think
we can at least keep the table . . . unlittered of *that*.

JULIA

(Sarcastic salute, not rising though)

Yes, sir.

AGNES *(Reasonable)*

And, if I shout, it's merely to be heard . . . above the awful din of your pri-
vacies and sulks . . . all of you. I am not being an ogre, am I?

TOBIAS *(Not anxious to argue)*

No, no; very . . . reasonable.

AGNES

If I am a stickler on certain points

(Just as JULIA's *mouth opens to speak)*

—a martinet, as Julia would have it, would you not, sweet? in fact, were
you not about to?—if I am a stickler on points of manners, timing, tact—
the graces, I almost blush to call them—it is simply that I am the one
member of this . . . reasonably happy family blessed and burdened with
the ability to view a situation objectively while I am in it.

JULIA *(Not really caring)*

What time is it?

AGNES *(A little harder now)*

The double position of seeing not only facts but their implications . . .

TOBIAS

Nearly ten.

AGNES

(Some irritation toward both of them)

. . . the longer view as well as the shorter. There *is* a balance to be main-
tained, after all, though the rest of you teeter, unconcerned, or uncaring,
assuming you're on level ground . . . by divine right, I gather, though that
is hardly so. And if I must be the fulcrum. . . .

(Sees neither of them is really listening, says in the same tone)

. . . I think I shall have a divorce.

(Smiles to see that her words have had no effect)

TOBIAS *(It sinks in)*

Have what? A *what?*

AGNES

No fear; merely testing. Everything is taken for granted and no one listens.

TOBIAS *(Wrinkling his nose)*

Have a divorce?

AGNES

No, no; Julia has them for all of us. Not even separation; that is taken care of, and in life: the gradual . . . demise of intensity, the private preoccupations, the substitutions. We become allegorical, my darling Tobias, as we grow older. The individuality we hold so dearly sinks into crotchet; we see ourselves repeated by those we bring into it all, either by mirror or rejection, honor or fault.

(To herself, really)

I'm not a fool; I'm really not.

JULIA

(Leafing a magazine; clear lack of interest but not insulting)

What's Claire up to?

AGNES

(Walking to TOBIAS, a hand on his shoulder)

Really not at all.

TOBIAS *(Looking up; fondness)*

No; really not.

AGNES

(Surprisingly unfriendly; to JULIA)

How would I know what she's doing?

JULIA *(She too)*

Well, you are the fulcrum and all around here, the double vision, the great balancing act. . . .

(Lets it slide away)

AGNES

(A little triste; looking away)

I dare say she's in her room.

JULIA *(Little girl)*

At least she has one.

AGNES

(Swinging around to face her; quite hard)

Well, why don't you run upstairs and claim your goddamn room back!

Barricade yourself in there! Push a bureau in front of the door! Take Tobias' pistol while you're at it! Arm yourself!

(A burst from an accordion; CLAIRE *appears in the archway, wearing it)*

CLAIRE

Barricades? Pistols? Really? So soon?

JULIA

(Giggling in spite of herself)

Oh, Claire . . .

AGNES *(Not amused)*

Claire, will you take off that damned thing!

CLAIRE

"They laughed when I sat down to the accordion." Take it off? No, I will not! This is going to be a festive night—from the smell of it, and sister Claire wants to do her part—pay her way, so to speak . . . justify.

AGNES

You're not going to play that dreadful instrument in here, and . . .

(But the rest of what she wants to say is drowned out by a chord from the accordion)

Tobias?

(Calm)

Do something about that.

TOBIAS *(He, too, chuckling)*

Oh, now, Agnes . . .

CLAIRE

So . . .

(Another chord)

. . . shall I wait? Shall I start now? A polka? What?

AGNES *(Icy, but to* TOBIAS*)*

My sister is not *really* lazy. The things she has learned since leaving the nest!: gaucherie, ingratitude, drunkenness, and even . . . this. She has become a musician, too.

CLAIRE *(A twang in her voice)*

Maw used to say: "Claire, girl" . . . she had an uncle named Claire, so she always called me Claire-girl—

AGNES *(No patience with it)*

That is not so.

CLAIRE

"Claire girl," she used to say, "when you go out into the world, get dumped outa the nest, or pushed by your sister . . ."

AGNES *(Steady, but burning)*

Lies.

(Eyes slits)

She kept you, allowed you . . . tolerated! Put up with your filth, your . . . "emancipated womanhood."

(To JULIA, *overly sweet)*

Even in her teens, your Auntie Claire had her own and very special ways, was very . . . advanced.

CLAIRE *(Laughs)*

Had a ball, the same as you, 'cept I wasn't puce with socially proper remorse every time.

(To JULIA)

Your mommy got her pudenda scuffed a couple times herself 'fore she met old Toby, you know.

TOBIAS

Your what?

AGNES *(Majesty)*

My pudenda.

CLAIRE *(A little grumpy)*

You can come on all forgetful in your old age, if you want to, but just remember . . .

AGNES *(Quiet anger)*

I am not an old woman.

(Sudden thought; to TOBIAS)

Am I?

TOBIAS *(No help; great golly-gosh)*

Well, you're my old lady. . . .

*(*AGNES *almost says something, changes her mind, shakes her head, laughs softly)*

CLAIRE *(A chord)*

Well, what'll it be?

JULIA *(Glum)*

Save it for Harry and Edna.

CLAIRE

Save it for Harry and Edna? Save it for them?

(Chord)

AGNES *(Nice)*

Please.

CLAIRE

All right; I'll unload.
   (Removes accordion)

AGNES

I dare say.
   (Stops)

·TOBIAS

What?

AGNES

No. Nothing.

CLAIRE *(Half-smile)*

We're waiting, aren't we?

TOBIAS

Hm?

CLAIRE

Waiting. The room; the doctor's office; beautiful unconcern; intensive study of the dreadful curtains; absorption in *Field and Stream,* waiting for the Bi-op-*see.*
   (Looks from one to the other)
No? Don't know what I mean?

JULIA *(Rather defiant)*

What *about* Harry and Edna?

CLAIRE *(Echo; half-smile)*

We don't want to talk about it.

AGNES

If they come back . . .

CLAIRE

If!?

AGNES *(Closes her eyes briefly)*

If they come back . . . we will . . .
   (Shrugs)

CLAIRE

You've only got two choices, Sis. You take 'em in, or you throw 'em out.

AGNES

Ah, how simple it is from the sidelines.

TOBIAS *(Sees through the window)*

We'll do neither, I'd imagine. Take in; throw out.

CLAIRE

Oh?

TOBIAS *(A feeling of nakedness)*

Well, yes, they're just . . . passing through.

CLAIRE

As they have been . . . all these years.

AGNES

Well, we shall know soon enough.

(Not too much pleasure)

They're back.

TOBIAS

(Rises, goes to the window with her)

Yes?

JULIA

I think I'll go up . . .

AGNES

You stay right here!

JULIA

I want to go to my . . .

AGNES

It is their room! For the moment.

JULIA *(Not nice)*

Among Doug's opinions, you might like to know, is that when you and your
ilk are blown to pieces by a Chinese bomb, the world will be a better place.

CLAIRE

Isn't ilk a lovely word?

AGNES *(Dry)*

You choose well, Julia.

JULIA

(Retreating into uncertainty)

That's what he says.

AGNES

Have, always. Did he include *you* as ilk, as well? Will you be with us when
"the fatal mushroom" comes. Are we to have the pleasure?

JULIA

(After a pause; as much a threat as a promise)

I'll be right here.

TOBIAS

Agnes!

JULIA

Would you like to know something else he says?

AGNES *(Patiently)*

No, Julia.

JULIA

Dad?

TOBIAS *(Some apology in it)*

Not right this minute, Julia. They have gone around to the back.

JULIA *(Defiance)*

Claire? You?

CLAIRE

Well, come on! You *know I'd* like to hear about it—love to—but Toby and Ag've got an invasion on their hands, and . . .

AGNES

We have no such thing.

CLAIRE

. . . and maybe you'd better save it for Harry and Edna, too.

AGNES

It does not concern Edna and Harry.

CLAIRE

Best friends.

AGNES

Tobias?

TOBIAS

(Reluctantly on his feet)

Where . . . what do you want me to do with everything? Every . . . ?

AGNES

(Heading toward the archway)

Well for God's sake! I'll do it.

(They exit)

JULIA

(As CLAIRE *moves to the sideboard)*

What . . . what do they want? Harry and Edna.

CLAIRE *(Pouring for herself)*

Hmm?

JULIA

You'll make Mother mad. Harry and Edna: what do they want?

CLAIRE

Succor.

JULIA *(Tiny pause)*

Pardon?

CLAIRE *(Brief smile)*

Comfort.

(Sees JULIA *doesn't understand)*

Warmth. A special room with a night light, or the door ajar so you can look down the hall from the bed and see that Mommy's door is open.

JULIA *(No anger; loss)*

But that's my room.

CLAIRE

It's . . . the *room.* Happens you were in it. You're a visitor as much as any-one, now.

(We hear mumbled conversation from the hallway)

JULIA *(Small whine)*

But I *know* that room.

CLAIRE *(Pointed, but kind)*

Are you home for good now?

*(*JULIA *stares at her)*

Are you home forever, back from the world? To the sadness *and* reassur-ance of your parents? Have you come to take my place?

JULIA *(Quiet despair)*

This is my home!

CLAIRE

This . . . ramble? Yes?

(Surprised delight)

You're laying claim to the cave! Well, I don't know how they'll take to that. We're not a communal nation, dear;

*(*EDNA *appears in the archway, unseen)*

giving, but not sharing, outgoing, but not friendly.

EDNA

Hello.

CLAIRE

(Friendly, but not turning to look at her)

Hello!

(Back to JULIA*)*

We submerge our truths and have our sunsets on untroubled waters.
C'mon in, Edna.

EDNA

Yes.

CLAIRE *(Back to* JULIA*)*

We live with our truths in the grassy bottom, and we examine aalllll the
interpretations of aalllll the implications like we had a life for nothing else,
for God's sake.

(Turns to EDNA*)*

Do *you* think we can walk on the water, Edna? Or do you think we sink?

EDNA *(Dry)*

We sink.

CLAIRE

And we better develop gills. Right?

EDNA

Right. We drove around the back. Harry is helping Agnes and Tobias get
our bags upstairs.

JULIA

(Slight schoolteacher tone)

Don't you mean Agnes and Tobias are helping Harry?

EDNA *(Tired)*

If you like.

(To CLAIRE*)*

What were you two up to?

CLAIRE

I think Julia is home for good this time.

JULIA

(Annoyed and embarrassed)

For Christ's sake, Claire!

EDNA

(Rather as if JULIA *were not in the room)*

Oh? Is it come to that?

CLAIRE

I always said she would, finally.

JULIA

(Under her breath, to CLAIRE*)*

This is family business!

EDNA (*Looking around the room*)

Yes, but I'm not sure Agnes and Tobias have seen it as clearly. I do wish Agnes would have that chair recovered. Perhaps now . . .

JULIA (*Exploding*)

Well, why don't you call the upholsterers! Now that you're living here!

CLAIRE (*Quiet amusement*)

All in the family.

EDNA

You're not a child anymore, Julia, you're nicely on your way to forty, and you've not helped . . . wedlock's image any, with your . . . shenanigans . . .

JULIA (*Full, quivering rage*)

YOU ARE A GUEST IN THIS HOUSE!!

EDNA

(*Lets a moment pass, continues quietly*)

. . . and if you *have* decided to . . .

(*Wistful*)

return forever? . . . then it's a matter of some concern for quite a few peo—

JULIA

You are a *guest!*

CLAIRE (*Quietly*)

As you.

EDNA

. . . for quite a few people . . . whose lives are . . . moved—if not necessarily touched—by your actions. Claire, where does Agnes have her upholstery done? Does she use . . .

JULIA

NO!

EDNA (*Strict, soft and powerful*)

Manners, young lady!

CLAIRE (*Pointed*)

Julia, why don't you ask Edna if she'd like something?

JULIA (*Mouth agape for a moment*)

NO!

(*To* EDNA)

You have no rights here. . . .

EDNA

I'll have a cognac, Julia.

(JULIA *stands stock still.* EDNA *continues; precise and pointed*)

My husband and I are your parents' best friends. We are, in addition, your godparents.

JULIA

DOES THIS GIVE YOU RIGHTS?!

CLAIRE *(Smile)*

Some.

EDNA

Some. Rights and responsibilities. Some.

CLAIRE

(Seeing HARRY *in the archway)*

Hello, there, Harry; c'mon in. Julia's about to fix us all something. What'll you . . .

HARRY

(Rubbing his hands together; quite at ease)

I'll do it; don't trouble yourself, Julia.

JULIA

(Rushes to the sideboard, her back to it, spreads her arms, protecting it, curiously disturbed and frightened by something)

No! Don't you come near it! Don't you take a step!

HARRY

(Patiently, moving forward a little)

Now, Julia . . .

JULIA

NO!

EDNA *(Sitting relaxing)*

Let her do it, Harry. She wants to.

JULIA

I DON'T WANT TO!!

HARRY *(Firm)*

Then I'll do it, Julia.

JULIA *(Suddenly a little girl; crying)*

Mother!? MOTHER!?

EDNA

(Shaking her head; not unkindly)

Honestly.

JULIA

MOTHER!?

CLAIRE

(*The way a nurse speaks to a disturbed patient*)
Julia? Will you let me do it? May I get the drinks?

JULIA (*Hissed*)

Stay away from it! All of you!

CLAIRE (*Rising*)

Now, Julia . . .

HARRY

Oh, come on, Julie, now . . .

EDNA

Let her go, Harry.

JULIA

MOTHER? FATHER! HELP ME!!

(AGNES *enters*)

AGNES (*Pained*)

Julia? You're shouting?

JULIA

Mother!

AGNES (*Quite conscious of the others*)

What *is* it, dear?

JULIA

(*Quite beside herself seeing no sympathy*)
THEY! THEY WANT!

EDNA

Forget it, Julia.

HARRY

(*A tiny, condescending laugh*)
Yes, for God's sake, forget it.

JULIA

THEY WANT!

AGNES

(*Kindly, but a little patronizing*)
Perhaps you *had* better go upstairs.

JULIA (*Still semi-hysterical*)

Yes? Where!? What room!?

AGNES (*Patient*)

Go up to my room, lie down.

JULIA *(An ugly laugh)*

Your room!

EDNA *(Calm)*

You may lie down in *our* room, if you prefer.

JULIA

(A trapped woman, surrounded)

Your room!

(To AGNES*)*

Your room? MINE!!

(Looks from one to another, sees only waiting faces)

MINE!!

HARRY

(Makes a move toward the sideboard)

God.

JULIA

Don't you go near *that!*

AGNES

Julia . . .

JULIA

I *want!*

CLAIRE *(Sad smile)*

What do you want, Julia?

JULIA

I . . .

HARRY

Jesus.

JULIA

I WANT . . . WHAT IS MINE!!

AGNES

(Seemingly dispassionate; after a pause)

Well, then, my dear, you will have to decide what that is, will you not.

JULIA

(A terrified pause; runs from the room)

Daddy? Daddy?

(A silence; HARRY *moves to the sideboard, begins to make himself a drink)*

AGNES

(As if very little had happened)

Why, I do believe that's the first time she's called on her father in . . . since her childhood.

CLAIRE

When she used to skin her knees?

AGNES *(A little laugh)*

Yes, and she would come home bloody. I *assumed* she was clumsy, but it crossed my mind a time or two . . . that she was religious.

EDNA

Praying on the gravel? A penance?

AGNES

(Chuckles, but it covers something else)

Yes. Teddy had just died, I think, and it was an . . . unreal time . . . for a number of us, for me.

(Brief sorrow clearly shown)

Poor little boy.

EDNA

Yes.

AGNES

It was an unreal time: I thought Tobias was out of love with me—or, rather, was tired of it, when Teddy died, as if that had been the string.

HARRY

Would you like something, Edna?

EDNA

(Her eyes on AGNES; *rather dreamy)*

Um-humh.

AGNES

(Not explaining and to none of them, really)

Ah, the things I doubted then: that I was loved—that *I* loved, for that matter!—that Teddy had ever lived at all—my mind, you see. That Julia would be with us long. I think . . . I think I thought Tobias was unfaithful to me then. Was he, Harry?

EDNA

Oh, Agnes.

HARRY *(Unsubtle)*

Come on, Agnes! Of course not! No!

AGNES *(Faint amusement)*

Was he, Claire? That hot summer, with Julia's knees all bloody and Teddy dead? Did my husband . . . cheat on me?

CLAIRE

(Looks at her steadily, toasts her; then)

Ya got me, Sis.

AGNES *(An amen)*

And that will have to do.

EDNA

Poor *Julia.*

AGNES *(Shrugs)*

Julia is a fool. Will you make me a drink, Harry, since you're being Tobias?
A Scotch?

HARRY *(Hands* EDNA *a drink)*

Sure thing. Claire?

CLAIRE

Why not.

AGNES *(An overly sweet smile)*

Claire could tell us so much if she cared to, could you not, Claire. Claire,
who watches from the sidelines, has seen so very much, has seen us all so
clearly, have you not, Claire. You were not named for nothing.

CLAIRE *(A pleasant warning)*

Lay off, Sis.

AGNES

(Eyes level on EDNA *and* HARRY; *precisely and not too nicely)*

What do you *want?*

HARRY

(After a pause and a look at EDNA*)*

I don't know what you mean.

EDNA *(Seemingly puzzled)*

Yes.

AGNES *(Eyes narrow)*

What do you *really . . . want?*

CLAIRE

You gonna tell her, Harry?

HARRY

I, *I* don't know what you mean, Claire. Scotch, was it, Agnes?

AGNES

I *said.*

HARRY *(Less than pleasant)*

Yes, but I don't re*member.*

EDNA *(Her eyes narrowing too)*

Don't talk to Harry like that.

AGNES

(About to attack, thinks better of it)

I . . . I'm sorry, Edna. I forgot that you're . . . very frightened people.

EDNA

DON'T YOU MAKE FUN OF US!

AGNES

My dear Edna, I am not mak—

EDNA

YES YOU ARE! YOU'RE MAKING FUN OF US.

AGNES

I assure you, Edna . . .

HARRY

(Handing AGNES *a drink; with some disgust)*

Here's your drink.

AGNES

I, I assure you.

CLAIRE *(Putting on her accordion)*

I think it's time for a little music, don't you, kids! I yodel a little, too, nowadays, if anybody . . .

AGNES *(Exasperated)*

We *don't* want music, Claire!

HARRY *(Horrified and amused)*

You, you *what!?* You *yodel!?*

CLAIRE

(As if it were the most natural thing in the world)

Well . . . sure.

EDNA *(Dry)*

Talent will out.

HARRY *(Continuing disbelief)*

You yodel!

CLAIRE *(Emphatic; baby talk)*

'ES!

*(*TOBIAS *has appeared in the archway)*

HARRY

She yodels!

CLAIRE *(Bravura)*

What would ya like, Harry? A chorus of "Take me to the greenhouse, lay me down . . ."?

AGNES

Claire!

TOBIAS

I . . . I wonder if, before the concert, one of you would mind telling me why, uh, my daughter is upstairs, in hysterics?

CLAIRE

Envy, baby; she don't sing, or nothin'.

(A chord)

TOBIAS

PLEASE!

(To the others)

Well? Will any of you tell me?

AGNES *(Controlled)*

What, what was she doing, Tobias?

TOBIAS

I told you! She's in hysterics!

AGNES *(Tight smile)*

That is a condition; I inquired about an action.

EDNA *(More sincere than before)*

Poor Julia.

HARRY

I don't understand that girl.

TOBIAS *(Quite miffed)*

An action? Is that what you want? O.K., how about

(Demonstrates this)

pressed against a corner of the upstairs hall, arms wide, palms back? Eyes darting? Wide?

(EDNA shakes her head)

How about tearing into Harry and Edna's room . . . ripping the clothes from the closets, hangers and all on the floor? The same for the bureaus?

AGNES *(Steady)*

I see.

TOBIAS

More?

AGNES *(Steady)*

All right.

TOBIAS

Or into your room next? Twisted on your bed, lots of breathing and the great wide eyes? The spread all gathered under her, your big lace pillow in her arms—like a lover—her eyes wide open, no tears now? Though if you come near her the sounds start and you think she'll scream if you touch her?

(Pause)

How's that?

CLAIRE *(Pause)*

Pretty good.

AGNES *(Pause)*

And accurate, I imagine.

TOBIAS *(Daring her)*

You're damned right! Now, why?

AGNES

(To TOBIAS *with a sad smile, ironic)*

Would it seem . . . incomplete to you, my darling, were I to tell you Julia is upset that Har—Edna and Harry are here, that . . .

HARRY *(Arms wide, helplessly)*

I was making myself a drink, for God's sake. . . .

EDNA

I asked her to *make* me something. . . .

TOBIAS

Oh, come on!

EDNA *(Some pleasure)*

She rose . . . like a silent film star, ran to the sideboard, defended it, like a princess in the movies, hiding her lover in the closet from the king.

CLAIRE

That sound incomplete to you, Toby?

TOBIAS *(Stern)*

Somewhat.

AGNES

Julia *has* been through a trying time, Tobias. . . .

HARRY *(A little apologetic)*

I suppose we did upset her some . . . .

EDNA *(Consoling)*

Of course!

TOBIAS

(To AGNES; *a kind of wondrous bewilderment)*

Don't you think you should go tend to her?

(The others all look to AGNES*)*

AGNES *(Shakes her head; lightly)*

No. She will be down or she will not. She will stop, or she will . . . go on.

TOBIAS *(Spluttering)*

Well, for God's sake, Agnes . . . !

AGNES *(An end to it; hard)*

I haven't the time, Tobias.

(Gentler)

I·haven't time for the four-hour talk, the soothing recapitulation. You don't go through it, my love: the history. Nothing is calmed by a pat on the hand, a gentle massage, or slowly, slowly combing the hair, no: the history. Teddy's birth, and how she felt unwanted, tricked; his death, and was she more relieved than lost . . . ? All the schools we sent her to, and did she fail in them through hate . . . or love? And when we come to marriage, dear: each one of them, the fear, the happiness, the sex, the stopping, the infidelities . . .

TOBIAS *(Nodding; speaks softly)*

All right, Agnes.

AGNES *(Shakes her head)*

Oh, my dear Tobias . . . my life is gone through more than hers. I see myself . . . growing old each time, see my own life passing. No, I haven't time for it now. At midnight, maybe . . .

(Sad smile)

when you're all in your beds . . . safely sleeping. Then I will comfort our Julia, and lose myself once more.

CLAIRE

(To break an uncomfortable silence)

I tell ya, there are so many martyrdoms here.

EDNA *(Seeing a hangnail)*

One to a person.

AGNES *(Dry)*

That is the usual,

(A glance at CLAIRE*)*

though I do believe there are some with none, and others who have known Job. The helpless are the cruelest lot of all: they shift their burdens so.

CLAIRE

If you interviewed a camel, he'd admit he loved his load.

EDNA *(Giving up on the hangnail)*

I wish you two would stop having at each other.

HARRY

Hell, yes! Let's have a drink, Tobias?

TOBIAS *(From deep in thought)*

Hm?

HARRY

What can I make yuh, buddy?

CLAIRE *(Rather pleased)*

Why, Edna; you've actually spoken your mind.

TOBIAS *(Confused as to where he is)*

What can *you* make *me?*

EDNA

I do . . . sometimes.

HARRY

Well, sure; I'm here.

EDNA *(Calm)*

When an environment is not all that it might be.

TOBIAS

Oh. Yeah; Scotch.

AGNES *(Strained smile)*

Is that for you to say?

CLAIRE *(A chord; then)*

Here we come!

AGNES

Stop it, Claire, dear.

   (To EDNA*)*

I said: Is that for you to say?

EDNA *(To* AGNES; *calm, steady)*

We must be helpful when we can, my dear; that is the . . . responsibility, the double demand of friendship . . . is it not?

AGNES *(Slightly schoolteacherish)*

But, when we are *asked.*

EDNA

   (Shakes her head, smiles gently)

No. Not only.

   (This heard by all)

It seemed to me, to us, that since we were living *here* . . .

(*Silence,* AGNES *and* TOBIAS *look from* EDNA *to* HARRY)

CLAIRE

That's my cue!

(*A chord, then begins to yodel, to an ump-pah base.* JULIA *appears in the archway, unseen by the others; her hair is wild, her face is tear-streaked; she carries* TOBIAS' *pistol, but not pointed; awkwardly and facing down*)

JULIA (*Solemnly and tearfully*)

Get them out of here, Daddy, getthemoutofheregetthemoutofheregetthemoutofheregetthemoutofheregetthemoutofhere. . . .

(*They all see* JULIA *and the gun simultaneously;* EDNA *gasps but does not panic;* HARRY *retreats a little;* TOBIAS *moves slowly toward* JULIA)

AGNES

Julia!

JULIA

Get them out of here, Daddy!

TOBIAS

(*Moving toward her, slowly, calmly, speaking in a quiet voice*)

All right, Julia, baby; let's have it now. . . .

JULIA

Get them out of here, Daddy. . . .

TOBIAS (*As before*)

Come on now, Julia.

JULIA

(*Calmly, she hands the gun to* TOBIAS, *nods*)

Get them out of here, Daddy.

AGNES (*Soft intensity*)

You ought to be horsewhipped, young lady.

TOBIAS

(*Meant for* both JULIA *and* AGNES)

All right, now . . .

JULIA

Do it, Daddy? Or give it back?

AGNES (*Turns on* JULIA; *withering*)

How dare you come into this room like that! How dare you embarrass me and your father! How dare you frighten Edna and Harry! How dare you come into this room like that!

JULIA

(To HARRY *and* EDNA; *venom)*
Are you going?

AGNES

Julia!

TOBIAS *(Pleading)*
Julia, please. . . .

JULIA

ARE YOU!?
(Silence, all eyes on HARRY *and* EDNA*)*

EDNA

(Finally; curiously unconcerned)
Going? No, we are not going.

HARRY

No.

JULIA *(To all)*
YOU SEE!?

HARRY

Coming down here with a gun like that . . .

EDNA *(Becoming* AGNES*)*
You return to your nest from your latest disaster, dispossessed, and suddenly dispossessing; screaming the house down, clawing at order . . .

JULIA

STOP HER!

EDNA

. . . willful, wicked, wretched girl . . .

JULIA

You are not my . . . YOU HAVE NO RIGHTS!

EDNA

We have rights here. *We* belong.

JULIA

MOTHER!

AGNES *(Tentative)*
Julia . . .

EDNA

We belong here, do we not?

JULIA *(Triumphant distaste)*

FOREVER!!

(Small silence)

HAVE YOU COME TO STAY FOREVER??

(Small silence)

EDNA

(Walks over to her, calmly slaps her)

If need be.

(To TOBIAS *and* AGNES, *calmly)*

Sorry; a godmother's duty.

(This next calm, almost daring addressed at, rather than to the others)

If we come to the point . . . we are at home one evening, and the . . . terror comes . . . descends . . . *if* all at once we . . . NEED . . . we come where we are wanted, where we know we are expected, not only where we want; we come where the table has been laid for us in such an event . . . where the bed is turned down . . . and warmed . . . and has been ready should we need it. We are not . . . transients . . . like some.

JULIA

NO!

EDNA *(To* JULIA)

You must . . . what is the word? . . . coexist, my dear.

(To the others)

Must she not?

(Silence; calm)

Must she not. This is what you have meant by friendship . . . is it not?

AGNES *(Pause; finally, calmly)*

You have come to live with us, then.

EDNA *(After a pause; calm)*

Why, yes; we have.

AGNES *(Dead calm; a sigh)*

Well, then.

(Pause)

Perhaps it is time for bed, Julia? Come upstairs with me.

JULIA *(A confused child)*

M-mother?

AGNES

Ah-ah; let me comb your hair, and rub your back.

(Arm over JULIA's *shoulder, leads her out. Exiting)*

And we shall soothe . . . and solve . . . and fall to sleep. Tobias?

(Exits with JULIA. *Silence)*

EDNA

Well, I think it's time for bed.

TOBIAS *(Vague, preoccupied)*

Well, yes; yes, of course.

EDNA

(She and HARRY *have risen; a small smile)*

We know the way.

(Pauses as she and HARRY *near the archway)*

Friendship *is* something like a marriage, is it not, Tobias? For better and for worse?

TOBIAS *(Ibid.)*

Sure.

EDNA *(Something of a demand here)*

We *haven't* come to the wrong place, *have* we?

HARRY *(Pause; shy)*

Have we, Toby?

TOBIAS *(Pause; gentle, sad)*

No.

(Sad smile)

No; of course you haven't.

EDNA

Good night, dear Tobias. Good night, Claire.

CLAIRE *(A half smile)*

Good night, you two.

HARRY

(A gentle pat at TOBIAS *as he passes)*

Good night, old man.

TOBIAS *(Watches as the two exit)*

Good . . . good night, you two.

*(*CLAIRE *and* TOBIAS *alone;* TOBIAS *still holds the pistol)*

CLAIRE *(After an interval)*

Full house, Tobias, every bed and every cupboard.

TOBIAS *(Not moving)*

Good night, Claire.

CLAIRE *(Rising leaving her accordion)*
Are you going to stay up, Tobias? Sort of a nightwatch, guarding? *I've done it.* The breathing, as you stand in the quiet halls, slow and heavy? And the special . . . warmth, and . . . permeation . . . of a house . . . asleep? When the house is sleeping? When the people *are* asleep?

TOBIAS
Good night, Claire.

CLAIRE *(Near the archway)*
And the difference? The different breathing and the cold, when every bed is awake . . . all night . . . very still, eyes open, staring into the dark? Do you know that one?

TOBIAS
Good night, Claire.

CLAIRE *(A little sad)*
Good night, Tobias.
   (Exit as the curtain falls)

ACT THREE

(Seven-thirty the next morning; same set. TOBIAS *alone, in a chair, wearing pajamas and a robe, slippers. Awake.* AGNES *enters, wearing a dressing gown which could pass for a hostess gown. Her movements are not assertive, and her tone is gentle)*

AGNES *(Seeing him)*

Ah; there you are.

TOBIAS

(Not looking at her, but at his watch; there is very little emotion in his voice)

Seven-thirty A.M., and all's well . . . I guess.

AGNES

So odd.

TOBIAS

Hm?

AGNES

There was a stranger in my room last night.

TOBIAS

Who?

AGNES

You.

TOBIAS

Ah.

AGNES

It was nice to have you there.

TOBIAS *(Slight smile)*

Hm.

AGNES

Le temps perdu. I've never understood that; *perdu* means lost, not merely . . . past, but it was nice to have you there, though I remember, when it was a constancy, how easily I would fall asleep, pace my breathing to your breathing, and if we were touching! ah, what a splendid cocoon that was. But last night— what a shame, what sadness—you were a stranger, and I stayed awake.

TOBIAS

I'm sorry.

AGNES

Were you asleep at all?

TOBIAS

No.

AGNES

I would go half, then wake—your unfamiliar presence, sir. I *could* get used to it again.

TOBIAS

Yes?

AGNES

I think.

TOBIAS

You didn't have your talk with Julia—your all-night lulling.

AGNES

No; she wouldn't let me stay. "Look to your own house," is what she said. You stay down long?

TOBIAS

When?

AGNES

After . . . before you came to bed.

TOBIAS

Some.
  (*Laughs softly, ruefully*)
I almost went into *my* room . . . by habit . . . by mistake, rather, but then I realized that your room is my room because my room is Julia's because Julia's room is . . .

AGNES

. . . yes.
  (*Goes to him, strokes his temple*)
And I was awake when you left my room again.

TOBIAS (*Gentle reproach*)

You could have said.

AGNES (*Curious at the truth*)

I felt shy.

TOBIAS (*Pleased surprise*)

Hm!

AGNES

Did you go to Claire?

TOBIAS

I never go to Claire.

AGNES

Did you go to Claire to talk?

TOBIAS

I never go to Claire.

AGNES

We must always envy someone we should not, be jealous of those who have so much less. You and Claire make so much sense together, talk so well.

TOBIAS

I never go to Claire at night, or talk with her alone—save publicly.

AGNES *(Small smile)*

In public rooms . . . like this.

TOBIAS

Yes.

AGNES

Have *never*.

TOBIAS

Please?

AGNES

Do we dislike happiness? We manufacture such a portion of our own despair . . . such busy folk.

TOBIAS

We are a highly moral land: we assume we have done great wrong. We find the things.

AGNES

I shall start missing you again—when you move from my room . . . if you do. I had stopped, I believe.

TOBIAS *(Grudging little chuckle)*

Oh, you're an honest woman.

AGNES

Well, we need *one* . . . in every house.

TOBIAS

It's very strange . . . to be downstairs, in a room where everyone has been, and is gone . . . very late, after the heat has gone—the furnace *and* the bodies: the hour or two before the sun comes up, the furnace starts again. And tonight especially: the cigarettes still in the ashtrays—odd, metallic smell. The odors of a room don't mix, late, when there's no one there, and I think the silence helps it . . . and the lack of bodies. Each . . . thing stands out in its place.

AGNES

What did you decide?

TOBIAS

And when you *do* come down . . . if you do, at three, or four, and you've left a light or two—in case someone should come in late, I suppose, but who is there left? The inn is full—it's rather . . . Godlike, if I may presume: to look at it all, reconstruct, with such . . . de*tach*ment, see your*self* you, Julia . . . Look at it all . . . play it out again, *watch.*

AGNES

Judge?

TOBIAS

No; that's being in it. Watch. And if you have a drink or two . . :

AGNES *(Mild surprise)*

Did you?

TOBIAS *(Nods)*

And if you have a drink or two, very late, in the quiet, tired, the mind . . . lets loose.

AGNES

Yes?

TOBIAS

And you watch it as it reasons, all with a kind of . . . grateful delight, at the same time sadly, 'cause you know that when the daylight comes the pressures will be on, and all the insight won't be worth a damn.

AGNES

What did you decide?

TOBIAS

You can sit and watch. You can have . . . so clear a picture, see everybody moving through his own jungle . . . an insight into all the reasons, all the needs.

AGNES

Good. And what did you decide?

TOBIAS *(No complaint)*

Why is the room so dirty? Can't we have better servants, some help who . . . help?

AGNES

They keep far better hours than we, that's all. They are a comment on our habits, a reminder that we are out of step—that is why we pay them . . . so very, very much. Neither a servant nor a master be. Remember?

TOBIAS

I remember when . . .

AGNES (*Picking it right up*)

. . . you were very young and lived at home, and the servants were awake whenever you were: six A.M. for your breakfast when you wanted it, or five in the morning when you came home drunk and seventeen, washing the vomit from the car, and you, telling no one; stealing just enough each month, by arrangement with the stores, to keep them in a decent wage; generations of them: the laundress, blind and always dying, and the cook, who did a better dinner drunk than sober. Those servants? Those days? When you were young, and lived at home?

TOBIAS (*Memory*)

Hmmm.

AGNES (*Sweet; sad*)

Well, my darling, you are not young now, and you do not live at home.

TOBIAS (*Sad question*)

Where do I live?

AGNES (*An answer of sorts*)

The dark sadness. Yes?

TOBIAS (*Quiet, rhetorical*)

What are we going to do?

AGNES

What did you decide?

TOBIAS (*Pause; they smile*)

Nothing.

AGNES

Well, you must. Your house is not in order, sir. It's full to bursting.

TOBIAS

Yes. You've got to help me here.

AGNES

No. I don't *think* so.

TOBIAS (*Some surprise*)

No?

AGNES

No. I thought a little last night, too: while you were seeing everything so clearly here. I lay in the dark, and I . . . revisited—our life, the years and years. There are many things a woman does: she bears the children—if there *is* that blessing. Blessing? Yes, I suppose, even with the sadness. She runs the house, for what that's worth: makes sure there's food, and not just anything, and decent linen; looks well; assumes whatever duties are demanded—if she is in love, or loves; and plans.

TOBIAS

(*Mumbled; a little embarrassed*)

I know, I know. . . .

AGNES

And plans. Right to the end of it; expects to be alone one day, abandoned by a heart attack or the cancer, *prepares* for that. And prepares earlier, for the children to become *adult* strangers instead of growing ones, for that loss, and for the body chemistry, the end of what the Bible tells us is our usefulness. The reins we hold! It's a team of twenty horses, and we sit there, and we watch the road and check the leather . . . if our . . . man is so disposed. But there are things we do not do.

TOBIAS (*Slightly edgy challenge*)

Yes?

AGNES

Yes.

(*Harder*)

We don't decide the route.

TOBIAS

You're copping out . . . as they say.

AGNES

No, indeed.

TOBIAS (*Quiet anger*)

Yes, you are!

AGNES (*Quiet warning*)

Don't you yell at me.

TOBIAS

You're copping *out!*

AGNES

(*Quiet, calm, and almost smug*)

We follow. We let our . . . men decide the moral issues.

TOBIAS (*Quite angry*)

Never! You've never done that in your life!

AGNES

Always, my darling. Whatever you decide . . . I'll make it work; I'll run it for you so you'll never know there's been a change in anything.

TOBIAS

(*Almost laughing; shaking his head*)

No. No.

AGNES *(To end the discussion)*

So, let me know.

TOBIAS *(Still almost laughing)*

I *know* I'm tired. I know I've hardly slept at all: I know I've sat down here, and thought . . .

AGNES

And made your decisions.

TOBIAS

But I have not *judged.* I told you that.

AGNES *(Almost a stranger)*

Well, when you have . . . you let me know.

TOBIAS *(Frustration and anger)*

NO!

AGNES *(Cool)*

You'll wake the house.

TOBIAS *(Angry)*

I'll wake the house!

AGNES

This is not the time for you to lose control.

TOBIAS

I'LL LOSE CONTROL! I have *sat* here . . . in the cold, in the empty cold, I have sat here alone, and . . .

   (Anger has shifted to puzzlement, complaint)

I've looked at *every*thing, *all* of it. I thought of you, and Julia, and Claire. . . .

AGNES *(Still cool)*

And Edna? And Harry?

TOBIAS *(Tiny pause; then anger)*

Well, of course! What do you think!

AGNES *(Tiny smile)*

I don't know. I'm listening.

   *(*JULIA *appears in the archway; wears a dressing gown; subdued, sleepy)*

JULIA

Good morning. I don't suppose there's . . . shall I make some coffee?

AGNES *(Chin high)*

Why don't you do that, darling.

TOBIAS (*A little embarrassed*)

Good morning, Julie.

JULIA (*Hating it*)

I'm sorry about last night, Daddy.

TOBIAS

Oh, well, now . . .

JULIA (*Bite to it*)

I mean I'm sorry for having embarrassed you.
(*Starts toward the hallway*)

AGNES

Coffee.

JULIA

(*Pausing at the archway; to* TOBIAS)
Aren't you sorry for embarrassing me, too?
(*Waits a moment, smiles, exits. Pause*)

AGNES

Well, isn't that nice that Julia's making coffee? No? If the help aren't up, isn't it nice to have a daughter who can put a pot to boil?

TOBIAS

(*Under his breath, disgusted*)
"Aren't you sorry for embarrassing me, too."

AGNES

You have a problem there with Julia.

TOBIAS

I? *I* have a problem!

AGNES

Yes.
(*Gentle irony*)
But at least you have your women with you—crowded 'round, firm arm, support. *That* must be a comfort to you. *Most* explorers go alone, don't have their families with them—pitching tents, tending the fire, shooing off the . . . the antelopes or the bears or whatever.

TOBIAS (*Wanting to talk about it*)

"Aren't you sorry for embarrassing me, too."

AGNES

Are you quoting?

TOBIAS

Yes.

AGNES

Next we'll have my sister with us—another porter for the dreadful trip.

(*Irony*)

Claire has never missed a chance to participate in watching. She'll be here.
We'll have us all.

TOBIAS

And you'll all sit down and watch me carefully; smoke your pipes and stir
the cauldron; watch.

AGNES (*Dreamy; pleased*)

Yes.

TOBIAS

You, who make all the decisions, really rule the game . . .

AGNES (*So patient*)

That is an *illusion* you have.

TOBIAS

You'll all sit here—too early for . . . *anything* on this . . . stupid Sunday—
all of you and . . . and *dare* me?—when it's just as much your choice as
mine?

AGNES

Each time that Julia comes, each clockwork time . . . do you send her back?
Do you tell her, "Julia, go home to your husband, try it again"? Do you?
No, you let it . . . slip. It's your decision, sir.

TOBIAS

It is not! I . . .

AGNES

. . . and I must live with it, resign myself one marriage more, and wait, and
hope that Julia's motherhood will come . . . one day, one marriage.

(*Tiny laugh*)

I am almost too old to be a grandmother as I'd hoped . . . too young to be
one. Oh, I had wanted that: the *youngest* older woman in the block. *Julia*
is almost too old to have a child properly, *will* be if she ever does . . . if she
marries again. *You* could have pushed her back . . . if you'd wanted to.

TOBIAS (*Bewildered incredulity*)

It's very early yet: that must be it. I've never heard such . . .

AGNES

Or Teddy! No? No stammering here? You'll let this pass?

TOBIAS (*Quiet embarrassment*)

Please.

AGNES *(Remorseless)*

When Teddy died?

(*Pause*)

We *could* have had another son; we could have tried. But no . . . those
months—or was it a year—?

TOBIAS

No more of this!

AGNES

. . . I think it was a year, when you spilled yourself on my belly, sir? "Please?
Please, Tobias?" No, you wouldn't even say it out: I don't want another
child, another loss. "Please? Please, Tobias?" And guiding you, *trying* to
hold you in?

TOBIAS *(Tortured)*

Oh, Agnes! Please!

AGNES

"Don't leave me then, like that. Not again, Tobias. Please? *I* can take care
of it: we *won't* have another child, but please don't . . . leave me like that."
Such . . . silent . . . sad, disgusted . . . love.

TOBIAS *(Mumbled, inaudible)*

I didn't want you to have to.

AGNES

Sir?

TOBIAS *(Numb)*

I didn't want you to have to . . . you know.

AGNES *(Laughs in spite of herself)*

Oh, that was thoughtful of you! Like a pair of adolescents in a rented
room, or in the family car. Doubtless you hated it as much as I.

TOBIAS *(Softly)*

Yes.

AGNES

But wouldn't let me help you.

TOBIAS *(Ibid.)*

No.

AGNES *(Irony)*

Which is why you took to your own sweet room instead.

TOBIAS *(Ibid.)*

Yes.

AGNES

The theory being pat: that a half a loaf is worse than none. That you are racked with guilt—stupidly!—and *I* must *suffer* for it.

TOBIAS *(Ibid.)*

Yes?

AGNES *(Quietly; sadly)*

Well, it was your decision, was it not?

TOBIAS *(Ibid.)*

Yes.

AGNES

And I have made the best of it. Have lived with it. Have I not?

TOBIAS *(Pause; a plea)*

What are we going to do? About everything?

AGNES *(Quietly; sadly; cruelly)*

Whatever you like. Naturally.
    (Silence. CLAIRE *enters, she, too, in a dressing gown)*

CLAIRE

(Judges the situation for a moment)

Morning, kids.

AGNES

(To TOBIAS, *in reference to* CLAIRE*)*

All I can do, my dear, is run it for you . . . and forecast.

TOBIAS *(Glum)*

Good morning, Claire.

AGNES

Julia is in the kitchen making coffee, Claire.

CLAIRE

Which means, I guess, I go watch Julia grind the beans and drip the water, hunh?
    (Exiting)
I tell ya, she's a real pioneer, that girl: coffee pot in one hand, pistol in t'other.
    (Exits)

AGNES *(Small smile)*

Claire is a comfort in the early hours . . . I have been told.

TOBIAS *(A dare)*

Yes?

AGNES
(Pretending not to notice his tone)
That is what I have been *told*.

TOBIAS *(Blurts it out)*
Shall I ask them to leave?

AGNES *(Tiny pause)*
Who?

TOBIAS *(Defiant)*
Harry and Edna?

AGNES *(Tiny laugh)*
Oh. For a moment I thought you meant Julia and Claire.

TOBIAS *(Glum)*
No. Harry and Edna. Shall I throw them out?

AGNES *(Restatement of a fact)*
Harry is your very best friend in the whole . . .

TOBIAS *(Impatient)*
Yes, and Edna is yours. Well?

AGNES
You'll have to live with it either way: do or don't.

TOBIAS *(Anger rising)*
Yes? Well, then, why *don't* I throw Julia and Claire out instead? Or better yet, why don't I throw the whole bunch out!?

AGNES
Or get rid of me! That would be easier: rid yourself of the harridan. Then you can run your mission and take out sainthood papers.

TOBIAS *(Clenched teeth)*
I think you're stating an opinion, a preference.

AGNES
But if you *do* get rid of me . . . you'll no longer have your life the way you want it.

TOBIAS *(Puzzled)*
But that's not my . . . that's not all the choice I've got, is it?

AGNES
I don't care very much what choice you've got, my darling, but I *am* concerned with what choice you *make*.
  (JULIA and CLAIRE enter; JULIA carries a tray with coffee pot, cups,
  sugar, cream; CLAIRE carries a tray with four glasses of orange juice)
Ah, here are the helpmeets, what would we do without them.

JULIA *(Brisk, efficient)*

The coffee is instant, I'm afraid; I couldn't find a bean: Those folk must lock them up before they go to bed.

(Finds no place to put her tray down)

Come on, Pop; let's clear away a little of the debris, hunh?

TOBIAS

P-Pop?

AGNES *(Begins clearing)*

It's true: we cannot drink our coffee amidst a sea of last night's glasses. Tobias, do be a help.

(TOBIAS *rises, takes glasses to the sideboard, as* AGNES *moves some to another table)*

CLAIRE *(Cheerful)*

And I didn't have to do a thing; thank God for pre-squeezed orange juice.

JULIA *(Setting the tray down)*

There; now that's much better, isn't it?

TOBIAS *(In a fog)*

Whatever you say, Julie.

(JULIA *pours, knows what people put in)*

CLAIRE

Now, I'll play waiter. Sis?

AGNES

Thank you, Claire.

CLAIRE

Little Julie?

JULIA

Just put it down beside me, Claire. I'm pouring, you can see.

CLAIRE

(Looks at her a moment, does not, offers a glass to TOBIAS*)*

Pop?

TOBIAS *(Bewildered, apprehensive)*

Thank you, Claire.

CLAIRE

(Puts JULIA's *glass on the mantel)*

Yours is here, daughter, when you've done with playing early-morning hostess.

JULIA

(Intently pouring; does not rise to the bait)

Thank you, Claire.

CLAIRE

Now; one for little Claire.

JULIA *(Still pouring; no expression)*

Why don't you have some vodka in it, Claire? To start the Sunday off?

AGNES *(Pleased chuckle)*

Julia!

TOBIAS *(Reproving)*

Please, Julie!

JULIA *(Looks up at him; cold)*

Did I say something wrong, Father?

CLAIRE

Vodka? Sunday? Ten to eight? Why not!

TOBIAS

(Quietly, as she moves to the sideboard)

You don't *have* to, Claire.

JULIA *(Dropping sugar in a cup)*

Let her do what she wants.

CLAIRE *(Pouring vodka into her glass)*

Yes I *do*, Tobias; the rules of the guestbook—be polite. We have our friends and guests for patterns, don't we?—known quantities. The drunks stay drunk; the Catholics go to Mass, the bounders bound. We can't have changes—throws the balance off.

JULIA *(Ibid.)*

Besides; you like to drink.

CLAIRE

Besides, I like to drink. Just think, Tobias, what would happen if the patterns changed: you wouldn't know where you stood, and the world would be full of strangers; that would never do.

JULIA *(Not very friendly)*

Bring me my orange juice, will you please.

CLAIRE *(Getting it for her)*

Oooh, Julia's back for a spell, I think—settling in.

JULIA *(Handing TOBIAS his coffee)*

Father?

TOBIAS (*Embarrassed*)

Thank you, Julia.

JULIA

Mother?

AGNES (*Comfortable*)

Thank you, darling.

JULIA

Yours is here, Claire; on the tray.

CLAIRE

(*Considers a moment, looks at* JULIA's *orange juice, still in one of her hands, calmly pours it on the rug*)

Your juice is here, Julia, when you want lt.

AGNES (*Furious*)

CLAIRE!

TOBIAS (*Mild reproach*)

For God's sake, Claire.

JULIA

(*Looks at the mess on the rug; shrugs*)

Well, why not. Nothing changes.

CLAIRE

Besides, our friends upstairs don't like the room; they'll want some alterations.

(CLAIRE *sits down*)

TOBIAS

(*Lurches to his feet; stands, legs apart*)

Now! All of you! Sit down! Shut up. I want to talk to you.

JULIA

Did I give you sugar, Mother?

TOBIAS

BE QUIET, JULIA!

AGNES

Shhh, my darling, yes, you did.

TOBIAS

I want to talk to you.

(*Silence*)

CLAIRE

(*Slightly mocking encouragement*)

Well, go *on*, Tobias.

TOBIAS *(A plea)*

You, too, Claire? Please.

> *(Silence. The women stir their coffee or look at him, or at the floor. They seem like children about to be lectured, unwilling, and dangerous, but, for the moment, behaved)*

Now.

> *(Pause)*

Now, something happened here last night, and I don't mean Julia's hysterics with the gun—be quiet, Julia!— though I *do* mean that, in part. I mean . . .

> *(Deep sigh)*

. . . Harry and Edna . . . coming here . . . (JULIA *snorts*)
Yes? Did you want to say something, Julia? No? I came down here and I sat, all night—hours—and I did something rather rare for this family: I *thought* about something. . . .

AGNES *(Mild)*

I'm sorry, Tobias, but that's not fair.

TOBIAS *(Riding over)*

I *thought*. I sat down here and I thought about all of us . . . and everything. Now, Harry and Edna have come to us and . . . asked for help.

JULIA

That is not *true*.

TOBIAS

Be quiet!

JULIA

That is not true! They have not *asked* for anything!

AGNES

. . . please, Julia . . .

JULIA

They have *told!* They have come in here and *ordered!*

CLAIRE *(Toasts)*

Just like the family.

TOBIAS

Asked! If you're begging and you've got your pride . . .

JULIA

If you're begging, then you may not have your pride!

AGNES *(Quiet contradiction)*

I don't think that's true, Julia.

CLAIRE

Julia wouldn't know. Ask me.

JULIA (*Adamant*)

Those people have no right!

TOBIAS

No right? All these years? We've known them since . . . for God's sake, Julia, those people are our *friends!*

JULIA (*Hard*)

THEN TAKE THEM IN!
(*Silence*)
Take these . . . intruders in.

CLAIRE (*To* JULIA: *hard*)

Look, baby; didn't you get the message on rights last night? Didn't you learn about intrusion, what the score is, who belongs?

JULIA (*To* TOBIAS)

You bring these people in here, Father, and I'm leaving!

TOBIAS (*Almost daring her*)

Yes?

JULIA

I don't mean coming and going, Father; I mean as *family!*

TOBIAS (*Frustration and rage*)

HARRY AND EDNA ARE OUR FRIENDS!!

JULIA (*Equal*)

THEY ARE INTRUDERS!!
(*Silence*)

CLAIRE (*To* TOBIAS, *laughing*)

Crisis sure brings out the best in us, don't it, Tobe? The family circle? Julia standing there . . . *asserting;* perpetual brat, and maybe ready to pull a Claire. *And* poor Claire! Not much help there either, is there? And lookit Agnes, talky Agnes, ruler of the roost, and maître d', *and* licensed wife—silent. All cozy, coffee, thinking of the menu for the week, *planning.* Poor Tobe.

AGNES (*Calm, assured*)

Thank you, Claire; I was merely waiting—until I'd heard, and thought a little, listened to the rest of you. I thought someone should sit back. Especially me: ruler of the roost, licensed wife, midnight . . . nurse. And I've been thinking about Harry and Edna; about disease.

TOBIAS (*After a pause*)

About what?

CLAIRE *(After a swig)*

About disease.

JULIA

Oh, for God's sake . . .

AGNES

About disease—or, if you like, the terror.

CLAIRE *(Chuckles softly)*

Unh, hunh.

JULIA *(Furious)*

TERROR!?

AGNES *(Unperturbed)*

Yes: the terror. Or the plague—they're both the same. Edna and Harry have come to us—dear friends, our very best, though there's a judgment to be made about that, I think—have come to us and brought the plague. Now, poor Tobias has sat up all night and wrestled with the moral problem.

TOBIAS *(Frustration; anger)*

I've not been . . . *wrestling* with some . . . abstract problem! These are *people!* Harry and Edna! These are our friends, God damn it!

AGNES

Yes, but they've brought the plague with them, and that's another matter. Let me tell you something about disease . . . mortal illness; you either are immune to it . . . or you fight it. If you are immune, you wade right in, you treat the patient until he either lives, or dies of it. But if you are *not* immune, you risk infection. Ten centuries ago—and even less—the treatment was quite simple . . . burn them. Burn their bodies, burn their houses, burn their clothes—and move to another town, if you were enlightened. But now, with modern medicine, we merely isolate; we quarantine, we ostracize—if we are not immune ourselves, or unless we are saints. So, your night-long vigil, darling, your reasoning in the cold, pure hours, has been over the patient, and not the illness. It is not Edna and Harry who have come to us—our friends—it is a disease.

TOBIAS

(Quiet anguish, mixed with impatience)

Oh, for God's sake, Agnes! It is our friends! What am I supposed to do? Say: "Look, you can't stay here, you two, you've got trouble. You're friends, and all, but you come in here *clean.*" Well, I can't do that. No. Agnes, for God's sake, if . . . if that's all Harry and Edna mean to us, then . . . then what about *us?* When we talk to each other . . . what have we meant? Anything? When we touch, when we promise, and say . . . yes, or please . . . with our*selves?* . . . have we meant, yes, but only if . . . if there's any condition, Agnes! Then it's . . . all been empty.

AGNES *(Noncommittal)*

Perhaps. But blood binds us. Blood holds us together when we've no more . . . deep affection for ourselves than others. I am *not* asking you to choose between your family and . . . our friends . . . .

TOBIAS

Yes you are!

AGNES *(Eyes closed)*

I am merely saying that there is *disease* here! And I ask you: who in this family is immune?

CLAIRE *(Weary statement of fact)*

I am. I've had it. I'm still alive, I think.

AGNES

Claire is the strongest of us all: the walking wounded often are, the least susceptible; but think about the rest of us. Are we immune to it? The plague, my darling, the terror sitting in the room upstairs? Well, if we are, then . . . on with it! And, if we're not . . .

(Shrugs)

well, why not be infected, why not die of it? We're bound to die of something . . . soon, or in a while. Or shall we burn them out, rid ourselves of it all . . . and wait for the next invasion. You decide, my darling.

(Silence. TOBIAS rises, walks to the window; the others sit. HARRY and EDNA appear in the archway, dressed for the day, but not with coats)

EDNA *(No emotion)*

Good morning.

AGNES *(Brief pause)*

Ah, you're up.

CLAIRE

Good morning, Edna, Harry.

(JULIA does not look at them; TOBIAS does, but says nothing)

EDNA

(A deep breath, rather a recitation)

Harry wants to talk to Tobias. I think that they should be alone. Perhaps . . .

AGNES

Of course.

(The three seated women rise, as at a signal, begin to gather the coffee things)

Why don't we all go in the kitchen, make a proper breakfast.

HARRY

Well, now, no; you don't have to . . .

AGNES

Yes, yes, we want to leave you to your talk. Tobias?

TOBIAS (*Quiet*)

Uh . . . yes.

AGNES (*To* TOBIAS; *comfortingly*)

We'll be nearby.
(The women start out)
Did you sleep well, Edna? Did you sleep at all? I've never had that bed,
but I know that when . . .
(The women have exited)

HARRY

(Watching them go; laughs ruefully)
Boy, look at 'em go. They got outa *here* quick enough. You'd think there
was a . . .
(Trails off sees TOBIAS *is ill at ease; says, gently)*
Morning, Tobias.

TOBIAS (*Grateful*)

Morning, Harry.
(Both men stay standing)

HARRY (*Rubs his hands together*)

You, ah . . . you know what I'd like to do? Something I've never done in
my life, except once, when I was about twenty-four?

TOBIAS (*Not trying to guess*)

No? What?

HARRY

Have a drink before breakfast? Is, is that all right?

TOBIAS

(Smiles wanly, moves slowly toward the sideboard)
Sure.

HARRY (*Shy*)

Will you join me?

TOBIAS (*Very young*)

I guess so, yes. There isn't any ice.

HARRY

Well, just some whiskey, then; neat.

TOBIAS

Brandy?

HARRY

No, oh, God, no.

TOBIAS

Whiskey, then.

HARRY

Yes. Thank you.

TOBIAS (*Somewhat glum*)

Well, here's to youth again.

HARRY

Yes.
(*Drinks*)
Doesn't taste too bad in the morning, does it?

TOBIAS

No, but I had some . . . before.

HARRY

When?

TOBIAS

Earlier . . . oh, three, four, while you all were . . . asleep, or whatever you
were doing.

HARRY (*Seemingly casual*)

Oh, you were . . . awake, hunh?

TOBIAS

Yes.

HARRY

I slept a *little*.
(*Glum laugh*)
God.

TOBIAS

What?

HARRY

You know what I did last night?

TOBIAS

No?

HARRY

I got out of bed and I . . . crawled in with Edna?

TOBIAS

Yes?

HARRY

She held me. She let me stay awhile, then I could see she wanted to, and I didn't . . . so I went back. But it was funny.

TOBIAS (*Nods*)

Yeah.

HARRY

Do you . . . do you, uh, like Edna . . . Tobias?

TOBIAS (*Embarrassed*)

Well, sure I *like* her, Harry.

HARRY (*Pause*)

Now, Tobias, about last night, and yesterday, and our coming here, now . . .

HARRY	TOBIAS
I was talking about it to Edna, last night, and I said, "Look, Edna, what do we think we're doing."	I sat up all night and I thought about it, Harry, and I talked to Agnes this morning, before you all came down.

HARRY

I'm sorry.

TOBIAS

I said, I sat up all night and I thought about it, Harry, and I talked to Agnes, too, before you all came down, and . . . By God, it isn't easy, Harry . . . but we can make it. . . if you want us to . . . . *I* can, I mean, I *think* I can.

HARRY

No . . . we're . . . we're going, Tobias.

TOBIAS

I don't know what help . . . I don't know *how* . . .

HARRY

I said: we're *going*.

TOBIAS

Yes, but . . . you're going?

HARRY (*Nice, shy smile*)

Sure.

TOBIAS

But, but you can *try* it here . . . or we can, God, I don't know, Harry. You can't go back there; you've got to . . .

HARRY

Got to what? Sell the house? Buy another? Move to the club?

TOBIAS

You came *here!*

HARRY *(Sad)*

Do you *want* us here, Tobias?

TOBIAS

You *came* here.

HARRY

Do you *want* us here?

TOBIAS

You *came! Here!*

HARRY *(Too clearly enunciated)*

Do you want us here?

(Subdued, almost apologetic)

Edna and I . . . there's. . . so much . . . over the dam, so many . . . disappointments, evasions, I guess, lies maybe . . . so much we remember we wanted, once . . . so little that we've . . . settled for . . . we talk, sometimes, but mostly . . . no. We don't . . . "like." Oh, sure, we *like* . . . but I've always been a little shy— gruff, you know, and . . . shy. And Edna isn't . . . happy—I suppose that's it. We . . . we like you and . . . and Agnes, and . . . well Claire, and Julia, too, I guess I mean . . . *I* like you, and you like me, I think, and . . . you're our best friends, but . . . I told Edna upstairs, I said: Edna, what if they'd come to us? And she didn't say anything. And I said: Edna, if they'd come to us like this, and even though we don't have . . . Julia, and all of that, I . . . Edna, I wouldn't take them in.

(Brief silence)

I wouldn't take them in, Edna; they don't . . . they don't have any right. And she said: yes, I know; they wouldn't have the right.

(Brief silence)

Toby, I wouldn't let *you* stay.

(Shy, embarrassed)

You . . . you don't *want* us, do you, Toby? You don't want us here.

TOBIAS

(This next is an aria. It must have in its performance all the horror and exuberance of a man who has kept his emotions under control too long. TOBIAS *will be carried to the edge of hysteria, and he will find himself laughing sometimes, while he cries from sheer release. All in all, it is genuine and bravura at the same time, one prolonging the other. I shall try to notate it somewhat)*

(Softly, and as if the word were unfamiliar)

Want?

(Same)

What? Do I what?

(Abrupt laugh; joyous)

> DO I WANT?

(More laughter; also a sob)

> DO I WANT YOU HERE!

(Hardly able to speak from the laughter)

> You come in here, you come in here with
> your . . . wife, and with your . . . terror!
> And you ask me if I want you here!

(Great breathing sounds)

> YES! OF COURSE! I WANT YOU
> HERE! THIS IS MY HOUSE! I WANT
> YOU IN IT! I WANT YOUR PLAGUE!
> YOU'VE GOT SOME TERROR WITH
> YOU? BRING IT IN!

(Pause, then, even louder)

> BRING IT IN!! YOU'VE GOT THE
> ENTREE, BUDDY, YOU DON'T NEED
> A KEY! YOU'VE GOT THE ENTREE,
> BUDDY! FORTY YEARS!

(Soft, now; soft and fast, almost a monotone)

> You don't need to ask me, Harry, you
> don't need to ask a thing; you're our
> friends, our very best friends in the
> world, and you don't have to ask.

(A shout)

> WANT? ASK?

(Soft, as before)

> You come for dinner don't you come for
> cocktails see us at the club on Saturdays
> and talk and lie and laugh with us and pat
> old Agnes on the hand and say you don't
> know what old Toby'd do without her and
> we've known you all these years and we
> love each other don't we?

(Shout)

> DON'T WE?! DON'T WE LOVE EACH
> OTHER?

(Soft again, laughter and tears in it)

> Doesn't friendship grow to that? To love?
> Doesn't forty years amount to anything?
> We've cast our lot together, boy, we're
> friends, we've been through lots of thick
> OR thin together. Which is it, boy?

(Shout)

WHICH IS IT, BOY?!
THICK?!
THIN?!
WELL, WHATEVER IT IS, WE'VE
BEEN THROUGH IT, BOY!

(Soft)

And you don't have to ask. I like you,
Harry, yes, I really do, I don't like Edna,
but that's not half the point, I like you
fine; I find my liking you has limits. . . .

(Loud)

BUT THOSE ARE MY LIMITS! NOT
YOURS!

(Soft)

The fact I like you well enough, but not
enough . . . that best friend in the world
should be something else—more—well,
that's my poverty. So, bring your wife,
and bring your terror, bring your plague.

(Loud)

BRING YOUR PLAGUE!

*(The four women appear in the archway, coffee cups in hand,
stand, watch)*

I DON'T WANT YOU HERE!
YOU ASKED?!
NO! I DON'T

(Loud)

BUT BY CHRIST YOU'RE GOING TO
STAY HERE!
YOU'VE GOT THE RIGHT!
THE RIGHT!
DO YOU KNOW THE WORD?
THE RIGHT!

(Soft)

You've put nearly forty years in it, baby;
so have I, and if it's nothing, I don't give
a damn, you've got the right to be here,
you've earned it

(Loud)

AND BY GOD YOU'RE GOING TO
TAKE IT!
DO YOU HEAR ME?!
YOU BRING YOUR TERROR AND YOU
COME IN HERE AND YOU LIVE WITH

                                US! YOU BRING YOUR PLAGUE!
                                YOU STAY WITH US!
                                I DON'T WANT YOU HERE!
                                I DON'T LOVE YOU!
                                BUT BY GOD . . . YOU STAY!!

(Pause)

                                STAY!

(Softer)

                                Stay!

(Soft, tears)

                                Stay. Please? Stay?

(Pause)

                                Stay? Please? Stay?

(A silence in the room. HARRY, *numb, rises; the women come into the room, slowly, stand. The play is quiet and subdued from now until the end)*

EDNA *(Calm)*

Harry, will you bring our bags down? Maybe Tobias will help you. Will you ask him?

HARRY *(Gentle)*

Sure.

(Goes to TOBIAS, *who is quietly wiping tears from his face, takes him gently by the shoulder)*

Tobias? Will you help me? Get the bags upstairs? (TOBIAS *nods, puts his arm around* HARRY. *The two men exit. Silence)*

EDNA

(Stirring her coffee; slightly strained, but conversational)

Poor Harry; he's not a . . . callous man, for all his bluff.

(Relaxing a little, almost a contentment)

He . . . he came to my bed last night, got in with me, I . . . let him stay, and talk. I let him think I . . . wanted to make love; he . . . it pleases him, I think—to know he would be wanted, if he . . . He said to me . . . He . . . he lay there in the dark with me—this man—and he said to me, very softly, and like a little boy, rather: "Do they love us? Do they love us, Edna?" Oh, I let a silence go by. "Well . . . as much as we love them . . . I should think."

(Pause)

The hair on his chest is very gray . . . and soft. "Would . . . would we let them stay, Edna?" Almost a whisper. Then still again.

(Kindly)

Well, I hope he told Tobias something simple, something to help. We mustn't press our luck, must we: test.

(Pause. Slight smile)

It's sad to come to the end of it, isn't it, nearly the end; so much more of it gone by . . . than left, and still not know—still not have learned . . . the boundaries, what we may not do . . . not ask, for fear of looking in a mirror. We *shouldn't* have come.

AGNES (A bit by rote)

Now, Edna . . .

EDNA

For our own sake; our own . . . lack. It's sad to know you've gone through it all, or most of it, without . . . that the one body you've wrapped your arms around . . . the only skin you've ever known . . . is your own—and that it's dry . . . and not warm.

(Pause. Back to slightly strained conversational tone)

What will you do, Julia? Will you be seeing Douglas?

JULIA (Looking at her coffee)

I haven't thought about it; I don't know; I doubt it.

AGNES

Time.

(Pause. They look at her)

Time happens, I suppose.

(Pause. They still look)

To people. Everything becomes . . . too late, finally. You know it's going on . . . up on the hill; you can see the dust, and hear the cries, and the steel . . . but you wait; and time happens. When you *do* go, sword, shield . . . finally . . . there's nothing there . . . save rust; bones; and the wind.

(Pause)

I'm sorry about the coffee, Edna. The help must hide the beans, or take them with them when they go to bed.

EDNA

Oooh. Coffee and wine: they're much the same with me—I can't tell good from bad.

CLAIRE

Would anyone . . . besides Claire . . . care to have a drink?

AGNES (Muttered)

Oh, really, Claire.

CLAIRE

Edna?

EDNA (Little deprecating laugh)

Oh, good heavens, thank you, Claire. No.

CLAIRE

Julia?

JULIA

(Looks up at her; steadily; slowly)
All right; thank you. I will.

EDNA

(As AGNES *is about to speak; rising)*
I think I hear the men.
*(*TOBIAS *and* HARRY *appear in the archway, with bags)*

TOBIAS

We'll just take them to the car, now.
(They do so)

EDNA

(Pleasant, but a little strained)
Thank you, Agnes, you've been . . . well, just thank you. We'll be seeing you.

AGNES

(Rises, too; some worry on her face)
Yes; well, don't be strangers.

EDNA *(Laughs)*

Oh, good Lord, how could we be? Our lives are . . . the same.
(Pause)
Julia . . . think a little.

JULIA *(A trifle defiant)*

Oh, I will, Edna. I'm fond of marriage.

EDNA

Claire, my darling, *do* be good.

CLAIRE

(Two drinks in her hands; bravura)
Well, I'll try to be quiet.

EDNA

I'm going into town on Thursday, Agnes. Would you like to come?
(A longer pause than necessary, CLAIRE *and* JULIA *look at* AGNES*)*

AGNES *(Just a trifle awkward)*

Well . . . no, I don't think so, Edna; I've . . . I've so much to do.

EDNA *(Cooler; sad)*

Oh. Well . . . perhaps another week.

AGNES

Oh, yes; we'll do it.
    (*The men reappear*)

TOBIAS

    (*Somewhat formal, reserved*)
All done.

HARRY (*Slight sigh*)

All set.

AGNES

    (*Going to* HARRY, *embracing him*)
Harry, my darling; take good care.

HARRY

    (*Kisses her, awkwardly, on the cheek*)
Th-thank you, Agnes; you, too, Julia? You . . . you be good.

JULIA

Goodbye, Harry.

CLAIRE (*Handing* JULIA *her drink*)
'Bye, Harry: see you 'round.

HARRY (*Smiles, a little ruefully*)
Sure thing, Claire.

EDNA (*Embraces* TOBIAS)
Goodbye, Tobias . . . thank you.

TOBIAS (*Mumbled*)
Goodbye, Edna.
    (*Tiny silence*)

HARRY

    (*Puts his hand out, grabs* TOBIAS', *shakes it hard*)
Thanks, old man.

TOBIAS (*Softly; sadly*)
Please? Stay?
    (*Pause*)

HARRY (*Nods*)
See you at the club. Well? Edna?
    (*They start out*)

AGNES (*After them*)
Drive carefully, now. It's Sunday.

EDNA'S AND HARRY'S VOICES

All right. Goodbye. Thank you.

(The four in the room together. JULIA *and* CLAIRE *have sat down;* AGNES *moves to* TOBIAS, *puts her arm around him)*

AGNES *(Sigh)*

Well. Here we all are. You all right, my darling?

TOBIAS *(Clears his throat)*

Sure.

AGNES

(Still with her arm around him)

Your daughter has taken to drinking in the morning, I hope you'll notice.

TOBIAS *(Unconcerned)*

Oh?

(Moves away from her)

I had one here . . . somewhere, one with Harry. Oh, there it is.

AGNES

Well, I would seem to have *three* early-morning drinkers now. I hope it won't become a club. We'd have to get a license, would we not?

TOBIAS

Just think of it as very late at night.

AGNES

All right, I will.

(Silence)

TOBIAS

I tried.

(Pause)

I was honest.

(Silence)

Didn't I?

(Pause)

Wasn't I?

JULIA *(Pause)*

You were very honest, Father. And you tried.

TOBIAS

Didn't I try, Claire? Wasn't I honest?

CLAIRE *(Comfort; rue)*

Sure you were. You tried.

TOBIAS

I'm sorry. I apologize.

AGNES *(To fill a silence)*

What I find most astonishing—aside from my belief that I will, one day . . . lose my mind—but when? Never, I begin to think, as the years go by, or that I'll not *know* if it happens, or maybe even *has*—what I find most astonishing, I think, is the wonder of daylight, of the sun. All the centuries, millenniums—all the history—I wonder if that's why we sleep at night, because the darkness still . . . frightens us? They say we sleep to let the demons out—to let the mind go raving mad, our dreams and nightmares all our logic gone awry, the dark side of our reason. And when the daylight comes again . . . comes order with it.

(Sad chuckle)

Poor Edna and Harry.

(Sigh)

Well, they're safely gone . . . and we'll all forget . . . quite soon.

(Pause)

Come now; we can begin the day.

CURTAIN

Everything in the Garden

FROM THE PLAY BY

GILES COOPER

To the memory of
Giles Cooper

FIRST PERFORMANCE

November 16, 1967, New York City, Plymouth Theatre

BARBARA BEL GEDDES *as* JENNY

BARRY NELSON *as* RICHARD

ROBERT MOORE *as* JACK

BEATRICE STRAIGHT *as* MRS. TOOTHE

RICHARD THOMAS *as* ROGER

MARY K. WELLS *as* BERYL

WHITEFIELD CONNOR as CHUCK

M'EL DOWD *as* LOUISE

TOM ALDREDGE *as* GILBERT

CHARLES BAXTER *as* PERRY

AUGUSTA DABNEY *as* CYNTHIA

Directed by PETER GLENVILLE

CHARACTERS

RICHARD
A pleasant-looking man, 43

JENNY
His wife, an attractive woman in her late thirties

ROGER
Their son, a nice-looking boy, 14 or 15

JACK
A neighbor, a pleasant-looking man, about 40

MRS. TOOTHE
An elegantly dressed, handsome lady, 50 or so

CHUCK AND BERYL

GILBERT AND LOUISE

CYNTHIA AND PERRY
Friends and neighbors,
very much like Richard and Jenny

THE SCENE

The living room and sunroom of a suburban house, a large and well-kept garden visible through the glass doors of the sunroom. This was an old house, and the sunroom is clearly an addition to the existing structure, though not jarring. There is no wealth evident in the set; taste and ingenuity have been used instead of money.

ACT ONE

SCENE ONE

(Stage empty, sounds of lawnmower (hand) out picture window. RICHARD *passes window, mowing; stops, mops; goes on.* JENNY *enters room from hall, looking for a cigarette; finds pack on mantel, finds it empty, is about to throw it away, remembers, removes coupons, then is about to throw pack in wastebasket when she spies another empty pack therein, shakes her head, stoops, takes it out, un-crumples it, removes coupons)*

JENNY

(Shakes her head; under her breath)
Honestly!
(Louder, but RICHARD *cannot possibly hear)*
You might remember!
*(*RICHARD *passes window again, mowing;* JENNY *opens glass door, speaks out to him)*
You might remember!
(He goes on mowing; irritated)
Richard!
(He stops)

RICHARD *(We really don't hear him)*
Hm?

JENNY
You might try to remember!
(Turns, comes back in, leaving glass door open)

RICHARD
(Follows her in, mopping neck with handkerchief)
I might what?

JENNY
You might remember.
(Leaves it at that)

RICHARD *(Thinks)*
All right. *(Pause)* I might remember what?

JENNY *(Still looking for a cigarette)*

When you throw them away.

RICHARD *(Considers that)*

Um-hum. *(Pause)* May I go back out now? *Some*body's got to get the damn
lawn mowed, and I don't notice any gardeners out there waiting for me to
tell them what . . .

JENNY

(Finding every cigarette box empty)

I've told you two thousand times: well, I've told you *two* things two thousand times: please keep cigarettes in the house . . .

RICHARD *(Used to it, but airy)*

You're running it.

JENNY

(Something of the strict schoolteacher creeping in)

When you finish a pack, do two things—I've told you . . .

RICHARD

—two thousand times—

JENNY

(Closes her eyes for a moment, goes on)

. . . first, when you finish a pack, look to see if it's the last one—the last
pack . . .

RICHARD *(Bored, impatient)*

Yes, ma'am.

JENNY *(Undaunted)*

And if it is, put it down to get some more, or tell *me* . . .

RICHARD *(Ibid.)*

O.K.; O.K.

JENNY

Whenever you *do* finish a pack, don't forget to take the coupons off.
Please? The coupons? We save them?

RICHARD

Did I *forget?*

JENNY

You *always* forget. We smoke these awful things just to get the coupons . . .

RICHARD *(Offhand)*

O.K.

JENNY *(After a small pause)*

Do you have any?

RICHARD

Coupons?

JENNY (*Not amused*)

Cigarettes!

RICHARD (*Feels*)

Um-hum.
   (*Suddenly aware*)
Want one?
   (*Offers her the pack*)

JENNY (*Sees the pack*)

Why, you dog! Those aren't . . . What are you—how dare you smoke *those*
cigarettes, those don't have coupons, you . . . Do you mean I sit in here,
ruining my lungs, piling up coupons, while you're sneaking around . . .

RICHARD (*Giggles at being caught*)

Caught me, huh?

JENNY

You little . . . twerp!

RICHARD (*Lighting for her*)

Big twerp. Good, aren't they?

JENNY (*Rue*)

Yes. (*Pause*) How's the lawn?

RICHARD

Growing.

JENNY

Remember what I told you: watch out for the tulips.

RICHARD (*Exaggerated contrition*)

Well, I gotta confess I got carried away, zooming along with the mower,
   (*Fast shiver sound*)
br-br-br-br-br-br-br, mowed 'em down; by the time I got control of
myself must have chopped up a good two dozen of 'em.
   (*Afterthought*)
Sorry.

JENNY (*Nods knowingly*)

Well, it wasn't funny that time you did.
   (*More-or-less to herself*)
Honestly, a grown man running a lawnmower through a tulip bed.

RICHARD (*Jaunty and proud*)

I rather liked it. Besides, what do you mean, "How's the lawn?" What do you care about the lawn? It could turn into one big dandelion patch for all you'd care so long as it didn't interfere with your hollyhocks and your tulips and your pink Williams, or whatever they are.

JENNY (*Superior, but friendly*)

We all do what we're equipped for. Some of us are fit for keeping a lawn cut, and others . . . well, how green is my thumb.

RICHARD (*Looks at it all*)

Looks good. Your scrambled eggs are a mess, but you sure can keep a garden.

JENNY (*Sweet-and-sour*)

I'm just an outdoor type.

RICHARD (*Kisses her forehead*)

Yes. You are.

(*Collapses in an easy chair; groans with fatigue*)

OOOOOHHHHhhhhhhhhhhhh, God!

JENNY

Hm?

RICHARD (*Sincere and sad*)

I *wish* we could afford things.

JENNY (*Muted; ironic*)

Keep smoking! Save those coupons!

RICHARD

Roger call? He get to school O.K.?

JENNY

Yes, he has three roommates this year, and they're going to let him have his bike.

RICHARD (*Very young again*)

I wish they'd let me have a power mower.

JENNY

Well, you can't have one, so just . . . (*Leaves it unfinished*)

RICHARD

I am probably the only natural-born citizen east of the Rockies who does not have a power mower.

JENNY

Well, you cannot *have* one, so let it be.

RICHARD

(*Points vaguely around, suggesting the neighborhood*)

Alan has one; Clinton; *Mark!* Mark's got one he trades *in* every . . .

JENNY *(Surprisingly sharp)*

No!

(Silence)

RICHARD *(To himself)*

Forty-three years old and I haven't even got a power mower.

(Silence)

JENNY

Do you want something? Some tea, or a sandwich?

RICHARD *(Sharp)*

Can we afford it?

JENNY *(Through her teeth)*

Barely.

RICHARD *(Gets up, paces; offhand)*

You, uh . . . you want to get a divorce? Get married again? Someone with money? Somebody with a power mower?

JENNY *(Weary, matter-of-fact)*

Not this week; I'm too busy.

RICHARD *(Abstracted)*

You let me know.

(Back to her)

How much?

JENNY

Hm?

RICHARD

How much do you spend? On, on seeds, and manure, and shears, and . . .

JENNY *(Gets up)*

Oh, for God's . . .

RICHARD

. . . and, and bulbs, and stakes to hold the damn plants up, and . . .

JENNY

(Angry, but, still, rather bravura)

Plow it up! Plow the whole damn garden under! Put in gravel! And while you're at it, get rid of the grass!

RICHARD *(Shrugs)*

Everybody has grass.

JENNY *(Furious)*

EVERYBODY HAS A GARDEN!

(Still angry, but softer)

I am willing; I am willing to scrimp, and eat what I don't really want to half the time, and dress like something out of a forties movie . . .

RICHARD (*Regretting the whole thing*)
All right; all right . . .

JENNY
. . . and *not* have a maid, and only have my hair done twice a month, and not say let's go away for the weekend . . .

RICHARD
All right!

JENNY
. . . to pay and pay on this god-damned house . . .

RICHARD
(*Soft, reasonable, but infuriating*)
. . . everybody has a house . . .

JENNY
. . . *and* the bloody car . . .

RICHARD
. . . we need a car . . .

JENNY
. . . *and* Roger's school . . .

RICHARD (*Ire up a little*)
When the public schools in this country . . .

JENNY
. . . *and* all the insurance . . .

RICHARD
We die, you know.

JENNY
. . . and everything else! Every money-eating thing!

RICHARD
Don't forget the government; *it's* hungry.

JENNY
I'll do it all, I'll . . . I'll smoke those awful cigarettes, I'll . . . but I *will* not. I *will* not give up my garden.

RICHARD (*Gentle: placating*)
I wouldn't *ask* you to.

JENNY
We live beyond our means, we have no right to be here, we're so far in the hole you'll have to rob a bank or something, we've . . .

RICHARD

I love your garden.

JENNY *(Quieting down some)*

There are some things I will just not do: and first in line is I will not give up my garden.

RICHARD

No; of course not.

JENNY

I *love* my garden.

RICHARD

Yes.

JENNY

The way the florist charges, if we had to buy *cut* flowers . . .

RICHARD

I *know;* I *know.*

JENNY

Now, if we had a greenhouse . . .

RICHARD

A greenhouse!

JENNY

Yes, well, a small one, just enough to raise some orchids in . . .
   (Sees RICHARD *rise, move off shaking his head)*
. . . Where are you going?

RICHARD

I'm going out to kill myself.

JENNY

But why!?

RICHARD *(Losing control)*

Do you know how much a greenhouse costs!?

JENNY *(Getting mad)*

I'M TRYING TO SAVE MONEY!

RICHARD *(Dismissing her)*

You're insane.

JENNY

Do you *know* how much cut flowers *cost?*

RICHARD *(Mimicking her)*

Do you *know* how much a greenhouse *costs?*

JENNY

I am *trying* to save *money.*

RICHARD *(Tiny pause, then)*

Then why don't you go to Paris and buy Christian Dior!? That way you won't have to pay for your dresses.

(Silence)

JENNY *(Preoccupied)*

Do you want some tea? Or a sandwich?

(RICHARD shakes his head; silence)

(A little sad, wistful, but reassuring)

We will have a greenhouse, someday. I'll make it nice; you'll have a living room full of flowering plants; you'll like it very much.

RICHARD *(Mildly ironic, sad)*

Can I have a power mower first?

JENNY *(Nice)*

You can have *everything.*

RICHARD *(Sighs)*

That will be nice.

JENNY *(Wistful)*

And so can I, and everything will be lovely.

RICHARD *(After a silence)*

The thing I don't like about being poor . . .

JENNY *(Correcting by rote)*

. . . about not having money . . .

RICHARD

The thing I don't like about being—about not having money . . .

JENNY

(A little embarrassed, as if someone might overhear)

We're not *starving.*

RICHARD

No, we eat, but if we didn't belong to the, the *(Points out the window)* club we'd eat a lot better.

JENNY *(Patient agreement)*

Yes.

RICHARD

If we didn't try to live like our friends we might put something away sometime.

JENNY *(Ibid.)*

Um-hum.

RICHARD

Friends we didn't have, by the way, until we moved here, took this place . . .

JENNY

But *friends.*

RICHARD

Oh, yeah, well, you find them. *(Tossed-off, but sincere)* We don't live right.

JENNY

(Throws her head back, laughs)
Oh God!

RICHARD

We don't!

JENNY

Poor baby.

RICHARD *(As if in a debate)*

You live in a forty-thousand-dollar house and you have to smoke bad cigarettes to get the coupons so you can afford a good vacuum so you can clean
it; you belong to the club so you can pay back dinner invitations from people
you wouldn't even know if you hadn't joined the club in the first place, and
you *joined* the club, *and* learned how to play tennis, because you decided to
move into a neighborhood where everybody belonged to the club.

JENNY *(Noncommittal)*

Except the Jews and the tradespeople.

RICHARD

Hm? You're up to hock in your eyebrows . . . *(Realizes what he has said,
tries to fix it, retaining dignity)* . . . *up* in hock to your . . . *in* hock up to
your eyebrows, and why!

JENNY *(Calm, nonplussed)*

Because you want to live nicely.

RICHARD

I do?

JENNY

(Eyes closed briefly in martyrdom)
Because *we* do, because we want to live nicely; because we want to live the
way a lot of people manage . . .

RICHARD

Yes; people who can afford it!

JENNY

No! The way a lot of other people *cannot* afford it, and still do. Do you think the mortgage department of the bank stays open just for us?

RICHARD

Look at Jack!

JENNY

Jack is rich! Look at everybody else.

RICHARD *(Pause; glum)*

I don't feel I belong anywhere.

JENNY

(Slightly patronizing commiseration)

Awww; poor Richard.

RICHARD

It *does*, by the way.

JENNY

(Very straightforward, even a little suspicious)

What does what?

RICHARD

The bank; the mortgage department; stays open just for us.

JENNY *(Laughs a little)*

You don't want a sandwich, or something?

RICHARD *(Preoccupied)*

No.

JENNY *(Clear they've had this before)*

I'm still able-bodied . . .

RICHARD *(Firm)*

No.

JENNY

Lots of wives do it.

RICHARD

No.

JENNY

Just part-time, only from . . .

RICHARD

You may *not* get a job!

JENNY

It would make all the difference in . . .

RICHARD *(Out of patience, now)*

No, now!

(Softer afterthought)

I'm not going to have a wife of mine trying to work at some job, *and* running a house, *and* looking after Roger when he's home from school . . .

JENNY

Roger is fourteen, he doesn't need any looking after.

RICHARD

No! Besides, he's fifteen.

JENNY

And if I *took* a job, then we could afford a maid, and . . .

RICHARD

I said *no*.

JENNY *(Exasperated)*

Well, it wouldn't be taking in laundry, for God's sake!

RICHARD *(Slightly nasty)*

No? What would it be?

JENNY *(She, too)*

Well, that may be all you think I'm good for . . .

RICHARD *(Voice rising)*

I didn't *say* that.

JENNY

Well, you *inferred* it!

RICHARD

Implied; not inferred. And I did not.

JENNY

Yes you did, for God's sake.

RICHARD

I said nothing of the sort.

JENNY

(Snotty, exaggerated imitation)

No? Well, what would it *be*? What could you do? *(Anger)* Is that all you think I'm good for?

RICHARD *(Trying patience now)*

I didn't say that all you could do was take in laundry; I merely meant that . . .

JENNY *(Starting to cry)*

I'm sorry you think so badly of me.

RICHARD *(Eyes to heaven)*

Oh, for Christ's . . .

JENNY

(Sniffling; the whole act which is not an act)

I'm sorry you think that's all I'm good for. I *try* to help you; I try to run a decent house . . .

RICHARD

It's a *lovely* house . . .

JENNY

. . . and bring up your son so he won't be some . . . some ruffian . . .

RICHARD

. . . *our* son . . .

JENNY

I try to *look* nice; I try to take care of myself, for *you*, for your friends . . .

RICHARD

What, what is this everything *mine* all of a sudden! Most of the time it's yours; all yours!

JENNY *(Real tears again)*

I try! I try!

RICHARD

Oh, Lord!

(Comes over, comforts her)

You do a *lovely* job; you run everything just . . . lovely; you look . . . you look good enough to eat.

(Snarls, tries to bite her neck)

JENNY *(Martyr)*

Don't, now.

(RICHARD repeats snarl, bite)

Just don't!

(RICHARD moves away)

Just . . . just go away.

RICHARD *(Pause; subdued)*

I didn't mean to . . . say anything to upset you.

JENNY

No, but you *meant* it!

RICHARD *(Anger rising)*

I did not *mean* it!

JENNY (*Angry, too*)

Then why did you *say* it!!?

RICHARD (*Eyes narrowed*)

What?

JENNY (*Cold*)

If you didn't mean it, then why did you say it?

RICHARD

I didn't say what . . . you implied that I . . .

JENNY

Inferred!

RICHARD

SKIP IT!
(*Silence*)

JENNY

(*Great soft-spoken dignity*)

I was merely trying to suggest that I might be able to help at the hospital one or two afternoons a week . . .

RICHARD (*Snorts*)

And make enough to pay a maid out of that?

JENNY (*Trying to stay calm*)

Or open a hat shop . . .

RICHARD

You're mad! You're absolutely mad!

JENNY (*Very sincere plea*)

I just want to help?
(*Silence*)

RICHARD (*With her again; nicely*)

I *know* you do. And you do as much as anyone; you do *more* than your share.

JENNY

No, no, I don't do *anything* to help you.

RICHARD (*Nuzzles*)

You do everything.

JENNY

You think I'm worthless.

RICHARD (*To make light of it*)

No, I imagine I could sell you for about . . . oh . . .

JENNY *(Won't go along)*

You think I'm a drag; I'm not a helpmeet. Lots of women have part-time jobs, just to help out, it . . .

RICHARD *(Final)*

No!

JENNY *(After a silence; sighs)*

Money, money, money.

RICHARD

That's how it's always been. That's how it *is*.

JENNY *(Comforting)*

You earn more than you used to.

RICHARD

Earn: yes. Taxes. Beware the steady man! Beware the slow rise through the respectable ranks.

> (JACK *appears in the french doors, enters, observes, lolls, speaks to the audience; becomes a part of the action only when he speaks directly to one or another of the characters*)

JENNY

I know; Mother told me I should marry a real-estate speculator.

RICHARD

(Going to the liquor cupboard)

Yes; well, well you should.

JENNY *(One more try)*

So, if I had just a *little* job . . .

RICHARD *(Looking among bottles)*

No!

JACK

(To the audience, while RICHARD *hunts among the bottles)*

Are they arguing about money? Poor things; they always do. They're very nice, though. Richard is decent, and Jenny is . . . good. Damn it; wish she weren't.

JENNY *(Unaware of* JACK*)*

What are you looking for?

RICHARD

(Ibid., not looking up from the bottles)

The vodka.

JENNY

There's some right there; right there in front of you.

RICHARD

Not *my* kind; not the Polish, only party stuff—American.

JENNY *("Get you")*

Oh; well, sorry.

RICHARD

It's empty anyway.

JACK *(To the audience)*

You see? That's it. The Polish vod is eight bucks a fifth. That's what makes the difference: taste; and taste is expensive. Poor children. *(A confidence)* I find Jenny *so attractive.* Not that I'm going to jump her, or anything. My letch is in the mind; *is; generally.*

RICHARD *(To* JENNY*)*

Decent vodka is not a luxury.

JENNY

Nor is a greenhouse.

RICHARD

Yes it is.

JACK *(To the audience)*

My uncle died and left *me* three-and-a-quarter mill. Which is very nice. Which means *I* can have a greenhouse, *and* the Polish vodka, *plus* the thirty-year scotch, plus . . . never worry—which is the nicest of all, don't you think?

(In the action now)

Hello, children!

RICHARD

Hm?

JENNY

(Piqued and pleased, her reaction to JACK *is always a combination of maternal and coquettish)*

Oh, for God's sake, Jack!

RICHARD

(His reaction to JACK *is a combination of slight mistrust, discomfort, and natural friendliness)*

Well, hello there, Jack.

JACK

(Sees they are a little embarrassed)

Ah, when I am wandering, footsore and loose, where do I always come? *Here.* And why? Well, for a warm and toasty welcome. How are you, children?

RICHARD

Poor.

JENNY

Fine!

JACK

Don't go together.

RICHARD

How've you been?

JACK

(*Kisses* JENNY *on the forehead*)

Stopped by the club to watch the heart attacks, looked in on the poker game and dropped a couple of hundred.

(*To* JENNY)

You . . . smell . . . lovely.

JENNY (*Pleased*)

Thank you.

JACK

And . . . thought I'd come over the fence and see you two.

RICHARD (*Nice, but an undertone*)

I'll bet you'd like a drink.

JENNY (*To cover*)

Ummm; me too!

JACK

Love one. Polish vod?

RICHARD (*A look at* JENNY)

Fresh out.

JENNY (*To* RICHARD)

Why don't you make us all a nice martini?

JACK (*Clucks; false disapproval*)

Drink drink drink.

RICHARD

No vermouth either.

JACK

Such hospitality; I *tell* you.

RICHARD

I'll go get some.

JACK

Perfect! That way I get to be alone with your wife.

JENNY

Oh, Jack!

RICHARD

(To suggest, "If you are, I'll go get some")
You staying long?

JENNY *(Cheerful admonition)*
Richard!

JACK
Well, what I thought I'd do is have one final drink with the two of you. You see, I've settled a quarter of a million on each of you, and after I had my drink I thought I'd go down in the cellar and kill myself.

JENNY
Awwwwww.

RICHARD *(A little grim)*
You ought to do it somewhere else; we might have trouble getting the money if . . .
(Leaves it unfinished)

JENNY *(Playing the game)*
Yes . . . they might . . . *you* know . . . ask questions.

JACK *(To the audience)*
He's right there, you know. Good mind.
(Back into action)
Oh.
(Pause)
Do you think? Yes; well, all right. I'll just have the drink, then.

RICHARD *(Slight, uncertain pause)*
O.K. *(Pause)* Well, I'll go get some.

JACK
Go, bucko; go.

JENNY *(Giggles)*
Oh, honestly, Richard; I'll be all right.

JACK
You have a faithful wife, Richard; never fear.
(To the audience)
He has, too. She's rare; she's a good woman.

RICHARD
(Moving to exit, through hallway)
I know; it's the only kind I ever marry.

JACK *(Genuine surprise)*

You been married before?

RICHARD *(Surprise)*

No. I was just . . .

    (At a loss for words)

. . . it was just a . . . something to say.

    (To JENNY*)*

You, you want anything? At the store?

JENNY *(Shakes her head)*

Unh-unh. Hurry back. Oh! Cigarettes!

RICHARD *(About to exit; a little bitter)*

Which kind?

JENNY *(A giving-up sigh and smile)*

The ones we like. Hurry, now.

    *(*RICHARD *exits)*

JACK *(To the departed* RICHARD*)*

By-ee!

    (To JENNY*, almost Groucho Marx)*

Quick! He'll be fifteen minutes even at a dog trot! Where's the guestroom?

JENNY *(Laughs)*

Oh, come on, Jack! Besides, you aren't even a guest.

JACK *(Seemingly surprised)*

No? What am I?

JENNY

A . . . uh . . . a fixture.

JACK

Something from the neighborhood? Bothersome Jack, here-he-comes-
again-probably-drunk-and-time-on-his-hands-so-why-not-waste-every-
body-else's-afternoon-while-he's-at-it?

JENNY

Mnnnnn.

JACK *(To the audience)*

Am, too. Like that, I mean. Time, time. God, the ambition you have to
have to overcome good fortune. I haven't *got* it.

    (Back to JENNY*)*

Let me paint your picture.

JENNY

    (Cheerful, but it's clear they've had this before)

No.

JACK

Won't cost you a penny.

JENNY

No.

JACK *(To the audience)*

I'm not a bad painter. Flattering portraits of the rich?
 (Back to JENNY*)*
What is it, then?

JENNY

I . . . just want to be different.

JACK *(Mild lechery)*

Oh, you *are,* Jenny.

JENNY

Every, every house I go into, every time Richard and I go out, there it is! Sybil,
Grace Donovan, Junie, Mrs. what's-her-name, Beachcomber, or something;
over the mantel, badly framed, the lady of the house; your portrait.

JACK *(Axiom)*

Ladies *like* to be painted, *I* paint ladies, ladies hang pictures.

JENNY *(Apologetic)*

It isn't proper.

JACK *(Brief laugh)*

Tell 'em in Newport; put me out of business.
 (Digging)
Besides, I bet I make more money in three good months up there than
Richard does in a whole . . .

JENNY

Oh, *money!*

JACK

 (Waits a moment; quietly, smiling)
Yes? Money?

JENNY

I just don't . . . I don't want to look at myself, that's all.

JACK *(Very elegant)*

If I were you . . . I would.
 (Normal tone)
What's the matter, love?

JENNY

Oh . . .
 (Very sincere, even plaintive, for a joke)

Would you do it, Jack? Go down in the cellar? I mean, leave Richard and me a quarter of a million each and then go kill yourself somewhere? I mean that nicely.

JACK

I'd do almost anything for you.
   (*Afterthought, but not flip*)
Unless it got in the way of what I wanted to do for me.
   (JENNY *laughs ruefully*)
What is it, puss?

JENNY (*Not going to talk about it*)

Tired. Just . . . tired.

JACK

Want a shoulder to cry on?

JENNY

Nope; just a quarter of a million and an easy mind.

JACK

   (*Shakes his head knowingly*)
Wouldn't help. Money's hungry, lonely, wants more of itself. Stay poor; you're better off.

JENNY (*Snorts*)

Crap!
   (*The doorbell rings;* JENNY *goes toward the hallway*)

JACK

Really; you are.

JENNY (*Going*)

You'd *know*.

JACK

I *watch*.
   (JENNY *has gone;* JACK *addresses the audience*)
I *have;* it *does;* money always wants more to keep it company. And a little money is a dangerous thing. Don't aim for a million: that's the danger point. If I were to *die* . . . I wouldn't leave them a quarter of a million each. Bad. *I'd* leave 'em the whole damn three. As a matter of fact, that isn't a bad idea at all. With three mill plus, they wouldn't have to worry. I think I'll do it. Yes; consider it done.
   (*Considers*)
I am *healthy*, though. They might not get it till it's way too late. Still . . . consider it done.

JENNY'S VOICE (*From the hallway*)

No, of course not, don't be silly.

(JENNY *appears, followed by* MRS. TOOTHE)

MRS. TOOTHE (*Entering*)

I *should* have phoned before just appearing at your door, but I thought that on . . . Ah, this must be your husband. How do you do, I'm Mrs. Toothe, and your wife has been kind enough to . . .

JENNY (*A little laugh*)

Oh, no, this isn't Richard—my husband, I mean . . .

MRS. TOOTHE

Ah. Well.

JENNY (*A little lame*)

This is just . . . Jack.

MRS. TOOTHE

(*Extends her hand to* JACK)

No matter. How do you do, just the same.

JACK

(*Takes hand, does curt little formal bow*)

Mrs. Toothe.

JENNY

(*Lame, and embarrassed by it*)

Jack was just . . . passing by.

MRS. TOOTHE (*Noncommittal*)

A friend of the family; of course.

JENNY

Yes.

JACK (*To* MRS. TOOTHE)

Not at all: a secret admirer of lovely Jenny. I only come round when Richard's out. We have a signal—panties on the laundry line.

JENNY

Jack!

MRS. TOOTHE

How divine!

JENNY

(*To* MRS. TOOTHE; *embarrassed and furious at being*)

There isn't a word of truth to what he says. There isn't a word of truth to *any*thing he says, *ever.*

JACK (*Still to* MRS. TOOTHE)

White panties if we've got one hour, yellow if we'll have to hurry, pink for those special occasions . . .

JENNY

Jack! Please!

JACK (*Shakes his head, sadly*)

I must confess it, madam, I am only what she says: a friend of the family . . . dropping by. Damned attractive, though. Wish it were true.

MRS. TOOTHE (*Pleased and sympathetic*)

Ahhhh.

JENNY

Why is everybody standing? Please sit down, Mrs. . . uh . . . Toothe.

MRS. TOOTHE (*Sits*)

Thank you.

JENNY

Jack, don't you think you should be . . . ?

JACK

(*Makes it obvious he has gotten the signal*)

By gum, I must be moving on! Different lines, more panties. There is no rest for the wicked in the suburbs. Mrs. Toothe, it's been . . .

MRS. TOOTHE

A great pleasure. And don't get your signals mixed.

(JENNY *accompanies* JACK *to the doors to the garden*)

JACK

Tell Richard I'll be back for that martini another day.

(*Sotto voce*)

Who is she, your fairy godmother?

JENNY

Will you go?

JACK

(*Pecks her on the forehead*)

Bye.

(*To the audience, a wave before quick exit*)

Bye.

(JACK *has gone;* JENNY *returns to* MRS. TOOTHE)

JENNY

You mustn't believe a thing Jack says, Mrs. . . . .

MRS. TOOTHE

(A hand up to silence her)
Oh, really. I can tell a lover from a friend.

JENNY

(Maybe even a little offended)
Oh? How?

MRS. TOOTHE *(Laughs)*
Because in this country they're very seldom the same.

JENNY

You're English.

MRS. TOOTHE

Yes. Very.
(Small silence)

JENNY
Would you like some tea . . . or a drink?

MRS. TOOTHE *(Very efficient)*
No thank you; this is business. Strictly business.

JENNY *(Pause)*

Oh?

MRS. TOOTHE

I'm told you need a job?

JENNY *(Somewhat confused)*
Who, who told you that?

MRS. TOOTHE *(Airy)*
Oh, one of your friends. A woman.

JENNY *(Curious, still puzzled)*
Oh? Who?

MRS. TOOTHE

No matter. Am I mistaken?

JENNY *(A little ill-at-ease)*
Well, no . . . that is, I *was* thinking about getting a job . . .

MRS. TOOTHE

Yes, well, I thought so.

JENNY

Not a . . . a career, you understand, just something . . .

MRS. TOOTHE

. . . part *time*, something to bring a little extra money in.

JENNY

Well, yes; you know how it is: my son's away at school, and I have the spare time. Besides, one can always use money, can't one?

MRS. TOOTHE

(*Looking about, noncommittally*)

Yes; one can.

JENNY

These days, with taxes, and the private school . . .

MRS. TOOTHE

Oh, yes; yes; quite. What does your husband do?

JENNY

(*Uncomfortable, as if being interviewed*)

Well, he . . . he's a research chemist, and . . .

MRS. TOOTHE

. . . and that, as so many good things, pays less than it should.

JENNY (*Protecting* RICHARD)

Well, he doesn't do *too* badly; I mean . . .

MRS. TOOTHE (*The laugh again*)

Of course not! But, still; you would like a job.

JENNY

(*Looks to the hallway, guilty*—RICHARD *might come back*)

Well, yes; one . . . one likes to feel useful.

MRS. TOOTHE

(*Looking into her handbag*)

Yes; useful.

(*She takes out a thick bundle of bills, shows them to* JENNY)

Money.

(JENNY *just looks at it, her mouth falling open a little*)

For you.

(*Makes to give it to her*)

JENNY

Yes, but . . .

(*Laughs a little, astounded*)

MRS. TOOTHE (*Nods her head*)

Yes, money. For *you*. A thousand dollars. Here, take it.

JENNY

(*Withdrawing a little from it*)

Well, no, I . . .

MRS. TOOTHE

Count it if you like. Here; a thousand dollars.

(*Tries to force it on her*)

JENNY (*A little panicked*)

No!

MRS. TOOTHE

Very well.

(*As calm as can be; rises, goes with the money to the fireplace, throws it on the burning logs*)

JENNY

(*Reflex, runs to the fireplace, almost puts her hands into the fire, makes a little yell; straightens up, holds on*)

Oh—I think you'd better go, Mrs. Toothe.

MRS. TOOTHE (*Enigmatic smile*)

Not yet. Let's begin again.

(*She takes another bundle of money from her handbag, makes as if to throw it in the fire; JENNY holds out her hand; MRS. TOOTHE quietly hands her the money, resumes her seat; JENNY stays standing*)

JENNY

(*Never taking her eyes off MRS. TOOTHE*)

You're quite mad.

MRS. TOOTHE

No. Very rich.

JENNY

(*Looks at the money, almost weighs it*)

Look, you . . . you can't just . . . *give* me money like this. I can't just . . . take money from you.

MRS. TOOTHE (*A little laugh*)

You have. It's yours. Isn't there something you'd like to buy? For yourself, for . . . what is his name? . . . Richard?

JENNY

People can't just give people money. I want to work.

MRS. TOOTHE

Good then. That's an advance of salary. You can work for me.

JENNY

But I haven't *said* I'd take a job at *all*. Richard is *very* much against it, and . . .

MRS. TOOTHE (*Daring her to refuse*)

I was told you needed money.

JENNY

Yes, but Richard wouldn't approve of anything like this, and . . .

MRS. TOOTHE

Like what?

(*Indicates the money*)

Wouldn't he approve of *that?*

JENNY

(*Looks at the money in her hands*)

I'm sorry; I didn't mean to be rude, but it's all so vague, isn't it? And . . . and so unexpected.

MRS. TOOTHE (*Shrugs*)

It's a job.

JENNY

(*Nervous laughter in her voice*)

Well, you'll have to tell me what it *is*. I mean, money isn't everything.

MRS. TOOTHE

No? What isn't money? Here we are; this house is money, that garden, that lovely garden, those clothes you're wearing, it's all *money,* isn't it?

JENNY

The job?

MRS. TOOTHE

What are your husband's hours?

JENNY

He leaves at eight and gets home from town at seven-thirty, but. . .

MRS. TOOTHE

Very good. *You'll* come in town, four afternoons a week, from one to five, say. You'll come to my address—lovely street: psychiatrist's office, doctors . . .

JENNY

Is this a . . . uh : . . a receptionist's job?

MRS. TOOTHE

Receptionist?

JENNY

Making, making appointments, and so on?

MRS. TOOTHE

I make appointments. For *you.*

JENNY (*Tiny pause*)

For me? Who with?

MRS. TOOTHE

Clients.

JENNY (*Innocent*)

What *for?*

MRS. TOOTHE

For a hundred dollars.

JENNY

No, I mean . . . A hundred dollars?

MRS. TOOTHE

More, sometimes—if they're generous.

JENNY

But these clients . . . who are they?

MRS. TOOTHE

Some businessmen, some visitors. All gentlemen; all rich.

JENNY

(*The knowledge is there but not admitted yet*)

What . . . exactly . . . what exactly would I do . . . for this money?

(MRS. TOOTHE *laughs lightly;* JENNY's *jaw drops with the admission; pause*)

(JENNY *picks up the bundle of money, holds it out to* MRS. TOOTHE; *even, hard*)

Get out of my house.

(MRS. TOOTHE *does nothing;* JENNY *drops the money on the table*)

I'll call the police.

MRS. TOOTHE

(*As calm as anything; a little superior*)

Whatever for?

JENNY (*Quivering*)

You know what for!

MRS. TOOTHE (*Smiles*)

I've said nothing.

JENNY

You know what you've suggested!

MRS. TOOTHE (*Shrugs*)

That you make money.

JENNY

THAT WAY!

MRS. TOOTHE

You have a friend who does.

JENNY

Who!

MRS. TOOTHE

Oh, no; we're very discreet.

JENNY (*Through her teeth*)

I don't believe you, not a word! People around here wouldn't do that sort
of *thing;* you don't realize; you don't know what we're like.

MRS. TOOTHE (*Unconcerned*)

Have it your way.

JENNY

One of the tradespeople, maybe; you're thinking of someone like that.

MRS. TOOTHE

I'm thinking of a friend of yours; a very nice woman with a lovely house,
who keeps it nicely—much more nicely than this, by the way—a woman
who has no more worries about money, who is very happy. So could you be.

JENNY

You're a filthy woman! IT'S DISGUSTING!!

MRS. TOOTHE (*Very calm*)

Nothing is disgusting, unless one is disgusted.

JENNY

YOU'RE EVIL!!

MRS. TOOTHE

Yes, yes . . .

JENNY

I'LL TELL THE POLICE!

MRS. TOOTHE

(*Stands up, stretches a little*)

Good. Then perhaps they'll arrest me.

JENNY

I hope they put you in prison!

MRS. TOOTHE

Yes, well, they probably will, and then I shall admit everything.

JENNY

Everything?

MRS. TOOTHE

Yes, how you approached me, and we discussed it, but the terms didn't suit you. The *money* wasn't enough.

JENNY

THAT'S NOT TRUE!

MRS. TOOTHE

Perhaps not. I think it would be believed, though. By enough people.

JENNY

GET OUT OF HERE!

MRS. TOOTHE

(Takes a calling card from her handbag)

Here is my card; address; telephone; let me know what you decide.

JENNY

(Change of tone; almost tearful)

Please? Please go?

MRS. TOOTHE

No police then; good.   .

(Sees JENNY *will not take the card, puts it down next to the bundle of money on the table)*

Don't telephone me before ten, though, please. I *do* like my sleep.

JENNY

Please? Go?

MRS. TOOTHE *(Smiles)*

I'll see myself out. It's been very nice to meet you.

(Looks one final time at the garden)

What a lovely garden. Do you have a greenhouse?

(Smiles, exits, leaving JENNY *standing in the center of the room)*

*(*JENNY *looks after* MRS. TOOTHE *for a long moment, not moving. Then she looks down at the table whereon sit the bundle of money and* MRS. TOOTHE'*s card. She picks up the card, reads it, moving her lips, then, with a grimace, rips the card in half and, as if she were carrying feces, takes it over to a wastebasket and drops it in. She comes back to the table, stares at the money, picks it up, looks at it with detached fascination; doesn't know quite what to do with it; finally, rather firmly, puts it in desk drawer, locks drawer, keeps key, starts toward french doors, looks back at locked drawer, goes, stands at french windows looking out)*

RICHARD'S VOICE *(From the hallway)*

Hell-oo-oo.

(He enters, with a paper bag of liquor)

Oh, there you are. And who the hell was *that* tripping down our path, that bit of old England? "How do you do?" she . . . Where the hell *is* he—Jack?

JENNY *(Sort of vacant)*

Oh. Hi.

RICHARD

(Puts liquor down, starts taking bottles out of bag)
Well, who *was* she—your fairy godmother?

JENNY *(Some alarm)*

My what?

RICHARD

The woman; the lady. Who was she?

JENNY *(Still preoccupied)*

Oh. Mrs. Toothe.

RICHARD

Mrs. what?

JENNY

Toothe; Toothe.

RICHARD

You're kidding. Where's Jack?

JENNY

It's a perfectly proper English name.
    (Pause)
I guess. Jack? He *went*.

RICHARD

Figures. Send me out to buy up the liquor store and off he goes.

JENNY

It was *your* idea to go.

RICHARD *(A little cross)*

Who *was* she?

JENNY

Mrs. Toothe?
    (Tosses it off)
Oh . . . committee; wants me for the hospital.

RICHARD

Free? Or pay?

JENNY *(Pause; casual)*

Pay.

RICHARD

No!

JENNY (*Pause; softly*)

All right.

RICHARD (*Looks at the liquor*)

Well, with all your rich guests gone, there's just us for drinks. What do you want . . . a martini?

JENNY (*Very sincere*)

Yes, I think that would be *nice*.

RICHARD

O.K.

(*Starts to make one; the ice is already there*)

You know what Tom Palmer said the other day?

JENNY

(*Preoccupied, and not exactly unpleasant, but not pleasant either*)

No, I don't; I didn't see Tom Palmer the other day. What did Tom Palmer say?

RICHARD

(*Looks up at* JENNY *for a moment, quizzically, then back to his work*)

He said Jack was at the club, at the bar . . . soused as usual . . .

JENNY

Jack isn't always drunk.

RICHARD (*A little annoyance*)

He's always drinking.

JENNY (*Dogmatic*)

That does *not* make him *drunk*.

RICHARD

I am merely repeating what Tom Palmer said.

JENNY

Tom Palmer's an old woman.

RICHARD (*Quite annoyed*)

I do *not* want to argue!

JENNY

All right!

(*Contrite*)

I'm sorry, darling.

(*Pause*)

You're a good, decent man and I love you.

RICHARD *(Grudging)*

Well, you're a good, decent woman, and I love you, too. As a matter of fact, I shall give you a house-special martini to show you how *much* I love you.

JENNY

Oh, I would like that.

(She comes for her drink, takes it from him, they put arms around each other, move toward the sofa; he kisses her on top of her head)

RICHARD

I think you smell even nicer than Jack does.

JENNY *(Purring)*

When have you smelled Jack?

RICHARD

Than *Jack* thinks you smell.

JENNY

Oh.

(RICHARD tries to nip her neck)

Ow! Now stop that; I'll spill my martini.

(They sit on the sofa, relax)

RICHARD *(A little bitter)*

You want to know something really funny?

JENNY

I don't *think* so. What?

RICHARD

I was in the liquor store . . .

JENNY

That's a riot.

RICHARD

Hush. I was in the liquor store, and Grady, who owns it, do you know what he told me?

JENNY

No; what?

RICHARD

He's getting a second car? Not trading one in; getting a second car.

JENNY

So?

RICHARD

Guy who owns a crummy little liquor store can have two cars? And we have to get by with . . .

JENNY

Did you bring the cigarettes back with you?

RICHARD

Hm? (*Gets them out*) Oh; yes; here.

JENNY

(*Takes one; so does he; he lights them both*)
I wonder which kills more people: liquor or cars?

RICHARD

Well, when you put them together it's pretty good. What's for dinner?
(*Pause*)

JENNY

Let's go *out* for dinner.

RICHARD

Where?

JENNY (*Expansive*)

Let's . . . let's go to Le Cavalier.

RICHARD (*Snorts*)

You must be out of your mind.

JENNY

No! Let's!

RICHARD

It'll cost twenty-five dollars each. After a drink, the wine, it'll cost twenty-
five each!
(*Pause*)

JENNY (*Cautiously*)

I've got some money.

RICHARD (*Half hearing*)

Hm?

JENNY

I said, *I've* got some money.

RICHARD (*Vaguely interested*)

How?

JENNY (*Very offhand*)

Oh, I've . . . put a little aside out of household. I keep a little bit each week.

RICHARD (*Mildly*)

Well, I'll be damned.

JENNY

Come on; let's go out; it'll do us good. Let's go to Le Cavalier. Let's live it up.

RICHARD

Let's pretend we can afford it?

JENNY

Sure! Come on; it'll do us both good.

RICHARD

You ingenious thing. How much have you got?

JENNY

Oh . . . enough. Come on now.

RICHARD

You clever girl.
   (Rises)
I'd better wash up. Really? You have enough?

JENNY *(Rises)*

Yes. Better put things away in the garden before you get cleaned up.

RICHARD

Right.
   (Moves to the french doors)
You very clever girl.
   (Goes outside)

   *(JENNY sees he is out of sight; goes slowly to the desk, unlocks the
   drawer, takes out the bundle of money, strips off several bills, puts
   them on the table, hesitates a moment, as to reconsider, then puts
   the rest of the money back in the drawer, locks it again, keeps the
   key. Stands for a moment; looks at the wastebasket, lifts it onto the
   table, takes the two halves of MRS. TOOTHE's card out, fits them together, looks at the card. RICHARD pokes his head inside; JENNY
   doesn't flinch or try to hide the card, knowing that RICHARD
   either can't see it or won't ask what it is)*

RICHARD

Jenny?

JENNY

Hm?

RICHARD *(Sort of wistful)*

Darling? How much does a greenhouse cost? You know . . . a little one?

JENNY

Why?

                    RICHARD
I just wondered.

                    JENNY *(Looks up)*
Quite a bit.

                    RICHARD
I just wondered.
    (Returns outside)

                    JENNY
    (Looks at the card again, shakes her head; some rue)
Quite a bit.

                    CURTAIN

SCENE TWO

(Six months later; scene the same; early afternoon; RICHARD *at the desk, paying bills; shakes his head occasionally, despair. Sound of front door opening, closing.* JENNY *comes in, with bundles)*

                    JENNY *(Cheerful)*
Hello.

                    RICHARD *(Glum)*
Hello.

                    JENNY
On Saturday you're supposed to rest; why aren't you out working in the garden?
    *(*RICHARD *laughs glumly)*
Or, or just . . . lying around?

                    RICHARD *(Wan smile)*
Paying bills.

                    JENNY
Oh.
    (Puts bundles down)
It figures, doesn't it: I go to the store and I forget half of what I want.

                    RICHARD
Didn't you make a list?

JENNY

Of course; I *got* everything on the list; I just didn't remember to put everything *on* the list.

RICHARD

Like what?

JENNY

Like what? Like . . . like root beer, and extra milk, and stuff for cookies,
and . . .

RICHARD

What for?

JENNY

We have a son. Right?

RICHARD *(Preoccupied)*

Um-huh.

JENNY *(Pause)*

He's coming *home* today!

RICHARD *(Puzzlement, pleasure)*

Roger? Today? Coming home?

JENNY *(As if he were addled)*

Yes. Vacation.

RICHARD

Well, I'll be damned.

JENNY

Mmmmmmm. And cornflakes and stuff, I suppose.

RICHARD

No camp this year.

JENNY

Hm?

RICHARD

No camp this year. For Roger. No camp. Can't afford it.

JENNY

(Noncommittal; her mind on something else)

Oh. Really?

RICHARD

Really.

JENNY *(Making her list)*

Well, afford or not, I thought it'd be nice if he was around *here* this summer. Get to know him.

RICHARD (*Adamantly grousing*)

Well, nice or not . . . necessary.

JENNY

Help *you,* help *me* . . .

RICHARD

While you're at it, get some more envelopes.

JENNY

There *are* some.

RICHARD

No, just that . . . that paper thing goes around them.

JENNY (*Notes it down*)

All right. He can help you in the garden.

RICHARD

Mmmm. Or maybe we can get him a magazine route.

JENNY

(*Mild disgust and indignation*)

Really!

RICHARD

Well, you're so keen for everybody to be working around here . . .

JENNY

He's just a child!

RICHARD

He's probably going steady already—got some local girl up at school—probably skips out at night, shacked up . . .

JENNY (*Protesting, embarrassed*)

Richard!

RICHARD

Kids grow up early nowadays.

JENNY

Roger is fourteen years old!

RICHARD

Well, if everything's functioning properly, there's no reason why he can't be getting laid, is there? Besides, he's fifteen.

JENNY

That's enough now.

RICHARD

Well, it's better that than lots of other things.

JENNY

ALL RIGHT!
  (*Silence*)

RICHARD

  (*Shakes his head, finally, a little sadly, smiles*)
I knew a girl once, when you and I were dating—not so as to say set the
alarm for seven, or anything like that, but . . .

JENNY (*A little stony*)

Don't regale me.

RICHARD

No; really. And I wasn't in on the good times, 'cause I was counting on
you . . .
  (JENNY *snorts*)
and you met her, I think, but I won't tell you who she was, cause she still
is . . . but she had the reputation as a proper put-out . . .

JENNY (*Some bored annoyance*)

Please, Richard.

RICHARD

No. *More* than proper: something of a dedicatee, guest bedrooms at parties, drawing blood, literally . . .

JENNY

Let the poor woman *alone.*

RICHARD (*Slight edge*)

I'm not *touching* her.
  (*Silence*)
I was planning, though, to compare her to *you.*

JENNY (*Sarcastic*)

Really.

RICHARD

To your ad*van*tage.

JENNY (*Dripping irony*)

Oooohhhh.

RICHARD

Socially—by which I mean out of bed, which is a euphemism for trash
heaps and coal bins—you'd think she was the Queen Mother. Staid? She
practically used the royal We. So proper; you'd never know.

JENNY (*Not nice*)

And what does that have to do with me?

RICHARD

Oh. It came up when I said Roger was probably going steady.

JENNY

Getting laid is what you said.

RICHARD

Same difference.

JENNY

Tell *that* to the sociologists.

RICHARD

They know. And I said Roger was probably going steady and you came on all funny and red and . . .

JENNY

I didn't see any need for you to shout the house down, and . . .

RICHARD *(Angry)*

Who's going to hear? The footmen?

JENNY

Don't you yell at me!

RICHARD

(Pause; shake of head; laugh-whimper)

All I wanted to do was say you're such a funny, silly, wonderful little . . .

JENNY

Nuts.

RICHARD

You are! You're a good wife and you're nice in bed, but you're funny and
. . . prim.

JENNY

Prim!?

RICHARD

Yes! Prim!

JENNY

I'm *sorry.*

RICHARD

And then I thought about, uh, what's-her-name; who came on like the Queen Mother, and how she was ridiculous and you were just a little silly about it, and . . . *(Mumbles)* aw, for Christ's sake, forget it. *(Pause)* I was just trying to pay you a *compl*iment! I was *try*ing to be *nice!*

JENNY

(Thinks about it, dismisses his reasoning)
I don't see why you brought her up in the *first* place.

RICHARD *(Frustrated anger)*
NEITHER DO I!
(Silence)

JENNY
I suppose I could learn a few dirty jokes, or start telling people about a couple of your peculiarities when it comes to . . .

RICHARD
Forget it!
(Silence)

JENNY *(Trying to hold back a smile)*
Who was she?
(RICHARD pouts, shakes his head)
Come on; who was she?

RICHARD
No, no.

JENNY *(Tickles him a little)*
Oh, come on!

RICHARD *(Happier)*
No; now, stop it.
(She tickles more, he grabs her, they wrestle, giggling, a little on the sofa, playing, ending in a kiss, then another, which prolongs, is far more serious)

JENNY
Unh-unh; not now.

RICHARD
Ooooohhhh . . .

JENNY
No; Roger'll come in, and . . .

RICHARD
Well, he'll be able to tell his friends we're still alive.

JENNY
Now, come *on. No.*

RICHARD *(Leans back; sighs)*
All right.

JENNY *(Pause)*

Who was she?

RICHARD *(Shakes his head)*

Unh-unh. I promised.

JENNY *(Eyes narrowing)*

Who?

RICHARD

Myself. Self-discipline.

JENNY *(Disentangling)*

Oh, honestly!

RICHARD

Well, a little doesn't hurt.

JENNY

(Looking at herself in the mirror, appraisingly, approvingly)

Did you see the paper today?

RICHARD *(Preoccupied)*

Mmmmm.

JENNY

They had an ad.

RICHARD *(Back to the desk)*

What are they doing, giving away money? I can sure use some, if they . . .

JENNY *(Still appraising)*

No, for a greenhouse, all-aluminum frame, curved glass . . .

RICHARD

(Slams a sheet of paper down)

For Christ's sake, Jenny!

(Pause, as she looks at him, a little haughtily)

I just finished telling you Roger isn't going to camp this year because we can't afford it, and . . .

JENNY *(Slight airy contempt)*

Oh, money-money-money.

RICHARD

Yes. Money.

(Shows bills)

Oil. The car. Con Ed—the bastards. An estimate on the attic—the leak.

(Doorbell rings)

JENNY

Doorbell.

RICHARD *(Back to work)*

Yes. Why don't you get it?

JENNY *(Tiny pause)*

Why don't you?

RICHARD

Hm?

JENNY

Why don't *you* get it?

RICHARD *(Slight whine)*

Because I'm working, darling; can't you see I'm . . .

JENNY

What if it's for you?

RICHARD *(Slight bewilderment)*

Then you can tell me who it *is*. Or *what*.

JENNY *(Pause, hesitation)*

Oh. Yes, that's true.
   (Doorbell again)

RICHARD

(Throws pen down, gets up, goes out)

Oh, for God's sake!
   (Maybe, offstage, we hear RICHARD *saying "Yes?" and then "Oh, O.K." While he is offstage* JENNY *moves about the room a little, practicing unconcern.* RICHARD *re-enters, with a small package: brown paper, wrapped with twine, lots of stamps, special delivery, etc.)*

JENNY

Who was it?

RICHARD

(Looking at package, with some curiosity and distaste)

Package.

JENNY

Oh, for me?

RICHARD

No. For me.
   (Shakes it, looks at it again)

JENNY *(Pause)*

Well. *(Pause)* Open it.

RICHARD

(Putting it down on the table, stares at it, hands on hips)
Wonder what it is.

JENNY *(Little laugh)*

Well, open it and see.

RICHARD

(Picks it up again, looks it over)
Special delivery, doesn't say where from.

JENNY

Well, open it, for heaven sakes.

RICHARD

(Tries to break twine, can't)
It's . . . tied up so . . .
    (Takes a pocket knife, saws through twine, begins to unwrap. JENNY
    keeps a distance. RICHARD *reveals contents. Slow awe in movements)*

JENNY *(Trying for unconcern)*

What, what *is* it?

RICHARD *(Wonder)*

Jenny! Look!

JENNY

Hm?

RICHARD

Jenny! It's money!

JENNY

It's what?

RICHARD

IT'S MONEY!!

JENNY

(Feigning disbelief and childish pleasure)
Money. It's money?

RICHARD *(Subdued; awe)*

Jenny; it's money. It's a great deal of money.

JENNY *(Taking a step closer)*

Well, for . . . for heaven sake.

RICHARD

Jenny, it's ten-dollar bills, wrapped in packages of five hundred dollars
each.

JENNY *(Beautiful bewilderment)*
Well . . . how *much?* How much *is* there?

RICHARD
(Starts counting, aloud then silently)
One, two, three, four, five, six, seven, eight, nine . . .

JENNY
(During his counting. Pauses between)
How . . . how incredible. I've . . . How absolutely incredible.

RICHARD
And wait . . . Here are hundred-dollar bills. One, two, three, four . . .
(Slight confusion)
Forty-nine hundred dollars.

JENNY *(Some confusion)*
Forty-nine?

RICHARD
Jenny, there's almost five thousand dollars here. Four thousand, nine hundred dollars. Jenny! Four thousand, nine hundred dollars!

JENNY
Well, that's incredible! Not five thousand?

RICHARD
(Sudden suspicion something's wrong)
I don't get it.

JENNY
Aren't you . . . aren't you pleased?

RICHARD
(Wry comment on her word)
Pleased!? I don't know whether I'm pleased or not.

JENNY *(Still not near the money)*
Is it real? Is it real money?

RICHARD *(Looks at a bill)*
Yes; of course it's real: real used hundred-dollar bills.

JENNY *(A kind of satisfaction)*
My God.

RICHARD
But . . . but *why?* I mean, there's no *sense* to it.

JENNY *(A protective step forward)*
Yes, but it *is* money.

RICHARD (*Looks at it glumly*)

It's money, all right. Too bad we can't keep it.

JENNY

What do you mean?

RICHARD (*No great enthusiasm*)

I mean we can't keep it. I'll take it to the police.

JENNY

No!

RICHARD

I *have* to, Jenny. There's something wrong here.

JENNY

What!

RICHARD (*At a loss for words*)

Well . . . I mean . . .

JENNY

It's addressed to you, isn't it? It came special delivery; it's not as though you *found* it, for God's sake.

RICHARD

Yes, I know, but . . .

JENNY (*As offhand as likely*)

Well, it seems to me someone wants you to have it. I . . . I can't think of any other reason for someone to send it to you.

RICHARD

Wants me to *have* it. Yes, but who?

JENNY

I . . . *I* don't know.

(*Shrugs*)

Someone.

RICHARD

Look, it could be something awful like . . .

JENNY

Like what?

RICHARD

Like, like the Mafia, or something, or bank robbers, or . . . sent it here for safekeeping, and . . .

JENNY (*Laughs gaily*)

Don't be ridiculous.

RICHARD *(Thinks about it; subdued)*

You think someone *sent* it to me?

JENNY

(The most obvious thing in the world)

Of *course.*

RICHARD

Yes, but *who?*

JENNY

Well . . . maybe . . . somebody you did something for.

RICHARD

Those sort of things don't happen . . . not to *me.*

JENNY

Well, *this* has happened.

RICHARD

(Holds the money out to her; quite childlike)

Don't you want to . . . touch it, or anything?

JENNY

Oh. Yes; of course.

(Goes to him, touches the money, smiles faintly)

I wonder who sent it to you.

RICHARD

I . . . I don't *know.* There's a man I sit next to on the train a lot. *He* seems very interested in me; older fellow, banker type. Keeps asking me about my work, how I manage. Maybe, maybe he's a millionaire, and maybe he's sort of crazy.

JENNY *(Unlit cigarette out)*

Match.

RICHARD

Hm? Oh, yeah.

(Is about to hand her the matchbook, thinks better of it, lights her cigarette)

It could come from somebody like him.

JENNY *(Slightest doubt)*

Well, yes, it could.

RICHARD *(Puzzled, a little deflated)*

And then again it couldn't. I mean, probably didn't.

JENNY *(Comforting)*

Yes. But someone.

RICHARD

Yes.

(*Considers, gives her a bill*)

Here. For you.

JENNY (*Tiniest pause*)

Thank you. You're . . . you're not going to turn it over to the police, then.

RICHARD

(*Pause, slight guilt, but bravura*)

No, I don't think so. (*Pause*) I guess someone wants me to have it. Someone *must*. It'd be silly not to keep it. (*Pause*) Don't you think so?

JENNY (*Nice smile*)

Yes. I think so.

RICHARD

I mean, it would be stupid to just . . . throw it away.

JENNY

Yes; it would be.

(*Cheerful*)

Let's have a drink: to celebrate?

RICHARD (*The sky has cleared*)

Yes! Let's.

JENNY (*Moves toward hall*)

I'll get the ice.

RICHARD

(*Moves toward the liquor cabinet*)

Good—And I'll make us a four-thousand-nine-hundred-dollar martini.

JENNY

Super!

(*Exiting*)

Call it five thousand even; sounds so much nicer.

(JACK *enters through the french doors after* JENNY *exits and* RICHARD *follows*)

JACK

(*Sauntering into the room; addresses the audience*)

The months turn; people live and die, but I just . . . wander around. I tell you, there are days when I admit to myself that I don't think I'm alive— never have been. *Un voyeur de la vie* . . . that's me. Look on; look in.

(*Propounds a great truth, with nothing other than objectivity*)

I've never felt really alive. It can't be only the isolation, the isolation of money, do you know? Naw, can't be that. I know lots of people with much more than I've got, and they've been alive . . . killed themselves and everything! Oh, by the way, I did what I said I was going to.

(*Nods*)

I made my will—remade it, to be technical—and left the whole kaboodle to Jenny and Richard here. Three million plus. I'd better not tell them, though. It's hard enough to like me as it is. I mean, I'm likable and all, but . . .

(*Spies the money on the table*)

My goodness.

(*Speaks loudly, is now in the action*)

My goodness! Look at all that money!

RICHARD (*Enters from kitchen*)

DON'T TOUCH THAT!

JACK (*Feigned affront*)

I'm sorry!

RICHARD

(*Still stern, advances toward the money*)

Just don't touch it.

JACK

Well. Shall I go back out and knock?

RICHARD (*Sighs, laughs a little*)

I'm sorry, Jack.

(JENNY *re-enters, with the ice bucket*)

JENNY

Here we go, five thousand dollars' worth of ice, an . . . oh. Jack.

JACK

(*Sees they are both ill at ease. To audience*)

My goodness.

JENNY

(*Tiny pause; show of great bonhomie*)

Hi!

RICHARD

Join us.

JACK

(*Smiles, waiting to have things explained*)

O.K.

RICHARD (*To* JENNY)

Jack, uh, noticed the money here, and . . .

JACK *(Very pleasantly)*
. . . and practically got my head snapped off.

JENNY
Oh. Well; there it is; money.

JACK *(Looks at it)*
Did you steal it, or make it in the basement on your own little press?

RICHARD
Neither, we . . .

JENNY
It arrived; it just . . . arrived.

RICHARD *(To explain further)*
In the mail.

JENNY
Yes.

RICHARD *(Ibid.)*
Special delivery.

JENNY
Yes.

JACK
(Tiny pause; clearly, there must be more explanation)
Well, that's very nice.

JENNY
Someone sent it to Richard.

JACK
Oh?

RICHARD
Yes.

JACK
Who?

JENNY
Well, we don't know, someone, we figure, who . . . well, appreciates him.
Admires him, maybe.

JACK
You mean you have no idea where it came from.

JENNY
No.

RICHARD
None.

JENNY

Absolutely none.

JACK

Is there a lot? Can I touch it?

RICHARD

(Involuntary gesture to protect money, withdraws it)
Sure.

JACK

(Touches it with one finger, looks at finger)
Perfectly dry.

JENNY

Of course; it's real.

RICHARD

(Sudden, none-too-happy thought)
Jack . . . *you* didn't do this, did you?

JACK

Do what?

RICHARD

You didn't. *You* didn't send us this money, did you?

JACK *(Tiny pause, then a laugh)*
Christ, no!

RICHARD

You're sure, because if you did . . .

JACK

I'm sure; I'm absolutely sure.
(To audience)
I didn't, by the way; I didn't send it to them.
(Back to them)
How much is there?

JENNY

Nearly . . .

RICHARD

Five thousand.

JACK

Well, that should prove it to you. I never deal in small amounts.

RICHARD *(Defensive)*
It might seem a small amount to *you*, but, to *some* people . . .

JENNY *(To change the subject)*

Why don't we all have a nice martini?

JACK

Splendid!

(RICHARD *sets about to make them.* JENNY *straightens up the room)*

I didn't mean to ridicule your . . . your windfall.

JENNY

Oh, now . . .

JACK

It's just splendid.

(To the audience)

And damned peculiar too, if you ask me.

(Back into the action)

Well, I *do* hope you're going to give a party.

(RICHARD *and* JENNY *look at one another, enthusiasm first)*

JENNY

Why, yes; we could!

RICHARD *(Hesitating)*

Well, I don't think we ought to *announce* that . . .

JACK

No, just a party for the hell of it. Live it up a little! Get some caviar! Serve champagne! Hire a butler! Give a garden party!

JENNY *(Entranced)*

A garden party!

RICHARD *(Giving over to it)*

Sure! Why not!

JACK

Sure! Why not!

(To the audience; shrugs)

Why not?

JENNY

What a super idea. When?

JACK

Now.

JENNY

Well, no . . . Next week, and . . .

RICHARD *(Wistful; a little sad)*

You know . . . people make plans, and . . .

JACK

No; *now.* This very minute: white heat. Get on the phone. Give a blow-out; just for the hell of it!

(*Gentler*)

Do something wild, and out-of-the-ordinary, and . . . the sort of thing you've always *wished* you could do.

JENNY

Yes! Let's! I'll call . . . who shall I call?

RICHARD

Well . . . Chuck and Beryl . . .

JENNY (*On her fingers; enthusiasm*)

Yes, Chuck and Beryl, and Cynthia and Perry, too, of course . . .

RICHARD

. . . yes. . .

JENNY

. . . and . . . and Gilbert and Louise. Who else?

RICHARD (*Little laugh*)

Hey, come on now. Let's not spend it all in one place.

JENNY

Is that enough? Six? Oh, and Jack; *you'll* come, Jack.

JACK

No, my darling; I've got a serious game of backgammon at the club.

JENNY

. . . oooohhhh . . .

JACK

No; *very* serious. High stakes. Wouldn't miss it for the world.

JENNY (*A colt*)

I'll go call. O.K.?

RICHARD (*Amused*)

O.K.

JENNY (*To* RICHARD)

You figure out what we need, how much liquor and all . . .

RICHARD

Not champagne?

JENNY

Yes! Of course! But some people don't like it. I'll go call.

(*Starts out of the living room*)

RICHARD

What time?

JENNY

Oh . . . six, six-thirty. What is it now?

RICHARD

Four.

JENNY *(Momentary pause)*

Oh. *(Resolve)* Well, better hurry. *(As she goes)* Bye, Jack!

JACK

Bye!
   (To RICHARD*)*
Does that mean I'm supposed to be gone by the time she gets back from phoning?

RICHARD

   (Merely laughs; hands JACK *his martini)*
Here.

JACK *(Takes it)*

Ice-cold, juniper-berried heaven. Thank you.
   (We will hear JENNY *faintly from the other room, talking to people on the phone. We will hear her enthusiasm)*

RICHARD

She's so excited. Cheers.

JACK

Double. Well, why shouldn't she be? Quite marvelous *getting* money this way.

RICHARD

Yes.

JACK

No tax, I mean. Tax-free?

RICHARD

Hm?

JACK

Well, you won't de*clare* it, of course . . . and that way there's no tax.

RICHARD *(He'd never thought of that)*

You're right! Free and clear. God!

JACK

And maybe there'll be *more.*

RICHARD (*A little puzzled*)

More? Why?

JACK

Well, good God . . . if someone's sending you money like this, why should they stop with one bundle? Maybe you'll get it every week.

RICHARD (*Almost blushes*)

Oh, come on.

JACK

No; I mean it!

RICHARD (*Worried frown*)

Jack, you won't . . . you won't tell anybody about this, will you?

JACK (*Jaunty*)

My dearest Richard . . . it'll fly out of mind in thirty seconds. No, of *course* I won't say anything. I don't want to screw it up for you.

RICHARD

I mean not even casually, or reference to it, you know, at the club, or . . .

JACK

. . . or when I've had a drink or two? No, Richard; I won't. I promise.

RICHARD

Thanks.

JACK (*Lolling*)

Money is a curious thing, isn't it, Richard?

RICHARD (*Small boy*)

I don't know; I've never had too much.

JACK

No: the thing and the symbol. It's a piece of paper, with ink on it . . . and the ink and the paper together aren't worth a quarter of a cent—less . . . yet if we didn't have it, the world would stop.

RICHARD

We could go back to barter.

JACK

Yes, I suppose we could. It's like painting. A stretch of canvas and some paint. Worth what? Four dollars? Five? Yet put a value on it. Let *me* do it, and it sells for a certain sum, or someone else, and ten times more . . . a hundred! A certain Picasso for half a million? Not a bad painting, *worth* it, maybe. Money. How much does a cow sell for?

RICHARD

I don't know . . . two hundred dollars?

JACK

Maybe. Let's say. One Picasso painting for twenty-five hundred cows. All
that milk. How many gallons does a cow give off in a day?

RICHARD

Fifteen?

JACK *(Some astonishment)*

Gallons?

RICHARD

No. Quarts. I think I read it.

JACK

O.K.
   (Figures in his head)
That comes to . . . fifteen times twenty-five hundred is . . .

RICHARD

You want a pencil and paper?

JACK *(Figures; waves him off)*

. . . figuring three hundred and *sixty* days a year, giving the cows holidays
off. Thirty-seven-five times thirty-six and carry all those zeros . . . comes to
. . . good God! Thirteen and a half million quarts of milk in a year.

RICHARD

You're kidding!

JACK

No; I'm not. Thirteen million and a half quarts of milk in one year.

RICHARD

That's incredible!

JACK

It is, isn't it. How much does milk go for wholesale?

RICHARD

Ten cents?

JACK

No, less. There's all that awful mark-up before it gets to us. Let's say five
cents. Thirteen-five by twenty . . . this is even *more* fascinating! Nearly
seven hundred thousand dollars a year for the milk alone!

RICHARD

What are you getting at?

JACK

Which would YOU rather have? The Picasso or the cows?

RICHARD

(Thinks, shakes his head; genuine)

I don't know. Another drink?

JACK

(Gulps his down, simultaneously shaking his head)

No. I've got to get to the club. Old Digby's waiting, panting at the backgammon board.

RICHARD

Oh. O.K.

JACK *(Both have risen; stops)*

Now that's the *interesting* thing. Old Digby. Do you know that he's eighty-seven, by the way? He *adores* money . . . and not as a symbol . . . as a *thing* in itself. I'll bet he's got sixty million if he's got one, but it's all a *thing* with *him.* It doesn't become Picassos or cows or . . . anything but just the paper as paper. Money as money.

RICHARD *(Pause, almost apologetic)*

Money *is* money, you know.

JACK *(Apologetic; gentle)*

I *know* it is.

RICHARD *(Quietly dogmatic)*

It's paying for this house, and a good education for Roger, and something every once in a while to make Jenny happy . . .

JACK

I *know; I know.*

RICHARD

(Indicates the money on the desk)

So, when something like *this* comes along . . . well, it means something.

JACK

I wasn't making fun of you.

RICHARD

Don't tell Jenny, but I might be able to get her some kind of greenhouse, a small one . . .

JACK

I told you: not a word about anything. Money? *What* money? I've got to go.

(Starts out french doors)

It just occurred to me that I don't think I've ever used the front door in this place. Is it nice?

RICHARD

The front door?

JACK

Mmm.

RICHARD

(He'd never really thought about it before)

Well, *yes* . . . it's all right, I guess.

JACK

I must do it someday.

RICHARD

Jack?

(JACK *stops, half out)*

Nothing.

JACK

(As RICHARD *turns away; to the audience)*

He's *right;* and I *wasn't* making fun of him. Money . . . is . . . money.
See you.

(Exits)

JENNY *(Bounces back in)*

Are you two . . . ? Oh. Is Jack gone?

RICHARD

Um-hum.

JENNY *(Sort of breathless)*

Chuck and Beryl are coming; they were going to just sort of sit around; and
I got Cynthia and Perry, or I got Cynthia, rather, and they had to get out
of something, but they'll be here, too, and I'm trying Gil and Louise but
their line keeps being busy, so I'll go back and finish *that* up.

RICHARD

O.K. You want a martini now?

JENNY

No; when I come back.

(As she goes again)

Roger should be arriving soon. He'll have to take a taxi from the station.

RICHARD

A *taxi!?*

JENNY

(Pauses her flight momentarily)

Yes; a taxi.

(Indicates the money)

Don't you think we can afford one?

RICHARD

(It sinks in; he laughs sheepishly)

Oh. Hunh! Yes, I guess we can.

(JENNY exits)

(RICHARD looks at the money, straightens it out; reaches in his pocket for a cigarette, finds none, looks around for one. Finds a cigarette box empty, looks some more)

RICHARD *(Half calling)*

Jenny, where did you put the cigarettes? Never mind, I can find them.

(Hands on hips for a moment, pondering. Goes to— what? a side table, maybe, opens a drawer, looks in, rummages, suddenly halts, frozen. Puts his hand on something, slowly brings it out. It is a bundle of money. He looks at it, looks over to the pile on the table, looks back at the money in his hand, drops the new bundle down on a chair, or the sofa, whichever is handier, and looks around the room, spies JENNY's sewing basket—say—and goes over to it; hesitates just a moment, then opens it, reaches in, takes out yet another bundle of money which he regards with a curious intensity as he takes it over and dumps it down where he put the last. Spies a box on the mantel and goes to it, opens it, and comes up with a fistful of money. He lets it fall, like confetti, all around him)

JENNY *(Re-enters)*

Well, that's done. Gilbert and Louise are coming, too, so that makes . . . *(She stops, sees what he has found)* . . . everybody we asked.

RICHARD *(In a kind of a fog)*

Jenny; look. What *is* it?

JENNY

Money, Richard.

RICHARD

But . . . is it . . . is it yours?

JENNY

There isn't time to tell you now, I . . .

RICHARD

Yes. There is. You must.

JENNY

We have so much to do before . . .

RICHARD

Wait!

(Points to the money on the table)

Did you send me that package?

JENNY

Actually, yes . . . well, I *had* to; there was *so* much, and I couldn't think of
any way to . . .

RICHARD

Have you been . . . have you been *gambling?*

JENNY *(Jumping on that)*

Yes!

RICHARD

Where? On what? Who through?

JENNY

There's . . . there's this man.

RICHARD

Called?

JENNY

What does it matter so long as I've been winning?

RICHARD *(Steelier)*

Called?

JENNY

Desorio.

RICHARD

That's a lie.

JENNY

Don't you *talk* to me like that!

RICHARD

Isn't it a lie?

JENNY

Well . . . sort of.

RICHARD

THEN IT'S A LIE!

JENNY *(Shrugs)*

Yes.

RICHARD

How much is there here? There's thousands!! Where did you get it?

JENNY *(Defensive)*

I didn't *steal* it.

RICHARD *(Steely)*

Where did you *get* it!?

JENNY

I earned it.

RICHARD

A job! You've got a job!

JENNY

Sort of.

RICHARD

I *told* you I didn't want you to take a *job*. No! You couldn't have earned this at a job. There's too much! There's thousands of dollars here, and . . .

JENNY

Six months!

RICHARD

(*Laughs ruefully and half hysterically*)

No, look, darling; look. Tell me. Did . . . did someone leave it to you? Did someone die and you haven't told me?

JENNY

Nobody died. I earned it.

(*Slight pause*)

In the afternoons.

RICHARD

Look; sweetheart: even if you worked full-*time* you couldn't have earned *this* kind of money. Come on now; *tell* me.

JENNY

(*Miffed and playing for time*)

Oh? Really? I guess *not* if all I'm supposed to be good for is a domestic or something.

RICHARD (*Gritting his teeth*)

Where did you *get* it?

JENNY (*Sighs, rattles it off*)

I make two hundred dollars an afternoon, four days a week, sometimes more. I've spent a little on clothes, but there hasn't been time to *spend* the rest, and . . . .

RICHARD

Nobody pays that sort of money! I mean you've no training.

JENNY

You don't *need* any.

RICHARD

(*Bewildered, and getting angry at the mystery*)

What *do* you need?

JENNY

Where's my martini? You promised me an ice-cold, super-special . . .

RICHARD *(Grabs her arm)*

Now tell me!

JENNY

Ow! Now let go of me!
   (He does; she rubs her arm as they glare at each other. Subdued)
There's nothing worth telling.

RICHARD

By God, you tell me or I'll make a bonfire of this money in the middle of the lawn!

JENNY *(Pleading underneath)*

Don't be ridiculous! It's money!

RICHARD

I want to know where it comes from!

JENNY *(Her voice rising, too)*

It comes from a job!

RICHARD

What *kind* of a job!?

JENNY *(Wild hunting)*

A . . . a receptionist.

RICHARD

For *that* kind of money?
   (Snorts- sneers)

JENNY

It's a very expensive place!

RICHARD

What *sort* of expensive place?!

JENNY

A . . . a doctor's office.

RICHARD

You expect me to believe you sit behind the desk at some god-damn doctor's office a couple of hours in the afternoon, and you get two hundred dollars a day for it?! You must think I'm crazy!!

JENNY

It's a very special and very expensive place!

RICHARD

   (A little fearful, a little disgusted)
What, what is it, some kind of . . . of abortionist office, or something?

JENNY

My God, you're disgusting!

RICHARD

Why! I've read in the paper of a man found out his wife worked for an abortionist, brought him patients, as a matter of fact.

JENNY

You're disgusting!!

RICHARD

Well, I'm *sorry;* but if you're going to be so damned secretive, what am I *supposed* to think? Hunh?

JENNY *(Trapped and furious)*

Think what you like!!
   (Quite cutting)
Don't you want the money?

RICHARD *(Both furious now)*

The money's got nothing to do with it!

JENNY

Oh yes it has! You don't think I do it for pleasure, do you?

RICHARD

Do what!? Sit behind a desk!?

JENNY

Yes; sit behind a desk!

RICHARD

What's the name of this place?

JENNY *(Daring him)*

No name; just a number.

RICHARD

Yeah? Well, what's the number?

JENNY

It's confidential!

RICHARD

I'm your husband!

JENNY

I'm your wife! Do you tell me everything?

RICHARD

I like being told the truth!

JENNY

How much do you talk about *your* job? To *me.*

RICHARD

It's a dull job!

JENNY

So's mine!

RICHARD

The money isn't! The money isn't so damn dull! Christ! It's four times what *I* get.

(*Contemptuous*)

Sitting behind the desk in a doctor's office . . . sounds more like a high-class whorehouse!

JENNY

I don't *like* that word.

RICHARD

Whorehouse! Call house! Cat house!

(*There is a silence.* JENNY *looks out toward the garden.* RICHARD *begins to realize he's hit on it*)

No; look; come on; what is it *really?*

JENNY

(*Looking away; sort of wistful, sad*)

Just a place.

RICHARD

A place.

JENNY

Where they pay me.

RICHARD (*Grabs her arm again*)

For God's sake! What do they pay me for!?

JENNY

It's *me* they *pay!*

(*Long pause; sort of lost*)

Don't you want the money?

RICHARD

(*Lets go of her arm, backs away a little, shakes his head; stuttered, almost laughing disbelief*)

I, I don't . . . I don't believe it. I, I don't believe it.

JENNY (*Quite light*)

Then don't.

RICHARD

(*Backs a bit further away; same confusion*)

I, I can't *believe* it. I CAN'T.

JENNY

(Coming toward him; the nicest smile)
Darling, it's going to make such a tremendous difference.

RICHARD

(Laughing mirthlessly at the irony)
Oh, by God it is!

JENNY *(Still happy; occupied)*
All the things we've been wanting for years . . .

RICHARD

We!

JENNY

We can have a second car, and . . .

RICHARD

There's no . . . I don't believe this!

JENNY

There's no what?

RICHARD

Room in the garage.
(Incredulous)
How could you *do* such a thing!?
(Pause)
Come on, it *isn't* true, *is* it?
(JENNY nods, slowly)
No; is it? Really?

JENNY

(Dogmatic; impatient)
It is for *us;* for everything we *want!*

RICHARD

(Between set teeth; quiet rage, letting it sink in firmly)
You are my wife; and Roger's mother; and you are a common *prostitute!?*

JENNY

That's a *horrid* way to *put* it.

RICHARD

HOW THE HELL AM I SUPPOSED TO PUT IT!!?

JENNY

I'm not the only *one,* you know. I'm not the only person in the world
who . . .

RICHARD

You're the only one who's married to *me!*

JENNY *(Triste reasoning)*

But it doesn't make any difference to *us,* and . . .

RICHARD *(Hard)*

Doesn't it?

(Walks over to her, slaps her hard across the face)

Doesn't it? How much do you charge for *that?*

*(She just stares at him, firm but maybe near tears way under-
neath. So he slaps her again, just as hard)*

I said: how much do you charge for that!!

JENNY

*(Says nothing, really, maybe a kind of growl-cry as she slaps him
back, just as hard as he hit her)*

RICHARD

(Cold, after a moment's pause)

Get out. Pack up and get out of here.

JENNY *(Equally cold)*

Where!

RICHARD

Anywhere! Or I will. No, by God, I won't! It's my house, I paid for it. I stay
here!

JENNY *(Curiously unemotional)*

I can't . . . just like that.

RICHARD

I said get out!

JENNY

A lot of things here are mine.

RICHARD

Take them! Take them!

JENNY *(Through her teeth)*

You certainly don't expect me to get everything together right now and . . .

RICHARD

I'll send it after you! Just . . . just get out!

JENNY

No, no, you wouldn't. I know *you:* you can never manage anything like that.
I'm the one who has to get the movers and arrange everything, and . . .

RICHARD

CRAP!!

JENNY

Well, it's perfectly true. When your aunt what's-her-name wanted her big, ugly breakfront back, you said you'd take care of it, and *weeks* went by and you didn't do a damn thing.

RICHARD

(Quietly, with controlled rage)

Get your things together and get out of this house!

JENNY *(Tired of it all)*

Oh, don't be silly.

RICHARD *(Fury and disbelief)*

Don't be *what!?*

JENNY

I said, don't be silly. Give me a cigarette.

RICHARD

You god-damn wanton bitch!

JENNY

I am *not* wanton! I told you: it's for the money! The money *you* don't make! The money we *need!* You think I get any enjoyment out of it?

RICHARD

Think!? I, I, I, I. I don't think anything! I *can't!* I'd go stark raving mad if I thought! Men kill their wives for this sort of thing!

JENNY *(Giggles)*

Oh, darling . . .

RICHARD

(Mocked, becomes uncontrollable)

You don't think they do?

(Starts toward her with serious intent)

Read the papers and find out! By God, read tomorrow's papers and find . . .

(They are both stopped by the sound of the front door slamming. ROGERS enters, from the hallway)

ROGER

Hi! I took a taxi; do you have any money?

JENNY

(As if she'd forgotten all about him and is sorry)

Roger!

ROGER

The taxi driver says he wants five dollars over the fare because it was such a long way.

RICHARD *(Fury turned on driver)*

Oh, he does, does he? *Well,* I'll fix that son of a bitch.

(RICHARD *exits, maybe pushing* ROGER *to one side as he goes)*

ROGER

(Looks at RICHARD's *exit, confused; back to* JENNY; *genuine affection)*

Hi, Mom.

JENNY *(Embarrassed, but covering)*

Darling! You're so . . . so terribly early.

ROGER *(Statement of fact)*

The train was on *time.*

JENNY *(A little flustered)*

Oh? Was it? Well, then . . . our clock must be slow.

ROGER

Must be.

(Goes to a chair, stands on its seat, looks out through french windows over fence.)

How's the tennis?

JENNY

What tennis?

ROGER *(Points)*

At the club.

(Angry voices from outside front door)

JENNY *(Looks off apprehensively)*

Oh, I . . . I don't pay much attention.

ROGER

Dad been playing? I hope the cab driver doesn't kill him.

JENNY *(Calling off; worried)*

Richard?

(To ROGER*)*

Get *down* off that before your father sees you!

ROGER

O.K. . . .

(Jumps down; sees the money)

Wow! Is that money?

JENNY (*Preoccupied, defensive*)

Yes, now . . . just leave it be.

ROGER

What is it, the sweepstakes?

JENNY

Just . . . don't concern yourself, now.

ROGER

Can I have a bunch?

JENNY (*Sudden anger*)

No! Now let it alone!

ROGER (*Hurt, some*)

I'm sorry.

(*Heavy-handed irony*)

Gee, am *I* glad *I* came home.

JENNY (*Apologetic*)

Oh, Roger, darling, I'm . . .

(RICHARD *reappears, a little mussed*)

RICHARD (*Vengefulness and pride*)

I hit him!

ROGER (*Shy*)

Hi, Dad.

RICHARD

(*To* JENNY, *since she caused it*)

I hit the son of a bitch!

JENNY (*Quite rebuking*)

Did you say hello to your son?

RICHARD

Hm?

ROGER (*Shy, pleased*)

Hi.

RICHARD

(*Really sees* ROGER *for the first time; sadness and pride*)

Hi.

(*Back to* JENNY; *quiet fury and glee*)

I hit that son of a bitch.

JENNY (*Quietly desperate*)

Why!

RICHARD

Why!!? He wanted nine dollars. The bastard wanted the regular fare and five dollars extra because . . .

JENNY

That is no reason to hit anyone!

RICHARD

WHO AM I SUPPOSED TO HIT!

(Less loud, but no less intense)

Who am I supposed to hit!

ROGER *(To fill a tiny silence)*

How's the tennis, Dad?

RICHARD *(To* ROGER*)*

What?

ROGER *(Intimidated)*

Tennis. How is it?

RICHARD *(Confused)*

I, I haven't . . . I, I, I, haven't played.

ROGER

Un huh . . .

JENNY

You'll get a lawsuit on us, you know.

RICHARD

(Deflated; embarrassed, even)

I only hit him on the shoulder. We . . . we just scuffled a little.

JENNY

(Pause, disappointment and relief)

Oh.

RICHARD *(A sneer)*

Not what I wanted to do.

*(*ROGER *has gone up on the chair again)*

ROGER

Wow! Right in the crotch!

RICHARD

Who! What!

JENNY

Roger, don't use words like that.

RICHARD *(Scoffs)*

Oh, Jesus!

ROGER

Serve took a bad bounce, hit him right in the . . . what word shall I use?

RICHARD

Don't ask your mother, she's too ladylike.

(*Realizes where* ROGER *is*)

GET THE HELL OFF THE GOD-DAMNED FURNITURE.

(ROGER *does so*)

ROGER *(Subdued, unhappy)*

Sorry.

RICHARD

You think we're made of money?

ROGER

(*Defensive, indicates money all over*)

It *looks* like it.

(*This sets in an embarrassed silence*)

RICHARD *(To change the subject)*

Did you have a good term?

ROGER

All right.

RICHARD

What's your average? What did you end up with?

ROGER

C plus.

RICHARD

What did you start out?

ROGER

C plus.

RICHARD *(Bitter)*

Keep it up: by the time you're eighteen we won't even be able to get you into an agricultural college!

JENNY

Be nice!

(RICHARD's *mouth drops open, but he doesn't say anything*)

Set the clock right.

RICHARD

It *is* right.

ROGER

It's twenty minutes slow.

RICHARD *(Furious)*

Then you set it right!

JENNY

Richard!

RICHARD

Shut up!
　(ROGER *goes to the mantel clock, takes it down*)

ROGER

What do I do?

RICHARD

Turn the knob; turn the god-damn knob!

JENNY

Richard, if you can't be . . .

RICHARD *(Between clenched teeth)*

I told you to shut up!
　(To ROGER*)*
No! Too far! That's tooo . . . DON'T TURN IT BACK.
　(Disgust, takes the clock, none too gently, from ROGER*)*
Here; give me the god-damn clock. NEVER TURN IT BACK! Don't ever
turn a clock back!

ROGER *(Flustered, confused)*

I'm sorry, I . . .

JENNY

Roger, darling, why don't you take your bag upstairs, and . . .

RICHARD

(Concentrating, excessively, on the clock; to himself as well as ROGER*)*
You *never* turn a clock back; *never.*

JENNY

Why don't you go unpack?

ROGER *(Sullen)*

O.K. You've got so much money, I don't see why you don't go *buy* a clock.

RICHARD

ALL RIGHT!

JENNY

Go unpack and then you can come down and *help* us.

ROGER

You want me to go upstairs, or would you rather I turned around and went right back to school?

RICHARD

GET UPSTAIRS!!

ROGER *(Under his breath)*

Christl!

RICHARD

And don't say that!

ROGER *(Standing up to him)*

Why not! YOU do! *(Exits)*
    (Small silence. RICHARD *hurls the clock down on the floor)*

JENNY *(Calm, displeased)*

That helps.

RICHARD

    (Intense, pounding his chest with his fingers)
It helps *me!* ME!!

JENNY

    (Closes her eyes for a moment; then all business)
I wish you'd make a list of what we need, what liquor we need.

RICHARD *(Stares at her; quietly)*

Whore.

JENNY *(Ignores it)*

We'll have champagne, but there are always some people don't like it, and . . .

RICHARD *(Ibid.)*

Whore!

JENNY

. . . and so you'd better check. If we're going to have *fresh* caviar, and I think we should, then I've got to go down to Blaustein's and get some . . .

RICHARD *(Ibid.)*

Filthy, rotten, no-good little whore!

JENNY *(Quite savage)*

Be quiet! You've got Roger in the house!

RICHARD *(Top of his voice)*

I'VE GOT A ROTTEN, FILTHY WHORE IN THE HOUSE!

JENNY

(Tiny pause; continues quietly)

Now make a list. They'll be here in about an hour . . .

RICHARD *(Laughing in disbelief)*

A party! We're going to have a party!

JENNY *(Level)*

Yes; we are.

RICHARD

*(The tears that finally come, tears of rage and despair, are incipi-
ent; we notice what is coming by a quivering in the voice)*

What, what shall we do? Make the announcement? Break it to the neighborhood? Tell them to tell their friends where they can go to get it? Hunh?

JENNY

Make a list.

RICHARD

Hunh? Is that what we should do? Is it? Whore?

(Tears nearer now)

JENNY

You can phone for the liquor, but we have to know what we need.

RICHARD *(Tears even nearer)*

Or, or maybe they already know. Maybe . . . maybe Chuck and Perry and
Gil . . . do they . . . do they know already?

JENNY

List.

RICHARD

L, l, list? We . . . all, all right, we need . . .

(Crying commences now)

v, v, v, vodka, and . . .

JENNY *(Gentle)*

American or Russian?

RICHARD *(Looks up; pleading)*

Both?

JENNY

Both, then.

RICHARD

. . . and . . . and . . . sc, sc, sc, scotch, and . . . bourbon, and . . .

(Full crying now)

. . . and gin, and . . . gin, and . . . gin, and . . .

(The word gin *takes a long time now, a long, broken word with gasps for breath and the attempt to control the tears)*

. . . g—i—i—i—n, and . . .

(Final word, very long, broken, a long howl)

G—i—i—i—n—n—n—n.

(Curtain falls slowly as the word continues)

ACT TWO

(Set the same; one hour later. RICHARD *alone on stage, sitting facing out at audience. It might be interesting if he looked the people in the audience right in the eye, but absently, seeing them, but thinking of something else. No attempt to set a new convention (with* RICHARD*), but it will give quite a few people an interesting sensation)*

*(*JENNY *enters, followed by* ROGER*, both laden with glasses, etc.)*

JENNY *(Pleasantly incredulous)*

What are you *doing?*

RICHARD

Hm?

JENNY

What are you *doing?* Roger, put those over there and be careful you don't break them.

ROGER

(Embarrassed at being warned)

O.K.

JENNY *(Puts her things down)*

I asked you what you thought you were doing. You've got guests coming over in about ten minutes, and . . .

RICHARD

(Ugly but quiet; a threat of explosion)

What am I supposed to do?

ROGER *(Breaks a glass)*

Damn!

JENNY

Oh, Roger . . .

RICHARD

That's right! Break the house up!

ROGER

It's only a glass, for God's sake, it . . .

RICHARD

We're not made . . . Do you know how much those things cost?

ROGER (*Standing his ground*)

No. How much?

RICHARD (*To* JENNY)

How much do they cost?

JENNY

Well, they're new, and . . .

RICHARD

(*Hint of hysteria; incipience*)

They're new!?

JENNY (*Calm*)

Yes, and they're crystal, and I suppose they . . . well, I think they were about four-fifty each . . .

RICHARD

(*After a pained look at* JENNY; *to* ROGER, *shaking his head and sneering*)

Four-fifty each. You broke a god-damn glass and they cost four . . .

ROGER (*Digs into his pocket*)

Well, here. Take it out of this.

RICHARD (*Unpleasant joy*)

Give it to your mother.

JENNY (*Laughing, covering*)

Don't be silly, darling. No, Roger, no.

ROGER (*Hand out of pocket again*)

Anything to keep peace in the house.

RICHARD

Don't be fresh!

JENNY (*Mollifying; to* ROGER)

Darling, go upstairs and change. People *will* be here soon, and I'll want you to help.

ROGER

Do I have to put on a tie?

RICHARD (*Furious*)

Yes!

JENNY (*All on* ROGER's *side*)

I'm afraid so, darling. Run along upstairs now.

ROGER

Tie?

RICHARD

Yes; *and* a shirt, *and* trousers, *and* socks, *and* shoes . . .

ROGER *(Going, shaking his head)*

Wow.

RICHARD

And don't hang out the window watching the tennis. Change.

ROGER *(Sloppy salute)*

Yes, sir!

(Exits)

RICHARD

And don't salute!

JENNY

(After a tiny pause; reasonable, calm)

It was only a glass.

RICHARD *(Turns on her; quiet wrath)*

What have you been doing: buying things behind my back? Crystal? Gold goblets? Clothes?

JENNY

Just a little.

RICHARD

Just a little what!

JENNY *(Sighs)*

A few clothes; those glasses; nicer sheets. Didn't you notice?

RICHARD *(Still furious)*

Notice what!

JENNY *(Quietly happy)*

The nice sheets. I thought they'd . . .

RICHARD

No! I didn't notice the nicer sheets, and by God I won't sleep on them! I won't sleep in the same room with you!

JENNY *(Cool)*

And where are you going to sleep?

RICHARD

What?

JENNY

I said, where are you going to sleep? Roger's home, there's no mattress in the guestroom . . .

RICHARD

Why not! Where is it!

JENNY

You threw it out. When you had the hepatitis and you slept in there you said it was awful—the mattress—so we threw it out.

RICHARD

Well, why didn't we get another one!

JENNY

(Shrugs, starts arranging things)
Oh . . . money, or something.

RICHARD

WELL, WE CAN DAMN WELL AFFORD ONE NOW!

JENNY *(Quiet, precise)*
I don't see the need. You've told me to get out.

RICHARD

(This stops him for the briefest instant only)
WELL, WHEN ARE YOU GOING!?

JENNY *(Stops what she is doing)*
Right now. Right this very minute.

RICHARD

You've got a party! You've got people coming over!

JENNY

(Pretending this complicates things)
Oh. Yes. Well then, I'll leave right after the party, right after everybody goes.

RICHARD

Fine.

JENNY *(Quietly withering)*
Or shall I stay and clean up first?

RICHARD

(Can think of nothing for a moment, finally)
Tramp.

JENNY

There's no need for that now.

RICHARD

I can't hold my head up in front of those people; I won't be able to look any of them in the eye. I might scream, or cry, or something.

JENNY

You'll hold your head up. In fact, I should think you might be *able* to look Chuck and Perry and Gil straight in the eye, maybe for the first time.

RICHARD

Why! Because my wife is a whore?

JENNY *(Sort of cajoling)*

No . . . well, because for once you won't be the poor relative, so to speak; you can talk about the new car you're going to get, and why don't we raise the dues at the club to keep the riffraff out, and Jenny and I were thinking about Antigua this winter—all those things.

RICHARD *(Some disgust)*

You're hopelessly immoral.

JENNY

Not at all! I'm talking about money—that thing that keeps us at each other's throats; that standard of judgment; that measure of a man's worth!

RICHARD

There are other standards!

JENNY

Well, not in the circles *we* move in! Not in *our* environment.

RICHARD

There are *kinds* of money!

JENNY

Yes! Three! Too little, too much, and just enough!

RICHARD

Corrupt!

JENNY

Too much money corrupts; too little corrupts. Just enough? Never.

RICHARD

It's how! *How!*

JENNY

Oh, don't tell me about how! Perry and that real estate he sells? Ten thousand for an acre out near, uh, near the track, and he doesn't even tell the god-damn fools there isn't any city water? Gilbert and his fancy publishing house? What's his advertising budget on trash? Thousands! How much does he spend on a halfway decent book . . . nothing!

RICHARD

All right, all right . . .

JENNY

And you in your research laboratory. All those government contracts? A little work on germ gas maybe?

RICHARD

I told you that in . . . I told you not to say a word about anything I told
you . . .

JENNY

You told me in confidence? Well, I'm telling you *back* in confidence! You
all stink, you're all killers and whores.

RICHARD

(*Nods several times rapidly*)

That's quite a performance.

JENNY

You're damned right.

RICHARD (*Great sarcasm*)

Bra-*vo!*

JENNY

At least! Come on! More!

RICHARD

With your theories on money, you should have married Jack.

JENNY (*Self-mocking rue*)

Unh-hunh; you may be right.

RICHARD

Though I don't necessarily think he'd take any better to having a whore for
a wife than I do.

JENNY (*Comforting*)

Well, if I'd married Jack none of it would have happened.

RICHARD

(*As* ROGER *re-enters; starts to go for her*)

Why, you . . .

ROGER

I'm dressed.

(*They both pause, for* ROGER's *tone has a curious impersonal disapproval to it*)

JENNY (*Recovering*)

And in good time, too. They'll start coming any second. My, don't you look
nice and grown-up.

ROGER

You've seen me in a tie before.

(*To* RICHARD)

Were you going to hit her?

RICHARD

Mind your own business.

ROGER (*Mildly puzzled*)

I thought it was.

RICHARD

Well, it's not. I don't suppose you washed.

ROGER

Well, I didn't have time for a sit-down bath, if that's what you mean. Why *isn't* it my business?

RICHARD

Because it isn't! Are your fingernails clean?

ROGER

(*To* JENNY, *the same mildly disapproving curiosity*)
Was he going to hit you?
(*Looks at his nails*)
Relatively.

JENNY

Don't be silly, darling; your father doesn't hit people bigger than he is. Come help me with things, now. Those glasses over there . . .

ROGER (*Grumbling, sort of*)

People always hit each other when other people are out of the room.

JENNY (*Decidedly offended*)

Roger!

RICHARD (*Snarl*)

Little monster.

ROGER

I wasn't complaining; I was just stating a fact.

RICHARD

Keep your facts to yourself.

JENNY

Nobody hits anybody around here.

RICHARD

Anyway, not above the belt.

JENNY (*"Not in front of Roger."*)

Richard!

RICHARD (*Subsiding*)

Sorry! Very sorry. Sorry about everything. Every single thing.

ROGER *(An aside, to* JENNY)

What's the matter with Dad?

JENNY

(RICHARD *can hear them both, of course*)

Oh, nothing; parties upset your father, that's all.

ROGER

(Goes to RICHARD: *genuine)*

I'll help.

RICHARD

(Looks at him for a moment, then, with a head-shaking laugh that could be confused with mockery, but isn't)

Oh, boy! Thanks!

ROGER *(Withdraws a little; stung)*

I'm sorry.

RICHARD *(Quite furious)*

Roger! I mean it! Thank you!

ROGER *(A little bewildered)*

O.K.

(Doorbell rings)

JENNY *(Sighs, girds herself)*

Well. Here we go.

RICHARD *(Little boy)*

I'm going to hate this.

ROGER

Hey, what shall I drink?

RICHARD

Ginger ale.

ROGER

Awww.

JENNY *(Exiting)*

I'll go.

RICHARD

Roger, do me a favor.

ROGER

Sure. What?

RICHARD

Grow up right.

(Sounds of greeting from hallway)

ROGER (*Offhand*)

O.K. Got any ideas?

RICHARD

Just . . . be good.

ROGER

As the twig is bent, as they say.

(JENNY *re-enters with* CHUCK *and* BERYL)

BERYL (*To* JENNY, *as they enter*)

No, it's been lovely, but I would love some rain. Our lawn is all brown and splotchy.

JENNY

Oh? Well, we manage ours.

BERYL

Green thumb, my darling.

CHUCK

Won't be any rain till we take off for . . . *Hel*lo, Richard!

RICHARD (*Shy*)

Hi, Chuck; Beryl?

BERYL

Are we too early? I told Chuck we'd be first here.

JENNY

Don't be silly.

CHUCK

And I said, so what? First to come, last to leave; no breeding. Roger!

ROGER

Hello.

BERYL (*To* ROGER; *some wonder*)

Do you grow each time I see you?

ROGER

Probably; I don't see you very much.

JENNY

He grows fresher each time you see him, I can tell you *that*.

CHUCK (*Formality*)

How's school, Roger?

ROGER

Fine.

CHUCK

Back for vacation? Now, that's a silly question. Got any silly answers?

ROGER

I keep those for exams.
(Some laughter)

RICHARD

How true. Hey! How about a drink? Champagne or proper stuff?

CHUCK *(Hearty)*

Champagne!

BERYL *(To* CHUCK*)*

You know what it does.
(To JENNY*)*
Keeps him up all night; bent double. Gas?

CHUCK *(To* RICHARD; *ruefully)*

I guess I better have some scotch.

RICHARD

Right. Beryl?
(Goes to her)

ROGER

Can I help?

BERYL

(Examining caviar; to JENNY*)*
Fresh, how nice. Do you get yours in the city?

JENNY

No, Blaustein's has the fresh.

BERYL *(To* RICHARD*)*

Gin, darling, and a little ice.
(Back to JENNY*)*
Well, fresh caviar can't keep, and I don't trust Blaustein's.

JENNY *(A tiny bit of pique)*

Oh, it's perfectly fresh.

BERYL *(Slight laugh)*

I'm sure it is. I just think Blaustein's cheats a little . . . keeps it on ice a day
or two more than they . . .

JENNY

Would you like some caviar, Chuck?

CHUCK

Sure would.
(Goes to it)
Toast? Toast?

JENNY

No; crackers.

BERYL

(Moving away from caviar, looks at garden, expansive)
How do you keep it!? How do you battle the weeds, and prune and dust . . . ?

JENNY *(Proud)*

Green *thumb.*

CHUCK

Cheers!

THE OTHERS *(Nearly simultaneously)*

Cheers!

BERYL

While I've got you now, I need you for the blood bank.

JENNY

Richard can't.

BERYL

Why?

JENNY

Hepatitis. And Roger shouldn't, either; he needs all he's got.

ROGER

I don't mind giving blood.

JENNY *(Light, but firm)*

I don't think you *should,* Roger.

BERYL

Well, Jenny, then you'll have to give for the whole family.

RICHARD

I don't think she should.

BERYL

Why ever not?

JENNY

Yes. Why not?

RICHARD *(Dogmatic)*

I just don't think you should.

JENNY *(A little annoyed)*

Well, do you have a reason? Or are you just hoarding everybody's blood.

RICHARD

(Too much attempt at a joke; only JENNY *will see what he means)*
Well, no; you . . . you might have some awful disease for all *you* know.

BERYL *(As* CHUCK *laughs)*
Oh, Richard! Really!
(Doorbell)

ROGER

Shall I go?

JENNY

(Exiting; a quick look at RICHARD*)*
I'll go. Help yourselves to the . . . *(Leaves it unfinished; exits)*

RICHARD *(The tiniest mockery)*
How's high finance, Chuck? How's the old market?

CHUCK

Oh, just like marriage . . . up and down, up and down.
*(*BERYL *and* RICHARD *laugh flimsily)*

ROGER

What does *that* mean?

RICHARD

Nothing.

ROGER

Then why did he say it?

RICHARD *(Annoyed)*
You know perfectly well what it means, so why did you ask?

ROGER *(Shrugs)*
I thought it was polite. You told me to help.
*(*JENNY *re-enters, with* GILBERT *and* LOUISE*)*

JENNY

Richard! It's Gilbert and Louise!

RICHARD

Well! Come on in! You know Beryl and Ch . . .

LOUISE

Yes, I think we've met at the club.

GILBERT

Yes, of course we have.

BERYL

How nice to see you both again.

CHUCK

Drinks are over here. There's champagne *and* the real stuff.

LOUISE

How nice you were to ask us. Oh, will you look at your garden! And the lawn! *How* do you do it?

BERYL

I was commenting before. I *don't* know how they do it.

GILBERT

Who's your gardener? Shropie?

RICHARD

Who?

GILBERT

Shropshire; he has a whole team, and . . .

JENNY

No, we've been doing it ourselves.

LOUISE

We have Shropshire, and they send two men, but we have six acres, too, so that makes a difference.

GILBERT

Charge an arm and a leg.

BERYL

But are they *good.* Chuck and I were thinking of using them, and . . .

CHUCK

Not going to get me mowing weekends . . .

JENNY

It sort of spoils the fun to farm it out—the work . . .

RICHARD (A *little tentative*)

We, we could have someone in, though.

JENNY (*Secret smile*)

Oh? Well, why don't we?

RICHARD (*Bitter at being caught*)

Spoils the fun.

JENNY (*To the others*)

We thought we might put a greenhouse in, though.

RICHARD

Did we!

LOUISE

Oh, you must. We're so glad *we* did.

JENNY

I've always wanted one.

CHUCK

You must be in the chips, Richard old boy: greenhouse, champagne, caviar . . .

RICHARD *(Laughs lightly)*

No; just . . .
(*Shrugs, leaves it unfinished*)

JENNY

No, just not scrimping.

BERYL *(Her eyes narrowing slightly)*

Oh, I'm glad.

ROGER *(Weary of asking)*

Can I help?

LOUISE

Roger, *dear!* I didn't even say hello to you. Gilbert! Roger's here.

GILBERT

Roger, my boy. Home from school?

ROGER *(False heartiness)*

Yes, Sir!

GILBERT

Doing O.K.?

ROGER

Holding my own, as they say.

GILBERT

Good boy; good boy. Hey, Rich; this is good caviar. Where'd you get it?

RICHARD

Jenny got it; it's Jenny's.

JENNY

I got it at Blaustein's, just as fresh as if you'd gone into town and . . .

GILBERT

Damn smart little kike, that Blaustein, putting in caviar and . . .

ROGER

We don't use words like that around here.
(*Everybody looks at him, not quite sure of what he means*)
At least, not in the family.
(*Doorbell again*)

JENNY (*Glad of the chance*)

I'll get it!

(*Exits*)

BERYL	LOUISE
(*Both just to say something*)	
I still say if you get it in town it's bound to be fresher.	The first year we had *our* greenhouse, I was amazed.

RICHARD

Drinks now! Come on, kids; the bar's open.

GILBERT

(*To* RICHARD *as they approach the bar*)

What did I say?

RICHARD	CHUCK
Nothing, nothing.	Your kid's sort of a wiseacre, hunh?

GILBERT (*Hurt*)

What did I say?

(*Simultaneous*)

RICHARD	BERYL
Nothing; forget it.	But aren't they a terrible chore?

CHUCK	LOUISE
I don't get the champagne. What for? What gives?	Well, no; not if you remember things, like water, and air, and heat, and . . .

(*Simultaneous*)

RICHARD	BERYL (*Laughs*)
What gives? Nothing.	Ah, just a few things like that!

CHUCK	LOUISE
Looks pretty festive to me.	It takes getting used to, that's all.

ROGER (*If anyone cares*)

I apologize.

(JENNY *re-enters, with* CYNTHIA *and* PERRY)

JENNY

The stragglers. Cynthia and Perry Straggler.

PERRY

Hi, folks.

ROGER *(To himself)*

Folk.

GILBERT

Well, if it isn't old Perry! Hi, Cyn!

CYNTHIA *(Generally)*

Hello there!

RICHARD

Bar's here, kids.

CYNTHIA

Well, will you look at all that!

CHUCK

Is it true what I heard, Perr?

PERRY

Probably. What?

CHUCK

You been selling lots to the black folk twice the going price?
   (Some laughter, for this is a joke)

PERRY

Not a word of it! Three times the going price, and at that I don't let 'em
have clear title.
   (More laughter)

ROGER

There are two Negro boys at school, on scholarship.

GILBERT *(None too pleasant)*

Oh yeah?
   (To RICHARD*)*
You ought to send your boy to Choate, Dick. That's a *good* school.

ROGER

There are Negro boys there, too.

GILBERT

You're kidding.

ROGER

Why not? I mean, why am I kidding?

BERYL *(Not snobbish)*

It *is* getting to be a problem.

CYNTHIA

I *know.*

LOUISE *(Very serious)*

Well . . . it's a time of change.

JENNY

It's time for a drink, that's what it's time for! Cynthia? Louise?

ROGER

Actually, there won't be any solution to the color problem— whatever *that* is—until we're all coffee-colored.

BERYL

Roger!

JENNY

Darling!

GILBERT

Where'd you pick up *that* theory?

ROGER

A book.

PERRY

A little knowledge is a dangerous thing, Roger.

CHUCK

Theories that come out of books ought to stay in books.

RICHARD *(To* ROGER*)*

Why don't you pass the caviar? I thought you wanted to help.

ROGER

I've been *ask*ing! I've been standing around on my two hind feet asking if I could be any help and everybody's been ignoring me!

RICHARD *(Put out)*

You've been standing around on your two hind feet *insult*ing everybody, that's what you've been standing around doing.

ROGER *(Something of a pout)*

That was after.

CYNTHIA

Oh, let him alone, for heaven sake! He's a sweet boy. How old are you, Roger, dear?

ROGER

I'm twelve.

JENNY

You're fourteen!

RICHARD

He *is* not; he's fifteen.

JENNY

I ought to know how old my own son is.

RICHARD

You ought; yes.

CHUCK

Where you going to put the greenhouse, Dick?

RICHARD

Hm? Oh . . . out there.
(*Gestures vaguely*)

JENNY (*Rather pointed*)

Show them *where*, darling.

RICHARD (*Trapped*)

Hm?

LOUISE

Oh, I'd love to see! Show us!

CYNTHIA

Yes! And I want to look at Jenny's roses.
(CYNTHIA *and* LOUISE *start out through french doors;* PERRY *automatically follows*)

CHUCK

Well, into the garden we go. Somebody bring a bottle of champagne.

GILBERT (*Following* CHUCK)

Nobody's *drinking* champagne.

CHUCK

Well . . . bring a bottle of scotch.
(*The two men laugh, follow the others out*)

JENNY (*To* RICHARD)

Well . . .

RICHARD (*Getting it straight*)

Show them where we're going to put the greenhouse.

JENNY (*Dazzling if mirthless smile*)

Yes.
(*Doorbell rings:* JENNY *starts*)
Who's that? We didn't ask anyone else.

RICHARD (*Exiting to garden*)

It's your party; you figure it out.

JENNY (*To* BERYL)

I can't imagine who it is. Roger, darling . . . go see.

(ROGER *exits through archway*)

Unless it's Jack Foster. He always drops in, and . . .

BERYL (*Starts exiting to garden*)

Well, if it is, I'll leave the two of you alone.

JENNY (*Annoyance showing through*)

And what is that meant to mean!

BERYL (*Throaty laugh, as she exits*)

Nothing, darling; nothing at all.

(*We will probably see one or more of the people out in the garden while they admire it and while* RICHARD *improvises where the greenhouse will be, but their backs will be to us, and they will not see inside until they return.*)

ROGER (*Re-entering*)

It's a woman to see you.

(MRS. TOOTHE *enters;* JENNY *stares at her, open-mouthed*)

MRS. TOOTHE

Good evening, my dear.

(JENNY *just stares*)

I said, good evening, my dear.

JENNY (*Still staring at her*)

Roger, go in the garden.

ROGER (*Bland*)

Why?

JENNY (*Turns, snaps*)

I said go in the garden!

ROGER

(*Some disgust, turns on his heel, goes*)

Good God!

JENNY (*Appalled*)

What do you want?

MRS. TOOTHE

I want to talk.

(*Sits*)

Ah! That feels good. I do so hate to walk.

JENNY

You can't *come* here; you *mustn't*.

MRS. TOOTHE

I know, my dear, it's very indiscreet, but most important.

JENNY

(Anger, and panic underneath)

I'm having a party! Guests!

MRS. TOOTHE

Yes, I see; fine, I'm one of them.

JENNY

No! I'm sorry; no!

MRS. TOOTHE

Why not?

JENNY

They're friends; Richard thinks you're on the hospital committee, and . . .

MRS. TOOTHE

Fine, I'm on the hospital committee.

JENNY

But these are local people, and Beryl is on the hospital committee, and . . .

MRS. TOOTHE

Beryl?

JENNY

Yes, and Louise is too . . . and, and . . .

MRS. TOOTHE

Well, you'll just have to make up something: I'm not from *here*, I'm from . . .

JENNY

Please! Leave!

MRS. TOOTHE *(Firm, coldly polite)*

I told you, my dear, it's a matter of considerable importance. Does your husband know?

JENNY

Yes, I told him today. Oh, my God, if he sees you and knows who you are, I don't know what he'll . . .

MRS. TOOTHE

Well, he will have to make the best of it. *(Pause, smile)* Will he not?

JENNY

(The final supplication of her life)

Please! *Please* leave!

(BERYL *and* CHUCK *have started back in*)

MRS. TOOTHE

Your guests are coming back.

(JENNY *wheels*)

BERYL

(*Not noticing* MRS. TOOTHE *yet*)

Jenny, my dear, Chuck and I agree: your husband is an angel; the green-house will be absolutely perfect; you'll . . .

JENNY *(Cutting in)*

Beryl, Chuck, this is Mrs. Toothe; Richard and I met her down in St. Thomas last year, and she's come by to say . . .

MRS. TOOTHE *(Quiet smile)*

Hello, Beryl, my dear; I have a bone to pick with you.

CHUCK

(*As* JENNY *watches, openmouthed*)

My God, what's she doing here?

BERYL *(Cool, calm)*

Oh? You have?

MRS. TOOTHE

Yes; indeed I have.

JENNY

(*Finally, to* BERYL, *flabbergasted*)

You!?

BERYL

(*As* MRS. TOOTHE *chuckles some, quite calm, with a tiny smile*)

Yes; and you, too, it would seem.

JENNY *(Awe)*

My God.

(*The others are coming in now,* LOUISE, CYNTHIA, PERRY, GILBERT *and* RICHARD; ROGER *is still outdoors*)

LOUISE

. . . and it seems to me that if you want the afternoon sun, well, then you'll have to make allowance for it, and . . .

(*Sees* MRS. TOOTHE)

RICHARD

(*All have seen* MRS. TOOTHE *save* RICHARD; *all are staring at her save him*)

It *could* be swung about, I suppose, though we'd have to dig up someth—

(He sees her, sees the silence; to MRS. TOOTHE*)*
Hello; I've seen you before, haven't I?

MRS. TOOTHE *(Very nice)*
Yes, but we didn't really meet; I'm Mrs. Toothe. Hello, Cynthia; Louise, my dear.
(They nod)

RICHARD *(Not getting it yet)*
Well, then, you all know each other, and . . .

MRS. TOOTHE
Where were you on Thursday, Beryl dear?

BERYL
I had, I had a headache, and . . .

MRS. TOOTHE
Well, that will cost you a hundred dollars. Someone was disappointed.

RICHARD *(Not quite dawn yet)*
You, you all know each other?

MRS. TOOTHE
Well, yes, I know all these ladies, and I've met their husbands, but I've known them, well, how shall I say . . . I don't think we've all known before that we all know each other.

JENNY *(Lame and unhappy)*
This is . . . Mrs. Toothe, darling.

GILBERT *(Rather pleased)*
Perry, you never told me.

LOUISE
Cynthia, dear, I'm surprised we haven't run into each other in town.

RICHARD *(Piecing it together)*
Look, now, does this mean . . .

PERRY *(He, too, rather pleased)*
Well, my God.

MRS. TOOTHE *(To* RICHARD*)*
And isn't it charming that all my suburban ladies should be under one roof.

RICHARD
All your ladies, and . . .
(To the women)
All of you?
(To the men)
And *you've* known about it?

GILBERT *(Not quite pleasant)*

Well, of course.

PERRY *(Slightly condescending)*

Yes; naturally.

BERYL

But how absolutely marvelous none of us has known about the other.

CYNTHIA *(To LOUISE: mock chiding)*

You and your shopping trips.

LOUISE *(Giggles a little; to BERYL)*

And all that museum-going.

MRS. TOOTHE *(Businesslike)*

Well. Here we all are.

RICHARD

(Backing off a little; quietly, as if facing a wall of strange shapes)

I don't believe it, I . . . I don't believe it, I . . .

JENNY *(Quietly pleading)*

. . . Richard . . .

CHUCK

(Shakes his head, chuckles)

Oh, boy! Oh, Jesus Christ! *(Full laughter)*

RICHARD *(To PERRY)*

You've . . . you've known? All the time?

GILBERT *(Slightly patronizing)*

What did you do, just find out?

RICHARD *(Tiny pause, a real scream)*

YES!!!!

(Pause)

CHUCK *(Calm, fairly stern)*

Get yourself a drink, boy. Quiet down.

(CHUCK pats RICHARD on the shoulder, makes for the bar)

RICHARD *(Softer; great loss in it now)*

Yes!

GILBERT *(Matter-of-fact)*

Well, now you know; and now we all know. (ROGER *enters*)

ROGER

Hi! You know, Venus is up already? The sun isn't even down yet, and . . .

JENNY

Roger; go get something.

ROGER

M-m'am?

JENNY

Richard? *Do* something?

PERRY *(Digs into his pocket)*

Roger, be a good fellow and run over to the club and get me some pipe
tobacco, will you?

ROGER *(Senses the silence)*

Well . . . sure.

PERRY

And get yourself a Coke, or something.

JENNY

That's a good boy.

ROGER *(Puzzled, slightly reluctant)*

O.K. . . . what, what kind?

PERRY

What?

ROGER

What kind of *pipe* tobacco?

PERRY

Ben at the desk; Ben knows; tell him it's for me.

ROGER

(Suspicion, confusion over, bounds out)

O.K. Be back!

RICHARD

Please, all of you, get out.

MRS. TOOTHE

As I said, I'm sorry I've had to come, but there's been trouble.

BERYL

What kind of trouble?

MRS. TOOTHE

So that I daren't use the phone; daren't call you.

PERRY

Police?

MRS. TOOTHE

Yes.

JENNY (*Quiet panic*)

Oh, my God.

MRS. TOOTHE

A man named Lurie; detective, I think.

CHUCK

Can't you buy him off?

MRS. TOOTHE

Won't be had.

GILBERT

That's damned odd.

MRS. TOOTHE

Yes; well; nonetheless, he won't.

(RICHARD *watches all of this from a distance; maybe sits*)

PERRY

Asking questions?

MRS. TOOTHE

No . . . telling me to clear out.

LOUISE

He didn't ask for *names*.

MRS. TOOTHE

It wasn't a *raid*. Besides, he wouldn't get them.

BERYL (*Sighs with relief*)

Well.

GILBERT

Yes; there is *that*.

MRS. TOOTHE (*Brightly*)

I don't believe I've been asked what I would like to drink.

(*Pause*)

Have I?

JENNY

(*Quite preoccupied, mostly with what* RICHARD *is thinking*)

Oh, no; I don't guess you have.

MRS. TOOTHE (*To* RICHARD)

Unless you have an objection to my . . . wetting my lips in your house.

RICHARD

(*Almost a monotone; a stunned quality*)

No, you go right ahead; have what you like; there's champagne, and . . .

MRS. TOOTHE (*A little laugh*)

Oh, heavens, no, I don't think so.

(*To* CHUCK, *who is still near the bar*)

Is there whiskey?

CHUCK

Sure. Neat?

MRS. TOOTHE

Very, and one cube.

CHUCK

No sooner said.

(*To* RICHARD; *an afterthought*)

O.K. if I . . . do the honors?

RICHARD (*As above*)

No, you go right ahead.

CYNTHIA

I think I'd like one, too. Perry?

PERRY

Right.

(*Some general movement to refill, hand drinks, etc.*)

GILBERT

(*To* MRS. TOOTHE; *asking more than just his question*)

I . . . I suppose you'll have to . . . move out.

MRS. TOOTHE

I'm gone! I've left already. There'll be a psychiatrist moving in.

BERYL (*Giggles*)

That'll be a surprise for the regulars.

CYNTHIA (*Laughing, too*)

Oh, Beryl! Really!

PERRY (*Stretching, breathing out*)

Well, I guess you'd better hold off on that greenhouse, Dick.

CYNTHIA

Yes, and put away the caviar.

LOUISE

What a shame.

(*Afterthought*)

What a shame for all of us!

RICHARD (*Barely registering*)

Hm?

GILBERT *(Fairly sententious)*

Yes . . . things are going to be a little harder for *all* of us.

MRS. TOOTHE *(Sipping her drink)*

Why?

(Good spirits)

This sort of thing happens. It's never the end.

BERYL

It's rather different for you: you're used to it.

MRS. TOOTHE *(Speculative)*

Ohhhh, one can get used to anything . . . I should say.

(To RICHARD*)*

Wouldn't you say?

RICHARD

Oh, God.

LOUISE

Yes, but one can't get used to the idea of jail, not to mention the newspapers and . . .

CHUCK

Cops are on to you.

PERRY

Where will you go?

MRS. TOOTHE *(Tiniest pause)*

Why not . . . out here?

SEVERAL *(Tones of shock, disbelief)*

Out here!

MRS. TOOTHE

Why not?

LOUISE *(Quite grand)*

Surely you're not serious.

MRS. TOOTHE

Very good train service; respectable . . . countryside . . .

CHUCK *(Not sure)*

Yes, there's very good train service, but . . .

MRS. TOOTHE

If one could find some suitable property.

(Looks at PERRY*)*

Do you think?

PERRY

No, no, this wouldn't do at all . . .

GILBERT

Absolutely not.

MRS. TOOTHE
(Makes as if to get up and go; very businesslike)

Well, then; I shall just have to find a more congenial city; somewhere where the police are fast asleep or . . . amenable. I shall miss you ladies, though.

BERYL *(Tentative)*

Of course . . .
(Stops)

PERRY, CYNTHIA, GILBERT
(More or less simultaneously)

Yes?

BERYL
(A little embarrassed, and pleased by the attention)

Well, I was going to say . . . it . . . it couldn't be right *here:* I mean right *here:* it could be . . . nearby.

JENNY
(She hasn't spoken for quite a while)

Well, *yes;* it would be . . . *(Leaves it unfinished)*

RICHARD *(As if hearing through fog)*

What did you say, Jenny?

JENNY
(Naked and embarrassed, but if you're in a nudist colony . . .)

I was going to say . . .

RICHARD

Yes. Go on.

JENNY
(If JENNY can physically blush, yet be resolute, fine)

I was going to say that if it could be out here then . . . then it would be handy.

RICHARD

What was that last word?

JENNY *(Tiniest pause)*

Handy . . . it would be handy.

RICHARD (*Nods, chuckles*)

Um-hum. Oh, yes.

(*Chuckles some more*)

Oh, God, yes.

(*A few defeated tears in the words*)

Especially with Roger home: you could make it back and do the jelly sand-wiches—now that he's not going to camp, 'cause we want him here, not 'cause we can't afford it.

MRS. TOOTHE

I think we'd best keep this to a business discussion. Don't you think?

PERRY

Yes; I think.

CHUCK

Good idea.

MRS. TOOTHE

Something to be talked about amongst us men. Jenny, why don't you go out and show the girls your roses?

JENNY

(*Occupied with observing* RICHARD)

Hm?

MRS. TOOTHE

Show the girls your roses.

BERYL (*Leading the way*)

Yes, why don't we see the garden again? There's so much there; so very much to see.

CYNTHIA

Yes; coming, Louise?

LOUISE

(*Gravely approving the proposition*)

Of course.

MRS. TOOTHE

Jenny?

JENNY

(*Loath to leave* RICHARD, *but going*)

Well, all right . . . I . . . all right.

(*Exits*) (*The men are left now, with* MRS. TOOTHE)

RICHARD

(*From where he sits; little emotion*)

You're a little high-handed, aren't you?

MRS. TOOTHE (*Cheerfully soothing*)
It's so much easier without them.

RICHARD
This *is* my house.

GILBERT
Oh, come off it, Richard.

CHUCK
We're lucky we're not all in jail.

MRS. TOOTHE
No, it won't come to that. Who will give me another drink?

PERRY (*Takes her glass*)
Whiskey and ice?

MRS. TOOTHE
Yes. *Thank* you. *One* cube.

GILBERT (*To* CHUCK)
How much do you stand to lose?

CHUCK (*Rueful laugh*)
Too *much;* damn *far* too much.

GILBERT (*Mulling*)
Yeeesss. Tax-free? Be able to retire early if you wanted to? If it kept up?
Louise and I talked it over.

RICHARD (*Coming in, now; a neophyte*)
You did? You talked it over? Just . . . talked it over?

GILBERT
Of course. Oh, I know how you *feel;* I felt that way . . . for a little.

CHUCK
Wanted to break the *place* up.

PERRY
(*Returning with* MRS. TOOTHE's *drink*)
I *did* break the place up. Gave us an excuse to redecorate.

CHUCK (*Settling*)
Funny how quickly you get used to the idea.

PERRY
Yes.

CHUCK
And, there *is* the money.

GILBERT

It's going to be a little tough to manage without it . . . *now.*

PERRY

I can't take Martin away from his school at *this* stage . . .

GILBERT

Same with Jeremy; and there's Jennifer's pony. I'm paying through the nose to keep it at that damn stable, but I can't sell it . . . she'd *kill* me.

CHUCK *(Fairly grim)*

Anybody want to buy a nearly paid-for Aston-Martin?

PERRY

That's the trouble: we're all involved in things. We can't . . . just stop.

GILBERT

And just between us, I don't mind admitting Louise and I get along together much better these days.

PERRY

So do Cyn and I. Most of our arguments were over money.

CHUCK

Yes.

MRS. TOOTHE *(To* RICHARD*)*

Do you begin to understand better now?

RICHARD *(Still rather numb)*

Oh yes; *I* understand.

MRS. TOOTHE

(Hears the women talking in the garden)

Listen to them. The girls chattering away.

PERRY *(Smiles)*

Yes.

MRS. TOOTHE

Shall we talk business?

GILBERT

Right! Richard? Will you be chairman?

RICHARD *(A haze)*

Will I what?

GILBERT

Be chairman. We want a proper business meeting.

CHUCK *(Moving in)*

Here you are. Besides, it's your chair.

GILBERT

Who will propose him?

CHUCK

I.

PERRY

Seconded.

GILBERT

Carried.

CHUCK

Call the meeting to order, Richard.

RICHARD *(Brief hesitation, then)*

Meeting come to order. *(Pause)* Well?

PERRY

Mr. Chairman, there *is* a property in our office that might suit Mrs. Toothe's needs, and ours, very well indeed.

GILBERT

Not *here*.

PERRY

No; two stops up. Big house, pretty cheap, too: it's only a couple of minutes' walk from the station.

MRS. TOOTHE

Sounds very good. How many rooms?

RICHARD

How many bedrooms, you mean, don't you?

MRS. TOOTHE

Will you be quiet!
  (Back to normal tone)
If the price is reasonable . . .

PERRY

Thirty-six.

MRS. TOOTHE

Twenty-eight. Yes, that will be all right. I shall look at it tomorrow. I don't want there to be too much of a gap in . . .
  (Smiles)
our services.
  *(*RICHARD *snorts)*
Look here: I've spent time, and money, and energy building up this enterprise, with a first-class clientele and . . .

RICHARD *(Mumbled)*

All right, all right, all right . . .

MRS. TOOTHE

Well, are there any questions?

CHUCK *(Satisfied)*

Fine.

GILBERT

Seems good.

MRS. TOOTHE

(To RICHARD; *none too pleasant)*

You?

RICHARD

(Again, an attempt at sarcasm)

Oh, a couple.

MRS. TOOTHE

(Impatient, but not hurried)

Well, let us have them.

CHUCK *(Chiding)*

Oh, Dick . . .

RICHARD

Doesn't it seem to bother any of you . . . Christ, everybody's going to know!
Inside of two weeks it'll be all over the . . . doesn't that *disturb* any of you?

MRS. TOOTHE

We don't advertise in the local paper.

RICHARD

There's a thing called word-of-mouth.

MRS. TOOTHE

Your wives will know if there is any danger. Believe me . . . I know what
I'm doing.

RICHARD

There's such a thing as messing on your own doorstep, isn't there?

GILBERT

That's a pretty rotten thing to say.

RICHARD

True.

GILBERT

Any other business?

CHUCK (*Guesses*)

No . . .

PERRY

No . . .

RICHARD (*Heavy sarcasm*)

Well, in that case, I declare the meeting closed.

MRS. TOOTHE

There is one other thing . . .

GILBERT

Mm?

PERRY

What is *that?*

MRS. TOOTHE

It's important that you carry on normally. You shouldn't talk about all this any more. I mean, even among yourselves.

GILBERT

We should forget it, you mean.

PERRY

Yes. We should forget it.

CHUCK

Quite right.

RICHARD

(*A little quivering laugh—rage in this*)

I don't quite see how we can . . . just forget it.

MRS. TOOTHE (*Wise counsel*)

Oh, yes you can. One can forget. If something isn't good to live with, or convenient, one can forget. After all, there are things you *have* to forget if you want to live at all.

RICHARD

Yes, but . . .

MRS. TOOTHE

But you all know this. You're men of family and education. You're not fools.

CHUCK

No; of course we're not.

PERRY

Quite right.

MRS. TOOTHE

(Rises, moves toward garden)

I think I'll go collect my ladies.

(Stops; to RICHARD*)*

One other thing for you to remember—one thing which might help you forget; two things: we do nobody any harm . . .

RICHARD

And the other?

MRS. TOOTHE

There's very little chance your wife will ever take a lover behind your back.

(She exits)

GILBERT *(After a small pause)*

Well, then; it's all set.

CHUCK *(Going to the bar)*

Shall we drink on it?

PERRY *(Raises his glass)*

Yes; here's to us.

GILBERT

To us.

(Notices RICHARD *is just looking at his glass)*

Richard? To us? To all of us?

RICHARD

(Pause, self-deprecating little laugh; raises glass)

Sure; to us.

GILBERT *(Older brother)*

You'll be all *right,* old man; you will be.

CHUCK AND PERRY *(Softly)*

Cheers.

RICHARD *(Little boy; something lost)*

Cheers.

(The ladies start coming back in)

BERYL

I find it quite hopeless to try to grow azaleas here, and I don't know why.

JENNY

It's the lime in the soil, I think, but you can take care of that.

BERYL

Ah, well; your thumb.

MRS. TOOTHE

Who will tend my garden? Are there local people?

CHUCK

Yes, good ones . . . but expensive.

MRS. TOOTHE

Ah, well, there will be enough . . . if everything works out. Jenny, dear, may I use your telephone?

JENNY

Of course; let me show you.

(JENNY *and* MRS. TOOTHE *exit*)

BERYL

Well, let us ladies all have another drink, and then we must go. It's all arranged, I understand.

CHUCK *(Moving to the bar)*

I'll do the honors. Yes; all fixed.

PERRY

Perfect set-up.

LOUISE

Fine.

CYNTHIA

I couldn't be happier.

BERYL

Richard, no one is drinking your champagne, what a shame; but I *will* have some of your caviar, crackers and all.

RICHARD *(Sarcasm intended)*

The champagne will keep; perhaps we can use it to christen Mrs. Toothe's new house.

(*General laughter as response; sarcasm not seen*)

CYNTHIA *(Giggling)*

Oh, Richard; really!

(JENNY *returns*)

JENNY

What did I miss?

LOUISE *(Her laughter dying)*

Oh, nothing; Richard said something funny.

JENNY *(Relieved)*

Oh. How very nice.

(ROGER *and* JACK *appear in the doorway to the garden;* JACK *is quite drunk, but, even so, he is exaggerating it)*

JACK

Hullo! Hullo! The gate-crasher is here; say hullo to the gate-crasher. Say hullo to the gate-crasher. Say hullo!

(They all turn, look at JACK; *complete silence from them)*

ROGER *(Giving tobacco to* PERRY*)*

Here's your tobacco; I hope it's right.

JACK

Young Roger found me by the club; well, *at* it, actually; *at* the club, and *at* the bar.

BERYL *(Cool)*

That's rather evident.

JACK

Ooohhh, *honestly,* Beryl! *(Generally again)* Annnddd so, I said to old Roger, how's the party, an' he told me, but I thought I'd come anyway. And here I am, and all my old friends, and isn't it wonderful.

JENNY *(Uncomfortable)*

I . . . I thought you had a game, or something.

JACK

Backgammon with old Digby . . . well, old Digby died; yes he did. Farnum was kneading away at him on the old massage table, finished up, slapped him gently on the ass and said, "All done, Mr. Digby, sir," and he just lay there. Died horizontal on a metal board, which is as splendid a way as any. Got the good vod out, Richard? Got it hidden?

PERRY *(As* JACK *makes for the bar)*

Go easy on the vodka, Jack.

JACK *(A dare)*

Your house? Your vodka?

PERRY

No; but, still . . .

JACK

Tell you what I'll do, Perr, old thing: next time you give a garden-type party, and I come unasked—which is the only way I'll make it, if old Cyn has anything to say about it, eh, kid?—*then* . . . I will go easy on the vod. O.K.?

LOUISE

Do you, uh . . . do you bring any *other* charming news from the club with you, dear Jack?

JACK

Anything other than poor old Digby? Weeellll . . . Oh! Yeah! They got rid of Harry Burns.

GILBERT

Got rid of him? How?

JACK

Dug back—someone did; found out it was short for Bernstein; asked him to go.

CHUCK (*Disbelief, but not offended*)

Oh, come *on*.

JACK

True; true.

LOUISE (*To* BERYL)

Is Monica Burns *Jewish?*

BERYL

Well; I *suppose.*

LOUISE (*Some wonder*)

I never would have *thought.*

CYNTHIA

She never let *on.*

LOUISE

Can you *imagine.*

JACK

For God's sake, you'd think she was a common prostitute, or something.
　　(*Small silence*)

BERYL (*Cold*)

A what?

JACK (*Wagging his head*)

A prostitootsie.
　　(*Another small silence*)

CYNTHIA

I can't say that Harry and Monica look . . .

LOUISE

No, no, they don't . . .

BERYL

Funny how you can sort of know, though . . .

JACK

After the fact, you mean.

PERRY (*Wincing a little*)

Threw him out of the club?

ROGER

Some people say we're *all* Jews.

JENNY (*Not offended; startled*)

What?

ROGER

The ten lost tribes.

GILBERT

Some people will say anything.

ROGER

And quite a lot of us are circumcised.
(*Silence, save* JACK, *who laughs softly*)

RICHARD (*Short, cold*)

Go to your room.

ROGER

What?

RICHARD

Go to your room!

ROGER

Why!?

JENNY

He didn't mean to say anything.

ROGER

What did I say?

RICHARD

I told you to go to your room!

ROGER (*Standing his ground*)

I want to know what I said wrong!

RICHARD

(*Feeling foolish; this, though, merely pushes him further*)

Don't you stand there and defy *me!!*

ROGER

It's not fair! You say much worse things!

RICHARD

I am your father and I tell you to go to your room. You're not fit to associate with decent people.

JACK (*Laughing, but serious*)

Oh, come on, Richard!

RICHARD (*To* JACK)

SHUT YOUR MOUTH! This is my house and my son! I tell him what to
do!

(*To* ROGER)

Go on!

ROGER

(*Supplication to the rest of the group*)

But it comes up all the time in the Bible.

RICHARD

So do the Ten Commandments. Do you know the Ten Commandments?

ROGER

Yes.

RICHARD

Say them.

ROGER

Now?

JENNY

Darling . . .

RICHARD (*Wheeling on her*)

Leave me something!

(*To* ROGER)

Now!

ROGER

Thou shalt not kill.

RICHARD

That's one. Go on.

ROGER

(*Looks to* JENNY *for help, but there is none there*)

Thou shalt not . . .

(*Falters*)

RICHARD (*To them all*)

There; and a liar as well. Go up to your room.

(ROGER *pauses, gives up, turns, begins going, shaking his head*)

JACK

The poor bastard didn't say anything.

RICHARD *(Following* ROGER)

Are you going to go to your room, or am I going to have to take you UP there?

JENNY *(To* RICHARD)

Darling, let him . . . let him go out, or something. Let him go to the club. Just . . . *(Between her teeth)* . . . get him *out* of here.

RICHARD *(Sighs)*

Oh . . . all right.

(Exiting, calling after ROGER)

Roger? Roger?

BERYL

They do need discipline.

GILBERT

A few licks with a belt from his father never did a boy any harm.

PERRY

Mine kept a riding crop.

GILBERT

And you never resented it, did you?

PERRY *(Can't recall)*

I . . . I guess not.

JACK

How savage you all are today. Savage . . . and strange. All embarrassed, and snapping. Have I caught you at something?

BERYL

What do you mean!

JACK *(To audience)*

Is there something going on here?

CHUCK

Have another drink, Jack.

JENNY

Yes! Let's everybody! Perry?

(General agreement and movement)

JACK

(Grabbing JENNY *by the arm as she moves by him)*

Jenny, my darling! Why do you all hate me? Why are you all trying to get me drunk?

JENNY *(Artificial little laugh)*

Jack!

JACK

What's going on, Jenny?

JENNY (*Transparently lying*)

Nothing, Jack. Nothing at all.

JACK

Do you still love me, Jenny?

JENNY (*Soothing the little boy*)

Yes, Jack; of course.

(RICHARD *re-enters*)

JACK

Ah! Thank God!

(*Rises*)

Kiss and make up.

(*He kisses her*)

RICHARD

I sent him out for a . . . What do you think you're doing!

JACK

I am kissing your beautiful wife.

RICHARD

Then stop it!

JACK

I *have* stopped.

RICHARD

I don't care for that sort of behavior.

JACK

Oh, come on, Richard. It might have been anyone. Hasn't Jenny been kissed before?

RICHARD

You are not to kiss her!!

JACK

What is the *matter* with all of you this evening?

BERYL

There is *nothing* the matter with us.

JACK

There is something . . . very wrong.

(MRS. TOOTHE *re-enters*)

MRS. TOOTHE

Well, my dear children, my flock, I have made the necessary calls, and I think we . . .

(Sees JACK)

Ah.

(Her eyes move from one person to another quickly)

I, uh . . . I do believe we've met before.

JENNY (Jumping in)

Jack, you do remember Mrs. Toothe; you met her . . . oh, six-seven months ago, and . . .

JACK (Staring at MRS. TOOTHE)

Yes; your fairy godmother.

MRS. TOOTHE (To JACK; very naturally)

How nice to see you again.

JACK

How nice to see you.

(Turns away, thinking)

MRS. TOOTHE (To the others)

I do think I should be off now. It was so nice meeting you all . . .

JACK (Suddenly remembering)

Yes!

(Turns around, a smile of fascination)

You're English, aren't you?

MRS. TOOTHE

(Playing it cool and natural)

British, yes.

JACK

And you lived in London . . . some, some time ago.

MRS. TOOTHE (Hedging)

Yes, I . . . well, I have lived in London, but . . .

JACK (Very pleased)

I do remember you, dear lady. By God, if I were sober, I doubt I would.

(Laughs greatly)

Oh yes! Do I remember you!

MRS. TOOTHE (Playing it through)

You must be mistaken. I never forget faces, and . . .

JACK

Oh, lady; I remember you well, I remember your . . .

(*Another fit of laughing*)

. . . your ladies, I . . .

(*Looks about the room, sees the trapped and embarrassed faces, breaks into more laughter*)

Oh no! No! Tell me it's not true! It is! It is true!

(*More laughter*)

BERYL

I don't know what you're thinking, Jack, but I suspect that you may have had a little too much to drink, and . . .

JACK

Has Madam found herself another group of ladies?

(*Laughter as he talks*)

Are we operating in the suburbs now?

(*Mock commiseration, laughter*)

Oh, my poor Beryl! Dear Cynthia! Proud Louise!

(*Sees* JENNY; *his tone now is a cross to disappointment and wonder at the future possibilities*)

And oh my darling Jenny!

RICHARD

Stay away from her.

JACK

And all that . . . and all that money lying on the . . .

(*Breaks into more laughter*) . . .

"Someone sent it to us in the mail?"

(*Laughter*)

Gentlemen . . . I don't know who arranged all this; but if you guys did, you're better businessmen than I ever thought you were.

(*Laughs, starts for french doors*)

MRS. TOOTHE (*Eyes narrowing*)

Stop him.

PERRY

Where do you think you're going?

JACK (*Still laughing*)

Hm?

PERRY

I said where do you think you're going?

JACK

Why, I thought I'd go back to the cl—

(Breaks down in laughter again)

MRS. TOOTHE

He'll talk.

(This was a command)

JENNY

Yes. He will.

MRS. TOOTHE

(Even more clear than before)

He'll talk.

(PERRY grabs JACK by the arm; CHUCK steps in front of him, barring his way)

PERRY

Hold on, old friend.

CHUCK

Easy now.

JACK *(Panic and anger rising)*

Let . . . Let me go. God damn it, let me . . .

(He begins to struggle; RICHARD and GILBERT come to the aid of PERRY and CHUCK)

GILBERT

Get him!

(They are on him, just restraining at first, but the more JACK struggles, the more they are on him)

JACK

Let me . . . Get your hands off me . . . Let! Me! God damn it! Let! Me!

(They have him down, are on top of him)

PERRY

Hold him! Hold him down!

JACK *(Really shouting)*

STOP IT! STOP IT!

MRS. TOOTHE

(On her feet, but not in a rush; a commander)

He's drunk; he'll talk. You must make him be quiet.

(JACK continues to struggle, bites CHUCK's hand)

CHUCK

(*In rage and reflex, strikes* JACK *across the face with the back of his hand*)

God damn you!

JACK

STOP! IT!

MRS. TOOTHE

Keep him quiet!

(RICHARD *grabs a pillow from the sofa and, together, two or three of them press it over* JACK's *face. His shouts become muffled as they hold the pillow on his face, stiff-armed. Finally there is silence. The men relax a little, slowly get off their knees, unwind some, look at* JACK's *prone, still form; they move about a little*)

GILBERT

He's out.

RICHARD (*Grim laugh*)

For a while.

MRS. TOOTHE

(*Goes over, bends over* JACK, *examines him for a moment, straightens up*)

No. Not for a while.

(*Begins to walk back to her chair*)

JENNY

(*Pitiful; moves toward* JACK)

Jack?

MRS. TOOTHE

(*Cruelly casual, but serious*)

Don't bother. He's dead.

GILBERT (*Offended*)

What do you mean he's dead!

MRS. TOOTHE

Look for your*self*. He's *dead*.

GILBERT (*Looks for himself*)

Yes. He is. He's dead.

(JENNY *and* CYNTHIA *begin to weep, quietly;* LOUISE *turns away; the men look at one another*)

BERYL (*Final; catatonic*)

Well.

CHUCK

I, I don't think we did that, he . . . We didn't do that.

GILBERT

No, we were just . . .

PERRY

He must have had a heart attack.

JENNY (*Going to him*)

Oh, my poor, darling Jack . . .

RICHARD

Stay away from him, Jenny.

CHUCK

What . . . what shall we do?

LOUISE (*Ordering it*)

He *can't* be dead; it doesn't happen.

CYNTHIA

He would have talked! It would have been all over town.

JENNY (*Defending* JACK)

Who says!?

BERYL

You said, for one.

JENNY (*Furious, and near tears*)

I did not! I said . . .

MRS. TOOTHE (*Calm*)

You said he would talk. You agreed he would.

GILBERT

No one meant to kill him . . .

PERRY

No, it was . . .

RICHARD (*Grim*)

I think I'd better call the police, hunh?

CHUCK (*Nodding*)

Yeah, yeah.

GILBERT

Yes; you'd better.

MRS. TOOTHE (*Calm, forceful*)

Do you think so?

RICHARD (*Sort of disgusted*)

What?

MRS. TOOTHE

Do you think you had better call the police?

RICHARD

There's a *dead* man there!

MRS. TOOTHE

I know; I can see. But what will you tell them? The police.

RICHARD

I'll, I'll tell them . . . we were having a party, and, and Jack came in, and he was drunk, and . . .

MRS. TOOTHE

And so you all smothered him?

RICHARD (*Furious*)

No! That he was drunk!

BERYL

. . . he kept on drinking . . .

GILBERT

. . . and he had a heart attack.
   (*Pause, they look to* MRS. TOOTHE)

CHUCK

No?

MRS. TOOTHE

You may call the police, if you want to. *Do* let me leave first, though. I wouldn't want to be listed among those present when the autopsy is done and they find the marks on him and the hemorrhage in the lungs. That happens when people are killed that way, you know; the lungs rupture.
   (*Silence*)

GILBERT

Oh.
   (*Silence*)

PERRY

I see.
   (*Silence*)

BERYL

Well. We can't take *that* chance, can we.
   (*Silence.* JENNY *weeps quietly*)

LOUISE (*Slowly*)

No. We can't.

RICHARD (*Quietly loathing*)

What do you suggest we do, then?

(*They all look to* MRS. TOOTHE, *save* JENNY)

MRS. TOOTHE (*To* RICHARD)

I know you think I'm a monster, so . . . if I ask you a question, it won't matter much.

RICHARD (*Waiting*)

Yes?

MRS. TOOTHE

What . . . what is the purpose of that deep trench you've dug near your brick wall?

(*Silence*)

RICHARD

(*Calm response; much underneath*)

I've been looking for the cesspool line.

MRS. TOOTHE

Have you found it?

RICHARD (*Still staring at her*)

No.

MRS. TOOTHE (*After a pause*)

Well, then. Bury him.

(*Silence. The guests look at each other, calmly, speculatively*)

RICHARD (*Slowly*)

You can't mean that.

MRS. TOOTHE (*To all the men*)

Go on; bury him.

RICHARD (*Smiling a little*)

No.

MRS. TOOTHE

All right, then. Call the police.

(*Silence; the men look at one another, slowly, steadily. Then, as if it had all been organized, they slowly move to work. They go to* JACK, *take him by the legs, arms, under the head, and take him out into the garden, disappear from our sight*)

JENNY

(After they have gone; rises, starts after them)
Jack! Richard!

MRS. TOOTHE

Jenny! Come here!
(BERYL and LOUISE go to JENNY, who is helplessly, quietly crying now, and gently bring her back to the group. They all sit)

JENNY

You . . . they just can't . . . do that.

MRS. TOOTHE

Hush, my dear. Hush.
(This is a wake and the ladies have sorrow on their faces)

LOUISE *(Sincere; helpless)*

Poor *Jack*.

BERYL

Yes; poor Jack.

LOUISE

At least it wasn't . . . one of us. I mean, someone, well . . . with a family, someone . . . regular.
(JENNY is quietly hysterical)

MRS. TOOTHE

You haven't put up with death, have you, Jenny?
(JENNY shakes her head)
I'm sorry to say you get used to it!

JENNY

N-never!

MRS. TOOTHE

You should have been in London in the war. You would have learned about death . . . and violence . . . All those nights in the shelters, with the death going on. Death and dying. Always take the former if you can.

LOUISE *(Nodding at the sad truth)*

Yes.

MRS. TOOTHE

You must help your husbands. You'll have to, I think . . . for a while. They may wake up at night; sweat, they may . . . lose heart. You'll have to be the strong ones . . . as usual.

BERYL

Yes.

MRS. TOOTHE
I wouldn't try to make them go on as if nothing has happened. For something *has* happened . . . very much so. One of the things that *does* happen . . . one of the accommodations that have to be made. Do you see, Jenny?

JENNY
I don't know.

MRS. TOOTHE *(Sweet; gentle)*
You can't go *back.* You have to make do with what is. And what is leads to what will be. You make the best as you go on. Like our looks, when we age, as we are doing, or will. Some of us have our faces lifted, I suppose, and we convince . . . some people—not as many as we'd like to—but we don't believe it ourselves, do we, Jenny?

JENNY (A *little girl at lessons*)
I shouldn't think so. No.

MRS. TOOTHE
No. We do what will help, which is all we can.

JENNY *(Instructed)*
Yes.
    (The men come back in, subdued, clothes a little awry, hands dirty)

GILBERT
All done.

PERRY
Finished.

CHUCK
You'd never know.

RICHARD
. . . unless you had a mind.

CHUCK
Unless you knew.

RICHARD
Yes.
    (Goes to JENNY; *in fact, all the men gravitate to their wives)*

CYNTHIA *(Kindly)*
Would any of you like a drink? Darling?

PERRY
No; no thanks.

LOUISE
Darling?

GILBERT

Yes. A quick one.

RICHARD (*To* JENNY; *comforting*)

You O.K.?

JENNY (*Brave smile*)

Sure. You?

RICHARD (*Empty*)

Considering.

MRS. TOOTHE

Well; you've all done very well. I think it's time I should be getting on.

BERYL

Yes; well, we all should.

GILBERT

Yes. What time are Don and Betty coming over?

LOUISE

Oh, my God! Eight o'clock. You're right, we've got . . .

CHUCK

Your husband is hungry.

BERYL

Well, all right then, I'll feed you.

MRS. TOOTHE (*To* PERRY)

I'll call you tomorrow and come to see the house?

PERRY

Yes; fine.

RICHARD

You're all just . . . leaving?

CHUCK (*What else?*)

Yes; I think we should.

PERRY

There's nothing we can do, is there?

RICHARD (*Quiet, intense*)

There's a body out there; Jack.

GILBERT

It's all *right,* Richard.

PERRY

Really, Richard; it's O.K.

BERYL

Yes, it *is*.

MRS. TOOTHE

Go home, children, it's all right.

CHUCK

Yes, well, I don't know what more we can do.

LOUISE

Yes, we do have Don and Betty coming over.

CYNTHIA

Do you mean Don and Betty Grainger?

LOUISE

Yes.

PERRY

I still can't get over Harry Burns.

GILBERT

Harry Bernstein, you mean.

(The guests have gone)

MRS. TOOTHE *(To* JENNY *and* RICHARD*)*

The grass will grow over; the earth will be rich, and soon— eventually—everything in the garden . . . will be as it was. You'll see.

*(*MRS. TOOTHE *exits, followed by* RICHARD *and* JENNY *seeing her out almost by reflex. Bare stage for a moment)*

*(*JACK *comes in from the garden, his clothes dirty, sod in his hair)*

JACK

(He will speak only to the audience from now on, even when RICHARD *and* JENNY *return; nor will they notice him, of course)*

Oh, don't get any ideas, now. I'm dead, believe me. I'm *dead*. It's amazing how dying sobers you up. Well, I certainly never thought it would be *this* way—like this; I'd imagined sliding gently from the bar stool at the club, or crashing into a truck on a curve some night, but never this. Shows you can't tell. God! Would you believe it? Mrs. Toothe, and Beryl and Cynthia and Louise? And poor Jenny? *I* wouldn't have; but, then, I'm rather selfish—self-concerned. *Was.* I must get *used* to that; past tense. Poor Jenny and Richard. They're the only ones I feel badly about—the guilt, and all the rest. That old Madam can take care of herself, and the others . . . who cares? But Jenny and Richard . . . that's a different matter. I *worry* for them.

*(*JENNY *and* RICHARD *re-enter, move about slowly.* JACK *puts a finger to his lips, to shush the audience, whether necessary or not)*

JENNY (*Timid*)

Well.

RICHARD (*Emptied*)

Yes.

JENNY (*Trying to be conversational*)

Where did you send Roger?

RICHARD

To the club. To swim.

JENNY (*Genuine*)

That was nice of you.

RICHARD

Stupid taking it out on him.

JENNY

Yes.

(*Pause*)

I think we'd better clean up—all the glasses and everything.

RICHARD

All right.

JACK

(*Watches them for a moment; back to the audience*)

Here's the *awful* irony of it.

JENNY (*Remembering*)

We're to say . . . nothing.

RICHARD

What will happen? He'll have just . . . disappeared?

JENNY

Yes; I guess so.

RICHARD

Roger *brought* him here.

JENNY

Yes, but we'll say Jack just stayed for a little, and then went on.

RICHARD

They'll ask?

JENNY

Someone will; someone's bound to—insurance people, somebody.

RICHARD

We must make a story.

JENNY

Yes. I'll talk to the others.

RICHARD

All right.

JENNY *(So sincere; explaining so much)*

Darling . . . I do *love* you.

RICHARD *(Timid)*

Yes; and I love you.

JACK

The irony; I was going to tell you the irony. Remember I said I'd made my will over, left it all to Richard and Jenny? Well, it was true; I wasn't kidding. Three and a half million; every penny, and my house here, *and* in Nassau. It's all theirs.

JENNY

Let's put the glasses on the tray here.

JACK

Problem now is, they'll have to wait. If I've just . . . vanished . . . disappeared from the face of the earth, it'll be seven years until I can be declared officially dead. And there'll *be* an investigation; you can be sure of that. I hope they make it stick—the story they tell. I imagine they will.

RICHARD

What shall I do with the caviar?

JENNY

Give it here; I'll cover it and put it in the fridge.

JACK

But seven years; that's a very long time. So much can happen. With all they're doing, in seven years their lives can be ruined. They have so much to live with.

(To RICHARD *and* JENNY*)*

You've got to be strong! You've got to hold on!

JENNY

Darling?

RICHARD

Mmm?

JENNY

I was thinking . . . that house Mrs. Toothe is taking.

RICHARD

What about it?

JENNY

I think it ought to be planted nicely, flowers and shrubs and all. Make it look like it's really lived in. It mustn't look like it's been let go. It might draw suspicion. You notice things like that.

RICHARD

Yes; you do.

JENNY

Gardens that have been let go. If people let them go, you know there's something wrong in the house.

RICHARD

Yes.

JENNY

I think it should be well planted and taken care of; kept up. I think it should look like all the others. Don't you think so?

RICHARD (*Straight*)

Yes; I think you're right.

JACK

Well . . . I think they'll make it.

CURTAIN

Box

AND

Quotations from Chairman Mao Tse-tung

TWO INTER-RELATED PLAYS

For Maeve Brennan
and Howard Moss

First performed at the Studio Arena Theatre, Buffalo, New York, March 6, 1968

BOX

THE VOICE OF RUTH WHITE

QUOTATIONS FROM CHAIRMAN MAO TSE-TUNG

CONRAD YAMA *as* CHAIRMAN MAO

LUCILLE PATTON *as* LONG-WINDED LADY

JENNY EGAN as OLD WOMAN

WILLIAM NEEDLES *as* MINISTER

Directed by ALAN SCHNEIDER

First performed in New York City at the Billy Rose Theatre, September 30, 1968

BOX

THE VOICE OF RUTH WHITE

QUOTATIONS FROM CHAIRMAN MAO TSE-TUNG

WYMAN PENDLETON *as* CHAIRMAN MAO

NANCY KELLY *as* LONG-WINDED LADY

SUDIE BOND *as* OLD WOMAN

GEORGE BARTENIEFF as MINISTER

Directed by ALAN SCHNEIDER

While it is true that these two short plays—*Box* and *Quotations from Chairman Mao Tse-tung*—are separate works, were conceived at different though not distant moments, stand by themselves, and can be played one without the company of the other, I feel that they are more effective performed enmeshed.

Even more . . . *Quotations from Chairman Mao Tse-tung* would most probably not have been written had not *Box* been composed beforehand, and *Mao* is, therefore, an outgrowth of and extension of the shorter play. As well, I have attempted, in these two related plays, several experiments having to do—in the main—with the application of musical form to dramatic structure, and the use of *Box* as a parenthesis around *Mao* is part of that experiment.

I may as well insist right now that these two plays are quite simple. By that I mean that while technically they are fairly complex and they do demand from an audience quite close attention, their content can be apprehended without much difficulty. All that one need do is—quite simply—relax and let the plays happen. That, and be willing to approach the dramatic experience without a preconception of what the nature of the dramatic experience should be.

I recall that when a play of mine called *Tiny Alice* opened in New York City a few years ago the majority of the critics wrote in their reviews—such as they were—that the play was far too complicated and obscure for the audience to understand. Leaving to one side the thoughts one might have about the assumption on the part of the critics that what they found confusing would necessarily confound an audience, this reportage had a most curious effect on the audiences that viewed the play. At the preview performances of *Tiny Alice* the audiences—while hardly to a man sympathetic to the play—found it quite clear; while later—after the critics had spoken on it—the audiences were very confused. The play had not changed one whit; a label had merely been attached to it, and what was experienced was the label and not the nature of the goods.

A playwright—unless he is creating escapist romances (an honorable occupation, of course)—has two obligations: first, to make some statement about the condition of "man" (as it is put) and, second, to make some statement about the nature of the art form with which he is working. In both instances he must attempt change. In the first instance—since very few serious plays are written to glorify the status quo—the playwright must try to alter his society; in the second instance—since art must move, or wither —the playwright must try to alter the forms within which his precursors have had to work. And I believe that an audience has an obligation to be interested in and sympathetic to these aims—certainly to the second of them. Therefore, an audience has an obligation (to itself, to the art form in which it is participating, and even to the playwright) to be willing to experience a work on its own terms.

I said before that these two plays are simple (as well as complex), and they *are* simple once they are experienced relaxed and without a weighing of their methods against more familiar ones.

—EDWARD ALBEE

BOX

Curtain rises in darkness. Lights go up slowly to reveal the outline of a large cube. The cube should take up almost all of a small stage opening. The side facing the audience is open, but we should see the other five sides clearly, therefore the interior of the cube should be distorted, smaller at the backstage side, for example; also, none of the sides should be exactly square in shape, but the angles of distortion should not be very great—not so great as to call attention to themselves and destroy the feeling of a cube. When the lights are fully up on the cube—quite bright light which stays constant until the final dim-out—there should be five seconds' silence.

VOICE

(The VOICE *should not come from the stage, but should seem to be coming from nearby the spectator—from the back or the sides of the theater. The* VOICE *of a woman; not young, but not ancient, either: fiftyish. Neither a sharp, crone's voice, but not refined. A Middle Western farm woman's voice would be best.*

Matter-of-fact; announcement of a subject)

Box.

(Five-second silence)

Box.

(Three-second silence)

Nicely done. Well put . . .

(Pause)

. . . together. Box.

(Three-second silence. More conversational now)

Room inside for a sedia d'ondalo, which, in English—for that is Italian—would be, is, rocking chair. Room to rock. *And* room to move about in . . . some. Enough.

(Three-second silence)

Carpentry is among the arts going out . . . or crafts, if you're of a nonclassical disposition. There are others: other arts which have gone down to craft and which are going further . . . walls, brick walls, music . . .

(Pause)

. . . the making of good bread if you won't laugh; living. Many arts: all craft now . . . and going further. But *this* is solid, perfect joins . . . good work. Knock and there's no give—no give of sound, I mean. A thud; no hollow. Oh, very good work; fine timber, and so fastidious, like when they shined the bottoms of the shoes . . . *and* the instep. Not only where you might *expect* they'd shine the bottoms if they *did* . . . but even the instep.

(Two-second silence. Grudging, but not very)

And other crafts have come up . . . if not to replace, then . . . occupy.

(Tiny laugh)

Nature abhors, among so many, so much else . . . amongst so much, us, itself, they say, vacuum.

(Five-second silence. A listing)

System as conclusion, in the sense of method as an end, the dice so big you can hardly throw them any more.

(Some awe, some sadness)

Seven hundred million babies dead in the time it takes, took, to knead the dough to make a proper loaf. Well, little wonder so many . . , went . . . cut off, said no instead of hanging on.

(Three-second silence)

Apathy, I think.

(Five-second silence)

Inevitability. And progress is merely a direction, movement.

(Earnest)

When it was *simple* . . .

(Light, self-mocking laugh)

Ah, well, yes, when it was simple.

(Three-second silence. Wistful)

Beautiful, beautiful box.

(Three-second silence)

And room enough to walk around in, take a turn.

(Tiny pause)

If only they had *told* us! Clearly! When it was clear that we were not only corrupt—for there is nothing that is not, or little—but corrupt to the self-ishness, to the corruption that we should die to keep it . . . go under rather than . . .

(Three-second silence. Sigh)

Oh, my.

(Five-second silence)

Or was it the milk? *That* may have been the moment: spilling and spilling and killing all those children to make a point. A penny or two, and a sym-

Box **265**

bol at that, and I suppose the children were symbolic, too, though they died, and couldn't stop. Once it starts—gets to a certain point—the momentum is too much. But spilling milk!

(*Two-second silence. Firmly felt*)

Oh, shame!

(*A little schoolmarmish*)

The *Pope* warned us; *he* said so. There are no possessions, he said; so long as there are some with nothing we have no right to anything.

(*Two-second silence*)

It's the *little* things, the *small* cracks. Oh, for every pound of milk they spill you can send a check to someone, but that does not unspill. That it *can* be *done* is the crack. And if you go back to a partita . . . ahhhhh, what when it makes you cry!? Not from the beauty of it, but from solely that you cry from loss . . . so precious. When art begins to hurt . . . when art begins to hurt, it's time to look around. Yes it is.

(*Three-second silence*)

Yes it is.

(*Three-second silence*)

No longer just great beauty which takes you more to everything, but a reminder! And not of what *can* . . . but what *has*. Yes, when art hurts . . .

(*Three-second silence*)

Box.

(*Two-second silence*)

And room enough to move around, except like a fly. That would be *very* good!

(*Rue*)

Yes, but so would so much.

(*Two-second silence. Schoolmarmish*)

Here is the thing about tension and the tonic—the important thing.

(*Pause*)

The release of tension is the return to consonance; no matter how far traveled, one comes back, not circular, not to the starting point, but a . . . setting down again, and the beauty of art is order—not what is familiar, necessarily, but order . . . on its own terms.

(*Two-second silence. Sigh*)

So much . . . flies. A billion birds at once, black net skimming the ocean, or the Monarchs that time, that island, blown by the wind, but going straight . . . in a direction. Order!

(*Two-second silence*)

And six sides to bounce it all off of.

(*Three-second silence. Brave start again*)

When the beauty of it reminds us of *loss*. Instead of the attainable. When it tells us what we cannot have . . . well, then . . . it no longer relates . . . *does* it. That is the thing about music. That is why we cannot listen anymore.

(Pause)

Because we cry.

(Three-second silence)

And *if* he says, or *she* . . . why are you doing that?, and, and your only honest response is: art hurts . . .

(Little laugh)

Well.

(Five-second silence)

Look! More birds! Another . . . sky of them.

(Five-second silence)

It is not a matter of garden, or straight lines, or even . . . morality. It's only when you can't come back; when you get in some distant key; that when you say, the tonic! the tonic! and they say, what is *that?* It's *then*.

(Three-second silence)

There! More! A thousand, and one below them, moving fast in the opposite way!

(Two-second silence)

What was it used to frighten me? Bell buoys and sea gulls; the *sound* of them, at night, in a fog, when I was very young.

(A little laugh)

Before I had ever seen them, before I had heard them.

(Some wonder)

But I knew what they *were* . . . a thousand miles from the sea. Landlocked, never been, and yet the sea sounds . . .

(Three-second silence. Very matter-of-fact)

Well, we can exist with *any*thing; with*out*. There's little that we need to have to go on . . . evolving. Goodness; we all died when we were thirty once. Now, much younger. Much.

(Suddenly aware of something)

But it *couldn't* have been fog, not the sea-fog. Not way back *there*. It was the memory of it, to be seen and proved later. And more! and more! they're all moving! The memory of what we have not known. And so it is with the fog, which I had never seen, yet knew it. And the resolution of a chord; no difference.

(Three-second silence)

And even that can happen here, I guess. But unprovable. Ahhhhh. That makes the difference, does it *not*. Nothing can seep here except the mem-

Box 267

ory of what I'll not prove.

> (*Two-second silence. Sigh*)

Well, we give up something for something.

> (*Three-second silence. Listing again; pleased*)

Sturdy, light . . . interesting . . . in its way. Room enough for a sedia d'on-dalo, which is the Italian of . . . or for . . . *of*, I prefer . . . The Italian of rocking chair.

> (*Three-second silence*)

When art hurts. That is what to remember.

> (*Two-second silence*)

What to look for. Then the corruption . . .

> (*Three-second silence*)

Then the corruption is complete.

> (*Five-second silence. The sound of bell buoys and sea gulls begins, faintly, growing, but never very loud*)

Nothing belongs.

> (*Three-second silence. Great sadness*)

Look; more of them; a black net . . . skimming.

> (*Pause*)

And just one . . . moving beneath . . . in the opposite way.

> (*Three-second silence. Very sad, supplicating*)

Milk.

> (*Three-second silence*)

Milk.

> (*Five-second silence. Wistful*)

Box.

> (*Silence, except for the sound of bell buoys and sea gulls. Very slow fading of lights to black, sound of bell buoys and sea gulls fading with the light*)

CURTAIN

The outline of the cube remains; the set for QUOTATIONS FROM CHAIRMAN MAO-TSE-TUNG *appears within the outlines of the cube during the brief blackout.*

CHARACTERS

CHAIRMAN MAO

Should be played, ideally, by an Asian actor who resembles Mao. However, the role can be played either with makeup or a face mask. In any event, an attempt should be made to make the actor resemble Mao as much as possible. Mao speaks rather like a teacher. He does not raise his voice; he is not given to histrionics. His tone is always reasonable, sometimes a little sad; occasionally a half-smile will appear. He may wander about the set a little, but, for the most part, he should keep his place by the railing. Mao always speaks to the audience. He is aware of the other characters, but he must never look at them or suggest in any way that anything they say is affecting his words. When I say that Mao always addresses the audience I do not mean that he must look them in the eye constantly. Once he has made it clear that he is addressing them he may keep that intention clear in any way he likes—looking away, speaking to only one person, whatever.

LONG-WINDED LADY

A lady of sixty. I care very little about how she looks so long as she looks very average and upper middle-class. Nothing exotic; nothing strange. She should, I think, stay pretty much to her deck chair. She never speaks to the audience. Sometimes she is clearly speaking to the Minister; more often she is speaking both for his benefit and her own. She can withdraw entirely into self from time to time. She uses the Minister as a sounding board.

OLD WOMAN

Shabby, poor, without being so in a comedy sense. She has a bag with her. An orange; an apple, one or two cans: beans, canned meat. She will eat from these occasionally. Her bag also contains a fork, or a spoon, a napkin, and a can-opener. She is aware of everybody, but speaks only to the audience. Her reading of her poem can have some emotion to it, though never too much. It should be made clear, though, that while the subject of her speeches is dear to her heart, a close matter, she is reciting a poem. She may look at the other characters from time to time, but what she says must never seem to come from what any of the others has said. She might nod in agreement with Mao now and again, or shake her head over the plight of the Long-Winded Lady. She should stay in one place, up on something.

MINISTER

Has no lines, and stays in his deck chair. He must try to pay close attention to the Long-Winded Lady, though— nod, shake his head, cluck, put an arm tentatively out, etc. He must also keep busy with his pipe and pouch and matches. He should doze off from time to time. He must never make the audience feel he is looking at them or is aware of them. Also, he is not aware of either Mao or the Old Woman. He is seventy or so, has white or gray hair, a clerical collar. A florid face would be nice. If a thin actor is playing the role, however, then make the face sort of gray-yellow-white.

GENERAL COMMENTS

For this play to work according to my intention, careful attention must be paid to what I have written about the characters: to whom they speak; to whom they may and may not react; how they speak; how they move or do not. Alteration from the patterns I have set may be interesting, but I fear they will destroy the attempt of the experiment: musical structure—form and counterpoint. Primarily the characters must seem interested in what they themselves are doing and saying. While the lines must not be read metronome-exact, I feel that a certain set rhythm will come about, quite of itself. No one rushes in on the end of anyone else's speech; no one waits too long. I have indicated, quite precisely, within the speeches of the Long-Winded Lady, by means of commas, periods, semi-colons, colons, dashes and dots (as well as parenthetical stage directions), the speech rhythms. Please observe them carefully, for they were not thrown in, like herbs on a salad, to be mixed about. I have underlined words I want stressed. I have capitalized for loudness, and used exclamation points for emphasis. There are one or two seeming questions that I have left the question mark off of. This was done on purpose, as an out-loud reading will make self-evident.

QUOTATIONS FROM CHAIRMAN MAO TSE-TUNG

The deck of an ocean liner. Bright daylight, that particular kind of brightness that is possible only in mid-ocean.

CHAIRMAN MAO

There is an ancient Chinese fable called "The foolish old man who removed the mountains." It tells of an old man who lived in Northern China long, long ago, and was known as the foolish old man of the north mountains. His house faced south and beyond his doorway stood the two great peaks, Taihand and Wangwu, obstructing the way. With great determination, he led his sons in digging up these mountains, hoe in hand. Another greybeard, known as the wise old man, saw them and said derisively, "How silly of you to do this! It is quite impossible for you few to dig up those two huge mountains." The foolish old man replied, "When I die, my sons will carry on; when they die there will be my grandsons, and then their sons and grandsons, and so on to infinity. High as they are, the mountains cannot grow any higher and with every bit we dig, they will be that much lower. Why can't we clear them away?" Having refuted the wise old man's wrong view, he went on digging every day, unshaken in his conviction. God was moved by this, and he sent down two angels, who carried the mountains away on their backs. Today, two big mountains lie like a dead weight on the Chinese people. One is imperialism, the other is feudalism. The Chinese Communist Party has long made up its mind to dig them up. We must persevere and work unceasingly, and we, too, will touch God's heart. Our God is none other than the masses of the Chinese people. If they stand up and dig together with us, why can't these two mountains be cleared away?

LONG-WINDED LADY

Well, I daresay it's hard to comprehend . . . I mean: *I* . . . at this remove . . . *I* find it hard to, well, not comprehend, but believe, or accept, if you will. So long ago! So much since. But there it was: Splash!

OLD WOMAN

"Over the Hill to the Poor-House."

LONG-WINDED LADY

Well, not splash, exactly, more sound than that, more of a . . .

(Little laugh)

no, I can't do that—imitate it: for I only *imagine* . . . what it must have sounded like to . . . an onlooker. An overseer. Not to *me;* Lord knows! Being *in* it. Or doing it, rather.

CHAIRMAN MAO

In drawing up plans, handling affairs or thinking over problems, we must proceed from the fact that China has six hundred million people, and we must never forget this fact.

OLD WOMAN

By Will Carleton.

LONG-WINDED LADY

No. To an onlooker it would not have been splash, but a sort of . . . different sound, and I try to imagine what it would have been like—*sounded* like—had *I* not been . . . well, so involved, if you know what I mean. And *I* was so *busy* . . . I didn't pay attention, or, if I did . . . that part of it doesn't re . . . recall itself. Retain is the, is what I started.

OLD WOMAN

"Over the Hill to the Poor-House"—a poem by Will Carleton.

CHAIRMAN MAO

Apart from their other characteristics, the outstanding thing about China's six hundred million people is that they are "poor and blank." This may seem a bad thing, but in reality it is a good thing. Poverty gives rise to the desire for change, the desire for action and the desire for revolution. On a blank sheet of paper free from any mark, the freshest and most beautiful characters can be written, the freshest and most beautiful pictures can be painted.

LONG-WINDED LADY

And so high!

OLD WOMAN

Over the hill to the poor-house—I can't quite make it clear!
Over the hill to the poor-house—it seems so horrid queer!
Many a step I've taken, a-toilin' to and fro,
But this is a sort of journey I never thought to go.

LONG-WINDED LADY

I'd never imagined it—naturally! It's not what one *would.* The *echo* of a sound, or the remembering of a sound having happened. No; that's not right either. For *them;* for the theoretical . . . onwatcher.

(Pause)

Plut! Yes!

CHAIRMAN MAO

Communism is at once a complete system of proletarian ideology and a new social system. It is different from any other ideological and social system, and is the most complete, progressive, revolutionary and rational system in human history. The communist ideological and social system alone is full of youth and vitality, sweeping the world with the momentum of an avalanche and the force of a thunderbolt.

LONG-WINDED LADY

Exactly: plut!

OLD WOMAN

Over the hill to the poor-house I'm trudgin' my weary way—
I, a woman of seventy, and only a trifle gray—
I, who am smart an' chipper, for all the years I've told,
As many another woman thats only half as old.

LONG-WINDED LADY

And then, with the wind, and the roar of the engines and the sea . . . maybe not even that, not even . . . plut! But, some slight sound, or . . . or the creation of one! The invention! What is that about consequence? Oh, *you* know! Everything has its consequence? Or, every action a reaction; something. But maybe nothing at all, no real sound, but the invention of one. I mean, if you see it happening . . . the, the thing . . . landing, and the spray, the sea parting, as it were . . . well, then . . . one makes a sound . . . in one's mind . . . to, to correspond to the sound one . . . didn't . . . hear. Yes?

CHAIRMAN MAO

Imperialism will not last long because it always does evil things.

OLD WOMAN

"Over the Hill to the Poor-House."

CHAIRMAN MAO

It persists in grooming and supporting reactionaries in all countries who are against the people; it has forcibly seized many colonies and semi-colonies and many military bases, and it threatens the peace with atomic war.

OLD WOMAN

By Will Carleton.

CHAIRMAN MAO

Thus, forced by imperialism to do so, more than ninety per cent of the people of the world are rising or will rise up in struggle against it.

OLD WOMAN

Over the hill to the poor-house I'm trudgin' my weary way—
I, a woman of seventy, and only a trifle gray.

CHAIRMAN MAO

Yet imperialism is still alive, still running amuck in Asia, Africa and Latin America. In the West, imperialism is still oppressing the people at home. This situation must change.

OLD WOMAN

I, who am smart an' chipper, for all the years I've told,
As many another woman that's only half as old.

CHAIRMAN MAO

It is the task of the people of the whole world to put an end to the aggression
and oppression perpetrated by imperialism, and chiefly by U.S. imperialism.

LONG-WINDED LADY

Yes. I think so.

CHAIRMAN MAO

Historically, all reactionary forces on the verge of extinction invariably con-
duct a last desperate struggle against the revolutionary forces, and some
revolutionaries are apt to be deluded for a time by this phenomenon of out-
ward strength but inner weakness, failing to grasp the essential fact that the
enemy is nearing extinction while they themselves are approaching victory.

LONG-WINDED LADY

I remember once when I broke my finger, or my thumb, and I was very little, and they said, you've broken your thumb, look, you've broken your
thumb, and there wasn't any pain . . . not *yet;* not for that first moment,
just . . . just an absence of sensation—an interesting lack of anything.

OLD WOMAN

"Over the Hill to the Poor-House."

LONG-WINDED LADY

When they said it again, look, you've broken your thumb, not only did I
scream, as if some knife had ripped my leg down, from hip to ankle, all
through the sinews, laying bare the bone . . . not only did I scream as only
children can—adults do it differently: there's an animal protest there, a
revenge, something . . . something other—not only did I scream, but I
manufactured the pain. Right then! Before the hurt could have come
through, I made it happen.
   (*Pause*)
Well; we do that.

OLD WOMAN

What is the use of heapin' on me a pauper's shame?
Am I lazy or crazy? am I blind or lame?
True, I am not so supple, nor yet so awful stout;
But charity ain't no favor, if one can live without.

LONG-WINDED LADY

Yes; we do that: we make it happen a little before it need.
   (*Pause*)
And so it might have been with someone watching—and maybe even to

those who *were*. Who *were* watching. And there were, or I'd not be here.

(*Pause*)

I daresay.

(*Pause*)

The sound manufactured. Lord knows, if *I* had been among the . . . non-participators I should have done it, too; no doubt. Plup! Plut! Whichever. I'm sure *I* should have . . . if I'd seen it all the *way,* now. I mean, if I'd caught just the final instant, without time to relate the event to its environment—the thing happening to the thing happened *to* . . . then I doubt I would have. Nor would anyone . . . or most.

CHAIRMAN MAO

The imperialists and their running dogs, the Chinese reactionaries, will not resign themselves to defeat in this land of China.

OLD WOMAN

What is the use of heapin' on me a pauper's shame?
Am I lazy or crazy? Am I blind or lame?

CHAIRMAN MAO

All this we must take fully into account.

LONG-WINDED LADY

But just imagine what it must have been like . . . to be one of the . . . watchers! How . . . well, is marvelous the proper word, I wonder? Yes, I suspect. I mean, how often? ! It's not too common an occurrence, to have it . . . plummet by! One is standing there, admiring, or faintly sick, or just plain throwing up, but how often is one *there.* Ever! Well, inveterates; yes; but for the casual crosser . . . not too often, and one would have to be exactly in place, at exactly the proper time, and alert! Very alert in . . . by nature, and able to relate what one sees to what is happening. Oh, I remember the time the taxi went berserk and killed those people!

CHAIRMAN MAO

Riding roughshod everywhere, U.S. imperialism has made itself the enemy of the people of the world and has increasingly isolated itself. Those who refuse to be enslaved will never be cowed by the atom bombs and hydrogen bombs in the hands of the U.S. imperialists. The raging tide of the people of the world against the U.S. aggressors is irresistible. Their struggle against U.S. imperialism and its lackeys will assuredly win still greater victories.

LONG-WINDED LADY

Well, it didn't go berserk, of course, for it *is* a machine: a taxi. Nor did the driver . . . go berserk. Out of control, though! The driver lost and out of control it went! *Up* on the sidewalk, bowling them down like whatchamacallems, then crash!, into the store front, the splash of glass and then on fire. How many dead? Ten? Twelve? And I had just come out with the crullers.

OLD WOMAN

I am ready and willin' an' anxious any day
To work for a decent livin', an' pay my honest way;
For I can earn my victuals, an' more too, I'll be bound,
If anybody is willin' to only have me 'round.

LONG-WINDED LADY

The bag of crullers, and a smile on my face for everyone liked them so, and
there it was! Careen . . . and dying . . . and all that glass. And I remember
thinking: it's a movie! They're shooting some scenes right here on the street.

(Pause)

They weren't, of course. It was real death, and real glass, and the fire, and
the . . . people crying, and the crowds, and the smoke. Oh, it was real
enough, but it took me time to know it. The mind does that.

CHAIRMAN MAO

If the U.S. monopoly capitalist groups persist in pushing their policies of
aggression and war, the day is bound to come when they will be hanged by
the people of the whole world. The same fate awaits the accomplices of
the United States.

OLD WOMAN

I am ready and willin' an' anxious any day
To work for a decent livin', an' pay my honest way;
For I can earn my victuals, an' more too, I'll be bound,
If anybody is willin' to only have me 'round.

LONG-WINDED LADY

They're making a movie! What a nice conclusion, coming out with the
crullers, still hot, with a separate little bag for the powdered sugar, of course
it's a movie! One doesn't come out like that to carnage! Dead people and the
wounded; glass all over and . . . confusion. One . . . concludes things—and
if those things and what is really there don't . . . are not the *same* . . . well!
. . . it would usually be better if it were so. The mind does that: it helps.

CHAIRMAN MAO

To achieve a lasting world peace, we must further develop our friendship
and cooperation with the fraternal countries in the socialist camp and
strengthen our solidarity with all peace-loving countries.

LONG-WINDED LADY

The mind does that.

CHAIRMAN MAO

We must endeavor to establish normal diplomatic relations, on the basis of
mutual respect for territorial integrity and sovereignty and of equality and
mutual benefit, with all countries willing to live together with us in peace.

LONG-WINDED LADY

It helps.

CHAIRMAN MAO

We must give active support to the national independence and liberation movement in Asia, Africa, and Latin America as well as to the peace movement and to just struggles in all the countries of the world.

VOICE, FROM **BOX**

Box.

LONG-WINDED LADY

So; if one happened to be there, by the rail, and not too discomfited, not in the sense of utterly defeated—though that would be more than enough— but in the sense of confused, or preoccupied, if one were not too preoccupied, and plummet! it went by! one, the mind, might be able to take it in, say: ah! there! there she goes!—or he; and manufacture the appropriate sound. But only then. And how many are expecting it!? Well, *I* am. *Now.* There isn't a rail I stand by, especially in full sun—my conditioning—that I'm not . . already shuddering . . . *and* ready to manufacture the sound.

(*Little laugh*)

Though not the sound *I* knew, for I was hardly thinking—a bit busy—but the sound I imagine someone else would have manufactured had *he* been there when I . . . WOOOOSSSH!! PLUT!!

(*Little laugh*)

VOICE, FROM **BOX**

Box.

OLD WOMAN

Once I was young an' han'some—I was, upon my soul—
Once my cheeks was roses, my eyes as black as coal;
And I can't remember, in them days, of hearin' people say,
For any kind of a reason, that I was in their way!

LONG-WINDED LADY

You never know until it's happened to you.

VOICE, FROM **BOX**

Many arts: all craft now . . . and going further.

CHAIRMAN MAO

Our country and all the other socialist countries want peace; so do the peoples of all the countries of the world. The only ones who crave war and do not want peace are certain monopoly capitalist groups in a handful of imperialist countries which depend on aggression for their profits.

LONG-WINDED LADY

Do you.

VOICE, FROM **BOX**

Box.

CHAIRMAN MAO

Who are our enemies? Who are our friends?

LONG-WINDED LADY

Do you.

CHAIRMAN MAO

Our enemies are all those in league with imperialism; our closest friends are the entire semi-proletariat and petty bourgeoisie. As for the vacillating middle bourgeoisie, their right wing may become our enemy and their left wing may become our friend.

LONG-WINDED LADY

Falling! My goodness. What was it when one was little? That when you fell when you were dreaming you always woke up before you landed, or else you wouldn't and you'd be dead. That was it, I think. And I never wondered why, I merely took it for . . . well, I *accepted* it. And, of course, I kept trying to dream of falling after I'd heard it . . . tried so hard! . . . and *couldn't,* naturally. Well, if we control the unconscious, we're either mad, or . . . dull-witted.

OLD WOMAN

Once I was young an' han'some—I was, upon my soul.

LONG-WINDED LADY

I think I dreamt of falling again, though, but after I'd stopped trying to, but I don't think I landed. Not like what I've been telling you, though that was more seaing than landing, you might say . . . if you like a pun. Once, though! Once, I dreamt of falling straight up . . . or out, all in reverse, like the projector running backwards, what they used to do, for fun, in the shorts.
   (*Some wonder*)
Falling . . . *up!*

CHAIRMAN MAO

In the final analysis, national struggle is a matter of class struggle. Among the whites in the United States it is only the reactionary ruling circles who oppress the black people.

LONG-WINDED LADY

Falling . . . *up!*

CHAIRMAN MAO

They can in no way represent the workers, farmers, revolutionary intellectuals and other enlightened persons who comprise the overwhelming majority of the white people.

VOICE, FROM **BOX**

Seven hundred million babies dead in half the time it takes, took, to knead the dough to make a proper loaf. Well, little wonder so many . . .

LONG-WINDED LADY

Not rising, you understand: a definite . . . falling, but . . . up!

OLD WOMAN

'Tain't no use of boastin', or talkin' over free,
But many a house an' home was open then to me;
Many a han'some offer I had from likely men,
And nobody ever hinted that I was a burden then!

LONG-WINDED LADY

Did I call them crullers? Well, I should *not* have; for they were not even doughnuts, but the centers . . . hearts is what they called them: the center dough pinched out, or cut with a cutter and done like the rest, but solid, the size of a bantam egg, but round. Oh, they were good, and crisp, and all like air inside; hot, and you'd dip them in the confectioner's sugar. One could be quite a pig; everyone was; they were so good! You find them here and about still. Some, but not often.

OLD WOMAN

"Over the Hill to the Poor-House."

CHAIRMAN MAO

All reactionaries are paper tigers. In appearance, the reactionaries are terrifying, but in reality they are not so powerful. From a long-term point of view, it is not the reactionaries but the people who are really powerful.

VOICE, FROM **BOX**

Apathy, I think.

LONG-WINDED LADY

My husband used to say, don't leave her next to anything precipitous; there's bound to be a do; something will drop, or fall, her purse, her*self*. And, so, he had people be careful of me. Not that I'm fond of heights. I'm not unfriendly toward them—all that falling—but I have no . . . great affection.

(*Little pause*)

Depths even less.

OLD WOMAN

By Will Carleton.

CHAIRMAN MAO

I have said that all the reputedly powerful reactionaries are merely paper tigers. The reason is that they are divorced from the people. Look! Was not Hitler a paper tiger? Was Hitler not overthrown? I also said that the czar of Russia, the emperor of China and Japanese imperialism were all paper tigers. As we know, they were all overthrown.

LONG-WINDED LADY

All that falling.

CHAIRMAN MAO

U.S. imperialism has not yet been overthrown and it has the atom bomb. I believe it also will be overthrown. It, too, is a paper tiger.

LONG-WINDED LADY

And it became something of a joke, I suppose . . . I suppose. Where is she? Watch her! Don't let her near the edge! She'll occasion a do!

OLD WOMAN

And when to John I was married, sure he was good and smart,
But he and all the neighbors would own I done my part;
For life was all before me, an' I was young an' strong,
And I worked my best an' smartest in tryin' to get along.

LONG-WINDED LADY

He was a small man—my husband, almost a miniature . . . not that I'm much of a giraffe. Small . . . and precise . . . and contained . . . quiet strength. The large emotions . . . *yes*, without them, what?—all there, and full size, full scope, but when they came, not a . . . spattering, but a single shaft, a careful aim. No waste, as intense as anyone, but precise. Some people said he was cold; or cruel. But he was merely accurate. Big people ooze, and scatter, and knock over things nearby. They give the impression—the illusion—of openness, of spaces through which things pass—excuses, bypassings. But small, and precise, and accurate don't . . . doesn't allow for that . . . for that *impression*. He wasn't cruel at all.

CHAIRMAN MAO

The socialist system will eventually replace the capitalist system; this is an objective law independent of man's will. However much the reactionaries try to hold back the wheel of history, sooner or later revolution will take place and will inevitably triumph.

OLD WOMAN

Over the hill to the poor-house—I can't quite make it clear.

LONG-WINDED LADY

Or cold. Neat; accurate; precise. In everything. All our marriage. Except dying. Except that . . . dreadful death.

CHAIRMAN MAO

The imperialists and domestic reactionaries will certainly not take their defeat lying down and they will struggle to the last ditch. This is inevitable and beyond all doubt, and under no circumstances must we relax our vigilance.

LONG-WINDED LADY

That dreadful death—all that he was not: large, random, inaccurate—in the sense of offshoots from the major objective. A spattering cancer! Spread enough and you're bound to kill *something*. Don't aim! Engulf! Imprecision!

VOICE, FROM **BOX**

When it was *simple* . . .

   (Light, self-mocking laugh)

Ah, well, yes, when it was simple.

OLD WOMAN

And so we worked together: and life was hard, but gay,
With now and then a baby to cheer us on our way;
Till we had half a dozen: an' all growed clean an' neat,
An' went to school like others, an' had enough to eat.

LONG-WINDED LADY

Don't let her near the edge!

CHAIRMAN MAO

Make trouble, fail, make trouble again, fail again . . . till their doom; that
is the logic of the imperialists and all reactionaries the world over in dealing with the people's cause, and they will never go against this logic. This
is a Marxist law.

LONG-WINDED LADY

Don't let her near the edge.

CHAIRMAN MAO

When we say "imperialism is ferocious," we mean that its nature will never
change, that the imperialists will never lay down their butcher knives, that
they will never become Buddhas, till their doom. Fight, fail, fight again,
fail again, fight again . . . till their victory; that is the logic of the people,
and they too will never go against this logic. This is another Marxist law.

LONG-WINDED LADY

But I hadn't thought I *was*. Well, yes, of course I *was* . . . but guarded . . .
well guarded. Or, so I *thought*. It doesn't happen terribly often—falling . . .
by indirection.

   (Pause)

Does it?

OLD WOMAN

An' so we worked for the child'rn, and raised 'em every one;
Worked for 'em summer and winter, just as we ought to've done;
Only perhaps we humored 'em, which some good folks condemn,
But every couple's child'rn's a heap the best to them!

VOICE, FROM **BOX**

Oh, shame!

LONG-WINDED LADY

Not death: I didn't mean death. I meant . . . falling off. *That* isn't done too
often by indirection. *Is* it! Death! Well, my God, of course; yes. Almost

always, 'less you take the notion of the collective . . . thing, which *must allow* for it, take it into account: I mean, if all the rest is part of a . . . pre-determination, or something that has already happened—in principle—well, under *those* conditions *any* chaos becomes order. Any chaos at all.

> VOICE, FROM **BOX**

Oh, shame!

> CHAIRMAN MAO

Everything reactionary is the same; if you don't hit it, it won't fall.

> VOICE, FROM **BOX**

Oh, shame!

> CHAIRMAN MAO

This is also like sweeping the floor; as a rule, where the broom does not reach, the dust will not vanish of itself. Nor will the enemy perish of himself. The aggressive forces of U.S. imperialism will not step down from the stage of history of their own accord.

> VOICE, FROM **BOX**

The *Pope* warned us; *he* said so. There are no possessions, he said; so long as there are some with nothing we have no right to anything.

> LONG-WINDED LADY

And the thing about boats is . . . you're burned . . . always . . . sun . . . haze . . . mist . . . deep night . . . all the spectrum down. Something. Burning.

> CHAIRMAN MAO

Everything reactionary is the same; if you don't hit it, it won't fall.

> LONG-WINDED LADY

I sat up one night—oh, *before* it happened, though it doesn't matter—I mean, on a deck chair, like this, well away from the . . . possibility, but I sat up, and the moon was small, as it always is, on the northern route, well out, and I *bathed* in the night, and perhaps my daughter came up from danc-ing, though I don't think so . . . dancing down there with a man, well, young enough to be her husband.

> OLD WOMAN

For life was all before me, an' I was young an' strong,
And I worked the best that I could in tryin' to get along.

> LONG-WINDED LADY

Though not. Not her husband.

> CHAIRMAN MAO

Classes struggle; some classes triumph, others are eliminated. Such is his-tory, such is the history of civilization for thousands of years. To interpret history from this viewpoint is historical materialism; standing in opposition to this viewpoint is historical idealism.

LONG-WINDED LADY

Though not. Not her husband.

CHAIRMAN MAO

No political party can possibly lead a great revolutionary movement to victory unless it possesses revolutionary theory and a knowledge of history and has a profound grasp of the practical movement.

LONG-WINDED LADY

And what I mean is: the burn; sitting in the dim moon, with not the sound of the orchestra, but the *possible* sound of it—therefore, I suppose, the same—the daughter, *my* daughter, and me up here, up *there*—this one? No.—and being burned! In that—what I said—that all seasons, all lights, all . . . well, one never returns from a voyage the same.

VOICE, FROM **BOX**

It's the *little* things, the *small* cracks.

OLD WOMAN

Strange how much we think of our blessed little ones!—
I'd have died for my daughters, I'd have died for my sons;
And God he made that rule of love; but when we're old and gray,
I've noticed it sometimes somehow fails to work the other way.

LONG-WINDED LADY

His scrotum was large, and not only for a small man, I think, as I remember back—and am I surmising my comparisons here, or telling you something loose about my past?
　(Shrugs)

CHAIRMAN MAO

Classes struggle; some classes triumph, others are eliminated.

LONG-WINDED LADY

What does it matter now, this late?—large, and not of the loose type, but thick, and leather, marvelously creased and like a neat, full sack. And his penis, too; of a neat proportion; ample, but not of that size which moves us so in retrospect . . . or is supposed to. Circumcised . . . well, no, not really, but trained back, *to* it; trained; like everything; nothing surprising, but always there, and ample. Do I shock you?

VOICE, FROM **BOX**

And if you go back to a partita . . .

CHAIRMAN MAO

Such is history.

LONG-WINDED LADY

Do I *shock* you?

CHAIRMAN MAO

The commanders and fighters of the entire Chinese people's Liberation Army absolutely must not relax in the least their will to fight; any thinking that relaxes the will to fight and belittles the enemy is wrong.

LONG-WINDED LADY

That is the last I have in mind. My intention is only to remember.

OLD WOMAN

Strange how much we think of our blessed little ones!

CHAIRMAN MAO

I hold that it is bad as far as we are concerned if a person, a political party, an army or a school is not attacked by the enemy, for in that case it would definitely mean that we have sunk to the level of the enemy.

LONG-WINDED LADY

That is the last I have in mind.

CHAIRMAN MAO

It is good if we are attacked by the enemy, since it proves that we have drawn a clear line of demarcation between the enemy and ourselves.

LONG-WINDED LADY

And the only desperate conflict is between what we long to remember and what we need to forget. No; that is not what I meant at all. Or . . . well, yes, it may *be;* it may be on the nose.

OLD WOMAN

Strange, another thing: when our boys an' girls was grown,
And when, exceptin' Charley, they'd left us there alone;
When John he nearer an' nearer come, an' dearer seemed to be,
The Lord of Hosts he come one day an' took him away from me!

LONG-WINDED LADY

But, wouldn't you think a death would relate to a life? . . . if not resemble it, *benefit* from it? Be *taught?* In *some* way? *I* would think.

OLD WOMAN

The Lord of Hosts He come one day an' took him away from me!

CHAIRMAN MAO

Whoever sides with the revolutionary people is a revolutionary. Whoever sides with imperialism, feudalism and bureaucrat-capitalism is a counter-revolutionary.

LONG-WINDED LADY

Be *taught?* In *some* way?

CHAIRMAN MAO

Whoever sides with the revolutionary people in words only but acts otherwise is a revolutionary in speech.

LONG-WINDED LADY

I would think.

CHAIRMAN MAO

Whoever sides with the revolutionary people in deed as well as in word is
a revolutionary in the full sense.

VOICE, FROM **BOX**

And if you go back to a partita . . . ahhh, what when it makes you cry!?

LONG-WINDED LADY

Savage how it can come, but, even more the preparations for it. No, not *for*
it, but the—*yes!* they *must* be preparations for it, unless we're a morbid
species—that, over the duck one day—the cold duck, with the gherkins and
the lemon slices, notched like a cog . . . and the potato salad, warm if you're
lucky, somebody suddenly says to your husband, when were you first aware
of death, and he's only forty! God!, and he looks, and he says, without even
that flick, that instant of an eye to me, odd you should ask me and I'm not
even . . . well, I'm thirty-nine, and I've begun, though if you'd asked me two
weeks ago, though you wouldn't have, and we saw you then—and it was true;
we had; two weeks ago; two weeks *before.* Is it something that suddenly
shows and happens at once? At one moment? When we are aware of it we
show we are? My God!, he said; I hadn't thought of dying since I was twelve,
and, then again, *what,* sixteen, *what,* when I wrote those sonnets, all on the
boatman, ironic, though. No! And the other man said, no: death, not dying.

VOICE, FROM **BOX**

And if you go back to a partita . . . ahhhh, what when it makes you cry!? Not
from the beauty of it, but from solely that you cry from loss . . . so precious.

OLD WOMAN

Still I was bound to struggle, an' never to cringe or fall—
Still I worked for Charley, for Charley was now my all;
And Charley was pretty good to me, with scarce a word or frown,
Till at last he went a-courtin', and brought a wife from town.

LONG-WINDED LADY

And another man there—an older man—someone my family had known,
some man we had at parties and once I'd called Uncle, though he wasn't,
some man I think my sister had been seen to go around with . . . someone
who was around, said, God, you're young! You think of death when you're
knee-high to a knicker, and dying when your cock gets decent for the first
or second time, and I mean *in* something, not the handy-pan, but when
you think of *dead!* And . . . he was drunk, though . . . what!—well, my lovely husband looked at him with a kind of glass, and he was a host then, and
he said, with a quiet and staid that I think is—well, what I have loved him
for, or what is of the substance of what I have loved him for . . . Straight In
The Eye! When I was young I thought of death; and then, when I was
older—or what I suddenly seemed to be . . . dying . . . with a kind of long-

ing: Ngggggg, with a look at me, as if he could go on . . . and by God!, he slapped away, and it was the first?, the only gesture I was . . . have, been . . . even . . . momentarily . . . DON'T TALK LIKE THAT!!

(Pause)

Slapped away with his eyes and said, I am suddenly dying, to which he added an it would seem, and while everybody tried to talk about death he wanted to talk about dying.

CHAIRMAN MAO

We should support whatever the enemy opposes and oppose whatever the enemy supports.

VOICE, FROM **BOX**

When art begins to hurt . . . when art begins to hurt, it's time to look around. Yes it is.

LONG-WINDED LADY

But, of course, my sister's . . . savior, or whatever you would have it, wouldn't not be still. *He* went *on!* Death!, he said. And then he would lapse . . . for nothing, that I could see, beyond the curious pleasure of lapsing . . . Death! Yes, my husband would say, or *said* : . . *said* this particular time—and Bishop Berkeley will be wrong, he added, and no one understood, which is hardly surprising—I am suddenly dying, and I want no nonsense about it! Death? You stop about death, finally, seriously, when you're on to *dying*. Oh, come on!, the other said; death is the whole thing. He drank, as . . . my sister did, too; she died. I think they got in bed together—took a bottle with them, made love perhaps. CRAP!—which quieted the room some . . . and me, too. He never did that. Death is nothing; there . . . there *is* no death. There is only life and dying.

CHAIRMAN MAO

A revolution is not a dinner party, or writing an essay, or painting a picture, or doing embroidery; it cannot be so refined, so leisurely and gentle, so temperate, kind, courteous, restrained and magnanimous. A revolution is an insurrection, an act of violence by which one class over-throws another.

VOICE, FROM **BOX**

When art begins to hurt, it's time to look around. Yes it is.

LONG-WINDED LADY

And *I*, he said, *I*—thumping his chest with the flat of his hand, slow, four, five times—*I* . . . am *dying*.

CHAIRMAN MAO

After the enemies with guns have been wiped out, there will still be enemies without guns; they are bound to struggle desperately against us, and we must never regard these enemies lightly. If we do not now raise and understand the problem in this way, we shall commit the gravest mistakes.

VOICE, FROM **BOX**

Yes it is.

LONG-WINDED LADY

And I, he said, I am dying. And this was long before he did. That night he told me: I was not aware of it before. We were resting . . . *before* sex—which we would not have that night; on our sides, his chest and groin against my back and buttocks, his hand between my breasts, the sand of his chin nice against my neck. I always knew I would die—I'm not a fool, but I had no sense of time; I didn't know it would be so soon. I turned; I cupped my hands around his lovely scrotum and our breaths were together. But, it won't be for so very *long*. Yes, he said; I know. Silence, then added; but always shorter.

OLD WOMAN

And Charley was pretty good to me, with scarce a word or frown,
Till at last he went a-courtin', and brought a wife from town.
She was somewhat dressy, an' hadn't a pleasant smile.

CHAIRMAN MAO

People all over the world are now discussing whether or not a third world war will break out. On this question, too, we must be mentally prepared and do some analysis. We stand firmly for peace and against war. But if the imperialists insist on unleashing another war, we should not be afraid of it.

LONG-WINDED LADY

And I, he said, I am dying.

CHAIRMAN MAO

If the imperialists insist on launching a third world war, the whole structure of imperialism will utterly collapse.

LONG-WINDED LADY

But what about *me!* Think about *me!*

OLD WOMAN

She was somewhat dressy, an' hadn't a pleasant smile—
She was quite conceity, and carried a heap o' style;
But if ever I tried to be friends, I did with her, I know;
But she was hard and proud, an' I couldn't make it go.

LONG-WINDED LADY

ME! WHAT ABOUT ME!

(*Pause*)

That may give the impression of selfishness, but that is not how I intended it, nor how it is . . . at all. *I* . . . am *left*.

(*Helpless shrug*)

He isn't. I'll not touch his dying again. It was long, and coarse, and ugly, and cruel, and tested the man beyond his . . . beyond *anyone's* capacities. I dare you! I dare anyone! Don't scream! Don't hate! I dare anyone.

(*Softer*)

All that can be done is turn into a beast; the dumb thing's agony is none the less, but it doesn't understand *why*, the agony. And maybe that's enough comfort: not to know why.

(*Pause; wistful; sad*)

But I am *left*.

VOICE, FROM **BOX**

And the beauty of art is order.

CHAIRMAN MAO

We desire peace. However, if imperialism insists on fighting a war, we will have no alternative but to take the firm resolution to fight to the finish before going ahead with our constriction. If you are afraid of war day in day out, what will you do if war eventually comes? First I said that the East Wind is prevailing over the West Wind and war will not break out, and now I have added these explanations about the situation in case war should break out. Both possibilities have thus been taken into account.

OLD WOMAN

She was somewhat dressy, an' hadn't a pleasant smile—
She was quite conceity, an' carried a heap o' style;
But if ever I tried to be friends, I did with her, I know.

LONG-WINDED LADY

Besides, his dying is all over; all gone, but his *death* stays. He said death was not a concern, but he meant his own, and for *him*. No, well, he was right: *he* only had his dying. I have both.

(*Sad chuckle*)

Oh, what a treasurehouse! I can exclude his dying; I can *not* think about it, except the times I want it back—the times I want, for myself, something less general than . . . tristesse. Though that is usually enough. And what for my daughter—*mine*, now, you'll notice; no longer ours; what box have I got for her? Oh . . . the ephemera: jewelry, clothes, chairs . . . and the money: enough. Nothing solid, except my dying, my death, those two, and the thought of her own. The former, though.

VOICE, FROM **BOX**

Not what is familiar, necessarily, but order.

CHAIRMAN MAO

War is the highest form of struggle for resolving contradictions, when they have developed to a certain stage, between classes, nations, states, or political groups, and it has existed ever since the emergence of private property and of classes.

LONG-WINDED LADY

(*A little stentorian; disapproving*)

Where were *you* those six last months, the time I did *not* need you, with my hands full of less each day; my arms.

(Sad, almost humorous truth)

If you send them away to save them from it, you resent their going and *they* want what they've missed. Well . . . I see as much of you as I'd like, my dear. Not as much as either of us should want, but as much as we do. Odd.

VOICE, FROM BOX

. . . and the beauty of art is order—not what is familiar, necessarily, but order . . . on its own terms.

OLD WOMAN

But she was hard and proud, an' I couldn't make it go.
She had an edication, an' that was good for her;
But when she twitted me on mine, 'twas carryin' things too fur;
An' I told her once, 'fore company (an' it almost made her sick),
That I never swallowed a grammar, or 'et a 'rithmetic.

LONG-WINDED LADY

(New subject)

And there I was! Falling!

CHAIRMAN MAO

Revolutionary war is an antitoxin which not only eliminates the enemy's poison but also purges us of our own filth.

VOICE, FROM BOX

That is the thing about music. That is why we cannot listen any more.

(Pause)

Because we cry.

LONG-WINDED LADY

We see each other less, she and I—my daughter—as I said, and most often on boats: something about the air; the burning. She was with me when I fell. Well: on *board*. When they . . . hauled me in—oh, what a spectacle *that* was!—there she was, looking on. Not near where I came in, exactly, but some way off: nearer where I'd done it; where it had been done. Red hair flying—not natural, a kind of purple to it, but stunning; quite stunning—cigarette; *always;* the French one. Nails the color of blood—artery blood, darker than the vein. The things one knows! Looking on, not quite a smile, not quite not. I looked up, dolphins resting on my belly, seaweed-twined, like what's-his-name, or hers . . . I'll bet all you'll say is Honestly, Mother!

(Slight pause)

And when she came to my cabin, after the doctor, and the welcome brandy, and the sedative, the unnecessary sedative . . . there she stood for a moment, cigarette still on, in her mouth, I think. She looked for a moment. Honestly, Mother!, she said, laughing a little in her throat, *at* it, humor *at* it. Honestly, Mother! And then off she went.

VOICE, FROM **BOX**

That is why we cannot listen any more.

OLD WOMAN

So 'twas only a few days before the thing was done—
They was a family of themselves, and I another one;
And a very little cottage one family will do,
But I never have seen a house that was big enough for two.

VOICE, FROM **BOX**

Because we cry.

LONG-WINDED LADY

Where is she now. This trip. Mexico. You'd better chain yourself to the
chair, she said to me, later, the day after. You *will* go on deck; put a long
cord on yourself. It's not a usual occurrence, I told her; not even for me.
No, but you're inventive, she said.

VOICE, FROM **BOX**

Look! More birds! Another . . . sky of them.

CHAIRMAN MAO

History shows that wars are divided into two kinds, just and unjust. We
Communists oppose all unjust wars that impede progress, but we do not
oppose progressive, just wars. Not only do we Communists not oppose just
wars, we actively participate in them. All wars that are progressive are just,
and all wars that impede progress are unjust. The way to oppose a war of
this kind is to do everything possible to prevent it before it breaks out and,
once it breaks out, to oppose war with war, to oppose unjust war with just
war, whenever possible.

OLD WOMAN

But I never have seen a house that was big enough for two.

LONG-WINDED LADY

Mexico; still; probably. I'm in Mexico, in case you care, she said. Four
A.M. First words, no hello, Mother, or sorry to wake you up if you're sleeping, if you're not lying there, face all smeared, hair in your net, bed jacket
still on, propped up, lights out, wondering whether you're asleep or not.
No; not that. Not even that. I'm in Mexico, in case you care.

VOICE, FROM **BOX**

Look! More birds! Another . . . sky of them.

LONG-WINDED LADY

Oh. Well . . . how very nice. I'm in Mexico, in case you care. I'm with two
boys. Sort of defiant. Oh? Well, how nice. Add 'em up and they're just my
age; one's twenty and the other's not quite that. Still defiant. Well, that's . . .
she lies a bit; she's forty-two. That's very *nice,* dear. They're both Mexican.
She sounded almost ugly, over the phone, in the dark. Well . . . They're both

uncircumcised, she said, and then waited. When this happens . . . when this happens, she will wait—not those very words, but something she hopes to affect me with, hurt me, shock, perhaps, make me feel less . . . well, I was going to say happy, but I am seldom that: not any more . . . make me feel less even. She'll wait, and I can hear her waiting, to see if I put the phone down. If I do *not,* after a certain time, of the silence, then she *will.* I put it down gently, when I do. She slams. This time, *I* put it down; gently. I've never known which makes her happier . . . if either does, though I suppose one must. Whether she is happier if she makes me do it, or if I pause too long, and she can. I would like to ask her, but it is not the sort of question one can ask a forty-two-year-old woman . . . daughter or no.

VOICE, FROM **BOX**

It's only when you can't come back; when you get in some distant key; that when you say, the tonic! the tonic! and they say, what is *that?* It's *then.*

OLD WOMAN

An' I never could speak to suit her, never could please her eye,
An' it made me independent, an' then I didn't try;
But I was terribly staggered, an' felt it like a blow,
When Charley turned ag'in me, an' told me I could go!

LONG-WINDED LADY

I *do wish* sometimes . . . just in general, I mean . . . I *do wish* sometimes . . .

CHAIRMAN MAO

Some people ridicule us as advocates of the "omnipotence of war." Yes, we are advocates of the omnipotence of revolutionary war; that is good, not bad, it is Marxist.

LONG-WINDED LADY

Just in general, I mean . . . I *do wish* sometimes . . .

CHAIRMAN MAO

Experience in the class struggle in the era of imperialism teaches us that it is only by the power of the gun that the working class and the laboring masses can defeat the armed bourgeoisie and landlords; in this sense we may say that only with guns can the whole world be transformed.

LONG-WINDED LADY

I suppose that's why I came this time . . . the Mexicans; the boys. Put an ocean between. It's not as far as a death, but . . . still.

OLD WOMAN

"Over the Hill to the Poor-House," by Will Carleton.

LONG-WINDED LADY

I remember, I walked to the thing, the railing. To look over. Why, I don't *know:* water never changes, the Atlantic, *this* latitude. But if you've been sitting in a chair, that is what you *do:* you put down the Trollope or James or sometimes Hardy, throw off the rug, and, slightly unsteady from suddenly up from horizontal . . . you walk to the thing . . . the railing. It's that simple. You look for a bit, smell, sniff, really; you look down to make sure it's moving, and then you think shall you take a turn, and you usually do not; you go back to your rug and your book. Or *not* to your book, but to your *rug*, which you pull up like covers and pretend to go to sleep. The one thing you do *not* do is fall off the ship!

VOICE, FROM **BOX**

There! More! A thousand, and one below them, moving fast in the opposite way!

OLD WOMAN

I went to live with Susan: but Susan's house was small,
And she was always a-hintin' how snug it was for us all;
And what with her husband's sisters, and what with child'rn three,
'Twas easy to discover that there wasn't room for me.

LONG-WINDED LADY

Here's a curious thing! Whenever I'm in an aeroplane—which I am not, often, for I like to choose my company: not that I'm a snob, heavens!, it's my daughter who will not see *me*, or, rather, not often. Not that I am a snob, but I feel that travel in rooms is so much nicer: boats and trains, where one can get away and then out again; people are nicer when you come upon them around corners, or opening doors. But whenever I'm up there, closed in, strapped to my seat, with all the people around, and the double windows, those tiny windows, and the great heavy door, bolted from the outside, probably, even when I'm plumped down in an inside seat—or aisle, as they call them—*then!* It's then that I feel that I'm going to fall out. Fall right out of the aeroplane! I don't know how I could possibly do it—even through the most . . . reprehensible carelessness. I probably couldn't, even if I felt I had to. But I'm sure I will! Always! Though, naturally, I never do.

VOICE, FROM **BOX**

What was it used to frighten me?

CHAIRMAN MAO

Revolutions and revolutionary wars are inevitable in class society, and without them it is impossible to accomplish any leap in social development and to overthrow the reactionary ruling classes and therefore impossible for the people to win political power.

OLD WOMAN

'Twas easy to discover that there wasn't room for me.

LONG-WINDED LADY

Coarse, and ugly, and long, and cruel. That dying. My lovely husband.
   (*Small pause*)
But I said I wouldn't dwell on that.

OLD WOMAN

An' then I went to Thomas, the oldest son I've got:
For Thomas's buildings'd cover the half of an acre lot;
But all the child'rn was on me—I couldn't stand their sauce—
And Thomas said I needn't think I was comin' there to boss.

LONG-WINDED LADY

Well! What can we say of an aging lady walks bright as you please from her
rug and her Trollope or her James or sometimes her Hardy right up to the
thing . . . the railing; walks right up, puts her fingers, rings and all, right on
the varnished wood, sniffs . . . that air!, feels the railing, hard as wood,
knows it's there—it *is* there—and suddenly, as sudden and sure as what
you've always known and never quite admitted to yourself, it is *not* there;
there is no railing, no wood, no metal, no buoy-life-thing saying S.S. or
H.M.S. whatever, no . . . nothing! Nothing at all! The fingers are claws, and
the varnish they rubbed against is air? And suddenly one is . . . well, what
would you expect?! One is suddenly leaning on one's imagination—which
is poor support, let me tell you . . . at least in *my* case—leaning on that,
which doesn't last for long, and over one goes!

VOICE, FROM **BOX**

. . . a thousand miles from the sea. Land-locked, never been, and yet the
sea sounds . . .

CHAIRMAN MAO

War, this monster of mutual slaughter among men, will be finally eliminated by the progress of human society, and in the not too distant future,
too.

VOICE, FROM **BOX**

A thousand miles from the sea. Land-locked.

CHAIRMAN MAO

But there is only one way to eliminate it and that is to oppose war with war,
to oppose counter-revolutionary war with revolutionary war, to oppose
national counterrevolutionary war with national revolutionary war, and to
oppose counter-revolutionary class war with revolutionary class war.

VOICE, FROM **BOX**

Never been, and yet the sea sounds.

CHAIRMAN MAO

When human society advances to the point where classes and states are
eliminated, there will be no more wars, counter-revolutionary or revolutionary, unjust or just. That will be the era of perpetual peace for mankind.

OLD WOMAN

But all the child'rn was on me—I couldn't stand their sauce—
And Thomas said I needn't think I was comin' there to boss.

LONG-WINDED LADY

Over one goes, and it's a long way, let me tell you! No falling *up;* no, siree;
or out! Straight down! As straight as anything! Plummet! Plut! Well, plummet for sure, plut conjectural. I wonder why I didn't kill myself. Exactly
what my daughter said: I wonder why you didn't kill yourself. Though her
reading was special. Had a note of derision to it.

OLD WOMAN

An' then I wrote to Rebecca, my girl who lives out West,
And to Isaac, not far from her—some twenty miles at best;
And one of 'em said 'twas too warm there for anyone so old,
And t'other had an opinion the climate was too cold.

VOICE, FROM **BOX**

Well, we give up something for something.

LONG-WINDED LADY

I did *not* kill myself, as *I* see it, through a trick of the wind, or chance, or
because I am bottom heavy. Straight down like a drop of shot! Except.
Except, at the very end, a sort of curving, a kind of arc, which sent me gently into a rising wave, or throw-off from the boat, angling into it just properly, sliding in so that it felt like falling on leaves—the pile of autumn
leaves we would make, or our brother would, and jump on, like a feather
bed. A gust of wind must have done that. Well . . . something did.

CHAIRMAN MAO

"War is the continuation of politics." In this sense war is politics and war itself
is a political action; since ancient times there has never been a war that did not
have a political character. "War is the continuation of politics by other means."

VOICE, FROM **BOX**

Something for something.

CHAIRMAN MAO

It can therefore be said that politics is war without bloodshed while war is
politics with bloodshed.

VOICE, FROM **BOX**

When art hurts. That is what to remember.

LONG-WINDED LADY

I try to recall if I recall the falling, but I'm never sure, I think I do, and
then I think I have not. It was so like being awake and asleep . . . at the
same time. But I *do* recall being in the water. Heavens! What a sight! *I*
must have been, too, but I mean what I *saw:* the sliding by of the ship,
green foam in the mouth—kind of exciting—green foam as the wake went
by. Lucky you missed the propellers, they said afterwards. Well, yes; lucky.

CHAIRMAN MAO

Without armed struggle neither the proletariat, nor the people, nor the

Communist Party would have any standing at all in China and it would be impossible for the revolution to triumph.

OLD WOMAN

And one of 'em said 'twas too warm there for anyone so old,
And t'other had an opinion the climate was too cold.

LONG-WINDED LADY

And sitting there! Sitting there in the water, bouncing around like a carton, screaming a little, not to call attention or anything like that, but because of the fright, and the surprise, and the cold, I suppose; and . . . well . . . because it was all sort of thrilling: watching the boat move off. My goodness, boats move fast! Something you don't notice till you're off one.

VOICE, FROM **BOX**

Then the corruption is complete.

OLD WOMAN

So they have shirked and slighted me, an' shifted me about—
So they have wellnigh soured me, an' wore my old heart out;
But still I've borne up pretty well, an' wasn't much put down,
Till Charley went to the poor-master, an' put me on the town.

LONG-WINDED LADY

And then . . . and then horns, and tooting, and all sorts of commotion and people running around and pointing . . .

  (Some disappointment)

and then the boats out, the launches, and dragging me in and hauling me up—in front of all those people!—and then the brandy and the nurse and the sedative . . . and all the rest.

  (Pause)

I lost my cashmere sweater . . . and one shoe.

CHAIRMAN MAO

We are advocates of the abolition of war; we do not want war; but war can only be abolished through war, and in order to get rid of the gun it is necessary to take up the gun.

LONG-WINDED LADY

You're a very lucky woman, I remember the chief purser saying to me, the next day; I was still groggy. You're a very lucky woman. Yes, I am, I said; yes; I am.

CHAIRMAN MAO

Every Communist must grasp the truth, "Political power grows out of the barrel of a gun."

VOICE, FROM **BOX**

Nothing belongs.

OLD WOMAN

But still I've borne up pretty well, an' wasn't much put down,
Till Charley went to the poor-master, an' put me on the town.

LONG-WINDED LADY

Then, of course, there were the questions. People don't fall off of ocean
liners very often. No, I don't suppose they do. Broad daylight and all,
people on deck. No; no; I don't imagine so. Do you think you slipped?
Surely not! Dry as paint. Have you . . . do you cross often? Oh, heavens,
yes! I've done it for years. Have you . . . has this sort of thing ever happened before? What do you take me for!? I'm lucky I'm back from this
one, I suppose. Then—gratuitously, and a little peevish, I'm afraid—and
I shall cross many times more! And I have—many times, and it's not happened again. Well, do you . . . do you think maybe you were—wincing
some here: them; not me—you were helped? Helped? What do you
mean? Well . . . aided. What do you mean, *pushed?* Bedside nod. Yes. A
laugh from me; a young-girl laugh: hand to my throat, head back.
Pushed! Good gracious, no! I had been *reading.* What were you reading—which struck me as beside the point and rather touching. Trollope,
I said, which wasn't true, for that had been the day before, but I said it
anyway.

(*Some wonder*)

They didn't know who Trollope was. Well, *there's* a life for you!

OLD WOMAN

Over the hill to the poor-house—my child'rn dear, good-by!
Many a night I've watched you when only God was nigh;
And God'll judge between us; but I will al'ays pray
That you shall never suffer the half I do today.

VOICE, FROM **BOX**

Look; more of them; a black net . . . skimming.

(*Pause*)

And just one . . . moving beneath . . . in the opposite way.

LONG-WINDED LADY

Isn't that *some*thing? You lead a whole life; you write books, or you do not;
you strive to do good, and succeed, sometimes, amongst the bad—the bad
never through design, but through error, or chance, or lack of a chemical
somewhere, in the head, or cowardice, maybe—you raise a family and live
with people, see them *through* it; you write books, or you do not, and you
say your name is Trollope . . . or whatever it may be, no matter what,
you say your name . . . and they have . . . never . . . heard of it. That *is* a
life for you.

VOICE, FROM **BOX**

Milk.

CHAIRMAN MAO

People of the world, unite and defeat the U.S. aggressors and all their running dogs! People of the world, be courageous, dare to fight, defy difficulties and advance wave upon wave. Then the whole world will belong to the people. Monsters of all kinds shall be destroyed.

OLD WOMAN

"Over the Hill to the Poor-House," by Will Carleton.

VOICE, FROM **BOX**

Milk.

LONG-WINDED LADY

Is there any chance, do you think . . . Hm? . . . I say, is there any chance, do you think, well, I don't know how to put it . . . do you think . . . do you think you may have done it on purpose? Some silence. I look at them, my gray eyes gently wide, misting a little in the edges, all innocence and hurt: *true* innocence; *true* hurt. That I may have done it on purpose? Yes; thrown yourself off.

(*Some bewilderment and hurt*)

. . . Me?

CHAIRMAN MAO

People of the world, unite and defeat the U.S. aggressors and all their running dogs.

LONG-WINDED LADY

Well; yes; I'm sorry. Thrown myself off? A clearing of the throat. Yes. Tried to kill yourself.

(*A sad little half-laugh*)

Good heavens, no; *I* have nothing to die for.

BOX

(Reprise)

Perhaps keep the figures from Quotations from Chairman Mao Tse-tung *still and put them in silhouette. Raise the light on the outline of the Box again.*

VOICE

If only they had *told* us! Clearly! When it was clear that we were not only corrupt—for there is nothing that is not, or little—but corrupt to the selfishness, to the corruption that we should die to keep it . . . go under rather than . . .

(Three-second silence. Sigh)

Oh, my.

(Five-second silence)

And if you go back to a partita . . . ahhhhh, what when it makes you cry!? Not from the beauty of it, but from solely that you cry from loss . . . so precious. When art begins to hurt . . . when art begins to hurt, it's time to look around. Yes it is.

(Three-second silence)

Yes it is.

(Three-second silence)

No longer just great beauty which takes you more to everything, but a reminder! And not of what *can* . . . but what *has*. Yes, when art hurts . . .

(Three-second silence)

Box.

(Two-second silence)

So much . . . flies. A billion birds at once, black net skimming the ocean, or the Monarchs that time, that island, blown by the wind, but going straight . . . in a direction. Order!

(Two-second silence)

When the beauty of it reminds us of *loss.* Instead of the attainable. When it tells us what we cannot have . . . well, then . . . it no longer relates . . . *does* it. That is the thing about music. That is why we cannot listen any more.

(Pause)

Because we cry.

Box **299**

(Five-second silence)

Look! More birds! Another . . . sky of them.

(Five-second silence)

What was it used to frighten me? Bell buoys and sea gulls; the *sound* of them, at night, in a fog, when I was very young.

(A little laugh)

Before I had ever seen them, before I had heard them.

(Some wonder)

But I knew what they *were* . . . a thousand miles from the sea. Land-locked, never been, and yet the sea sounds . . .

(Three-second silence)

But it *couldn't* have been fog, not the sea-fog. Not way back *there*. It was the memory of it, to be seen and proved later. And more! and more! they're all moving! The memory of what we have not known. And so it is with the fog, which I had never seen, yet knew it. And the resolution of a chord; no difference.

(Three-second silence)

And even that can happen here, I guess. But unprovable. Ahhhhh. That makes the difference, does it *not*. Nothing can seep here except the memory of what I'll not prove.

(Two-second silence. Sigh)

Well, we give up something for something.

(Three-second silence)

When art hurts. That is what to remember.

(Two-second silence)

What to look for. Then the corruption . . .

(Three-second silence)

Then the corruption is complete.

(Five-second silence. The sound of bell buoys and sea gulls begins, faintly, growing, but never very loud)

Nothing belongs.

(Three-second silence. Great sadness)

Look; more of them; a black net . . . skimming.

(Pause)

And just one . . . moving beneath . . . in the opposite way.

(Three-second silence. Very sad, supplicating)

Box.

(Silence, except for the sound of bell buoys and sea gulls. Very slow fading of lights to black, sound of bell buoys and sea gulls fading with the light)

CURTAIN

All Over

For
Bernard and Rebecca Reis

FIRST PERFORMANCE

March 27, 1971, Martin Beck Theater, New York City

JESSICA TANDY *as* THE WIFE

MADELEINE SHERWOOD *as* THE DAUGHTER

COLLEEN DEWHURST *as* THE MISTRESS

NEIL FITZGERALD *as* THE DOCTOR

JAMES RAY *as* THE SON

GEORGE VOSKOVEC *as* THE BEST FRIEND

BETTY FIELD *as* THE NURSE

JOHN GERSTAD, CHARLES KINDL, *and* ALLEN WILLIAMS
as TWO PHOTOGRAPHERS AND A REPORTER

CHARACTERS

THE WIFE 71; *small-boned, not heavy. Dresses well, if conservatively; gray-haired, probably.*

THE MISTRESS 61; *auburn or dark blond hair; a great beauty fading some; more voluptuous than* THE WIFE, *maybe a bit taller; given to soft, pastel clothes.*

THE SON 52; *a heavy-set man, soft features; dark hair, business clothes.*

THE DAUGHTER 45; *angular; once attractive, now a little ravaged; doesn't care much about how she dresses.*

THE BEST FRIEND 73; *an erect, good-looking gray-haired man, thin to middling; well dressed, well groomed.*

THE DOCTOR 86; *a tiny, shrunken white-haired man; needn't be tiny, but it would be nice.*

THE NURSE 65; *a large woman, graystreaked blond hair; wears a nurse's uniform.*

TWO PHOTOGRAPHERS AND A REPORTER; *no matter; middle-aged, or whoever understudies the male principals.*

ONE IDEA OF A SET: *A paneled bed-sitting room. The bed—a huge, canopied four-poster on a raised platform to the rear. Back there, an armoire, perhaps a bureau, a hospital stand for instruments and medicines, a hospital screen hiding the occupant of the bed. In the sitting-room part, a huge fireplace in the stage-right wall, and a door leading to a bathroom upstage of it. In the stage-left wall, a door leading to the hall. The room is solid and elegant, a man's room. The furniture, all of which is good and comfortable, is most probably English. Several chairs, a sofa, side tables, lamps. A tapestry, eighteenth-century family portraits. An Oriental carpet.*

TIME: *The present.*

ACT ONE

THE DOCTOR *at the bed with the patient;* THE NURSE *at the foot of the bed. The others about, the three women probably sitting,* THE SON *and* THE BEST FRIEND *maybe not.*

Unless otherwise indicated, the characters will speak in a conversational tone, without urgency, more languorously than not. But there will be no whispering; the languor is not boredom, but waiting. The fireplace has an ebbing fire in it; the room is warm.

THE WIFE (*Gazing at the fire*)

Is he dead?

THE DAUGHTER

(*A gentle admonishment: not a rebuke*)

Oh, mother.

THE MISTRESS

I wish you wouldn't say that: is he dead?

THE WIFE (*Too polite; small smile*)

I'm *sorry.*

THE MISTRESS

It's not your curiosity I mind; it is a wifely right, and I know it's not impatience. It's the *form.* We talked about it once, I remember—he and I did—though not how it came up; I don't remember that, but let me see. He put down his fork, one lunch, at *my* house . . . what had we been talking about? Maeterlinck and that plagiarism business, I seem to recall, and we had done with that and we were examining our salads, when all at once he said to me, "I wish people wouldn't say that other people 'are dead.'" I asked him why, as much as anything to know what had turned him to it, and he pointed out that the verb to be was not, to his mind, appropriate to a state of . . . non-being. That one cannot . . . *be* dead. He said his objection was a quirk—that the grammarians would scoff—but that one could be dying, or have died . . . but could not . . . be . . . dead.

THE WIFE (*Quiet amusement*)

Maeterlinck?

THE MISTRESS (*Lightly*)

Oh, well; that was just one day. I'm sorry for having taken issue.

THE WIFE (*Gazing into the fire again*)

No matter. Let me rephrase it, then.

(Raises her head, inclines it slightly toward THE DOCTOR*)*
Has he . . . *died?*

THE DOCTOR *(Pause)*
Not yet.

THE WIFE *(Pressing a small point)*
Will he die *soon?*

THE SON *(Faint distaste)*
Please, mother.

THE WIFE *(Tiny laugh)*
I would like to know. Merely that.

THE DOCTOR
Relatively.

THE WIFE
To?

THE DOCTOR
To the time it has taken him so far.

THE DAUGHTER
Then what was the urgency?

THE DOCTOR
Hunch.

THE BEST FRIEND
(More curiosity than reproach)
Don't you *want* to be here?

THE DAUGHTER
(Considering it for the first time)
Well . . . I don't *know.*
*(*THE MISTRESS *laughs gently)*

THE BEST FRIEND
It's not required that you *do* know. It *is* more or less required that you *be*
. . . I think: here. Family. Isn't it one of our customs? That if a man has not
outlived his wife and children—will not outlive them . . . they gather?

THE WIFE *(To* THE BEST FRIEND*)*
And his closest friend, as well.
*(*THE BEST FRIEND *bows slightly, cocks his head.* THE WIFE *indi-
cates* THE MISTRESS*)*
And don't forget *her.*

THE BEST FRIEND
(Matter-of-fact, but friendly)
And his . . . very special friend, too.

THE MISTRESS (*Smiles*)

Thank you.

THE BEST FRIEND

And we do it—custom—wanted, or not. We wait until we cannot be asked—unless there is something written, or said, refusing it—and we . . . gather, often even *if* we are refused.

THE WIFE

And is that *so?* In your lawyerish way . . .

THE BEST FRIEND

No; we have not been refused.

THE WIFE (*To* THE DOCTOR)

A hunch. *Nothing* more . . . technical than that? More medical? Your hunch it will be *soon?* Your intuition if you were a woman, or are doctors graced with that?

(*To her* DAUGHTER; *somewhat chiding*)

We've not *come* any distance. Is it just we're in the room with him—not at the hotel, or downstairs?

THE DAUGHTER

I suppose. And that we lived here once.

THE WIFE (*To* THE DAUGHTER)

That was another century.

(*To* THE DOCTOR)

Hunch.

THE DOCTOR (*To* THE WIFE)

I can't give it to you to the minute. Did I predict when she would be born?

(*Refers to* THE DAUGHTER)

The hour—the day, for that matter? Or him?

(*Refers to* THE SON)

THE MISTRESS (*Back to the point*)

Though you have *reason.*

THE DOCTOR

Yes.

(*Pause*)

THE WIFE

(*A little as though she were speaking to a backward child*)

And what *is* it?

THE NURSE

(*Fact more than reproach*)

You should let him die in the hospital.

THE DAUGHTER

Yes!

THE WIFE *(Quietly indignant)*

Hooked up?

THE NURSE *(Shrugs)*

Whatever.

THE MISTRESS

(Soft-smiling; shaking her head; faintly ironic)

Yes, of course We should have.

(To THE WIFE*)*

Can you imagine it?

THE WIFE

Tubes; wires. All those machines, leading to and from? A central gadget?

(To them all, generally)

That's what he had become, with all those tubes and wires: one more machine.

(To THE MISTRESS*)*

Back me up.

THE MISTRESS

Oh, far more than *that.*

THE WIFE

A city seen from the air? The rail lines and the roads? Or, an octopus: the body of the beast, the tentacles electrical controls, recorders, modulators, breath and heart and brain waves, and the tubes!, in either arm and in the nostrils. Where had he gone!? In all that . . . equipment. I thought for a moment *he* was keeping *it* . . . functioning. Tubes and wires.

THE NURSE

They help to keep time, to answer your questions easier.

(Shakes her head)

That's all.

THE MISTRESS

The questions are very simple now. A stopwatch should do it, a finger on the wrist . . .

THE DAUGHTER *(Fairly arch)*

We are led to understand . . .

THE MISTRESS *(No nonsense)*

He *said . . .* here.

THE DAUGHTER *(None too pleasant)*

We have your word for it.

THE WIFE (*Shrugs*)

We have her word for *every*thing.

THE MISTRESS (*Not rising to it*)

He *said* . . . *here*. When it becomes hopeless . . . no, is that what he said?
Pointless! When it becomes pointless, he said . . . have me brought back
here. I want a wood fire, and a ceiling I have memorized, the knowledge
of what I could walk about in, *were* I to. I want to leave from some place
. . . I have known.

(*Changed tone; to* THE DAUGHTER)

You have my *word* for it; yes, you have only my word . . . for so very much
. . . if he loved you, for example . . . any more.

(*To them all; triste*)

You *all* have my word, and that is all. I translate for you, as best I can; I tell
you what I remember, or think I remember, and I lie sometimes, and give
you what he would have said . . . *had* he: thought to . . . or bothered.

THE DAUGHTER

(*Dogged, but not forceful*)

That will not do.

THE SON (*Quiet*)

Please?

THE DAUGHTER (*Scoffing*)

You!

THE WIFE

When I came there, to the hospital—the last time, before the . . . removal
here—I said . . .

(*Turns to* THE MISTRESS)

you were not there, were shopping, or resting, I think . . .

(*Turns back generally*)

looking at him, all wired up, I stood at the foot of the bed—small talk all gone,
years ago—I shook my head, and I clucked, I'm afraid—tsk-tsk-tsk-tsk—for
he opened his eyes a little, baleful, as I suppose my gaze must have seemed to
him, though it was merely . . . objective. This won't do at all, I said. Wouldn't
you rather be somewhere else? Do you want to be here? He kept his eyes half
open for a moment or so, then closed them, and nodded his head, very
slowly. Well, which?, I said, for I realized I'd asked two questions, and a nod
could mean either yes or no. Which is it?, I said; do you want to be here? Slow
shake of the head. You *would* rather be somewhere else. Eyes opened and
closed, twice, in what I know—from eons—to be impatience; then . . . nodding.
Well, naturally, I said, in my bright business tone, of course you don't want to
be here. Do you want to go home? No reply at all, the eyes burning at me.
Your own home, I mean, not mine certainly. Or hers. Perhaps you want to go
there. Shall I arrange something? Eyes still on me, no movement. Do you

want *her* to arrange it? Still the eyes, still no movement. Has it been arranged? Has she arranged it already? The eyes lightened; I could swear there was a smile in them. She *has*. Well; good. If it is done, splendid. All I care is whether it is *done*. I no longer feel possessive, have not for . . . and the eyes went out—stayed open, went out . . .

(*To* THE MISTRESS)

That is one of those things . . .

THE DAUGHTER

(*Possessive, in a very female way*)
MOTHER!

THE WIFE

Do not . . . *deflect* me.

THE DAUGHTER

(*More a whine, but protective*)
MOTHER.

THE WIFE (*As cool as possible*)

Yes?

(*Pause*)

Out. Stayed open, went out.

THE MISTRESS

Ah, well; that happened often.

THE WIFE

(*Quiet, almost innocent interest*)
Yes?

THE MISTRESS

Ah; well, yes.

THE WIFE

Odd I don't remember it. The opening and closing . . . of course, the . . . impatience, but . . . out.

THE MISTRESS (*Gently*)

Ah, well; perhaps you should have noticed. It must have happened.

THE WIFE (*A small smile*)

Well, yes, perhaps I should have. Doubtless it did.

THE MISTRESS

It was always—for me . . .

THE DAUGHTER

Was? The past tense? Why not *is*?

THE MISTRESS

(Not rising to it; calm)

He has not, for some time. You *were* a little girl. Are you still?

(THE DAUGHTER turns away)

THE WIFE *(A little laugh)*

Semantics from a C minus?

THE SON *(Softly)*

Leave her alone.

THE WIFE *(Not harsh)*

Was it not? At school? A C minus, if that? *You* were little better.

THE MISTRESS

It was always—for me—an indication that . . .

THE DOCTOR *(No urgency)*

Nurse.

(Some reaction from them all; not panic, but a turning of heads; a quickening)

THE WIFE *(A little breathless)*

Something?

THE DOCTOR

(Looks up at them; a slight smile; some surprise)

Oh . . . oh, *no.* Just . . . business.

(Slight pause)

THE MISTRESS

(Not pressing; continuing)

. . . an indication that . . . some small fraction had gone out of him, some . . . faint shift from total engagement. Or, if not that, a warning of it: impending.

THE WIFE *(A smile)*

Ah. Then I *do* know it . . . the sense of it, and probably from what you describe, without knowing I was aware of it.

THE BEST FRIEND

I have been aware of it.

THE WIFE

(Referring to her husband)

In *him?*

THE BEST FRIEND

No. In myself.

THE WIFE *(Mildly mocking)*

You *have?*

THE BEST FRIEND *(Smiles)*

Yes; I have.

THE WIFE *(Smiling, herself)*

How extraordinary.

   (Thinks about it)

When?

THE BEST FRIEND *(To THE WIFE)*

In relation to my wife, when I was wavering on the divorce, during that time you and I were—how do they put it?—comforting one another; that secret time I fear that everyone knew of.

THE MISTRESS

He never knew of it. *I* did. I didn't tell him.

THE WIFE *(Sad; smiling)*

Well, there wasn't very much to tell.

THE BEST FRIEND

No; but some; briefly. It was after I decided not to get the divorce, that year . . . until I committed her. Each thing, each . . . incident—uprooting all the roses, her hands so torn, so . . . killing the doves and finches . . . setting fire to her hair . . . all . . . all those times, those things I knew were pathetic and not wanton, I watched myself withdraw, step back and close down some portion of . . .

THE MISTRESS

Ah, but that's not the same.

THE WIFE

   (Not unkindly; objectively)

No, not at all; she was *insane* . . . your wife.

THE MISTRESS

And that is not what we meant at all.

THE WIFE

No, not at all.

THE BEST FRIEND

It is what you were talking about.

THE MISTRESS *(Laughs a little; sadly)*

No. It's when it happens calmly and in full command: the tiniest betrayal— nothing so calamitous as a lie held on to in the face of fact, or so niggling as a fantasy during the act of love, but in between—and it can be anything, or nearly nothing, except that it moves you back into yourself a little, the knowledge that all your sharing has been . . .

THE WIFE

. . . arbitrary . . .

THE MISTRESS

. . . willfull, and that nothing has been inevitable . . . or even necessary.
When the eyes close down; go out.

THE SON (*Intense*)

My father is dying!

THE WIFE (*After a tiny pause*)

Yes. He is.

THE DOCTOR

If you want to go back downstairs, any of you . . .

THE DAUGHTER

. . . to the photographers? The people from the papers? I put my foot on
the staircase and they're all around me: Has it happened yet? *Is* he? May
we go up now? Eager. Soft voices but very eager.

THE WIFE (*Soothing*)

Well, they have their families . . . their wives, their mistresses.

THE DAUGHTER (*Generally*)

Thank you: I'll stay up here; I'll sit it out.

THE WIFE

(*With a wrinkling of her nose*)

Neat.

THE DAUGHTER

(*Slightly incredulous*)

Did you say neat?

THE MISTRESS

Yes; she did.

THE DAUGHTER (*To* HER MOTHER)

Because I said sit it out?

THE WIFE

(*Without expression; waiting*)

Um-humm.

THE DAUGHTER (*Startlingly shrill*)

WELL, WHAT ARE YOU DOING!?

THE WIFE

(*Looks up at her, smiles vaguely, speaks softly*)

I am waiting out a marriage of fifty years. I am waiting for my *hus*band to
die. I am thinking of the little girl I was when he came to me. I am thinking

of . . . do you want me to stop? . . . almost everything I can except the two
of you—you and your . . . unprepossessing brother—

(*Light, to* THE SON)

Do forgive me.

(*Back*)

I am sitting it out. *I* . . . am sitting it out.

(*To* THE DAUGHTER)

And *you* are?

THE DAUGHTER

Enjoying it less than you.

THE MISTRESS

(*To* THE DAUGHTER; *a quiet discovery; as if for the first time, almost*)

You are not a very kind woman.

THE WIFE (*Passing it off*)

She has been raised at her mother's knee.

THE DAUGHTER

(*To* THE MISTRESS)

And am I suddenly *your* daughter?

THE MISTRESS

Oh; my stars! No!

THE DAUGHTER

Well, you have assumed so much . . .

THE WIFE

(*Announcement of a subject*)

The little girl I was when he came to me.

THE MISTRESS

So much?

(*To* THE WIFE)

Interesting: it's only the mother who can ever really know whose child it is.
Well, the husband knows his wife is *having* the baby . . .

THE WIFE (*Laughs gaily*)

He took me aside one day—before you and he had made your liaison; they
were grown, though—and, rather in the guilty way of "Did I *really* back
the car through the *whole* tulip bed?", asked me, his eyes self-consciously
focusing just off somewhere . . . "*Did* I make these children? Was it *our*
doing: the two of us alone?" I laughed, with some joy, for while we *were*
winding down we were doing it with talk and presence: the silences and
the goings off were later; the titans were still engaged; and I said, "Oh, yes,
my darling; yes, we did; they are our very own."

(She chuckles quietly. Brief pause; THE DAUGHTER *rises, almost languidly, walks over to where* THE WIFE *is sitting, slaps her across the face, evenly, without evident emotion, returns to where she is sitting. After a pause; to* THE MISTRESS; *small smile)*

Excuse me.

(She rises, just as languidly, walks over to where THE DAUGHTER *is sitting, slaps her across the face, evenly, without evident emotion, returns to where she is sitting. After a noncommittal sigh at* THE DAUGHTER, *who is glaring straight ahead, over her shoulder, to* THE DOCTOR)

And what do you think now?

THE DOCTOR *(Patient smile)*

Are you back at my intuition again? My hunch? Your funny names for all the years I've watched you come and go? Both your parents, both of his. My sixty years of practice.

(Indicates THE NURSE)

The forty years she's come here with me to sit up nights with you all?

THE WIFE

Yes.

THE MISTRESS *(Some wonder)*

Sixty years of *something.*

THE WIFE *(Still to* THE DOCTOR)

Even on the chance of frightening the horses, or being taken as heartless—which I am *not*—are you holding him back, or are you seeing him through to it?

*(*THE DAUGHTER *stiffens, turns on her heel, moves to the door, opens it, exits, slams it after her)*

THE DOCTOR

(Watching this before he answers)

I've stopped the intravenous feeding. We're letting him . . . starve, if you will. He's breathing very slowly now . . . like sleep. His heart is . . .

(Shrugs)

. . . well, weak . . . bored is close to it. He's bleeding . . . internally. Shall I go on?

THE WIFE *(No expression)*

Please do.

THE DOCTOR

If you'd like to come and look . . . he seems to have diminished every time I turn my head away and come back. There'll be precious little left for the worms.

THE MISTRESS

The flames.

THE WIFE

(Having heard something on the wind)

Oh? Yes?

THE MISTRESS

He will be burned. "And you are not to snatch my heart from the flames,"
he said, "for it is not a tasty organ."

THE WIFE *(Schoolmarmish)*

Per*haps*. Per*haps* he will be burned.

THE BEST FRIEND

(Quite serious; really!)

Surely he didn't suggest an outdoor event . . . a funeral pyre!

(He is stopped by a concert of THE WIFE *and* THE MISTRESS *in
rather cold, knowing, helpless laughter)*

THE SON *(Finally)*

Don't you . . . *have* something? Some papers?

THE WIFE

(Rather helpless in quiet, terrible laughter)

You *must!*

THE SON

(Doubtless the most intense in his life)

You MUST!

THE MISTRESS

Yes!

THE BEST FRIEND

(After an embarrassed pause)

There . . . *are* . . . papers . . . envelopes I've not opened, on instruction;
there may be . . .

THE MISTRESS *(Adamant; cool)*

It was a verbal . . . envelope.

THE BEST FRIEND

I will go by what is *down*.

THE WIFE

(Half sardonic, half leaning)

Of *course* he will.

THE MISTRESS

(Cold; a diamond hardness, yet womanly)

Oh, Christ; you people! You will go by what I tell you; finally; as I have told you.

THE WIFE

(Almost as if improvising; bright)

No! We will go with what *is*, with what resides. Goodness, if a man desires to go up in flames, let him put it down—on a tablet! Or shall we go over and shake him . . . wake him to the final glory before the final glory, and have two women at him, with a best friend overhead, and make him make his *mind* up! "My darling, we merely want to know! Is it flame or worm? Your mistress tells me you prefer the flame, while I, your merely wife of fifty years, the mother of your doubted children—true, oh, true, my darling—wants you to the worms. Do tell us. Yes? Open your awful lips for a moment, or do your eyes: open and close them, put them on and out; let us . . . finally! . . . misunderstand."

*(*THE MISTRESS *smiles, slowly applauds. Five sounds; seven; always an odd number.*

Brief pause following the applause, during which THE WIFE *nods her head gently toward* THE MISTRESS*)*

THE DOCTOR

(To himself, but not sotto voce)

Death is such an old disease.

(Realizes he is being listened to; speaks to THE WIFE *and* THE MISTRESS, *laughs a little)*

That being so, it must be a comfort having someone as old as I am by the bed: familiar with it, knowing it so well.

THE MISTRESS

Well, let me discomfort you. I was *not* pleased to have you. Get a younger man, I said to him . . .

THE WIFE

Be kind.

THE BEST FRIEND

There are customs . . .

THE DOCTOR

(Not hurt; not angry; shrugs)

And you had them . . . the surgeons, the consultants, younger—well, not brash, but I doubt you'd have wanted that . . .

THE WIFE

. . . some bouncy intern with a scalpel in one hand, a racquet under his arm . . .

THE MISTRESS *(Mildly annoyed)*

Don't be ridiculous.

THE DOCTOR *(Chuckles)*

I'm rather like a priest: you have me for the limits, for birth and dying, *and* for the minor cuts and scratches in between. If that nagging cough keeps nagging, now it's not *me* opens up the throat or the chest; not *me*. *I* send you on to *other* men . . . and very quickly. I am the most . . . general of practitioners.

THE MISTRESS

I'm sorry.

THE DOCTOR

'Course, if you think some younger man would do better here, have him back on his feet and at the fireplace, clinking the ice in a bourbon, looking better than ever . . .

THE MISTRESS *(Wants no more of it)*

No! I *said* I am sorry. Just . . . railing against it.
  (Gently)
I *am* sorry.

THE BEST FRIEND

  (To THE MISTRESS, *really; but, to* THE DOCTOR, *and to the others)*
The custom of the house. And it *has* been, for so long. "You end up with what you start out with."

THE WIFE

  (Quiet, choked laughter)
Oh; God! "The little girl I was when he came to me."

THE MISTRESS *(After a pause)*

The house? The custom of which house?

THE BEST FRIEND

  (Dogged, not unpleasant)
Of wherever he is: the house he carries on his back, or in his head.

THE MISTRESS

  (Mildly assertive; slightly bewildered)
Well . . . I thought I knew it *all*: having been so . . . having participated so fully.

THE WIFE *(To* THE BEST FRIEND*)*

Is it written on one of your lovely things? . . . your pieces of paper? That we end up with what we start out with? Or that *he* does?

THE BEST FRIEND *(Quiet smile)*

No.

THE WIFE

I thought not, for Dr. Dey, who brought him into this world . . . into all this, went down with that boat, ship, rather—the iceberg one, or was it the German sub; the iceberg, I think.

THE SON

Titanic.

THE WIFE

Thank you.

THE NURSE

Dey did not go down with a ship.

THE WIFE AND THE BEST FRIEND
(*Slightly overlapping, almost simultaneously*)

He did *not?*

THE NURSE (*To* THE DOCTOR)

May I? . . .

(THE DOCTOR *nods*)

. . . Dey went down with what we all go down with, and one *day,* you will
forgive the pun, he realized the burning far too up in the chest, and the
sense of the kidneys saying they can not go on, and the sudden knowledge
that it has all gone on . . . from what central, possibly stoppable place—like
eating that last, unwanted shard, that salad, breathing that air from the top
of . . . where?—that one thing we are born to discover and never find.

(*Pause*)

He locused in on his killer, and he looked on it, and he said, "I will not have
you."

(*Pause*)

And so he booked on the Titanic, of *course.*

THE SON (*Abstracted*)

Well . . . that is what I thought.

THE MISTRESS (*Sensing something*)

Of course.

THE NURSE (*Lighter*)

Or something like it. I mean, if the cancer's on you and you're a doctor to
boot and know the chances *and* the pain, well . . . what do you do save
book on a boat you think's going to run into an iceberg and sink.

THE SON (*Frowning*)

Oh. Then he did *not* go down on the Titanic.

THE NURSE

No; he went to Maine, to his lodge, and fished . . . for about a week. Then
he killed himself.

THE WIFE

And the story of the ship . . .

THE NURSE

. . . was a fiction, invented by his wife and agreed to by his mistress, by the
happy coincidence that the Titanic *did* go down when he did. Oh, nobody
believed it, you understand; the obituaries were candid; but it became a
euphemism and was eventually accepted.

THE WIFE

Poor woman.

THE MISTRESS

Poor *women*.

THE WIFE

Who was his mistress? I didn't know he had one.

THE NURSE (*Casual*)

I was.

THE WIFE

My gracious; you're . . . *old, aren't* you.

THE NURSE

Yes; very.

THE WIFE

(*After the slightest pause*)

It never occurred to me before. You've always been such a . . . presence. I
don't believe a single word you've told us.

THE NURSE (*Shrugs*)

I don't care.

(*Returns to her place by the bed.*)

(*Pause*)

THE DOCTOR

You see . . .

THE MISTRESS (*Quite annoyed*)

You *always* say that!

THE WIFE

(*Not sure, but interested*)

Does he?

THE DOCTOR

You see, I did my tithe all at once, in the prisons, when I was young. After
my internship; I went to help.

THE WIFE

We never knew that.

THE MISTRESS

No.

THE DOCTOR

No?

(*Shrugs, chuckles*)

It was a while ago: it was before our minds had moved to the New Testament, or our reading of it. Men would die, then—for their killings—soon, if . . . well, perhaps not decently, but what passed for decently if burning a man alive survived the test . . . we were all Old Testament Jews, and we still are, two hundred million of us, save the children, for we believe what we no longer practice . . . *if: if* the justice was merciful, for that is what sets us medicine men apart from jurors: we are not in a hurry. But, I was with them; stayed with them; helped them have what they wanted for the last time. I would be with them, and they were alone in the death cells, no access to each other, and the buggery was over, had it ever begun, the buggery and the rest; and there were some, in the final weeks, who had abandoned sex, masturbation, for God, or fear, or some enveloping withdrawal, but not all; some . . . some made love to themselves in a frenzy—indeed, I treated more than one who was bleeding from it, from so much—and several confided to me that their masturbation image was their executioner . . . some fancy of how he looked.

THE WIFE
(Remembering an announcement)
The little girl I was when he came to me.

THE DOCTOR
You see:

THE WIFE *(Laughing a little)*
You see? No one cares.

THE DOCTOR
I . . . am eighty-six . . . which, I was informed by my grandson, or perhaps my great-nephew—I confuse them, not the two, but the . . .
(Confiding)
well, they look alike, and have what I confess I think of as wigs, though I know they are not . . .
(Some, though not fruity, longing here)
. . . long, lovely . . . turning down and underneath at the shoulders . . . blond and grail-like hair . . . but they said . . . or one of them did . . .
(Not loud, but emphasized)
. . . "Eighty-six! Man, that means going out!" Well, of course, I knew what they meant, but I was coy with it— and I asked them why—what does that make me? "Eighty-six and out." Does that make me . . . and suddenly I knew! I knew I wanted to lie in the long blond hair, put my lips there in the back of the neck, with the blond hair over me . . .

THE SON *(Great urgency)*
I don't *follow* you!

THE DOCTOR
I was completing what I had begun before: how we become enraptured by it . . .

(Small smile)

. . . by the source of our closing down. You see: I suddenly loved my exe-
cutioners . . . well, figurative; and in the way of . . . nestling up against
them, huddling close—for we do seek warmth, affection even, from those
who tell us we are going to die, or when.

THE MISTRESS *(After a pause)*

I believe in the killing; *some* of it; for *some* of them.

THE WIFE

Of *course*. Give us a theory and we'll do it in.

THE BEST FRIEND *(Quiet distaste)*

You *can't* believe in it.

THE WIFE

See . . . your own wife.

THE BEST FRIEND

(Gut betrayal, but soft-keyed)

You *can't* do that. There was no killing there.

THE WIFE

Just . . . divorce. It wasn't *us* that did her in—our . . . late summer . . .
arrangement: there had been others. *Our* . . . mercy to each other, by the
lake, the city . . . *that* didn't take a wild woman who could still bake bread
and give a party half the time and send her spinning back into the animal
brain; no, my dear; fucking—as it is called in public by everyone these
days—is not what got at her; yours and mine, I mean. Divorce: leave *alone*.
So don't tell *me* you don't believe in murder. You *do*. *I* do.

(Indicates THE MISTRESS*)*

She does, and admits it.

THE SON *(Without moving)*

I WANT TO TALK TO HIM!

THE BEST FRIEND

(To THE WIFE, *quiet; intense)*

You said she was insane. You *all* said it.

THE WIFE *(Rather dreamy)*

Did I? Well, perhaps I meant she was *going*.

(Enigmatic smile)

Perhaps we all did.

(To THE SON*)*

Then talk to him. You can preface every remark by saying "for the first and
last time." And you'll get no argument—there's *that*. I'd not *do* it, though.

(Dry)

You'd start to cry; you've little enough emotion in you: I'd save it.

THE SON

(To his mother; frustration; controlled rage)
He's *dying!*

THE WIFE

(Sad; comforting; explaining)
I *know.*

THE BEST FRIEND

(Quiet; more or less to himself)
It was progressive. I *asked* them. The violence was transitional.
(To THE WIFE*)*
I saw her not two months ago.

THE MISTRESS

(Seeing that THE WIFE *is preoccupied)*
Did you!

THE BEST FRIEND

I had been to the club, and was getting in my car; another pulled up along-
side and someone said—coolly, I think—"Well; I declare." It was a voice I
knew, and I turned my head and it was her sister behind the wheel, with
another woman in the death seat beside her, as it is called. "I *do* declare," she
said—definitely cool—and I perceived it in an instant, before I looked, that
my wife was in the back, my ex-wife, and the woman in the front was from
the hospital: no uniform, but an attendant of some sort. "Look who we have
here!" That was the way she talked, the smile set, the eyes madder than my
wife's could ever be—a sane woman, though. The attendant was smoking, I
remember that. Of course I looked, and indeed she *was* there, in the back,
catercorner, a fur rug half backdrop, half cocoon, and how small she was in
it! "Look who's here," her sister said, this time addressing *her,* her head
turned to catch both our expressions. The windows were down and I put my
hands on the sill—if that *is* what car doors have—and bent down some.
"Hello," I said, "how are you?", realizing as I said it that if she laughed in my
face, or screamed, or went for me I would not have been surprised. She
smiled, though, and stroked the fur beside her cheek with the back of her
hand. Her voice was calm, and extremely . . . rested. "It's fine in here," she
said, "how is it out there?" I didn't reply: I was so aware of her eyes on me,
and her sister's, and the attendant not turned, but looking straight ahead, and
smoking. She went on: "Oh, it would be so nice to say to you, 'Come closer,
so I can whisper something to you.' That way I could put my hand to the back
of your head and say very softly, 'Help me'; either that or rub my lips against
your ear, the way you like, and then *grab* you with my teeth, and hold on as
you pulled away, blood, and ripping." It was so . . . objective, and without ran-
cor, I didn't move at all; the attendant did, I remember; she turned. "I can't
do that, though," my wife said—sadly, I think. "Do you know why?" "No, I

don't know why." "Because," she said, "when I look at your ear I see the rump
and the tail of a mouse coming out from it; he must be chewing very deeply."
I didn't move; my fingers stayed where they were. It could be I was trying to
fashion some reply, but there *is* none to that. Her sister gunned the motor
then; having seen me when she parked, she must have thought to keep it
idling. "Nice to see you," she said to me, the same grim smile, mad eyes, and
she backed out, curving, shifted, and moved off. And what I retain of their
leaving, most of all, above the mouse, my wife, my*self*, for that matter, is the
sound of her sister's bracelet clanking against the steering wheel—a massive
gold chain with a disc suspended from it, a large thin disc, with her first name,
in facsimile, scrawled across one face of it; that; clanking as she shifted.

   (Pause)

THE WIFE

(Having listened to almost all the story)
Then I'm sorry.

THE BEST FRIEND

(Quietly; a little weary)
It's all right.
   (Pause)

THE SON

It's not true, you know: there's more emotion in me than you think.

THE WIFE *(Gentle, placating)*

Well, I hope so.
   (Pause; to THE MISTRESS*)*
You're very silent.

THE MISTRESS

I was *wondering* about that: why I *was*. I'd *noticed* it and was rather puzzled. It's not my *way*.

THE WIFE *(Agreeing)*

No.

THE MISTRESS

Outsider, I guess.

THE WIFE *(Friendly)*

Oh, stop!

THE MISTRESS

No; really; yes. In this context. Listening to you was a capping on it, I suppose: *God;* that was effective as you did it, and I dare say you *needed* it.
Maybe that's how we keep the nineteenth century going for ourselves: pretend it exists, and . . . well . . . outsider.

THE WIFE

(Objective curiosity, but friendly)

What will you *do?*

THE MISTRESS

(Thinks about that for a while)

I don't *know.* I really don't. Give me a schedule. Who runs to the coverlet first? And who throws her arms where, and where, and where does it matter? Who grabs the shoulders, to shake the death out of them, and who collapses at the knees?

THE WIFE *(Not sure, herself)*

You don't *know.*

THE MISTRESS *(Laughs, so sadly)*

Oh, God, the little girl you were when he came to you.

THE WIFE *(Sad truth)*

Yes!

THE MISTRESS *(Sad truth)*

I don't *know.*

(THE DAUGHTER *enters; her swift opening of the door jars them all to quiet attention; she chuckles a little, unpleasantly, at their reaction, and moves to the fireplace without a word; she rests her hands on the mantel, and stares into the fire)*

Ultimately, an outsider. I was *thinking* about that, and I concluded it was ritual that made it so.

(Looking about; almost amused)

This is . . . ritual, is it not?

(Normal tone)

Twenty years without it, except an awkwardness at Christmas, perhaps.

(To THE WIFE*)*

I remember one December in particular, when it was in the papers you were suing for divorce. Glad you didn't, I think; it would have forced him to marry me . . . or not. Move off.

(Generally)

He missed you all then. Oh, he always *has* . . . mildly, but *that* Christmas— we were at the lodge; it was the next year we took to the islands, to avoid the season as much as anything, though it *was* good for his back, the sun— that one in particular, we sat before the great fire, with all the snow and the pines, and I knew he missed . . . well: family.

(Small laugh)

He missed the ritual, I think.

(Not unkindly)

I doubt you were very good with Christmas, though; hardly . . . prototypical: wassail, and chestnuts.

THE SON (*Slightly triste*)

Once. Chestnuts.

THE WIFE (*To* THE MISTRESS; *a smile*)

You *are* right.

THE MISTRESS

In front of the fire; Christmas Eve. We *had* been holding hands, but were *not;* not at that moment, and did he sigh? Perhaps; but there was a great . . . all of a sudden, a . . . slack, and I caught his profile as he stared into the fire, that . . . marvelous granite, and it was as if he had . . . deflated, just perceptibly. I took his hand, and he turned to me and smiled: came back. I said, "You should spend it with *them;* every *year.*" He said he thought not, and it was not for *my* sake.

THE DAUGHTER

(*Still staring into the fire; she intones the word, spreads it*)

Drone. Drone!

THE MISTRESS

(*Looks up at* THE DAUGHTER's *back, pauses a moment, looks out at nothing; continues*)

It *is* the ritual, you see, that gives me the sense. The first few times I wouldn't go to his doctorates, until he *made* me do it, and the banquets when he *spoke!* Naturally, I've never thought of myself as a secret—for I am not a tart, and I would never have been good at it—but the rituals remind me of what I believe is called my . . . status. To be something so fully, and yet . . . well, no matter.

(*A quick, bright laugh; the next directed to* THE WIFE)

I wonder: if I had been *you*—the little girl you were when he came to you—would you have come along, as I did? Would *you* have come to take *my* place?

THE DAUGHTER

(*As* THE WIFE *is about to speak; turns, but stays at the fireplace*)

They're all down there! The cameramen, the television crews, the reporters. They gave me a container of coffee.

THE WIFE

Well, why aren't they being *looked* after? Didn't you tell them in the kitchen to see what was needed, and . . .

THE DAUGHTER

The ones out*side:* the crews with their trucks and lights. *They* gave me the coffee.

(*Laughs, but it is not pleasant*)

It's like a *fungus.* The TV people are on the stoop, with all their equipment on the sidewalk, and you and your tubes and wires! Like a fungus: all of those outside, and the photographers have assumed the entrance hall, like a stag line—nobody sits!, and the newspapermen have taken the library, for that is where the Scotch is.

THE WIFE *(To* THE BEST FRIEND*)*
Go down and *do* something!

THE DAUGHTER
(It is clear she's enjoying it, in a sad way)
Don't bother! It's all been set. Touch it and you'll have it on the landing. Leave it.
(Looks toward her father's bed; overplayed)
Who *is* this man?

THE WIFE *(Trailing off)*
Well, I suppose . . .

THE DAUGHTER
I forgot to mention the police.

THE WIFE *(Mild anxiety)*
The police!

THE DAUGHTER *(Very much "on")*
For the people. Well, there aren't many there now, people, twenty-five, maybe—the kind of crowd you'd get for a horse with sunstroke, if it were summer. The TV has brought them out, the trucks and the tubes. They're lounging, nothing better to do, and if it weren't a weekend, I doubt they'd linger. I mean, God, we don't have the President in here, or anything.

THE SON *(Quiet, but dismayed)*
Don't talk like that.

THE WIFE *(To* THE BEST FRIEND*)*
Shouldn't you go down?

THE BEST FRIEND *(Shakes his head)*
No; it's a public event; *will* be.

THE NURSE
That's the final test of fame, isn't it, the degree of it: which is newsworthy, the act of dying itself, or merely the death.

THE MISTRESS *(Aghast)*
MERELY!

THE NURSE *(Almost a reproach)*
I wasn't speaking for me, *or* you. *Them.* The public; whether it's enough for them to read about it in the papers without a kind of anger at having

missed the dying, too. They were cheated with the Kennedys, both of them, *and* with King. It happened so fast; all people could figure for themselves was they'd been clubbed in the face by history. Even poor Bobby; he took the longest, but everybody knew he was dead before he died. Christ, that loathsome doctor on the tube kept telling us.

(*Imitation of a person despised*)

"There's no chance at *all* as I see it; the hemorrhaging, the bullet where it is. No chance. No chance." Jesus, you couldn't even *hope*. It was a disgusting night; it made me want to be young, and a man, and violent and unreasoning—rage so that it meant something. Pope John was the last one the public could share in—two weeks of the vilest agony, and conscious to the very end, unsedated, because it was something his God wanted him to experience. I don't know, maybe a bullet *is* better. In spite of everything.

THE WIFE

Perhaps.

THE MISTRESS (Quiet sadness)

What a sad and shabby time we live in.

THE WIFE

Yes.

THE DAUGHTER

(*Begins to laugh; incredulous, cruel*)

You . . . hypocrites!

THE WIFE

Oh?

THE DAUGHTER

You pious hypocrites!

(*Mocking*)

The sad and shabby time we live in. "Yes." You dare to sit there and shake your heads like that!?

(*To* THE WIFE)

To hell with you with your . . . affair with him, though that's not bad for sad and shabby, *is* it.

(*Points to* THE MISTRESS)

But what about *her!*

THE WIFE (Curious)

What *about* her?

THE MISTRESS (She, too)

Yes; what *about* me?

THE DAUGHTER

Mistress is a pretty generous term for what it's all about, isn't it? So is *kept*.

Isn't that *another* euphemism? And how much do you think she's gotten from him? Half a million? A million?

THE MISTRESS

There are things you do *not* know, little girl.

THE WIFE (*Steel*)

You live with a man who will not divorce his wife, who has become a drunkard because of him, and who is doubtless supplied with her liquor gratis from *his liquor* store—a business which is, I take it, the height of his ambition—who has taken more money from you than I like to think about, who has broken one rib that I know of, and blackened your eyes, and has *dared* . . . *dared* to come to me and suggest I intercede with your father . . .

THE DAUGHTER (*Furious*)

ALL RIGHT!

THE WIFE

. . . in a political matter which *stank* of the Mafia . . .

THE DAUGHTER (*A scream*)

ALL RIGHT!

THE WIFE

(*A change of tone to loss*)

You know a lot about sad and shabby; you know far too much to turn the phrase on others, especially on those who do *not* make a point of doing what they will or must as badly as possible. That is probably what I have come to love you so little for—that *you* love yourself so little. Don't ever tell *me* how to make a life, or *anyone* who does things out of love, or even affection.

(*Pause*)

You were beautiful, you know. You really were. Once.

(THE DAUGHTER *opens her mouth as if to respond; thinks otherwise; moves away. Silence as they think on this*)

THE MISTRESS

(*Some delight; really to bring them all back*)

My parents are both still alive—I suddenly remember. They are neither . . . particularly *limber*, they keep to themselves more than not, and my father's eyesight is such that when he dares to drive at all it is down the center line of the road. Oh, it makes the other drivers cautious. She's learned that snapping at him does no good at all, and the one time she put her hand on the wheel, thinking—she told me later—that his drift to the left was becoming more pronounced than ever, he resisted her, and the result was weaving, and horns, and a ditch, or shoulder, whichever it is, and a good deal of heavy breathing.

THE BEST FRIEND

Why doesn't *she* drive?

THE MISTRESS

(Smiles a little)

No; she could learn, but I imagine she'd rather sit there with him and see things his way.

THE DAUGHTER *(Dry)*

Why doesn't she walk, or take a taxi, or just not go?

THE MISTRESS

(Knows she is being mocked, but prefers to teach rather than hit back)

Oh; she loves him, you see.

(Laughs again)

My *grand*father died only last *year.*

THE DAUGHTER *(Spat out)*

Oh, *stop* it!

THE MISTRESS *(Controlled)*

Please stop telling me to stop it.

(Generally)

He was a hundred and three, my mother's father, and he was not at all like those centenarians you're always reading about: full head of snow-white hair, out chopping wood all the time when they weren't burying their fourth wife or doing something worthy in the Amazon; not a bit of it. He was a wispy little man, whom none of us liked very much—not even my mother, who would be a saint one day, were it not for Luther; a tiny man, with the face of a starving child, and blond hair of the type that white does not become, and very little of that, and bones, it would appear, of the finest porcelain, for he fell, when he was seventy-two, and did to his pelvis what you would do to a teapot were you to drop it on a flagstone floor.

THE DOCTOR *(Factual; nothing else)*

The bones dry out.

THE MISTRESS

Indeed they must, for he took to his bed—or was taken there—and remained in it for thirty-one years. He wanted to be read to a lot.

THE WIFE

(She tries to get the two words out sensibly, but breaks up during it into a helpless laughter; she covers her mouth, and her eyes dart from person to person; the words are:)

Poor man!

(Finally she quiets herself, but a glance at her daughter staring at her with distaste sends her into another outburst; this one she controls rather more easily)

THE MISTRESS

(After the second outburst has quieted; very serious)

Shh, now. As I said, he wanted to be read to a lot.

*(*THE WIFE *smothers giggles occasionally during this)*

This was not easy for his family and fast-diminishing set of friends, for he was hard of hearing and one had to shout;

(She holds her right index finger up)

plus; plus, everyone knew he had the eyesight of a turkey buzzard.

*(*THE BEST FRIEND *starts to giggle a bit, too, now)*

THE DAUGHTER

Stop it!

THE MISTRESS

So, finally, of course, one had to start hiring people.

THE DAUGHTER

(As THE WIFE *laughs)*

Stop it!

THE WIFE

(She can no longer control her hysteria)

A turkey buzzard!?

(Her newest explosion of laughter is enough to set THE SON *off as well, and, to a lesser degree,* THE DOCTOR *and* THE NURSE*)*

THE DAUGHTER

Stop it!

THE WIFE

It's not *true, is* it!

THE MISTRESS *(As she breaks up, herself)*

No; not a word of it!

(Note: While this laughter should have the look, to those who have watched it, and the feel, to those who have experienced it, of the self-generating laughter possible under marijuana, we should be aware that it is, in truth, produced by extreme tension, fatigue, ultimate sadness and existentialist awareness: in other words . . . the reason we always react that way. Further note: The ones who have laughed least freely should stop most precipitously, though THE SON *might keep his mirth awhile longer than most.* THE WIFE *and* THE MISTRESS *have an arm around one another)*

THE DAUGHTER

(She has been saying, "Stop it, stop it; stop it, you fucking bitches!" all through the ultimate laughter, mostly to THE WIFE *and* THE

MISTRESS, *but at* THE SON, THE NURSE, THE BEST FRIEND *and* THE DOCTOR *as well. Clearly, she has meant it for them all, for, as they stop, not without a whoop or two at her from time to time, her volume stays constant, so that, finally, hers is the voice we hear, and hers only*)

Stop it; stop it; stop it, you bitches, you filthy . . . you filth who allow it . . . you . . . you . . .

(*Stop*)

THE WIFE

(*She is the one who stops first, becomes fixed on* THE DAUGHTER)

You! *You* stop it!

THE DAUGHTER

You bitches! You fucking . . .

(*Stops; realizes*)

THE WIFE

(*A quiet, post-hysterical smile*)

Why don't you go home to your *own* filth? You . . . you . . . issue!

(*Sits back, eyes her coldly*)

THE DAUGHTER (*Rage only, now*)

Your morality is . . . it's incredible; it really is; it's a model for the world. You're smug, and excluding. You're incredible! All of you!

THE WIFE (*Calm; seemingly detached*)

Well, since you've nothing else to do, why don't you run downstairs and tell the waiting press about . . . *our* morality? And while you're at it . . . tell them about your own as well.

THE DAUGHTER

(*So intense she can barely get it through her teeth*)

This woman has come and taken . . . my . . . *father!*

THE WIFE

(*After a pause; not sad; a little weary; empty, perhaps*)

Yes. My *hus*band. Remember?

(*Sighs*)

And that makes all the difference. Perhaps your fancy man has people who care for him, who worry after him; they are not my concern. They may be *yours*, but I doubt it. *I* . . . *care*; about what happens *here*. This woman loves my husband—as *I* do—and she has made him happy; as *I* have. She is good, and decent, and she is not moved by envy and self-loathing . . .

THE DAUGHTER (*Close to rage again*)

. . . like some people?!! . . .

THE WIFE

... Indeed. Like *some* people.

THE DAUGHTER *(A stuck record)*

Like *you!?* Like *you!?* Like *you!?*

THE WIFE

(Shuts her eyes for a moment, as if to shut out the sound)

Somewhere, in the rubble you've made of your life so far, you must have an instinct tells you why she's part of us. No? She *loves* us. And we love *her.*

THE DAUGHTER *(A rough, deep voice)*

Do *you* love *me?*

(Pause; her tone becomes fiercer)

Does *anyone* love me?

THE WIFE

(A bright little half-caught laugh escapes her; her tone instantly becomes serious)

Do *you* love anyone?

(A silence.

THE DAUGHTER *stands for a moment, swaying, quivering just perceptibly; then she turns on her heel, opens the door and slams it behind her)*

THE BEST FRIEND

(As THE WIFE *sighs, reaches for* THE MISTRESS' *hand)*

Will she? Will she go down and tell the waiting press?

THE WIFE *(True curiosity)*

I don't *know.* I don't think she would; but I don't *know.*

(Laughs as she did before)

I laughed before, because it was so unlikely. I had an aunt, a moody lady, but with cause. She died when she was twenty-six—died in the heart, that is, or whatever portion of the brain controls the spirit; she went on, all the appearances, was snuffed out, finally, at sixty-two, in a car crash, all done up in jodhpurs and a derby, yellow scarf with the foxhead stickpin, driving in the vintage car, the old silver touring car, the convertible with the window between the front and back seats, back from the stable, from jumping, curved, bashed straight into the bread truck, Parkerhouse rolls and blood, her twenty-six-year heart emptying out of her sixty-two-year body, on the foxhead pin and the metal and the gasoline, and all the cardboard boxes sprawled on the country road.

(Slight pause)

"Does anyone love me?" she asked, once, back when I was nine, or ten. There were several of us in the room, but they were used to it. "Do *you* love anyone?" I asked her back. Slap! Then tears—hers *and* mine; mine not from the pain but the ... effrontery; hers ... both; effrontery *and* pain.

THE MISTRESS *(After a short silence)*

Hmmmm. Yes.

(The door bursts open, and THE DAUGHTER *catapults into the room, leaving the door wide)*

THE DAUGHTER

YOU tell them!

*(*TWO PHOTOGRAPHERS AND A REPORTER *enter tentatively; in the moment it takes for the people assembled to react, they have moved a step or two in.*

Then the room moves into action. THE DOCTOR *and* THE NURSE *stay where they are, but transfixed;* THE SON *rises from his chair;* THE BEST FRIEND *takes a step or two forward;* THE WIFE *and* THE MISTRESS *rise, poised)*

THE BEST FRIEND

Get back downstairs; you can't come . . .

(But it is THE WIFE *and* THE MISTRESS *who move)*

THE WIFE

(A beast's voice, really)

Get . . . out . . . of . . . here!

(The two women attack, fall upon the intruders with fists and feet, and there is an animal fury within them which magnifies their strength. The struggle is brief, but intense; one of the cameramen has his camera knocked to the floor, where he leaves it as the three men retreat. THE WIFE *forces the door shut, turns, leans against it.* THE DAUGHTER *has her back to the audience, with* THE WIFE *and* THE MISTRESS *to either side of her, facing her. No words; heavy breathing; almost a tableau.*

Finally; it is an animal's sound; rage, pain)

AARRRGGGHHH.

(Two seconds silence)

CURTAIN

ACT TWO

The scene: the same as before, a couple of hours later. THE DOC-
TOR *and* THE NURSE *are at the bed, half asleep on their feet, or
perhaps* THE DOCTOR *has fallen asleep on a chair near the bed.*
THE BEST FRIEND *is by the fireplace, gazing into it;* THE WIFE *is
dozing in a chair;* THE MISTRESS *is in a chair near the fireplace;*
THE DAUGHTER *is in a chair somewhat removed from the others,
facing front;* THE SON *is massaging her shoulders.*

*It seems very late: the exhaustion has overwhelmed them; even
awake they seem to be in a dream state. What one says is not
picked up at once by another.*

THE SON *(Gently)*

You shouldn't have done that. You know you shouldn't.

THE DAUGHTER

(Really not anxious to talk about it)

I know I shouldn't. Gentler.

THE SON

No matter how you feel.

THE DAUGHTER

I *know.* I *said* I *know.*

THE SON

If they'd gotten in . . .

THE DAUGHTER

Not with our sentries; you'd need an army for that.

THE SON

No matter *how* you feel.

THE DAUGHTER *(Languid)*

I feel . . . well, how you must have felt when you were young, at school,
and you'd fail, or be dismissed, to make some point you didn't know quite
what. Like that.

(Quite without emotion)

I feel like a child, rebellious, misunderstood and known oh, so very well;
sated and . . . empty. I'm *on* to myself; there's no mistake there. I'm all the
things you think of me, every one of you, and I'm also many more.

(An afterthought)

I wonder why they didn't kill me, the two of them.

THE SON

There's enough death going here.

THE DAUGHTER

Oh, I don't know. God knows, I can probably go my own way now, without a word or a look from any of you. Non grata *has* its compensations. Go my own way. What a relief.

(Ironic)

Back to that "degradation" of mine. Imagine her!, degrading a family as famous as this, up by its own bootstraps—well, the only one of it who mattered, anyway—all the responsibility to itself, the Puritan moral soul. How does it go?: "Since we have become what we are, then the double edge is on us; we cannot back down, for we are no longer private, and the world has its eye on us." Christ, you'd think we were only nominally mortal, *he* at any rate; he's the only one who matters, and *he's* mortal enough, is going to prove to be. Well, I'll be glad when he's gone— no, no, not for the horrid reasons, not for all of your mistakes about me, but simply that the tintype can be thrown away, the sturdy group, and I can be what I choose to be with only half of the disapproval, no longer the public. *You* won't get in the press because you're someone's son, unless you get arrested for something serious, *or* newsworthy. Nor will I. I'll have my man—such as he is and such as I want him for—and only mother will really mind. We'll see each other less, all of us, and finally not at all, I'd imagine—except on . . . occasions. Whatever we disdain will be our own affair. You can, too, probably, very soon . . . when all *this* is finished.

THE SON

Do *what.*

THE DAUGHTER

Resign . . . You'll be rich enough, or do you want to go on with it, even when he's gone? Isn't it pointless for you there? Aren't you useless?

THE SON *(Wry little laugh)*

Probably. I don't like it very much; I don't feel *part* of it, though it's a way of getting through from ten to six, and avoiding all I know I'd be doing if I didn't have it . . .

(Smiles a bit)

those demons of mine.

THE DAUGHTER *(Laughs a little)*

Ah, those demons. You're no different.

(Turns toward THE BEST FRIEND*)*

Will you keep him on—

    (*Mildly mocking*)

at the *firm*—after . . . all this is finished, and you've no more obligation to our father, or did you make a bond to keep it up forever?

                THE BEST FRIEND (*Quietly*)

There's no bond; your brother isn't with me as a charity.

    (*To* THE SON)

You don't think that, do you? You fill your position nicely and you're nicely paid for doing it. If you choose to leave, of course, nothing will falter, nor, for that matter, will I feel any . . . particular loss, but we know that about each other, don't we. But no one's waiting to throw you down. That's your sister's manner.

    (*To* THE DAUGHTER)

Don't ask me to talk about it now.

                   THE SON

    (*To* THE BEST FRIEND; *very simple*)

I didn't know that you didn't care for me. I suppose I always assumed . . . well, that we were all a form of family, and . . .

    (*Shrugs*)

              THE DAUGHTER (*Sad advice*)

Don't assume.

                 THE SON

Well; no matter.

          THE BEST FRIEND (*A little impatient*)

Did I say I didn't *care* for you? I thought I said I'd feel no loss if you were gone. I'm pretty much out of loss.

    (*He turns back to the fire*)

                 THE SON

Sorry; that *is* what you said.

    (*To* THE DAUGHTER)

Enough? More?

               THE DAUGHTER

The base of the neck, and slowly, very slowly. Uh hunh.

    (*Sensuous, as he massages her neck*)

They were animals, and I had a moment of . . . absolutely thrilling dread, very much as when I read of the Chinese, and how they are adept at keeping a man alive and conscious, *conscious,* for hours, while they strip the skin from his body. They tie him to a pole.

                 THE SON

What for?

THE DAUGHTER

So he won't wander off, I'd imagine. I'm not your usual masochist, in spite of what *she* thinks. I mean, a broken rib really *hurts,* and everybody over twelve knows what a black eye on a lady *means.* I don't fancy any of that, but I do care an awful lot about the guilt I can produce in those that do the hurting.

(*Suddenly a little girl*)

Mother?

THE SON

She's sleeping.

THE DAUGHTER

(*Turns to* THE MISTRESS)

You're not.

THE MISTRESS (*Coming back*)

Hm?

THE DAUGHTER

You're not, *are* you. Sleeping.

THE MISTRESS

(*Not hostile; still half away*)

No. I'm far too exhausted.

THE DAUGHTER

(*To* THE SON; *plaintive*)

Wake mother up.

THE BEST FRIEND (*Sotto voce*)

Let her sleep, for God's sake!

THE MISTRESS (*Voice low; cool*)

Do you want to start in again? Do you have some new pleasure for us?

THE DAUGHTER (*Heavy sigh*)

I want to tell her that I'm sorry.

THE MISTRESS

I dare say she knows that; has, for years.

THE DAUGHTER

Still . . .

THE MISTRESS

Nobody's a fool here.

THE DAUGHTER (*Mildly biting*)

You were never a mother.

THE MISTRESS (*Smiles*)

No, nor have you been, but you've been a woman.

THE DAUGHTER (*Ironic*)

And the old instinct's always there, right?

THE MISTRESS

Right.

THE DAUGHTER

But you have been a wife, haven't you, twice as I remember, not to count your adventures in mistresshood. How many men have you gone through, hunh? No divorces, you; just bury them.

THE MISTRESS (*Calm, but intent*)

Listen to me, young lady, there are things you have no idea of, matters might cross your mind were you not so . . . self-possessed. You lash out—which can be a virtue, I dare say, stridency aside, if it's used to protect and not just as a revenge . . .

THE DAUGHTER (*To cut it off*)

O.K. O.K.

THE MISTRESS

. . . but you're careless, not only with facts, but of your*self.* What words will you ever have left if you use them all to kill? What words will you summon up when the day *comes,* as it may, poor you, when you suddenly discover that you've been in love—oh, for a week, say, and not known it, not having been familiar with the symptoms, being such an amateur? Love with mercy, I mean, the kind you can't hold back as a reward, or use as any sort of weapon. What vocabulary will you have for that? Perhaps you'll be mute; many are—the self-conscious—in a foreign land, with only the phrases the guidebook gives them, or maybe it will be dreamlike for you—nightmarish—lockjawed, throat constricted, knowing that whatever word you use, whatever phrase you might say will come out, not as you mean it then, but as you have meant before, that "I love you; I need you," no mat-ter how joyously meant, will be the snarl of a wounded and wounding ani-mal. You'd better go back to grade school.

THE DAUGHTER

(*Contempt and self-disgust*)

Oh, I'm far too old for that, aren't I?

THE MISTRESS (*Shrugs*)

Perhaps you are. It would serve you right.

THE DAUGHTER

There's ignorance enough in you, too, you know. You've not been that much in touch—except with *him,* and he's hardly one to keep you up to date.

THE MISTRESS

So true. But—and I *do* hate to say it, I really do—unless you're some kind of unique, I've seen your type before.

THE DAUGHTER *(Quietly)*

Fuck yourself.

(To THE SON*)*
You've stopped.

THE SON *(Not starting again)*

Yes. My fingers ache.

THE DAUGHTER

(Quietly, without emotion)
You never were much good at anything.

THE MISTRESS

(To THE BEST FRIEND; *mock ingenuous)*
How am I supposed to do that, I wonder?

THE BEST FRIEND *(Dry, weary)*

It's usually said to men, but even there it's a figure of speech.

(He shakes his head, turns back to the fire)
Don't involve me; please.

*(*THE DOCTOR *has moved toward them; he stands for a moment)*

THE DOCTOR *(Quietly)*

That's very interesting; it *is*.

THE SON *(Soft, but frightened)*

What is?

THE DOCTOR

His heart stopped beating . . . for three beats. Then it started again.

THE DAUGHTER *(To* THE SON; *anxious)*

Wake mother!

THE DOCTOR *(With a gesture)*

No; no; it *began* again.

THE DAUGHTER

Maybe you were asleep: you're old enough.

THE DOCTOR

Surely, but I wasn't. Fall asleep with the stethoscope to his chest, dream of stop and go? Wake immediately, jolted back by the content? No. His heart stopped beating . . . for three beats. Then it started again. Nothing less than that. I thought I'd report it.

(He starts to turn back; returns)

It's interesting when it happens, but it's nothing to write home about. Just thought I'd report it, that's all.

THE MISTRESS

What does it signify? It must, something.

THE DOCTOR *(Thinks, shrugs)*

Weakening. What did you mean, something conscious like fighting it off?

THE MISTRESS *(Wistful)*

Maybe.

THE DOCTOR *(Gentle; a smile)*

Nooooo. You're better than that.
(He moves back whence he came)

THE DAUGHTER

They tell you more on television.
*(*THE MISTRESS *laughs a little)*

They do!

THE MISTRESS

In a way.

THE SON *(Sober)*

Just think: it could have been finished then.
(Quickly)

I don't mean anything but the wonder of it.

THE MISTRESS *(Dry)*

Why, don't you believe in suffering?

THE DAUGHTER

Does he know he is? Suffering?

THE MISTRESS

I didn't mean him.
(Refers first to THE DAUGHTER, *then* THE SON*)*

I meant you . . . and you. I *do:* believe in suffering.

THE DAUGHTER *(Quiet scorn)*

What *are* you, a fundamentalist, one of those "God designed it so it must be right" persons, down deep beneath the silvery surface?

THE SON

She didn't mean that.

THE DAUGHTER *(Ibid.)*

How would *you* know? You're not much good at anything.

THE SON *(To* THE MISTRESS*)*

Did you? *Mean* that?

THE MISTRESS

I meant at least two things, as I usually do.

(*To* THE DAUGHTER)

No divorces, I just bury them? Well; what would you have me do? I know, you meant it as a way of speaking; you were trying to be unkind, but keep it in mind should your lover be rid of his wife, marry you, and die. You've been a woman, but you haven't been a wife. It isn't very nice, you know, to get it all at once—for both my deaths were sudden: heart attack, and car.

(*Sighs, almost begins to laugh*)

Well, maybe it's better than . . .

(*Indicates the room with a general gesture*)

this. It's all done at once, and you're empty; you go from that to grief without the intervening pain. You can't suffer with a man because he's dead; his dying, yes. The only horror in participating is . . .

(*Thinks better of it*)

. . . well, another time.

(*Pause; shift of tone*)

Look here! You accused me before of being—what is that old-fashioned word?—a gold digger, of having insinuated myself into . . .

THE DAUGHTER

I said you *probably!*

THE MISTRESS

Yes, of course, but you're imprecise and I know what you meant. That I am expecting something less than I have received from your father—money, in other words, a portion of what you are expecting for having permitted yourselves to be born.

(*Turns to* THE BEST FRIEND, *takes his hand; he still stares into the fire*)

May I engage you?

(THE BEST FRIEND *shakes his head, leaves his hand where it is; she removes hers*)

No? All right.

(*Back to* THE DAUGHTER)

You will see, in good time.

(*Laughs*)

I remember a family once, two children, both well into their fifties, with a dying mother, eighty-something. These children—and there is no allegory here; read yourselves in if you want, but I hope not—these elderly children didn't like each other very much; the daughter had married perhaps not wisely for her second time—penniless, much younger than she, rather fruity to the eye and ear, but perhaps more of a man than most, you never know—but the reasons went further back, the dislike, to some genesis I came upon them too late for, and in the last months of their mother's life they did battle for a percentage of her will, for her estate. But fifty-fifty wouldn't do, and it would shift from that to sixty-forty—seventy-thirty once, I'm told! The mother, you see, had loved them both, and either one who came to her would tilt the balance. But she ended it exactly where she'd started it—half to each—and all that had happened was damage. The daughter was the one at fault, or more grievously, for she had been spoiled in a way that sons are seldom. But all of this is to tell you that I'm not an intruder in the dollar sense. I've more than enough—I was born with it. Don't you people ever take the trouble to scout? And I told your father I wanted nothing beyond his company . . . *and* love. He agreed with me, you'll be distressed to know, said *you needed* it. So. I am not your platinum blonde with the chewing gum and the sequined dress.

THE DAUGHTER *(After a pause)*
I'm supposed to like you now, I take it, fall into your arms and cry a little and choke out words like sorry and forgive. Well, you've got the wrong lady.

THE MISTRESS *(Light)*
I wouldn't expect it, and I really don't much care. I've more important things.
  (Less light)
He taught me a sense of values, you know, beyond what I'd thought was adequate. Cold, I suppose, but right on the button. Took a little while, but I guess I knew I'd go through this someday; so I learned. And you know something else? I'll be there at the funeral, ashes if I have my way—if *he* has *his*—but either way. It's one . . . ritual I'll not defer for.

THE DAUGHTER
You wouldn't dare!

THE MISTRESS
You don't know me, child.

THE DAUGHTER
I won't *have* it.

THE SON *(Gently)*
Be calm.

THE MISTRESS *(Laughs a little)*
It's not a mind gone mad with power, or a dip into impropriety, or the need to reopen a wound—for the wound *is* closed, you know, your mother knows; *you* do, too; you're railing because you never saw it open; *you* can't even find a scar; you don't know where it *was;* that *must* be infuriating—none of those things, but simply that I'll not be put down by sham, and I'll *be* there, dressed in my gray and white, a friend of the family. There'll be none of your Italian melodrama, with all the buzz as to who is that stranger off to one side, that woman in black whom nobody knows, wailing louder than the widow and the family put together. None of that. I have always known my place, and I shall know it then. Don't wake her. Let her sleep.

THE DAUGHTER

(As THE NURSE *approaches, tapping a cigarette)*

You're right: I *am* an amateur.

THE NURSE

May I join you?

(Nobody replies; she eases into a chair, clearly exhausted. She lights her cigarette, inhales, exhales with a great, slow breath)

Sensible shoes help, but when you're well up into the 'teens, like me, there's nothing for it but this, sometimes.

THE MISTRESS *(Looking away)*

Any change?

THE NURSE

No; none. Well, of course, some. Procession, but nothing, really.

(Looks at THE SON*)*

You're much too fat; heavy, rather.

THE SON *(Matter-of-fact)*

I'm sedentary.

THE NURSE

Eat less; do isometrics. You won't last out your fifties.

THE SON

(Quiet; an echo of something)

Maybe not?

THE NURSE

It's different for a woman: our hearts are better. Eat fish and raw vegetables and fruit; avoid everything you like.

(An afterthought)

Except sex; have a lot of that: fish, raw vegetables, fruit and sex.

THE SON *(Embarrassed)*

Th-thank you.

THE NURSE

Eggs, red flesh, milk-cheese-butter, nuts, most starches 'cept potatoes and rice . . . all bad for you; ignore them. Two whiskies before dinner, a glass of good burgundy *with* it, and sex before you go to sleep. That'll do the trick, keep you going.

THE SON

For?

THE NURSE

(Rather surprised at his question)

Until it's proper time for you to die. No point in rushing it.

THE DAUGHTER

(Eyes upward, head rolling from side to side; through her teeth)
Death; death; death; death; death . . .

THE NURSE

(Taking a drag on her cigarette)
Death, yes; well, it gets us where we live, doesn't it.

(A sound startles them. It comes from THE WIFE; *it is a sharp, exhaled "Ha-ah." The first one comes while she is still asleep in her chair. She bolts upright and awake. She does it again: "Haah")*

THE WIFE

(Fully awake, but still a trifle bewildered)
I was *asleep.* I *was asleep.* I was dreaming, and I dreamt I was asleep, and it wakened me. Have—have I . . . is every—every . . .

THE NURSE

It's all right; go back to sleep.

THE WIFE

No, I mustn't; I can't.

(She rises, a little unsteady, and begins to move toward THE DOCTOR)
Is everything all right, is . . .

THE DOCTOR

Everything is all right. Really.

*(*THE WIFE *moves toward the grouping, sees* THE DAUGHTER, *pauses, eyes her with cold loathing, moves to* THE MISTRESS *and* THE BEST FRIEND, *puts a hand absently on* THE MISTRESS' *shoulder, looks at* THE BEST FRIEND's *back, then at* THE NURSE)

THE WIFE

(To THE NURSE; *no reproach)*
Shouldn't you be back there?

THE NURSE *(Smiles)*

If I should be, I would be.

THE WIFE

Yes; I'm sorry.

(Generally; to no one, really)
I was dreaming of so many things, odd and . . . well, that I was shopping, for a kind of thread, a brand that isn't manufactured any more, and I knew it, but I thought that they might have some in the back. I couldn't remember the name of the maker, and of course that didn't help. They showed me several that were very much like it, one in particular that I almost settled on, but didn't. They tried to be helpful; it was what they used to call a dry goods store,

and it was called that, and I remember a specific . . . not smell, but scent the place had, one that I only remember from being little, so I was clearly in the past, and when they couldn't help, I asked if I could go in the back, the stock. They smiled and said of course, and so I went through a muslin curtain, into the stock, and it was not at all what I'd expected—shelves of cardboard boxes, bales of twine, bolts of fabric, some of the boxes with labels, some with buttons pasted to the end, telling what was there—none of it; it was all canned fruit, and vegetables, peas and carrots and string beans and waxed beans, and bottles of chili sauce and catsup, and canned meats, and everything else I'd not expected and was not a help to me. So I walked back through the muslin and into the living room my family'd had when I was twelve or so, a year before we moved. It was the room my aunt had slapped me in, and I sensed that I was asleep, and it woke me.

THE SON
(*Moves toward a door beside the fireplace, upstage*)

Excuse me.

THE MISTRESS (*Wistful*)

Dreams.

THE WIFE (*A little sad*)

Yes.

> (THE SON *closes the door behind him.* THE WIFE *turns to* THE BEST FRIEND)

Are you all right?

THE BEST FRIEND
(*Straightens up, turns, finally, sighs*)

I suppose. Trying to shut it all out helps. I felt a rush of outrage—back awhile—not over what *she* brought on,

> (*Indicating* THE DAUGHTER)

or my wife's sister, or *myself*, for that matter, or

> (*Indicates generally*)

. . . all this, but very generally, as if my brain was going to vomit, and I thought that if I was very still—as I was when I was a child, and felt I was about to be sick over something—it would go away. Well, no, not go away, but . . . recede.

> (*Smiles, sadly*)

It has, I think; some.

THE DAUGHTER (*Shy, tentative*)

Mother?

THE WIFE
(*Tiniest pause, to indicate she has heard; speaks to* THE BEST FRIEND)

I upset you, then. I'm sorry; what I said wasn't kind. You *do* understand it as well as the next.

THE DAUGHTER

(Still pleading quietly, but with an edge to it)

Mo-ther.

THE WIFE *(As before)*

And *excluding* you was never my intention, for any cruel reason, that is. Oh, I may have wanted to join the two of us together

(Indicates THE MISTRESS*)*

as close as we were but had not admitted, or discussed, certainly, for we have so much to learn from each other . . .

THE DAUGHTER

(A growl of frustration and growing anger)

Mooootherrrr!

THE BEST FRIEND

You'd better answer her: she'll go downstairs again.

THE WIFE *(Calm, smiling a little)*

No; she's done that once and won't succeed with it again, for no reason other than you wouldn't let her out the door . . . would you.

(Pause, as THE BEST FRIEND *winces, smiles sadly)*

Besides, it wouldn't be shocking any more, merely tiresome; she'd be pounding her fists on the wind.

THE DAUGHTER

(Bolt upright in her chair, hands grasping the arms, neck tendons tight; a howl)

MOOOOTHERRRRR!!

THE MISTRESS

(After a pause; gently)

Do answer her.

THE WIFE

(Pats THE MISTRESS *gently on the shoulder; looks at* THE DAUGHTER; *speaks wistfully, eyes always on her)*

I may never speak to her again. I'm not certain now—I have other things on my mind—but there's a good chance of it: I seldom speak to strangers, and if one should try to be familiar at a time of crisis, or sorrow, I'd be enraged.

(Talks to THE MISTRESS *now)*

Well, I suppose were I to stumble on the way to the gravesite and one—she—were to take my elbow to keep me from falling, I might say thank you, looking straight ahead. Unlikely, though, isn't it . . . stumbling.

(Small smile; quietly triumphant)

No; I don't think I shall speak to her again.

(THE DAUGHTER *rises;* THE WIFE *and* THE MISTRESS *watch.* THE
DAUGHTER *seems drained and very tired; she stands for a
moment, then slowly moves to the upstage chair or sofa recently
abandoned by* THE WIFE; *she throws herself down on it, turns over
on her back, puts one arm over her eyes, is still. Softly)*

So much for that.

(*Directly to* THE MISTRESS' *back-of-the-head)*

You notice I *did* say gravesite, and I am not speaking of an urn of ashes.

THE MISTRESS (*Small smile*)

I know; I heard you.

THE WIFE (*Almost apologetic*)

I *will* do battle with you there, no matter what you tell me, no matter what
an envelope may say, I will have my way. Not a question of faith, or a
repugnance; merely an act of will.

THE MISTRESS (*Gently*)

Well, I won't argue it with you now.

(THE SON *emerges, closes the door, leans against it, pressed flat, his
head up, his eyes toward the ceiling. He is wracked by sobbing,
and there is a crumpled handkerchief in his hand)*

THE SON

(*Barely able to get it out, for the sobs*)

It's all . . . still there . . . all . . . just as it . . . was.

(*Quite suddenly he manages to control himself. This effect is not
comic. It is clear an immense effort of will has taken place. His voice
is not quite steady, falters once or twice, but he is under control)*

I'm sorry; I'm being quite preposterous; I'm sorry. It's just that . . . it's all
still there, just as I remember it, not from when I may have seen it last—
when? twenty years?—but as it was when I was a child: the enormous sink;
the strop; the paneling; the pier glass; the six showerheads and the mosa-
ic tile; and . . . the . . . the white milkglass bottles with the silver tops, the
witch hazel and cologne, the gilt lettering rubbed nearly off; and . . .

(*Softer; sadder*)

. . . the ivory brushes, and the comb.

(*Shakes his head rapidly, clearing it; full control*)

Sorry; I'm sorry.

(*Pause*)

THE WIFE

(*Sighs, nods several times*)

It would take *you, wouldn't* it. Choose anything, any of the honors, the
idea of a face in your mind, something from when he took you somewhere

once, or came halfway round the world when you were burning up and the
doctors had no way of knowing what it was, then, in those times, sat by
your bed the four days till it began to slacken, *then* slept.

(Her anger, her contempt, really rising)

No! Not any of it! Give us you, and you find a BATHROOM . . . *MOVING?*

(Pause. Softer, a kind defeat)

Well . . . I can't expect you to be the son of your father and *be* much: it's
too great a *burden;* but to be so little is . . .

(Dismisses him with a gesture, paces a little)

You've neither of you had children, thank God, children that I've *known* of.

(Harsh)

I hope you never marry . . . *either* of you!

(Softer, if no gentler)

Let the line end where it is . . . at its zenith.

THE SON *(A rasped voice)*

Mother! Be kind!

THE WIFE

(To THE MISTRESS; *rather fast, almost singsong)*

We made them both; remember how I told you that he asked me that? If
it were true? And how I laughed, and said, oh, yes? Remember?

*(*THE MISTRESS *nods, without looking at her)*

THE SON

(Moves toward the stage-left door, stops by THE DAUGHTER;
speaks to her)

I'm going across the hall, to the solarium.

*(*THE WIFE *turns to notice this exchange)*

THE DAUGHTER *(Without moving)*

All right.

THE SON

So you'll know where I am.

THE DAUGHTER

All right.

THE SON

In case.

THE DAUGHTER

All right.

THE WIFE

(As THE SON *reaches the door to the hallway; mocking, but without vigor)*

Aren't you up to it?

THE SON *(Mildly; matter-of-fact)*

Not up to you, mother; never was.

(He exits)

THE WIFE *(At something of a loss)*

Well.

(Pause)

Well.

(Pause)

Indeed.

(THE DAUGHTER speaks next; while she does, THE WIFE moves about, listening, looking at THE DAUGHTER occasionally, but generally at furniture, the floor, whatever)

THE DAUGHTER

(Never once removing her arm from across her eyes)

Dear God, why can't you leave him alone? Why couldn't you let him be, this *once*. Everyone's the target of something, something unexpected and maybe even stupid. You can shore yourself up beautifully, guns on every degree of the compass, a perfect surround, but when the sky falls in or the earth gives way beneath your feet . . . so what? It's all untended, and what's it guarding? Those movies—remember them?—way back, India, usually, or in the west, the forts against the savages: the rescue party finally got there, and there was the bastion, guns pricking out from every window and turret, the white caps of the soldiers, the flag of the regiment blowing, but something was wrong; the Max Steiner music had stopped and the only sound was the blowing of the sand; and then the head of the rescue party would shoot off his pistol as a signal to those inside, and wait; still, just the blowing of the sand, and no Max Steiner music; they'd approach, go in, and there it all was, just as all of us except the rescue party knew it would be—every last soldier dead, propped up into position as some kind of grisly joke by the Tughees, or the Sioux, or whatever it was. Why couldn't you have just left him alone? He's spent his grown life getting set against everything, fobbing it all off, covering his shit as best he can, and so what if the sight of one unexpected, ludicrous thing collapses it all? So *what!* It's proof, isn't it? Isn't it proof he's not as . . . little as you said he was? It is, you know.

(Slight pause)

You make me as sick as I make you.

(Pause. THE WIFE looks at THE DAUGHTER for a little, opens her mouth as if to speak, doesn't, looks back at THE DOCTOR, who seems to be dozing, turns to THE NURSE)

THE WIFE *(To THE NURSE)*

You . . .

(Has to clear her throat)

. . . you'd better go back, I think; he may have fallen asleep.

THE NURSE

(Swivels in her chair, looks back)

Doubt it; it's a trick he has, allows patient to think he isn't watching.

THE WIFE *(Abrupt)*

Don't be ridiculous!

THE NURSE *(Calm)*

Don't be *rude*.

THE WIFE *(Sincerely)*

I'm sorry.

THE DOCTOR

(From where he is, without raising his head)

If I *am* dozing—which *is* possible, though I don't think I've slept in over forty years—if I *am*, then I imagine my intuition would snap me back, if anything needed doing, wouldn't you think? My famous intuition?

THE WIFE *(Sings it back to him)*

Sor-ry.

(To THE MISTRESS*; wryly)*

That's all I seem to say. Shall I apologize to you for anything?

THE MISTRESS

(Smiles; shakes her head)

No thank you.

THE WIFE

I may—just automatically—so pay no attention.

THE MISTRESS *(Stretches)*

You *could* answer my question, though.

THE WIFE

Have I forgotten it?

THE MISTRESS

Probably. I was wondering, musing: If I had been *you*—the little girl you were when he came to you—would you have come along as I did? Would *you* have come to take *my* place?

THE WIFE

(Smiles as she thinks about it)

Hmmmmm. No; I don't think so. We function so differently. I function as a wife, and you—don't misunderstand me—you do not. Married twice, yes, you were, but I doubt your husbands took a mistress, for you were *that*, too. And no man who has a mistress for his wife will take a wife as mistress.

*(*THE MISTRESS *laughs, softly, gaily)*

We're different kinds; whether I had children or not, I would always be a wife and mother, a symbol of stability rather than refuge. Both your husbands were married before they met you, no?

THE MISTRESS

Um; yes.

THE WIFE *(Light)*

Perhaps you're evil.

THE MISTRESS

No, I don't think so; I never scheme; I have never sought a man out, said, I think I will have this one. Oh, *is* he married? *I* see; well, no matter, that will fall like a discarded skin. I am not like that at all. I have cared for only three men—my own two husbands . . . and yours. My, how shocking that sounds. Well, three men and one boy. That was back, very far, fifteen and sixteen. God!, we were in love: innocent, virgins, both of us, and I doubt that either of us had ever told a lie. We met by chance at a lawn party on a Sunday afternoon, and had got ourselves in bed by dusk. You may not call that love, but it was. We were not embarrassed children, awkward and puppy-rutting. No; fifteen and sixteen, and never been before, but our sex was a strong and practiced and assisting . . . "known" thing between us, from the very start. Fumbling, tears, guilt? No, not a bit of it. He was the most . . . beautiful person I have ever seen: a face I will not try to describe, a lithe, smooth swimmer's body, and a penis I could not dismiss from my mind when I was not with him—I am not one of your ladies who pretends these things are of no account. We were a man and woman . . . an uncorrupted man and woman, and we made love all the summer, every day, wherever, whenever.

(Pause)

And then it stopped. *We* stopped.

THE DAUGHTER

(After a moment; same pose)

What happened? Something tragic? Did he die, or become a priest?

THE MISTRESS

(Ignoring her tone; remembering)

No, nothing like it. We had to go back to school.

THE DAUGHTER *(Snorts)*

Christ!

THE MISTRESS

We had to go back to *school.* Could anything be simpler?

THE DAUGHTER

(Raising herself half-up on her elbows; mildly unpleasant tone)

No burning correspondence, love and fidelity sworn to eternity? Surely a weeping farewell, holding hands, staring at the ceiling, swearing your passion until Christmas holidays.

THE MISTRESS (*Still calm*)

No, not that at all. We made love, our last day together, kissed, rather as a brother and *sister* might, and said: "Goodbye; I love you." "Goodbye; I love you."

THE DAUGHTER

A couple of horny kids, that's all.

THE MISTRESS (*Smiles a little*)

No, I think you're wrong there. Oh, we were *that*, certainly, but I also think we were very wise. "Leave it; don't touch it again." I told you; it was very simple: we had to go back to school; we were *children*.

THE DAUGHTER

(*Reciting the end of a fairy tale*)

And you never saw him again.

THE MISTRESS

True. He was from across the country, had been visiting that summer.

THE WIFE (*Very nice*)

What became of him?

THE MISTRESS (*Waves it away*)

Oh . . . things, things I've read about from time to time; nothing.

THE DAUGHTER

Oh, come on! What became of him!?

THE MISTRESS

(*Irritated, but by the questioner, not the question*)

Whatever you like! He died and became a priest! *What* do *you* care?

THE DAUGHTER

I don't.

THE MISTRESS

Then shut it up.

(THE DAUGHTER *sinks back to her previous position*)

THE WIFE (*After a pause*)

Four men, then.

THE MISTRESS

Hm? Oh; well, yes; yes, I suppose he *was* a man. Four men, then. Not too bad, I guess; spread out, not all bunched together.

THE WIFE

Yes.

(*Slowly; something of a self-revelation*)

I have loved only . . . once.

THE MISTRESS *(Nods, smiles; kindly)*

Yes.

THE BEST FRIEND *(Swings around)*

What if there *is* no paper? What if all the envelopes are business, and don't say a thing about it? What if there *are* no instructions?

THE WIFE *(Dry, but sad)*

Then it is in the hands of the wife . . . is it not?

THE BEST FRIEND

Yes, certainly, but . . . still.

THE WIFE *(On her guard)*

Still?

THE BEST FRIEND *(Pained)*

After a time, it . . . after a time the prerogative becomes *only* legal.

THE WIFE

Only, and *legal?* Those two words *next* to each other? From you?

THE BEST FRIEND *(Helpless)*

I can't stop you.

THE WIFE

Why would you want to, and why are we playing "what if"? He's a thorough man, knows as much law as you, or certainly *some* things. I am not a speculator.

THE BEST FRIEND

Those envelopes are not from yesterday.

THE WIFE

I dare say not. How *old* were you when you became aware of death?

THE BEST FRIEND

Well . . . what it meant, you mean.

(Smiles, remembering)

The age we all become philosophers—fifteen?

THE WIFE

(Mildly impatient; mildly amused)

No, no, when you were aware of it for yourself, when you knew you were at the top of the roller-coaster ride, when you knew half of it was probably over and you were on your *way* to it.

THE BEST FRIEND

Oh.

(Pause)

Thirty-eight?

THE WIFE

Did you make a will then?

THE BEST FRIEND (*A rueful smile*)

Yes.

THE WIFE

Instructions in it?

THE BEST FRIEND

(*Curiously angry*)

Yes! But not about that! Not about what was to be *done* with me. Maybe that's something women think about more.

THE WIFE

(*Surprised, and grudging a point*)

May-*be*.

THE BEST FRIEND (*He, too*)

And maybe it's something I never thought to *think* about.

THE WIFE

Do I sound absolutely *tribal?* Am I wearing feathers and mud, and *are* my earlobes halfway to my shoulders? I wonder! My rationale has been perfectly simple: you may lose your husband while he is alive, but when he is not, then he is yours again.

THE DAUGHTER (*Same position*)

He still *is*.

(THE WIFE *opens her mouth to reply, stops herself*)

THE BEST FRIEND

What.

THE DAUGHTER

Alive.

THE BEST FRIEND (*Controlling his anger*)

We *know* that.

THE DAUGHTER

Wondered; that's all.

THE MISTRESS (*Gently*)

Let's not talk about it any more. We're misunderstood.

THE BEST FRIEND

It's just that . . . well, never mind.

THE WIFE (*Nicely*)

That you're his best friend in the world, and you care about what happens to him?

THE BEST FRIEND (*Glum*)

Something like that.

THE WIFE

Well, there are a number of his best friends here, and we all seem quite concerned. That we differ is incidental.

THE BEST FRIEND

Hardly. I warn you: if there *is* no paper, and I doubt there is, and you persist in having your way, I'll take it to court.

THE WIFE (*Steady*)

That will take a long time.

THE BEST FRIEND

No doubt.

THE WIFE

Well.

(*Pause*)

It was pleasant having you as my lawyer.

THE BEST FRIEND

Don't be like that.

THE WIFE (*Furious*)

Don't *be* like that!? Don't *be* like that!? We are talking of *my husband*. Surely you've not forgotten. You were a guest in our house—in the days when we *had* a house together. We entertained you. Here! You and your wife spent Christmas with us; many times! Who remembered to bring you your cigars from Havana whenever we were there? Who went shopping with you to surprise your wife, to help you make sure it was right and not the folly you husbands make of so many things? Me! *Wife!* Remember!?

(THE BEST FRIEND *goes to her where she sits, kneels beside her, takes her hands, puts them to his lips*)

I think I shall cry.

THE BEST FRIEND

No, now.

THE WIFE

(*Wrenches her hands free, looks away; weary*)

Do what you want with him; cast him in bronze if you like. I won't do battle with you: I like you both too much.

THE MISTRESS

I told you what he wants, that's all, or what he wanted when he told me. Let's not fall out over the future.

THE BEST FRIEND (*Gentle*)

If I retract, will you hire me back again?

THE WIFE

You were never fired; what would I do without you? Rhetoric.

THE DAUGHTER *(Same position)*

Join hands; kiss; sing.

THE WIFE

(Rather light tone, to THE BEST FRIEND*)*

What *is* it if you kill your daughter? It's matricide if *she* kills *you*, and infanticide if you do her in when she's a tot, but what if she's all grown up and beginning to wrinkle? Justifiable homicide, I suppose.

*(*THE NURSE *half emerges from behind the screen)*

THE NURSE

Doctor!?

(He joins her, and they are only partially visible. THE WIFE *stays where she is, grips the arms of her chair, closes her eyes.* THE MISTRESS *rises, stays put.* THE BEST FRIEND *moves toward the bed.* THE DAUGHTER *rises, stays where she is)*

THE NURSE *(Reappearing)*

Stay back; it's nothing for you.

(She goes back to the bed. THE DAUGHTER *sits again;* THE BEST FRIEND *goes into a chair.* THE DAUGHTER *returns to her sofa)*

THE DAUGHTER

(She pounds her hands on the sofa, more or less in time to her words; her voice is thick, and strained and angry. She must speak with her teeth clenched)

Our Father, who art in heaven; hallowed be thy name; thy kingdom come, thy will be done on earth as it is in heaven; give us this day!

(They are all silent.

THE NURSE *reappears; her uniform is spotted with blood, as if someone had thrown some at her with a paint brush. There is blood on her hands, too)*

THE NURSE

It's all right; it's a hemorrhage, but it's all right.

THE WIFE *(Eyes still closed)*

Are you certain!

THE NURSE

(Forceful, to quiet them)

It's all right!

(She returns to the bed)

THE MISTRESS

(To THE WIFE, *after a pause)*

Tell me about something; talk to me about anything—anything!

THE WIFE

(Struggling for a subject)

We . . . uh . . . the . . . the garden, yes, the garden we had, when we had our house in the country, outside of Paris. We were in France for nearly three years. Did you . . . did he tell you that?

THE MISTRESS

Yes; was it lovely?

THE WIFE

He couldn't, he couldn't have taken you there. It was lovely; it burned down; they wrote us.

THE MISTRESS

What a pity.

THE WIFE

Yes; it was lovely.

(She struggles to get through it)

It wasn't just a garden; it was a world . . . of . . . floration. Is that a word? No matter. It was a world of what it was. One didn't walk out into a garden—in the sense of when they say to you: "Come see what we've done." None of any of that. Of *course.* It had been planned, by careful minds—a woman *and* a man, I think, for it was that kind, or several; generations— and it resembled nothing so much as an environment.

(Head back, loud, to THE DOCTOR *and* THE NURSE)

IS ANYONE TELLING ME THE TRUTH!?

THE NURSE *(Reappearing briefly)*

Yes.

(Goes back)

THE WIFE *(Quietly)*

Thank you.

THE MISTRESS

The garden.

THE WIFE

Yes.

(Pause, while she regathers)

The . . . the house, itself, was centuries old, rather Norman on the outside, wood laid into plaster, but not boxy in the Norman manner, small, but rambling; stone floors; huge, simple mantels, great timbers in the ceilings, a

kitchen the size of a drawing room—*you* know. And all about it, clinging
to it, spreading in every way, a tamed wilderness of garden. No, not tamed;
planned, a planned wilderness. Such profusion, and all the birds and
butterflies from miles around were privy to it. *And* the bees. One could
walk out and make bouquets Redon would have envied.

(*Pause*)

I don't think I want to talk about it any more.

(THE DOCTOR *appears, finishing drying his hands with a towel. He
comes forward*)

THE DOCTOR

Close, but all right; there's no predicting those. May I join you?

(*He sits with* THE WIFE *and* THE MISTRESS)

That's better. I suddenly feel quite old . . .

(*Chuckles*)

. . . which could pass for a laugh, couldn't it?

THE MISTRESS

Are you going to retire, one day?

THE DOCTOR

Couldn't, now; I'm way past retirement age. I should have done it fifteen
years ago. Besides, what would I do?

THE WIFE

(*Not looking at* THE DOCTOR)

Did it . . . hasten it?

THE DOCTOR (*Pause*)

Sure. What else would you expect? Every breath diminishes; each heartbeat is taking a chance.

THE MISTRESS

(*An attempt to change the subject*)

I've never understood how you doctors stay so well in the midst of it all—
the contagions. You must rattle from the pills.

THE DOCTOR

Oh, it's easier now; used to be a day, though. Still, it's interesting. In Europe,
in the time of the black plague—and I *read* about it, don't be thinking
fresh—when eighty percent of a town would go, wiped out in a week, the
doctors, such as they were, would lose only half. There wasn't much a doctor could do, in those days, against the bubonic—and especially the pneu-
monic—but saddling up and running wouldn't have helped, postponed,
maybe, so they stayed, tried to get the buboes to break, nailed some houses
shut with all the living inside if there was a case, and preceded the priests by
a day or two in their rounds. The priests had the same break as the doctors,

the same percentages. Might *mean* something; probably not.
(Pause)
Want some more history?

THE WIFE
(Shakes her head, smiles a little)
No.

THE MISTRESS *(Ibid.)*
Not really.

·THE DOCTOR *(Rises, with an effort)*
I'll go back, then. If you do, let me know; I'm up on it.
(Starts back, passes THE DAUGHTER, *recumbent)*
Got a headache, or something?
(Moves on)

THE DAUGHTER
(Rises, swiftly; under her breath)
Christ!
(Generally)
I'll be in the solarium, too.
(She exits, slamming the door after her. Some silence)

THE WIFE
(To THE MISTRESS *gently)*
What *will* you do?

THE MISTRESS *(Smiles sadly)*
I don't *know.* I've *thought* about it, of course, and nothing seems much good.
I'm not a drinker, and I'm far too old for drugs. I've thought of taking a very
long trip, of going places I've not been before—*we've* not been—but there's
quite a lot against that, too. Do I want to forget, or do I want to remember? If
the choice comes down to masochism or cowardice, then maybe best do nothing. Though, I must do *something.* The sad thing is, I've seen so many of them,
the ones who are suddenly without their men, going back to places they have
known together, sitting on terraces and looking about. They give the impression of wanting to be recognized, as if the crowd in Cannes that year had all
the people from the time before and someone would come and say hello.
They overdress, which is something they never would have done before: at
three in the afternoon they're wearing frocks, and evening jewelry, and their
make-up is for the dim of the cocktail lounge, and not the sun. I'm not talking
of the women who fall apart. No, I mean the straight ladies who are mildly
startled by everything, as if something they could not quite place were not
quite right. Well, it is all the things they have come there to not admit—that
the present is not the past, that they must order for themselves, and trust no

one. And the groups are even worse, those three or four who make the trips together, those coveys of bewildered widows, talking about their husbands as if they'd gone to a stag, or were at the club. There's a coarsening in that, a lack of respect for oneself, ultimately. I *shall* go away; I *know* that; but it won't be to places unfamiliar, either. There are different kinds of pain, and being once more where one has been, and shared, *must* be easier than being where one *cannot* ever . . . I think what I shall do is go to where I've been, *we've* been, but I shall do it out of focus, for indeed it will be. I'll go to Deauville in October, with only the Normandie open, and take long, wrapped-up walks along the beach in the cold and gray. I'll spend a week in Copenhagen when the Tivoli's closed. And I'll have my Christmas in Venice, where I'm told it usually snows. Or maybe I'll just go to Berlin and stare at the place where the wall once was. We were there when they put it up. There's so much one can do. And so little.

(*Long pause; finally, with tristesse*)

What will *you* do?

THE WIFE (*Pause*)

It's very different. I've been practicing widowhood for so many years that I don't know what effect the fact will have on me. Maybe none. I've settled in to a life which is comfortable, interesting, and useful, and I contemplate no change. You never know, though. It may be I have told myself . . . all lies and I am no more prepared for what will happen—when? tonight? tomorrow morning?— than I would be were he to shake off the coma, rise up from his bed, put his arms about me, ask my forgiveness for all the years, and take me back. I can't predict. I know I want to feel something. I'm waiting to, and I have no idea what I'm storing up. You make a lot of adjustments over the years, if only to avoid being eaten away. Anger, resentment, loss, self-pity— *and* self-loathing—loneliness. You can't live with all that in the consciousness very long, so, you put it under, *or* it gets well, and you're never sure which. Worst might be if there's nothing there any more, if everything has been accepted. I'm not a stoic by nature, by any means—I would have killed for my children, back when I cared for them, and he could please me and hurt me in ways so subtle and complex I was always more amazed at *how* it had happened than I was by *what.* I remember once: we were in London, for a conference, and, naturally, he was very busy.

(*Pause*)

No; I don't want to talk about *that*, either. Something *must* be stirring: it's the second time I've balked.

THE MISTRESS (*Nicely*)

You won't mind.

THE WIFE

Well, I won't know till it's too late, will I?

(*Turns to* THE BEST FRIEND)

You're going to ask me to marry you, *aren't* you.

THE BEST FRIEND *(From where he sits)*

Certainly.

THE WIFE *(Smiles)*

And I shall *refuse,* shall I *not.*

THE BEST FRIEND

Certainly; I'm no bargain.

THE WIFE

Besides; fifty years married to one man, I wouldn't be settling on three or
four with another—or even ten, if you outwit all the actuaries. And
besides—though listen to how it sounds from someone *my* age, *my* condition—I am devoted to you, sir, but I am not in love with you. Fill my
mouth with mould for having said it, but I love my husband.

THE MISTRESS *(Smiles, nicely)*

Of course you do.

THE BEST FRIEND

(As if nothing else had entered his mind and he is not disputing it)

Of course you do.

THE WIFE

(A bit put off by their acquiescence)

Yes. Well.

(Shakes her head, slowly, sadly)

Oh, God; the little girl.

(Does she move about? Perhaps)

Eighteen . . .

(To THE MISTRESS*)*

and none of yours, no summer lovemaking; no thought to it, or anything
like it; alas.

(Pause, gathers herself again)

Some would-be beaux, but, like myself, tongue-tied and very much their
ages. They would come to call, drink lemonade with my mother there, an
aunt or so, an uncle; they would take me walking, play croquet, to a dance.
I didn't fancy any of them.

THE MISTRESS *(Smiles)*

No; you were waiting.

THE WIFE

(Shakes her head, laughs)

Of course! For Prince Charming!

*(*THE MISTRESS *chuckles.* THE WIFE *shrugs)*

And then—of course—he came *along,* done with the university, missing the war in France, twenty-four, already started on his fortune—just begun, but straight ahead, and clear. We met at my rich uncle's house, where he had come to discuss a proposition, and he made me feel twelve again, or younger, and . . . comfortable, as if he were an older brother, though . . . different; very different. I had never felt threatened, by boys, but he was a man, and I felt secure.

THE MISTRESS

Did you fall in love at once?

THE WIFE

Hm?

(*Thinks about it*)

I don't *know;* I knew that I would marry him, that he would ask me, and it seemed very . . . right. I felt calm. Is that an emotion? I suppose it is.

THE MISTRESS

Very much.

THE WIFE (*Sighs heavily*)

And two years after that we were married; and thirty years later . . . he met *you.* Quick history. Ah, well.

(*A quickening*)

Perhaps if I had been . . .

(*Realizes*)

No; I don't suppose so.

(*A silence*)

THE DOCTOR

(*Emerging from where the bed has hidden him; to* THE BEST FRIEND)

Where are the others?

THE BEST FRIEND (*Rising*)

In the solarium.

THE DOCTOR (*Level*)

You'd best have them come in.

THE WIFE (*Pathetic; lost*)

No-o!

THE BEST FRIEND

(*Moving toward the door; to* THE DOCTOR)

I'll get them.

THE WIFE (*Ibid.*)

Not yet!

THE BEST FRIEND (*Misunderstanding*)

They should *be* here.

THE WIFE (*Ibid.*)

I don't mean them!

THE BEST FRIEND (*Hard to breathe*)

I'll get them.

(*He exits*)

THE WIFE

(*Turning back to* THE DOCTOR; *as before; pathetic, lost*)

Not yet!

THE MISTRESS

(*Takes* THE WIFE's *hand*)

Shhhhhhhhh; be a rock.

THE WIFE (*Resentful*)

Why!

THE MISTRESS

They need you to.

THE WIFE (*Almost sneering*)

Not you?

THE MISTRESS (*Matter-of-fact*)

I'll manage. It would help, though.

THE WIFE

(*Takes her hand away; hard*)

You be; *you* be the rock. I've *been* one, for all the years; steady. It's profit-less!

THE MISTRESS

Then, just a little longer.

THE WIFE (*Almost snarling*)

You be; *you've* usurped!

(*Pause; finally; still hard*)

I'm sorry!

THE MISTRESS

That's not fair.

THE WIFE (*Still hard*)

Why? Because I no longer had what you up and took?

THE MISTRESS (*Her tone hard, too*)

Something like that.

THE WIFE

(A sudden, hard admitting, the tone strong, but with loss)

I don't love *you.*

*(*THE MISTRESS *nods, looks away)*

I don't love *anyone.*

(Pause)

Any more.

(The door opens; THE DAUGHTER *enters, followed by* THE SON, *followed by* THE BEST FRIEND. THE BEST FRIEND *moves wearily, the other two shy, as if they were afraid that by making a sound or touching anything the world would shatter.* THE BEST FRIEND *quietly closes the door behind him; the other two move a few paces, stand there.*

On her feet, now; to THE DAUGHTER, *same tone as before)*

I don't love *you,*

(To THE SON*)*

and I don't love *you.*

THE BEST FRIEND *(Quietly)*

Don't do that.

THE WIFE

(Quieter, but merciless)

And you know I don't love *you.*

(An enraged shout which has her quivering)

I LOVE MY HUSBAND!!

*(*THE NURSE *has moved forward;* THE DAUGHTER *moves to her, buries herself in* THE NURSE*'s arms.* THE SON *falls into a chair, covers his face with his hands, sobs. To* THE SON*)*

STOP IT!!

(THE SON abruptly ceases his sobbing, doesn't move)

THE MISTRESS *(Steady)*

You stop it.

(Silence; THE BEST FRIEND *moves to the fireplace;* THE MISTRESS *and* THE WIFE *are both seated;* THE SON *stays where he is;* THE DAUGHTER *returns to the sofa;* THE DOCTOR *is by the bed;* THE NURSE *stands behind the sofa and to one side, eyes steady, ready to assist or prevent. Nobody moves from these positions, save* THE DOCTOR, *from now until the end of the play)*

THE WIFE

(Calm, now, almost toneless. A slow speech, broken with long pauses)

All we've done . . . is think about ourselves.

(*Pause*)

There's no help for the dying. I suppose. Oh my; the burden.

(*Pause*)

What will become of *me* . . . and *me* . . . and *me*.

(*Pause*)

Well, we're the ones have got to go on.

(*Pause*)

Selfless love? *I* don't think so; we love to *be* loved, and when it's taken away
. . . then why *not* rage . . . or pule.

(*Pause*)

All we've *done* is think about ourselves. Ultimately.

(*A long silence. Then* THE WIFE *begins to cry. She does not move,
her head high, eyes forward, hands gripping the arms of her
chair. First it is only tears, but then the sounds in the throat begin. It is controlled weeping, but barely controlled*)

THE DAUGHTER

(*After a bit; not loud, but bitter and accusatory*)

Why are you crying!

THE WIFE

(*It explodes from her, finally, all that has been pent up for thirty
years. It is loud, broken by sobs and gulps of air; it is self-pitying
and self-loathing; pain, and relief*)

Because . . . I'm . . . unhappy.

(*Pause*)

Because . . . I'm . . . unhappy.

(*Pause*)

BECAUSE . . . I'M . . . UNHAPPY!

(*A silence, as she regains control. Then she says it once more,
almost conversational, but empty, flat*)

Because I'm unhappy.

(*A long silence. No one moves, save* THE DOCTOR, *who finally removes
the stethoscope from* THE PATIENT'*s chest, then from his ears. He
stands, pauses for a moment, then walks a few steps forward, stops*)

THE DOCTOR (*Gently*)

All over.

(*No one moves*)

CURTAIN

Seascape

For
Ella Winter
and
Donald Ogden Stewart
with love

The first performance of SEASCAPE was presented by Richard Barr, Charles Woodward, and Clinton Wilder on Sunday, January 26, 1975, at the Sam S. Shubert Theatre, New York City.

DEBORAH KERR *as* NANCY

BARRY NELSON *as* CHARLIE

FRANK LANGELLA *as* LESLIE

MAUREEN ANDERMAN *as* SARAH

Directed by EDWARD ALBEE

Scenery and Lighting by JAMES TILTON

Costumes by FRED VOELPEL

General Manager, MICHAEL KASDAN

Production Stage Manager, MARK WRIGHT

ACT ONE

The curtain rises. NANCY *and* CHARLIE *on a sand dune. Bright sun. They are dressed informally. There is a blanket and a picnic basket. Lunch is done;* NANCY *is finishing putting things away. There is a pause and then a jet plane is heard from stage right to stage left—growing, becoming deafeningly loud, diminishing.*

NANCY

Such noise they make.

CHARLIE

They'll crash into the dunes one day. I don't know what good they do.

NANCY

(Looks toward the ocean; sighs)
Still . . . Oh, Charlie, it's so nice! Can't we stay here forever? Please!

CHARLIE

Unh-unh.

NANCY

That is not why. That is merely no.

CHARLIE

Because.

NANCY

Nor is that.

CHARLIE

Because . . . because you don't really mean it.

NANCY

I do!

CHARLIE

Here?

NANCY *(Expansive)*

Yes!

CHARLIE

Right here on the beach. Build a . . . a tent, or a lean-to.

NANCY (*Laughs gaily*)

No, silly, not this very spot! But *here,* by the shore.

CHARLIE

You wouldn't like it.

NANCY

I would! I'd love it here! I'd love it right where we are, for that matter.

CHARLIE

Not after a while you wouldn't.

NANCY

Yes, I *would.* I love the water, and I love the air, and the sand and the dunes and the beach grass, and the sunshine on all of it and the white clouds way off, and the sunsets and the noise the shells make in the waves and, oh, I love every bit of it, Charlie.

CHARLIE

You wouldn't. Not after a while.

NANCY

Why wouldn't I? I don't even mind the flies and the little . . . sand fleas, I guess they are.

CHARLIE

It gets cold.

NANCY

When?

CHARLIE

In the winter. In the fall even. In spring.

NANCY (*Laughs*)

Well, I don't mean this one, literally . . . not all the time. I mean go from beach to beach . . . live by the water. Seaside nomads, that's what we'd be.

CHARLIE (*Curiously hurt feelings*)

For Christ's sake, Nancy!

NANCY

I mean it! Lord above! There's nothing binding us; you *hate* the city . . .

CHARLIE

No.

NANCY (*Undaunted*)

It would be so lovely. Think of all the beaches we could see.

CHARLIE

No, now . . .

NANCY

Southern California, and the Gulf, and Florida . . . and up to Maine, and what's-her-name's—Martha's—Vineyard, and all those places that the fancy people go: the Riviera and that beach in Rio de Janeiro, what is that?

CHARLIE

The Copacabana.

NANCY

Yes, and Pago Pago, and . . . Hawaii! Think, Charlie! We could go around the world and never leave the beach, just move from one hot sand strip to another: all the birds and fish and seaside flowers, and all the wondrous people that we'd meet. Oh, say you'd like to do it, Charlie.

CHARLIE

No.

NANCY

Just *say* you'd like to.

CHARLIE

If I did you'd say I meant it; you'd hold me to it.

NANCY *(Transparent)*

No I wouldn't. Besides, you have to be pushed into everything.

CHARLIE

Um-hum. But I'm not going to be pushed into . . . into *this*—this new business.

NANCY *(Private rapture)*

One great seashore after another; pounding waves and quiet coves; white sand, and red—and black, somewhere, I remember reading; palms, and pine trees, cliffs and reefs, and miles of jungle, sand dunes . . .

CHARLIE

No.

NANCY

. . . and all the people! Every . . . language . . . every . . . race.

CHARLIE

Unh-unh.

NANCY

Of course, I'd never push you.

CHARLIE

You? Never!

NANCY *(Gay)*

Well, maybe a hint here; hint there.

CHARLIE

Don't even do that, hunh?

NANCY

That's all it takes: figure out what you'd really like— what you want without knowing it, what would secretly please you, put it in your mind, then
make all the plans. *You* do it; *you* like it.

CHARLIE *(Final)*

Nancy, I don't want to travel from beach to beach, cliff to sand dune, see
the races, count the flies. Anything. I don't want to do . . . anything.

NANCY *(Testy)*

I see. Well.

CHARLIE

I'm happy . . . doing . . . nothing.

NANCY

   (Makes to gather some of their things)
Well then, we'd best get started. Up! Let's get back!

CHARLIE *(Not moving)*

I just . . . want . . . to . . . do . . . nothing.

NANCY *(Gathering)*

Well, you're certainly not going to do that.
   (Takes something from him, a pillow, perhaps)
Hurry now; let's get things together.

CHARLIE *(Aware)*

What . . . Nancy, what on earth are you . . .

NANCY *(Busy)*

We are *not* going to be around forever, Charlie, and you may *not* do nothing. If you don't want to do what *I* want to do—which doesn't matter—
then we will do what *you* want to do, but we will not do nothing. We will
do *something*. So, tell me what it is you want to do and . . .

CHARLIE

I *said*. Now give me back my . . .

NANCY

You said, "I just want to do nothing; I'm happy doing nothing." Yes? But is
that what we've . . . come all this way for?
   (Some wonder and chiding)
Had the children? Spent all this time together? All the sharing? For nothing? To lie back down in the crib again? The same at the end as at the
beginning? Sleep? Pacifier? Milk? Incomprehensible once more?
   (Pause)

Sleep?
   (*Pause*)
Sleep, Charlie? Back to sleep?

CHARLIE

Well, we've earned a little . . .

NANCY

. . . rest.
   (*Nods, sort of bitterly*)
We've earned a little rest. Well, why don't we act like the old folks, why
don't we sell off, and take one bag apiece and go to California, or in the
desert where they have the farms—the retirement farms, the old folks'
cities? Why don't we settle in to waiting, like . . . like the camels that we
saw in Egypt—groan down on all fours, sigh, and eat the grass, or whatever it is. Why don't we go and wait the judgment with our peers? Take our
teeth out, throw away our corset, give in to the palsy, let our mind go dim,
play lotto and canasta with the widows and the widowers, eat cereal . . .
   (CHARLIE *sighs heavily, exasperatedly*)
Yes! Sigh! Go on! But once you get there, once you *do* that, there's no
returning, that purgatory *before* purgatory. No thank you, sir! I haven't
come this long way.

CHARLIE (*Chuckles a little, resigned*)
What do you want to do, Nancy?

NANCY

Nor have you! Not this long way to let loose. All the wisdom—by accident,
by accident, some of it—all the wisdom and the . . . unfettering. My God,
Charlie: See Everything Twice!

CHARLIE (*Settling back*)
What do you want to do?

NANCY

You are *not* going to live forever, to coin a phrase. Nor am I, I suppose,
come to think of it, though it would be nice. Nor do I imagine we'll have
the satisfaction of doing it together—head-on with a bus, or into a mountain with a jet, or buried in a snowslide, if we ever *get* to the Alps. No. I
suppose I'll do the tag without you. Selfish, aren't you—right to the end.

CHARLIE

   (*Feeling for her hand, taking it*)
What do you want to do?

NANCY (*Wistful*)
If you get badly sick I'll poison myself.
   (*Waits for reaction, gets none*)
And you?

CHARLIE *(Yawning)*

Yes; if you get badly sick I'll poison *my*self, too.

NANCY

Yes, but then if I *did* take poison, you'd get well again, and there I'd be, laid out, all for a false alarm. I think the only thing to do is to *do* something.

CHARLIE *(Nice)*

What would you like to do?

NANCY *(Faraway)*

Hm?

CHARLIE

Move from one sand strip to another? Live by the sea from now on?

NANCY *(Great wistfulness)*

Well, we have nothing holding us, except together; chattel? Does chattel mean what I think it does? We *have* nothing we *need* have. We could do it; I would so like to.

CHARLIE *(Smiles)*

All right.

NANCY *(Sad little laugh)*

You're humoring me; it *is* something I want, though; maybe only the principle.
(Larger laugh)
I suspect our children would have us put away if we announced it as a plan—beachcombing, leaf huts. Even if we did it in hotels they'd have a case—for our *reasons*.

CHARLIE

Mmmmmmm.

NANCY

Let's merely have it for today . . . and tomorrow, and . . . who knows: continue the temporary and it becomes forever.

CHARLIE *(Relaxed; content)*

All right.
(The sound of the jet plane from stage right to stage left—growing, becoming deafeningly loud, diminishing)

NANCY

Such noise they make!

CHARLIE

They'll crash into the dunes one day; I don't know what good they do.

NANCY *(After a pause)*

Still . . . Ahhh; breathe the sea air.

(Tiny pause; suddenly remembers)

Didn't you tell me? When you were a little boy you wanted to live in the sea?

CHARLIE

Under.

NANCY *(Delighted)*

Yes! Under the water—in it. That all your friends pined to have wings? Icarus? Soar?

CHARLIE

Uh-huh.

NANCY

Yes, but you wanted to go under. Gills, too?

CHARLIE

As I remember. A regular fish, I mean fishlike—arms and legs and every-thing, but able to go under, live down in the coral and the ferns, come home for lunch and bed and stories, of course, but down in the green, the purple, and big enough not to be eaten if I stayed close in. Oh yes; I *did* want that.

NANCY

(Considers it, with some wonder)

Be a fish.

(Lightly)

No, that's not among what *I* wanted—when *I* was little, not that I remem-ber. I wanted to be a pony once, I think, but not for very long. I wanted to be a *woman*. I wanted to grow up to be *that,* and all it had with it.

(Notices something below her in the distance, upstage. Offhand)

There are some people down there; I thought we were alone. In the water; some people, I think.

(Back)

And, I suppose I *have* become that.

CHARLIE *(Smiling)*

You have.

NANCY

In any event, the appearances of it: husband, children—precarious, those, for a while, but nicely settled now—to all appearances—and the grand-children . . . here, and on the way. The top of the pyramid! Us two, the children, and all of theirs.

(Mildly puzzled)

Isn't it odd that you can build a pyramid from the top down? Isn't that dif-ficult? The engineering?

CHARLIE

There wasn't anyone before us?

NANCY *(Laughs lightly)*

Well, yes, but everybody builds his own, starts fresh, starts up in the air, builds the base around him. Such levitation! Our own have started *theirs*.

CHARLIE

It's all one.

NANCY *(Sort of sad about it)*

Yes.

(Bright again)

Or maybe it's the most . . . difficult, the most . . . breathtaking of all: the whole thing balanced on one point; a reversed *pyramid,* always in danger of toppling over when people don't behave themselves.

CHARLIE *(Chuckling)*

All right.

NANCY *(Above it)*

You have no interest in imagery. None.

CHARLIE *(Defiance; rue)*

Well, I used to.

NANCY

The man who married a dumb wife; not you! Was that Molière? Beaumarchais?

CHARLIE

Anatole France.

NANCY

Was it?

CHARLIE *(Continuing from before)*

I used to go way down; at our summer place; a protected cove. The breakers would come in with a storm, or a high wind, but not usually. I used to go way down, and try to stay. I remember before that, when I was tiny, I would go in the swimming pool, at the shallow end, let out my breath and sit on the bottom; when you let out your breath—all of it—you sink, gently, and you can sit on the bottom until your lungs need air. I would do that—I was so young—sit there, gaze about. Great trouble for my parents. "Good God, go get Charlie; he's gone and sunk again." "Will you look at that child? Put him in the water and he drops like a stone." I could swim perfectly well, as easy as walking, and around the same time, but I used to love to sink. And when I was older, we were by the sea. Twelve; yes, or thirteen. I used to lie on the warm boulders, strip off . . .

(Quiet, sad amusement)

. . . learn about my body; no one saw me; twelve or thirteen. And I would go into the water, take two stones, as large as I could manage, swim out a bit, tread, look up one final time at the sky . . . relax . . . begin to go down. Oh, twenty feet, fifteen, soft landing without a sound, the white sand clouding up where your feet touch, and all around you ferns . . . and lichen. You can stay down there so long! You can build it up, and last . . . so long, enough for the sand to settle and the fish come back. And they do—come back—all sizes, some slowly, eyeing past; some streak, and you think for a moment they're larger than they are, sharks, maybe, but they never are, and one stops being an intruder, finally—just one more object come to the bottom, or living thing, part of the undulation and the silence. It was very good.

NANCY

Did the fish talk to you? I mean, did they come up and stay close, and look at you, and maybe nibble at your toes?

CHARLIE *(Very shy)*

Some of them.

NANCY *(Enthusiastic)*

Why don't you go and do it! Yes!

CHARLIE *(Age)*

Oh, no, now, Nancy, I couldn't.

NANCY

Yes! Yes, you could! Go do it again; you'd love it!

CHARLIE

Oh, no, now, I . . .

NANCY

Go down to the edge; go in! Pick up some stones . . .

CHARLIE

There're no coves; it's all open beach.

NANCY

Oh, you'll find a cove; go on! Be young again; my God, Charlie, be young!

CHARLIE

No; besides, someone'd see me; they'd think I was drowning.

NANCY

Who's to see you?! Look, there's no one in the . . . no, those . . . people, they've come out, the ones were in the water, they're . . . well, they're lying on the beach, to sun; they're prone. Go on down; I'll watch you from here.

CHARLIE

(Firm, through embarrassment)

No! I said no!

NANCY

(Undaunted; still happy)

Well, I'll come with you; I'll stand by the edge, and if anyone comes by and says, "Look, there's a man drowning!" I'll laugh and say, "La! It's my husband, and he's gone down with two stones to sit on the bottom for a while."

CHARLIE

No!

NANCY

The white sand clouding, and the ferns and the lichen. Oh, do it, Charlie!

CHARLIE

I wouldn't like it any more.

NANCY *(Wheedling, taunting)*

Awwww, how long since you've done it?!

CHARLIE *(Mumbles)*

Too long.

NANCY

What?

CHARLIE *(Embarrassed; shy)*

Not since I was seventeen?

NANCY

(This time pretending not to hear)

What?

CHARLIE

(Rather savage; phlegm in the throat)

Too long.

(Small pause)

Far too long?

(Silence)

NANCY *(Very gentle; not even urging)*

Would it be so very hard now? Wouldn't you be able to? Gently? In some sheltered place, not very deep? Go down? Not long, just enough to . . . reconfirm.

CHARLIE *(Flat)*

I'd rather remember.

NANCY

If *I* were a man—What a silly thing to say.

CHARLIE

Yes. It is.

NANCY

Still, if I were . . . I don't think I'd let the chance go by; not if I had it.

CHARLIE *(Quietly)*

Let it go.

NANCY

Not if *I* had it. There isn't that much. Sex goes . . . diminishes; well, it becomes a holiday and rather special, and not like eating, or going to sleep. But that's nice, too—that it becomes special—

(Laughs gaily)

Do you know, I had a week when I thought of divorcing you?

CHARLIE

(Quite surprised, vulnerable; shakes his head)

No.

NANCY

Yes. You were having your thing, your melancholia— poor darling—and there I was, brisk and thirty, still pert, learning the moles on your back instead of your chest hairs.

CHARLIE *(Relieved, if sad)*

Ah. Then.

NANCY *(Nods)*

Um-hum. Then. Rereading Proust, if I have it right. Propped up in bed, all pink and ribbons, smelling good, not all those creams and looking ten years married as I might have, and who would have blamed me, but fresh, and damned attractive, if I have to say it for myself; propped up in bed, literate, sweet-smelling, getting familiar with your back. One, two, three moles, and then a pair of them, twins, flat black ones . . .

CHARLIE *(Recalling)*

That time.

NANCY *(Nods)*

. . . ummmm. The ones I said should *go*—*still* think they should—not that it matters: they haven't done anything. It was at the . . . center of your thing, your seven-month decline; it was *then* that I thought of divorcing you. The deeper your inertia went, the more *I* felt alive. Good wife, patient, see him through it, whatever it is, wonder if it isn't something *you* haven't done, or have; write home for some advice, but oh, so busy, with the children and the house. Stay neat; don't pry; weather it. But right in the center, three and a half months in, it occurred to me that there was nothing wrong, save perhaps another woman.

CHARLIE *(Surprised; hurt)*

Oh, Nancy.

NANCY

Well, one has a mind, and it goes about its business. If one is happy, *and* content, it doesn't mean that everyone else is; never assume that. Maybe he's found a girl; not even looking, necessarily; maybe he turned a corner one afternoon and there was a girl, not prettier even, maybe a little plain, but unencumbered, or lonely, or lost. That's the way it starts, as often as not. No sudden passion over champagne glasses at the fancy ball, or seeing the puppy love again, never like that except for fiction, but something . . . different, maybe even a little . . . less: the relief of that; simpler, not quite so nice, how much nicer, for a little.

CHARLIE

Nothing like that.

NANCY (*Laughs a little*)

Well, *I* know.

CHARLIE

Nothing at *all.*

NANCY

Yes, but the *mind.* And what bothered me was not what *you* might be doing—oh, well, certainly; *bothered,* yes— not entirely what you might be doing, but that, all of a sudden, *I* had not. *Ever.* Had not even thought of it. A child at thirty, I suppose. Without that time I would have gone through my entire life and never thought of another man, another pair of arms, harsh cheek, hard buttocks, pleasure, never at all.

(Considers that)

Well, I might have, and maybe this was better. All at once I thought: it was over between us—not our life together, that would go on, and we would be like a minister and his sister—the . . . active part of our life, the rough-and-tumble in the sheets or in the grass when we took our picnics, that all of that had stopped between us, or would become cursory, and I wouldn't have asked why, nor would you have said, or if I *had*—asked why—you would have said some lie, or truth, would have made it worse, and I thought back to before I married you, and the boys I would have done it with, if I had been that type, the firm-fleshed boys I would have taken in my arms had it occurred to me. And I began to think of them, Proust running on, pink and ribbons, looking at your back, and your back would turn and it would be Johnny Smythe or the Devlin boy, or one of the others, and he would smile, reach out a hand, undo my ribbons, draw me close, ease on. Oh, that was a troubling time.

CHARLIE (*Sad remembrance*)

You were never one for the boys, were you?

NANCY (*She, too*)

No.

(Pause)

But I thought: well, if he can turn his back on me like this—nice, isn't it, when the real and the figurative come together—*I* can turn, too—if not my back, then . . . back. I can have me a divorce, I thought, become eighteen again.

(Sudden thought)

You know, I think that's why our women want divorces, as often as not—to be eighteen again, no matter how old they are; and daring. To do it differently, and still for the first time.

(Sighs)

But it was only a week I thought about that. It went away. You came back . . . eventually.

CHARLIE

(A statement of fact that is really a question)

You never thought I went to anyone else.

NANCY

She said to me—wise woman—"Daughter, if it lasts, if you and he come back together, it'll be at a price or two. If it lasts there'll be accommodation, wandering; if he doesn't do it in the flesh, he'll think about it; one night, in the dark, if you listen hard enough, you'll hear him think the name of another woman, kiss *her,* touch *her* breasts as he has his hand and mouth on you. *Then* you'll know something about loneliness, my daughter; yessiree; you'll be halfway there, halfway to compassion."

CHARLIE *(After a pause; shy)*

The other half?

NANCY

Hm?

(Matter-of-fact)

Knowing how lonely *he* is . . . substituting . . . using a person, a body, and wishing it was someone else—almost anyone. *That* void. *Le petit mort,* the French call the moment of climax? And that lovely writer? Who talks of the sadness after love? After intimate intercourse, I think he says? But what of *during?* What of the loneliness and death *then? During.* They don't talk of that: the sad fantasies; the substitutions. The thoughts we have.

(Tiny pause)

One has.

CHARLIE *(Softly, with a timid smile)*

I've never been with another woman.

NANCY *(A little laugh)*

Well, *I* know.

CHARLIE (*Laughs ruefully*)

I think one time, when you and I were making love—when we were near-ly there, I remember I pretended it was a week or so before, one surpris-ing time we'd had, something we'd hit upon by accident, or decided to do finally; I pretended it was the time before, and it was quite good that way.

NANCY (*Some wonder*)

You pretended I was me.

CHARLIE (*Apology*)

Well . . . yes.

NANCY

(*Laughs delightedly; thinks*)
Well; perhaps I was.
(*Pause*)
So much goes, Charlie; we shouldn't give up until we have to.
(*Gentle*)
Why don't you go down; why don't you find a cove?

CHARLIE (*Smiles; shakes his head*)

No.

NANCY

It's something *I've* never done; you could teach me. You could take my hand; we could have two big stones, and we could go down together.

CHARLIE

(*Not a complaint; an evasion*)
I haven't got my suit.

NANCY

Go bare! You're quite presentable.

CHARLIE

(*Mildly put off, and a little pleased*)
Nancy!

NANCY (*Almost shy*)

I wouldn't mind. I'd like to see you, pink against the blue, watch the water on you.

CHARLIE

Tomorrow.

NANCY

Bare?

CHARLIE

We'll see.

NANCY *(Shrugs)*

I'm used to that: we'll see, and then put off until it's forgotten.

   (Peers)

I wonder where they've gone.

CHARLIE *(Not interested)*

Who?

NANCY

Those people; well, those that were down there.

CHARLIE

Gone in.

NANCY

The water? Again?

CHARLIE

No. Home.

NANCY

Well, I don't think so. I thought maybe they were coming up to us.

CHARLIE

Why?

NANCY

They . . . looked to be. I mean, I thought . . . well, no matter.

CHARLIE

Who were they?

NANCY

You know my eyes. I thought they were climbing, coming up to see us.

CHARLIE

If we don't know them?

NANCY

Some people are adventurous.

CHARLIE

Mmmmm.

NANCY

I wonder where they've gone.

CHARLIE

Don't spy!

NANCY *(Looking down)*

I'm not; I just want to . . . Lord, why couldn't my ears be going instead? I think I see them halfway up the dune. I think I can make them out; rest-ing, or maybe sunning, on an angle for the sun.

CHARLIE

A lot of good *you'd* be under water.

NANCY

(*Considers what she has seen*)

Rather odd.

(*Dismisses it*)

Well, that's why you'll have to take me if I'm going to go down; you wouldn't want to lose me in the fernery, and all. An eddy, or whatever that is the tide does underneath, might sweep me into a cave, or a culvert, and I wouldn't know *what* to do. No, you'll have to take me.

CHARLIE

You'd probably panic . . . if I took you under.

(*Thinks about it*)

No; you wouldn't; you'd do worse, most likely: start drowning and not let on.

(*They both laugh*)

You're a good wife.

NANCY (*Offhand*)

You've been a good husband . . . more or less.

CHARLIE (*Not aggressive*)

Damned right.

NANCY

And you courted me the way I wanted.

CHARLIE

Yes.

NANCY

And you gave me the children I wanted, as many, and when.

CHARLIE

Yes.

NANCY

And you've provided a sturdy shoulder and a comfortable life. No?

CHARLIE

Yes.

NANCY

And I've not a complaint in my head, have I?

CHARLIE

No.

NANCY (*Slightly bitter*)

Well, we'll wrap you in the flag when you're gone, and do taps.

(*A fair silence*)

CHARLIE *(Soft; embarrassed)*

We'd better . . . gather up; . . . We should go back now.

NANCY

(Nudges him on the shoulder)

Ohhhhhhhh . . .

(CHARLIE shakes his head, keeping his eyes averted.)

NANCY

Ohhhhhhhhh . . .

CHARLIE

I don't want to stay here any more. You've hurt my feelings, damn it!

NANCY *(Sorry)*

Ohhh, Charlie.

CHARLIE *(Trying to understand)*

You're not cruel by nature; it's not your way. Why do you *do* this? Even so rarely; *why?*

NANCY

(As if it explained everything)

I was being *pe*tulant.

CHARLIE

(More or less to himself, but not sotto voce)

I *have* been a good husband to you; I *did* court you like a gentleman; I *have* been a good lover . . .

NANCY *(Light)*

Well, of course I have no one to compare you with.

CHARLIE *(Preoccupied; right on)*

. . . you *have* been comfortable, and my shoulder *has* been there.

NANCY *(Gaily)*

I *know;* I *know.*

CHARLIE

You've had a good *life.*

NANCY

Don't *say* that!

CHARLIE

And you'll not pack it up in a piece of cloth and put it away.

NANCY

No! Not if *you* won't! Besides, it was hyperbole.

CHARLIE *(Slightly testy)*

I knew that. Not if *I* won't, eh? Not if I won't what?

NANCY

Pack it up in a piece of cloth and put it away. When's the last time you were stung by a bee, Charlie? Was it that time in Maine . . . or Delaware? When your cheek swelled up, and you kept saying, "Mud! Get me some mud!" And there wasn't any mud that *I* could see, and you said, "Well, *make* some."

CHARLIE

Delaware.

NANCY

After all the years of making you things, my mind couldn't focus on how to make *mud*. What *is* the recipe for *that*, I said to myself . . . What sort of *pan* do I use, for one; water, yes; but water and . . . what? Earth, naturally, but what *kind* and . . . oh, I felt so foolish.

CHARLIE *(Softer)*

It was Delaware.

NANCY

So foolish.

CHARLIE *(Mildly reproachful)*

The whole cheek swelled up; the eye was half closed.

NANCY *(Pedagogic)*

Well, that's what a bee sting does, Charlie. And that's what brings on the petulance—mine; it's just like a bee sting, and I re*mem*ber, though it's been years.

CHARLIE *(To reassure himself)*

Crazy as a loon.

NANCY

No; not at all. You asked me about the petulance—why it comes on me, even rarely. Well, it's like the sting of a bee: something you say, or do; or don't say, or don't do. And it brings the petulance on me—not that I like it, but it's a healthy sign, shows I'm still nicely alive.

CHARLIE *(Not too friendly)*

Like when? Like what?

NANCY

What brings it on, and when?

CHARLIE *(Impatient)*

Yes!

NANCY

Well, so many things.

CHARLIE

Give me *one*.

NANCY

No; I'll give you several.

CHARLIE

All *right.*

NANCY

"You've had a good life."
  (Pause)

CHARLIE *(Curiously angry)*
All right. *Go* on.

NANCY

Do you know what I'm *saying?*

CHARLIE

You're throwing it up to me; you're telling me I've had a . .

NANCY

No-no-no! I'm saying what you *said,* what you told *me.* You told me, you
said to me, "You've had a good life." I wasn't talking about *you,* though you
have. I was saying what you said to me.

CHARLIE *(Annoyed)*
Well, you have! You *have* had!

NANCY *(She, too)*
Yes! Have *had!* What *about* that!

CHARLIE

What about it!

NANCY

Am not *having.*
  (Waits for reaction; gets none)
Am not *having?* Am not *having* a good life?

CHARLIE

Well, of *course!*

NANCY

Then why say had? Why put it that way?

CHARLIE

It's a way of speaking!

NANCY

No! It's a way of thinking! *I* know the language, and I know *you.* You're not
careless with it, or didn't used to be. Why *not* go to those places in the
desert and let our heads deflate, if it's all in the past? Why not just *do* that?

CHARLIE

It was a way of speaking.

NANCY

Dear God, we're *here*. We've served our time, Charlie, and there's nothing telling us do *that,* or any conditional; not any more. Well, there's the arthritis in my wrist, of course, and the eyes have known a better season, and there's always the cancer or a heart attack to think about if we're bored, but besides all these things . . . what is there?

CHARLIE *(Somewhat triste)*

You're at it again.

NANCY

I am! Words are lies; they *can* be, and you *use* them, but I know what's in your gut. I *told* you, didn't I?

CHARLIE *(Passing it off)*

Sure, sure.

NANCY *(Mimicking)*

Sure, sure. Well, they are, and you do. What *have* we got left?

CHARLIE

What! You mean besides the house, the kids, *their* kids, friends, all that? What?!

NANCY

Two things!

CHARLIE

Yeah?

NANCY

Ourselves and some time. Charlie—the pyramid's building by itself; the earth's spinning in its own fashion without any push from us; we've done all we ought to—and isn't it splendid we've enjoyed so much of it.

CHARLIE *(Mild irony)*

We're pretty splendid people.

NANCY

Damned right we are, and now we've got each other and some time, and all *you* want to do is become a vegetable.

CHARLIE

Fair, as usual.

NANCY *(Shrugs)*

All right: a lump.

CHARLIE

We've earned . . .

NANCY (*Nods*)

. . . a little rest. My God, you say that twice a day, and sometimes in between.

(*Mutters*)

We've earned a little *life,* if you ask *me.*

(*Pause*)

Ask me.

CHARLIE (*Some rue*)

No; you'd tell me.

NANCY

(*Bold and recriminating*)

Sure! Course I would! When else are we going to get it?

CHARLIE

(*Quite serious; quite bewildered*)

What's to be gained? And what would we really get? There'd be the same sounds in the dark—or similar ones; we'd have to sleep and wonder if we'd waken, either way. It's six of one, except we'll do it on familiar ground, if *I* have *my* way. I'm not up to the glaciers and the crags, and I don't think you'd be . . . once you got out there.

NANCY (*Grudging*)

I do admit, you make it sound scary—first time away to camp, sleeping out, the hoot owls and the goblins. Oh, that's scary. Are you telling me you're all caved in, Charlie?

CHARLIE (*Pause; considers the fact*)

Maybe.

NANCY

(*Pause while she ponders this*)

All closed down? Then . . . what's the difference? You make it ugly enough, either way. The glaciers and the crags? At least we've never *tried that.*

CHARLIE

(*Trying to justify, but without much enthusiasm*)

There's comfort in settling in.

NANCY (*Pause*)

Small.

CHARLIE (*Pause, final*)

Some.

(*A silence*)

(LESLIE *appears, upper half of trunk pops up upstage, from*

behind the dune. Neither CHARLIE *nor* NANCY *sees him.* LESLIE
looks at the two of them, pops back down out of sight)

NANCY

(To bring them back to life again)
Well. I've got to do some postcards tonight; tell all the folks where we are.

CHARLIE
Yes?

NANCY

. . . what a time we're having. I've got a list . . . somewhere. It wouldn't be nice not to. They do it for us, and it's such fun getting them.

CHARLIE
Um-hum.

NANCY
You do some, too?

CHARLIE
You do them for both of us.

NANCY *(Mildly disappointed)*
Oh.
    (Pause)
All right.

CHARLIE *(Not very interested)*
What do you want to do, then?

NANCY

(While NANCY *speaks,* LESLIE *and* SARAH *come up on the dune, behind* CHARLIE *and* NANCY, *but some distance away. They crawl up; then they squat down on their tails.* NANCY *stretches)*
Oh, I don't know. Do you want to have your nap? Cover your face if you do, though; put something on it. *Or* . . . we could go on back. *Or* . . . we *could* do a stroll down the beach. If you won't go in, we'll find some pretty shells . . . *I* will.

CHARLIE *(Small smile)*
What a wealth.

NANCY *(Fairly cheerful)*
Well . . . we make the best of it.

    *(*CHARLIE *senses something behind him. He turns his head, sees* LESLIE *and* SARAH. *His mouth falls open; he is stock-still for a moment; then, slowly getting on all fours, he begins, very cautiously, to back away.* NANCY *sees what* CHARLIE *is doing, is momentarily puzzled. Then she looks behind her. She sees* LESLIE *and* SARAH)

NANCY

(*Straightening her back abruptly*)

My goodness!

CHARLIE

(*On all fours; ready to flee*)

Ohmygod.

NANCY (*Great wonder*)

Charlie!

CHARLIE

(*Eyes steady on* LESLIE *and* SARAH)

Oh my loving God.

NANCY (*Enthusiasm*)

Charlie! What *are* they?!

CHARLIE

Nancy, get back here!

NANCY

But, Charlie . . .

CHARLIE

(*Deep in his throat; trying to whisper*)

Get back here!

(NANCY *backs away until she and* CHARLIE *are together.*)

NOTE: CHARLIE *and* NANCY *are now toward stage right,* LESLIE *and* SARAH *toward stage left. They will not hear each other speak until indicated.*

(*Whispering*)

Get a stick!

NANCY (*Interest and wonder*)

Charlie, what are they?

CHARLIE (*Urgent*)

Get me a stick!

NANCY

A what?

CHARLIE (*Louder*)

A stick!

NANCY (*Looking about; uncertain*)

Well . . . what *sort* of stick, Charlie?

CHARLIE

A stick! A wooden *stick!*

NANCY *(Begins to crawl stage right)*

Well, of course a wooden stick, Charlie; what other kinds of sticks *are* there, for heaven's sake? But what sort of stick?

CHARLIE

(Never taking his eyes off LESLIE *and* SARAH*)*

A big one! A big stick!

NANCY

(None too happy about it)

Well . . . I'll *look.* Driftwood, I suppose . . .

CHARLIE

Well, of course a *wooden* stick, Charlie; what other kinds of sticks . . .

*(*LESLIE *moves a little, maybe raises an arm)*

GET ME A GUN!

NANCY *(Astonished)*

A *gun,* Charlie! Where on earth would anyone find a gun up here.

CHARLIE *(Shrill)*

Get me a stick!

NANCY *(Cross)*

All right!

CHARLIE

*(*SARAH *moves toward* LESLIE; CHARLIE *stiffens, gasps)*

Hurry!

NANCY

I'm looking!

CHARLIE

(A bleak fact, to himself as much as anything)

They're going to come at us, Nancy . . .

(An afterthought)

. . . and we're arguing.

NANCY

(Waving a smallish stick; thin, crooked, eighteen inches, maybe)

I found one, Charlie; Charlie, I found one!

CHARLIE

(Not taking his gaze off LESLIE *and* SARAH; *between his teeth)*

Well, bring it here.

NANCY

(Crawling to CHARLIE *with the stick between her teeth)*

It's the best I could do under the circumstances. There was a big trunk or
something . . .

CHARLIE *(His hand out)*

Give it to me!

NANCY

Here!

(Gives the stick to CHARLIE, *who, without looking at it, raises it in
his right hand)*

Charlie! They're magnificent!

CHARLIE

(Realizes what he is brandishing, looks at it with distaste and loss)

What's *this?*

NANCY

It's your stick.

CHARLIE *(Almost crying)*

Oh my God.

NANCY

(Eyes on LESLIE *and* SARAH*)*

Charlie, I think they're absolutely beautiful. What *are* they?

CHARLIE

What am I supposed to *do* with it?!

NANCY

You *asked* for it, Charlie; you said you wanted it.

CHARLIE *(Snorts: ironic-pathetic)*

Go down fighting, eh?

*(*LESLIE *clears his throat; it is a large sound, rather like a growl or
a bark. Instinctively,* CHARLIE *gathers* NANCY *to him, all the while
trying to brandish his stick)*

NANCY

(Not at all sure of herself)

Fight, Charlie? Fight? Are they going to hurt us?

CHARLIE

(Laughing at the absurdity)

Oh, God!

NANCY *(More vigor)*

Well, at least we'll be together.

> (LESLIE *clears his throat again, same sound;* CHARLIE *and* NANCY *react a little, tense.* LESLIE *takes a step forward, stops, bends over and picks up a large stick, four feet long and stout; he brandishes it and clears his throat again)*

Now, *that's* an impressive stick.

CHARLIE *(Shakes his stick at her)*

Yeah; thanks.

NANCY *(Some pique)*

Well, thank *you* very much. If I'd known I was supposed to go over there and crawl around under their flippers, or pads, or whatever they have . . .

CHARLIE

(Final words; some haste)

I love you, Nancy.

NANCY

(The tiniest pause; a trifle begrudging)

Well . . . I love *you*, too.

> (LESLIE *slowly, so slowly, raises his stick above him in a gesture of such strength that should he smite the earth it would tremble. He holds the stick thus, without moving)*

CHARLIE

Well, I certainly hope so: here they come.

> (LESLIE *and* SARAH *slowly begin to move toward* CHARLIE *and* NANCY. *Suddenly the sound of the jet plane again, lower and louder this time.* LESLIE *and* SARAH *react as animals would; frozen for an instant, tense seeking of the danger, poised, every muscle taut, and then the two of them, at the same instant and with identical movement—paws clawing at the sand, bellies hugging the earth— they race back over the dune toward the water.*
> CHARLIE *and* NANCY *are as if struck dumb; they stare, open-mouthed, at the now-vacated dune)*

NANCY *(Finally, with great awe)*

Charlie!

(Infinite wonder)

What have we *seen?!*

CHARLIE

The glaciers and the crags, Nancy. You'll never be closer.

NANCY

All at *once!* There they *were*, Charlie!

CHARLIE

It was the liver paste. That explains everything.

NANCY *(Tolerant smile)*

Yes; certainly.

CHARLIE

I'm sure it was the liver paste. I knew it. When you were packing the lunch this morning, I said what is that? And you said it's liver paste, for sandwiches; what's the matter, don't you like liver paste any more? And I said what do we need *that* for? For sandwiches, you said. And I said yes, but what do we *need* it for?

NANCY

But, Charlie . . .

CHARLIE

You've got a roasted chicken there, and peaches, and a brie, and bread and wine, what do we need the sandwiches for, the liver paste?

NANCY

You might want them, I said.

CHARLIE

But, with all the rest.

NANCY

Besides, I asked you what would happen if you picked up the roasted chicken and dropped it in the sand. What would you do—rinse it off with the wine? Then I'd have to make iced tea, too. Miles up on the dunes, no fresh water anywhere? Bring a thermos of iced tea, too, in case you dropped the chicken in the sand?

CHARLIE

When have I dropped a chicken in the sand? *When* have I done that?

NANCY *(Mildly piqued)*

I wasn't suggesting it was a thing you *did;* I wasn't pointing to a history of it; I said you *might.* But, Charlie . . . at a time like *this* . . . they may come back.

CHARLIE

Liver paste doesn't keep; I *told* you that: goes bad in a minute, with the heat and all.

NANCY

Wrapped up in silver foil.

CHARLIE

Aluminum.

NANCY

. . . whatever; wrapped up and perfectly safe, it keeps.

CHARLIE

It goes bad in a minute, which is what it did: the liver paste clearly went bad. It went bad in the sun and it poisoned us.

NANCY

Poisoned us?!

    (Disbelieving, and distracted)

And *then* what happened?

CHARLIE

    (Looks at her as if she's simple-minded)

Why . . . we *died*, of course.

NANCY

We died?

CHARLIE

We ate the liver paste and we died. That drowsy feeling . . . the sun . . . and the wine . . . none of it: all those night thoughts of what it would be like, the sudden scalding in the center of the chest, or wasting away; milk in the eyes, voices from the other room; none of it. Chew your warm sandwich, wash it down, lie back, and let the poison have its way . . .

    (LESLIE and SARAH reappear over the dune; formidable, upright.

    NANCY *begins laughing)*

. . . talk—*think* you're talking—and all the while the cells are curling up, disconnecting . . . Nancy, don't do that! . . . it all goes dim . . . Don't laugh at me! . . . and then you're dead.

    (Between her bursts of laughter)

How can you *do* that?

    (LESLIE and SARAH move toward CHARLIE and NANCY, cautiously

    and intimidatingly; NANCY sees them, points, and her laughter

    changes its quality)

How can you laugh when you're dead, Nancy? Now, don't *do* that!

NANCY

We may be dead already, Charlie, but I think we're going to die again. Here they come!

CHARLIE

Oh my *dear* God!

    (LESLIE and SARAH approach, but stop a fair distance away from

    CHARLIE *and* NANCY; *they are on their guard)*

NANCY *(After a pause)*

Charlie, there's only one thing for it. Watch me now; watch me carefully.

CHARLIE

Nancy . . .

(She smiles broadly; with her feet facing LESLIE *and* SARAH, *she slowly rolls over on her back, her legs drawn up, her hands by her face, fingers curved, like paws. She holds this position, smiling broadly)*

NANCY

Do *this*, Charlie! For God's sake, do *this!*

CHARLIE *(Confused)*

Nancy . . .

NANCY

It's called "submission," Charlie! I've seen it in the books. I've read how the animals do it. Do it, Charlie! Roll over! Please!

*(*CHARLIE *hesitates a moment, looks at* LESLIE *and* SARAH*)*

Do it, Charlie!

(Slowly, charlie smiles broadly at LESLIE *and* SARAH, *assumes* NANCY's *position)*

CHARLIE *(Finally)*

All right.

NANCY

Now, Charlie, smile! And mean it!

*(*LESLIE *and* SARAH *begin to look at each other.)*

CURTAIN

ACT TWO

The curtain rises. The set: the same as the end of ACT ONE. CHARLIE, NANCY, LESLIE, *and* SARAH *as they were. All are stock-still for a moment.*

LESLIE

(Turns his head toward SARAH*)*
Well, Sarah, what do you think?

SARAH *(Shakes her head)*
I don't know, Leslie.

LESLIE

What do you think they're doing?

SARAH

Well, it *looks* like some sort of a submission pose, but you never know; it might be a trick.

LESLIE

I'll take a look.

SARAH

Well, be very careful.

LESLIE *(A weary sigh)*
Yes, Sarah.
(LESLIE *starts moving over to where* CHARLIE *and* NANCY *lie in their submission postures)*

CHARLIE

Oh my God, one of them's coming.

NANCY

Stay very still.

CHARLIE

What if one of them touches me?

NANCY

Smile.

CHARLIE

I'll scream.

NANCY

No, don't do *that.*

CHARLIE
(Whispers out of the side of his mouth)
It's coming! It's coming!

NANCY
Well . . . hold on, and don't panic. If we had a tail, this'd be the perfect time to wag it.
(LESLIE is very close)

CHARLIE
Oh, God.
(LESLIE stops, leans forward toward CHARLIE, and sniffs him several times. Then he straightens up and pokes CHARLIE in the ribs with his foot-paw. CHARLIE makes an involuntary sound but holds his position and keeps smiling. LESLIE looks at NANCY, sniffs her a little, and pokes her, too. She holds her position and wags her hands a little. LESLIE surveys them both, then turns and ambles back to SARAH)

SARAH
Well?

LESLIE
Well . . . they don't look very . . . formidable—in the sense of prepossessing. Not young. They've got their teeth bared, but they don't look as though they're going to bite. Their hide is funny—feels soft.

SARAH
How do they smell?

LESLIE
Strange.

SARAH
Well, I should suppose *so*.

LESLIE *(Not too sure)*
I guess it's *safe*.

SARAH
Are you *sure*?

LESLIE *(Laughs a little)*
No; of course not.
(Scratches his head)

NANCY *(Sotto voce)*
What are they doing?

CHARLIE
It poked me; one of them poked me; I thought it was all over.

NANCY (*Not to be left out*)

Well, it poked *me*, too.

CHARLIE

It *sniffed* at *me*.

NANCY

Yes. Keep where you are, Charlie; don't move. It sniffed at *me*, too.

CHARLIE

Did you smell it?

NANCY

Yes; fishy. And beautiful!

CHARLIE

Terrifying!

NANCY (*Agreeing*)

Yes; beautiful.

LESLIE

Well, I suppose I'd better go over and . . .
    (*Sort of shrugs*)

SARAH (*Immediately*)

I'll come with you.

LESLIE

No; you stay here.

SARAH (*Determined*)

I *said* I'll come *with* you.

LESLIE (*Weary*)

Yes, Sarah.

SARAH

There's no telling what kind of trouble you'll get yourself into.

LESLIE

Yes, Sarah.

SARAH

If you're going to take *that* attitude, we might as well . . .

LESLIE (*Rather abrupt*)

All *right*, Sarah!

SARAH (*Feminine, submissive*)

All right, Leslie.

CHARLIE

What's happening?

NANCY

'I think they're having a discussion.

LESLIE

Are you ready?

SARAH (*Sweet*)

Yes, dear.

LESLIE

All right?
  (SARAH *nods*)
All right.
  (*They slowly advance toward* CHARLIE *and* NANCY)

CHARLIE

Here they come!

NANCY

We're making history, Charlie!

CHARLIE (*Snorts; fear and trembling*)
The sound of one hand clapping, hunh?
  (LESLIE *and* SARAH *are before them.* LESLIE *raises paw to strike* CHARLIE)

SARAH

Don't hurt them.
  (LESLIE *gives* SARAH *a disapproving look, pokes* CHARLIE)

CHARLIE

OW!

NANCY (*Chiding*)

Charlie! Please!

CHARLIE

It poked me!

LESLIE

  (*To* CHARLIE *and* NANCY; *clears his throat*)
Pardon me.

CHARLIE (*To* NANCY)
What am I supposed to do if it pokes me?

LESLIE (*Louder*)
Pardon me.

NANCY (*Indicating* LESLIE)
Speak to it, Charlie; answer it.

CHARLIE

Hm?

NANCY

Speak to it, Charlie!

CHARLIE

"Don't just lie there," you mean?

NANCY

I guess.

    (*Sits up and waves at* SARAH, *tentatively*)

Hello.

SARAH (*To* NANCY)

Hello.

    (*To* LESLIE)

It said hello. Did you hear it?

LESLIE

    (*His attention still on* CHARLIE)

Um-hum.

NANCY

Go on, Charlie.

SARAH

Speak to the other one.

LESLIE

I've spoken to it twice; maybe it's deaf.

NANCY

Go on.

CHARLIE

No; then I'd have to accept it.

SARAH

Maybe it's shy—or frightened. Try once again.

LESLIE (*Sighs*)

All right.

    (*Prods* CHARLIE; *says, rather too loudly and distinctly*)

Pardon me!

NANCY (*Stage whisper*)

Go *on*, Charlie.

CHARLIE (*Pause; then, very direct*)

Hello.

    (*Turns to* NANCY)

All right?

(*Back to* LESLIE)

Hello!

(*Brief silence*)

SARAH

(*Overlapping with* NANCY's *following*)

There! You see, Leslie, everything's going to be . . .

NANCY

Good for you, Charlie! Now, that wasn't so . . .

(*A raised paw and a growl from* LESLIE *silences them both in mid-sentence*)

LESLIE

(*Moves a step toward* CHARLIE, *eyes him*)

Are you unfriendly?

(SARAH *and* NANCY *look to* CHARLIE. CHARLIE *lowers his legs and comes up on one elbow*)

CHARLIE

Well . . .

NANCY

Tell him, Charlie!

CHARLIE

(*To* NANCY, *through clenched teeth*)

I'm thinking of what to say.

(*To* LESLIE)

Unfriendly? Well, no, not by nature. I'm certainly on my guard, though.

LESLIE

Yes, well, so are we.

SARAH

Indeed we are!

CHARLIE

I mean, if you're going to kill us and eat us . . . then we're unfriendly: we'll . . . resist.

LESLIE

(*Looks to* SARAH *for confirmation*)

Well, I certainly don't think we were planning to do *that*. *Were* we?

SARAH (*None too sure*)

Well . . . no; at least, I don't *think* so.

NANCY

Of course you weren't! The very idea! Charlie, let's introduce ourselves.

LESLIE

After all, you're rather large . . . and quite unusual.
   (*Afterthought*)
Were you thinking of eating *us?*

NANCY (*Almost laughs*)

Good heavens, no!

SARAH

Well, we don't know your habits.

NANCY

I'm Nancy, and this is Charlie.

CHARLIE

How do. We don't know *your* habits, either. It'd be perfectly normal to assume you ate whatever . . . you ran into . . . you know, whatever you ran into.

LESLIE (*Cool*)

No; I don't know.

SARAH (*To* NANCY)

I'm Sarah.

NANCY

Hello, Sarah.

CHARLIE

   (*Somewhat on the defensive*)
It's perfectly simple: we don't eat . . . we're not cannibals.

LESLIE

What is this?

CHARLIE

Hm? We do eat other flesh . . . you know, cow, and pigs, and chickens, and all . . .

LESLIE (*To* SARAH, *very confused*)

What are *they?*
   (SARAH *shrugs*)

CHARLIE

I guess you could put it down as a rule that we don't eat anything that . . . well, anything that *talks;* you know, English, and . . .

NANCY (*To* CHARLIE)

Parrots talk; some people eat parrots.

CHARLIE

Parrots don't *talk;* parrots *imitate.* Who eats parrots?

NANCY

In the Amazon; I'm sure people eat parrots there; they're very poor, and . . .

LESLIE

What are you *saying?!*

CHARLIE *(Frustrated)*

I'm trying to tell you . . . we don't eat our own kind.

SARAH *(After a brief pause; flat)*

Oh.

LESLIE *(Rather offended)*

Well, we don't eat our own kind, either. Most of us. Some.

NANCY *(Cheerful)*

Well. You see?

LESLIE *(Dubious)*

Well . . .
 (To make the point)
You see . . . you're *not* our kind, so you can understand the apprehension.

NANCY

Besides, we cook everything.

SARAH

Pardon?

NANCY

We cook everything. Well, most things; *you* know . . . no, you don't, do you?

SARAH

This is Leslie.

NANCY *(Extending her hand)*

How do you do, Leslie?

LESLIE *(Regards her gesture)*

What is that?

NANCY

Oh; we . . . well, we shake hands . . . flippers, uh . . . Charlie?

CHARLIE

When we meet we . . . take each other's hands, or whatever, and we . . . touch.

SARAH *(Pleased)*

Oh, that's *nice*.

LESLIE *(Not convinced)*

What for?

SARAH *(Chiding)*

Oh, Leslie!

LESLIE *(To* SARAH, *a bit piqued)*

I want to know what *for*.

CHARLIE

Well, it *used* to be, since most people are right-handed, it used to be to prove nobody had a weapon, to prove they were friendly.

LESLIE *(After a bit)*

We're ambidextrous.

CHARLIE *(Rather miffed)*

Well, that's *nice* for you. Very nice.

NANCY

And some people used to hold on to their sex parts, didn't you tell me that, Charlie? That in olden times people used to hold on to their sex parts when they said hello . . . their own?

CHARLIE

I don't think I told you quite that. Each other's, maybe.

NANCY

Well, no matter.

(To LESLIE*)*

Let's greet each other properly, all right?

(Extends her hand again)

I give you my hand, and you give me your . . . what *is* that? What is that called?

LESLIE

What?

NANCY

(Indicating LESLIE's *right arm)*

That there.

LESLIE

It's called a leg, of course.

NANCY

Oh. Well, we call this an arm.

LESLIE

You have four arms, I see.

CHARLIE

No; she has two arms.
  (Tiny pause)
And two legs.

SARAH

(Moves closer to examine NANCY *with* LESLIE*)*
And which are the legs?

NANCY

These here. And these are the arms.

LESLIE *(A little on his guard)*
Why do you differentiate?

NANCY

Why do we differentiate, Charlie?

CHARLIE *(Quietly hysterical)*
Because they're the ones with the hands on the ends of them.

NANCY *(To* LESLIE*)*
Yes.

SARAH

(As LESLIE *glances suspiciously at* CHARLIE*)*
Go on, Leslie; do what Nancy wants you to.
  (To NANCY*)*
What is it called?

NANCY

Shaking hands.

CHARLIE

Or legs.

LESLIE *(Glowers at* CHARLIE*)*
Quiet.

CHARLIE *(Quickly)*
Yes, sir.

LESLIE *(To* NANCY*)*
Now; what is it you want to do?

NANCY

Well . . .
  (A glance at CHARLIE, *both reassuring and imploring)*

. . . you give me your . . . that leg there, that one, and I'll give you my . . . leg, or arm, or whatever, and we'll come together by our fingers . . . these are your fingers . . .

LESLIE

Toes.

NANCY

Oh, all right; toes.
(Shakes hands with LESLIE*)*
And we come together like this, and we do this.
(They continue a slow, broad handshake)

LESLIE

Yes?

NANCY

And now we let go.
(They do)
There! You see?

LESLIE

(Somewhat puzzled about it)
Well, that's certainly an unusual thing to want to do.

SARAH

Let *me! I* want to!
*(*SARAH *shakes hands with* NANCY, *seems happy about doing it)*
Oh, my; that's very interesting.
(To LESLIE*)*
Why haven't *we* ever done anything like that?

LESLIE *(Shrugs)*

Damned if *I* know.

SARAH

(To LESLIE, *referring to* CHARLIE*)*
You do it with *him,* now.
*(*CHARLIE *smiles tentatively, holds his hand out a little;* LESLIE *moves over to him)*

LESLIE

Are you *sure* you're friendly?

CHARLIE *(Nervous, but serious)*

I *told* you: you'll never meet a more peaceful man. Though of course if I thought you were going to *go* at me, or Nancy here, I'd probably defend myself . . . I mean, I *would.*

LESLIE

The danger, as *I* see it, is if one of us panics.

(CHARLIE *gives a hollow laugh*)

I think I'd like to know what frightens you.

(CHARLIE *laughs again*)

Please?

NANCY (*Nicely*)

Tell him, Charlie.

SARAH

Please?

CHARLIE

(*A pause, while the nature of his questioner sinks in*)

What frightens me? Oh . . . deep space? Mortality? Nancy . . . not being with me?

(*Chuckles ruefully*)

Great . . . green . . . creatures coming up from the sea.

LESLIE

Well, that's it, you see: what we don't *know.* Great green creatures, and all, indeed! You're pretty odd yourselves, though you've probably never looked at it that way.

CHARLIE

Probably not.

LESLIE

You're not the sort of thing we run into every day.

CHARLIE

Well, *no* . . .

LESLIE (*Points at* CHARLIE)

What's all *that?*

CHARLIE (*Looks at himself*)

What?

LESLIE

(*Touches* CHARLIE's *shirt; says it with some distaste*)

All *that.*

CHARLIE

This? My shirt.

("*Naturally*" *implicit*)

LESLIE

What *is* it?

NANCY

Clothes; they're called clothes; we put them on; we . . . well, we cover our skins with them.

LESLIE

What for?

NANCY

Well . . . to keep warm; to look pretty; to be decent.

LESLIE

What is *that?*

NANCY

Which?

LESLIE

Decent.

NANCY

Oh. Well . . . uh, not to expose our sexual parts. My breasts, for example.
(*Touches them*)

CHARLIE

Say "mammaries."

NANCY

What?

SARAH (*Fascinated*)

What *are* they?

NANCY

Well, they . . . no, you don't seem to have them, do you? They're . . . secondary sex organs.
(*Realizes it's hopeless as she says it*)
No? well . . .
(*Beckons* SARAH, *begins to unbutton her blouse*)
Come here, Sarah.

CHARLIE

Nancy!

NANCY

It's all *right*, Charlie. Come look, Sarah.

SARAH

(*Puts one paw on* NANCY's *blouse, peers in*)
My gracious! Leslie, come see!

CHARLIE

Now just a minute!

NANCY *(Laughs)*

Charlie! Don't be silly!

LESLIE *(To* CHARLIE; *ingenuous)*

What's the matter?

CHARLIE

I don't want you looking at my wife's breasts, that's all.

LESLIE

I don't even know what they are.

NANCY *(Buoyant)*

Of course not! Are you *jealous,* Charlie?

CHARLIE

Of course not! How could I be jealous of . . .

   (Indicates LESLIE *with some distaste)*

. . . how *could* I be?

NANCY *(Agreeing with him)*

No.

CHARLIE *(Reassuring himself)*

I'm *not.*

SARAH *(No overtones)*

I think Leslie *should* see them.

NANCY

Yes.

LESLIE *(To* CHARLIE; *shrugs)*

It's up to *you;* I mean, if they're something you *hide,* then maybe they're
embarrassing, or sad, and I shouldn't *want* to see them, and . . .

CHARLIE *(More flustered than angry)*

They're not embarrassing; *or* sad; They're lovely! Some women . . . some
women Nancy's age, they're . . . some women . . .

   (To NANCY, *almost spontaneously bursting into tears)*

I *love* your breasts.

NANCY *(Gentle)*

Yes; *yes.* Thank you.

   (More expansive)

I'm not an exhibitionist, dear, as you very well know . . .

CHARLIE

. . . except that time you answered the door stark naked . . .

NANCY *(An old story)*

We'll not discuss that now.

(*To* LESLIE *and* SARAH)

It was nothing.

CHARLIE (*By rote*)

So *she* says.

NANCY (*To the others*)

It was nothing. Really.

(*To* CHARLIE)

What I was trying to say, Charlie, was—and prefacing it with that I'm not an exhibitionist, as you very well know—that if someone . . .

CHARLIE (*To* NANCY)

Stark naked.

NANCY

. . . has *not* . . . has gone through life and *not* seen a woman's breasts . . . why, it's like Sarah never having seen . . . the sky. Think of the wonder of *that,* and think of the wonder of the other.

CHARLIE (*Rather hurt*)

One of the wonders, hunh?

NANCY

I didn't *mean* it that way!

(*Shakes her head; buttons up*)

Well . . . no matter.

LESLIE (*Shrugs*)

It's up to you.

SARAH

They're really very interesting, Leslie; I'm sorry you didn't see them.

LESLIE

Well, another time, maybe.

SARAH (*Delighted and excited*)

I suddenly remember something! Leslie, do you remember when we went way north, and it was very cold, and the scenery changed, and we came to the edge of a deep ravine, and all at once we heard those strange and terrible sounds . . .

LESLIE

(*Disturbed at the memory*)

Yes; I remember.

SARAH

Oh, it was a frightening set of sounds, echoing . . . all around us; and then we saw them . . . swimming by.

LESLIE

Enormous . . .

SARAH

Huge! Huge creatures; ten of them, maybe more. I'd never seen the size.
They were of great girth.

CHARLIE

They were whales; I'm sure they were whales.

LESLIE

Is *that* what they were?

SARAH

We observed them, though, and they had young with them; young! And it
was most interesting: the young would attach themselves to what I assume
was the female—the mother—would attach themselves to devices that I
think were very much like those of *yours;* resemble them.

NANCY

Of course! To the mammaries! Oh, Sarah, those *were* whales, for whales
are mammals and they feed their young.

SARAH

Do you remember, Leslie?

LESLIE *(Nods)*

Yes, I think I do.
   (To NANCY*)*
And you have those? That's what *you* have?

NANCY

Yes; well . . . very much like them . . . In principle.

LESLIE

My gracious.

CHARLIE *(To clear the air; brisk)*

Do you, uh . . . do *you* have any children? Any young?

SARAH *(Laughs gaily)*

Well, of course I have! Hundreds!

CHARLIE

Hundreds!

SARAH

Certainly; I'm laying eggs all the time.

CHARLIE *(A pause)*

You . . . lay eggs.

SARAH

Certainly! Right and left.
  (*A pause*)

NANCY

Well.

LESLIE (*Eyes narrowed*)

You, uh . . . you *don't* lay eggs, hunh?

CHARLIE (*Incredulous*)

No; of course not!

LESLIE (*Exploding*)

There! You see?! What did I tell you?! They don't even lay eggs!

NANCY

  (*Trying to save the situation*)
How many . . . uh . . . eggs have you laid, Sarah?

SARAH (*Thinks about it for a bit*)

Seven thousand?

NANCY (*Admonishing*)

Oh! Sarah!

SARAH

No?

NANCY

Well, I dare say! Yes! But, really!

SARAH

I'm sorry?

NANCY

No! Never that!

CHARLIE

  (*To* LESLIE, *with some awe*)
Seven thousand! Really?

LESLIE

  (*Gruff; the usual husband*)
Well, *I* don't know. I mean . . .

NANCY

What do you *do* with them, Sarah? How do you take *care* of them?

SARAH

Well . . . they just . . . float away.

NANCY (Chiding)

Oh, Sarah!

SARAH

Some get eaten—by folk passing by, which is a blessing, really, or we'd be inundated—some fall to the bottom, some catch on growing things; there's a disposition.

NANCY

Still!

SARAH

Why? What do you do with them?

NANCY (Looks at her nails briefly)

It's different with us, Sarah. In the birthing, I mean; I don't know about . . . well, how you go about it!

SARAH (Shy)

Well . . . we couple.

LESLIE

Shhh!

NANCY

Yes; I thought. And so do we.

SARAH (Relieved)

Oh; good. And then—in a few weeks—

NANCY

Oh, it takes a lot longer for us, Sarah: nine months.

SARAH

Nine months! Leslie!

LESLIE

Wow!

SARAH

Nine months.

NANCY

And then the young are born. Is born . . . usually.

SARAH

Hm?

NANCY

Is. We usually have one, Sarah. One at a time. Oh, two, occasionally; rarely three or more.

SARAH *(Commiserating)*

Oh, Nancy!

LESLIE *(To* CHARLIE*)*

If you have only one or two, what if they're washed away, or eaten? I mean, how do you . . . perpetuate?

NANCY *(Gay laugh)*

That never happens. We keep them with us . . . till they're all grown up and ready for the world.

SARAH

How long is that?

CHARLIE

Eighteen . . . twenty years.

LESLIE

You're not serious!

NANCY

Oh, we *are!*

LESLIE

You *can't* be.

CHARLIE *(Defensive)*

Why not?!

LESLIE

Well . . . I mean . . . *think* about it.

CHARLIE *(Does)*

Well . . . it *is* a long time, I suppose, but there's no other way for it.

NANCY

Just as you let them float away, or get caught on things; there's no other way for it.

SARAH

How many have you birthed?

NANCY

Three.

LESLIE

Pfft!

SARAH

(Still with the wonder of that)

Only three.

NANCY

Of course, there's *another* reason we keep them with us.

SARAH

Oh? What is that?

NANCY *(Puzzled at her question)*

Well . . . we *love* them.
(*Pause*)

LESLIE

Pardon?

CHARLIE

We *love* them.

LESLIE

Explain.

CHARLIE

What?

LESLIE

What you said.

CHARLIE

We said we love them.

LESLIE

Yes; explain.

CHARLIE *(Incredulous)*

What love means?!

NANCY *(To* SARAH*)*

Love? Love is one of the emotions.
(*They look at her, waiting*)
One of the *emotions,* Sarah.

SARAH *(After a tiny pause)*

But, what *are* they?!

NANCY *(Becoming impatient)*

Well, you *must* have them. You *must* have *emotions.*

LESLIE *(Quite impatient)*

We may, or we may not, but we'll never know unless you define your
terms. Honestly, the imprecision! You're so thoughtless!

CHARLIE *(Miffed)*

Well, we're sorry!

LESLIE

You have to make allowances!

CHARLIE

All *right!!*

LESLIE

Just . . . thoughtless.

CHARLIE

All *right!*

SARAH

Help us, Nancy.

NANCY (*To* SARAH *and* LESLIE)

Fear. Hatred. Apprehension. Loss. Love.

(*Pause*)

Nothing?

(*A bedtime story*)

We keep them with us because they need us to; and we feel possessive toward them, and grateful, and proud . . .

CHARLIE (*Ironic*)

And lots of *other* words describing emotions. You can't *do* that, Nancy; it doesn't help.

NANCY (*Annoyed*)

Then *you* do it! And when we get back home, I'm packing up and taking a good long trip. *Alone.* I've been married to you far too smoothly for far too long.

CHARLIE (*To* LESLIE)

That's an example of emotion: frustration, anger . . .

NANCY (*To herself*)

I'm too *old* to have an affair.

(*Pause*)

No, I'm not.

(*Pause*)

Yes, I am.

CHARLIE (*Chuckling*)

Oh, come on, Nancy.

(*To* LESLIE *and* SARAH)

Maybe *I* can do it. How did you two get together? How'd ya meet?

LESLIE

Well, I was just going along, one day, minding my own business . . .

SARAH

Oh, Leslie!

(To CHARLIE)

I was reaching my maturity, and so, naturally, a lot of males were paying attention to me—milling around—you know, preening and snapping at each other and generally showing off, and I noticed one was hanging around a little distance away, not joining in with the others . . .

LESLIE

That was me.

SARAH

. . . and I didn't pay too much attention to him, because I thought he was probably sickly or something, and besides, there were so many others, and it was time to start coupling . . .

LESLIE

You noticed me.

SARAH

. . . when, all of a sudden! There he was, right in the middle of them, snapping away, really fighting, driving all the others off. It was quite a rumpus.

LESLIE *(An aside,* to CHARLIE)

They didn't *amount* to much.

SARAH *(Shrugs)*

And so . . . all the others drifted away . . . and there he was.

LESLIE

They didn't *drift* away: I drove them away.

SARAH

Well, I suppose that's true.
   (Bright)
Show them your scar, Leslie!
   (To CHARLIE *and* NANCY)
Leslie has a marvelous scar!

LESLIE *(Proud)*

Oh . . . some other time.

SARAH

And there he *was* . . . and there *I* was . . . and here we *are*.

CHARLIE

Well, yes! That proves my point!

LESLIE

What?

CHARLIE *(Pause)*

About *love*.

(Pause)

He *loved* you.

SARAH

Yes?

CHARLIE

Well, *yes.* He drove the others away so he could have *you.* He wanted *you.*

SARAH

(As if what CHARLIE *has said proves nothing)*

Ye-es?

CHARLIE

Well . . . it's so *clear.* Nancy, isn't it clear?

NANCY

I don't *know.* Don't talk to me; you're a terrible person.

CHARLIE *(Under his breath)*

Oh, for God's sake! Leslie! *Why* did you want Sarah?

LESLIE

Well, as I told you: I was just going along one day, minding my own business, and there was this great commotion, with all the others around her, and so I decided *I* wanted her.

CHARLIE *(Losing, but game)*

Didn't you think she was . . . pretty—or whatever?

LESLIE

I couldn't really see, with all the others hovering. She *smelled* all right.

CHARLIE

Have you ever, you know, coupled with anyone else since you met Sarah?

NANCY

Charlie!

LESLIE *(Pause; too defensive)*

Why should I?

CHARLIE *(Smiles)*

Just asking.

(Patient)

Is that your *nature?* Not to go around coupling whenever you feel like it, whatever female strikes your fancy?

SARAH *(Fascinated)*

Very interesting.

LESLIE (*To shut her up*)

It is *not*!
>(*To* CHARLIE)

I've coupled in my time.

CHARLIE

Since you met Sarah?

LESLIE

I'm not going to *answer* that.

SARAH (*Hurt*)

You *have?*

CHARLIE

No; he means he hasn't. And he's embarrassed by it. What about you, Sarah? Have you been with anyone since Leslie?

LESLIE

Of *course* she hasn't!

NANCY

What an *awful* question to ask Sarah! You should be *ashamed* of yourself!

CHARLIE

It's not an awful question at all.

NANCY

It *is!* It's dreadful! Of course she hasn't.

CHARLIE (*Annoyed*)

What *standards* are you using? How would *you* know?

NANCY (*Up on her high horse*)

I just know.

CHARLIE

Things might be different, you know . . .
>(*Gestures vaguely around*)

. . . down . . . *there*. I don't think it's dreadful at *all*.

SARAH (*To* NANCY *and* CHARLIE)

The truth of the matter is: no, I haven't.

LESLIE

What are you getting at?!

CHARLIE

It's hard to explain!

LESLIE

Apparently.

CHARLIE

Especially to someone who has no grasp of conceptual matters, who hasn't heard of half the words in the English language, who lives on the bottom of the sea and has green scales!

LESLIE

Look, buddy . . . !

SARAH	NANCY
Leslie . . .	Now you two boys just . . .

CHARLIE *(Half to himself)*

Might as well be talking to a fish.

LESLIE

(Really angry; starts toward CHARLIE*)*

That does it!

NANCY

Charlie! Look out! Sarah, stop him!

SARAH *(Stamps her paw)*

Leslie! You be nice!

LESLIE *(To* SARAH*)*

He called me a fish!

SARAH

He did not!

NANCY

No he didn't; not quite. He said he might as well.

LESLIE

Same thing.

CHARLIE *(A glint in his eye)*

Oh? What's the matter with fish?

NANCY *(Sotto voce)*

Calm down, Charlie . . .

CHARLIE *(Persisting)*

What's the matter with fish, hunh?

SARAH

Be good, Leslie . . .

LESLIE

(On his high horse—so to speak)
We just don't think very highly of fish, that's all.

CHARLIE

(Seeing a triumph somewhere)
Oh? You don't like fish, hunh?

NANCY

Now, *both* of you!

CHARLIE

What's the matter with fish all of a sudden?

LESLIE

(Real middle class, but not awful)
For one thing, there're too many of them; they're all over the place . . .
racing around, darting in front of you, *picking* at everything . . . moving in,
taking over where you live . . . and they're stupid!

SARAH *(Shy)*

Not all of them; porpoises aren't stupid.

LESLIE *(Still wound up)*

All right! Except for porpoises . . . they're stupid!
(Thinks about it some more)
And they're dirty!

CHARLIE

(Mouth opens in amazement and delight)
You're . . . you're prejudiced! Nancy, he's . . . You're a bigot!
(Laughs)
You're a goddamn bigot!

LESLIE *(Dangerous)*

Yeah? What's that?

NANCY

Be careful, Charlie.

LESLIE *(Not amused)*

What *is* that?

CHARLIE

What? A bigot?

LESLIE

I don't know. Is that what you said?

CHARLIE *(Right on with it)*

A bigot is somebody who thinks he's better than somebody else because they're different.

LESLIE *(Brief pause; anger defused)*

Oh; well, then; that's all right. I'm not what you said. It's *not* because they're different: it's because they're stupid and they're dirty and they're all over the place!

CHARLIE

(Parody of studying and accepting)

Oh. Well. That's all right, then.

NANCY *(Wincing some)*

Careful, Charlie.

LESLIE

(Absorbed with his own words)

Being different is . . . interesting; there's nothing implicitly inferior or superior about it. *Great* difference, of course, produces natural caution; and if the differences are too extreme . . . well, then, reality tends to fade away.

NANCY *(An aside; to* CHARLIE*)*

And so much for conceptual matters.

CHARLIE

(Dismissing it with bravado)

Ooooooooh, he probably read it somewhere.

SARAH

(Looks at the sky, and about her, expansively)

My! It *is* quite something out here, isn't it? You can see! So very far!

(She sees birds with some consternation)

What are those?

*(*LESLIE *sees them. Tenses. Does an intake of breath)*

NANCY *(looking up)*

Birds. Those are birds, Sarah.

*(*LESLIE *in reaction to the birds starts moving up the dune)*

SARAH

Leslie! Leslie!

*(*LESLIE *continues to move to top of the dune; growling)*

NANCY

What's he doing?

SARAH

He's . . .

(*Shrugs*)

. . . well, he does it everywhere we go, so why not up here? He checks things out, makes sure a way is open for us . . .

CHARLIE

It's called instinct.

SARAH

(*Polite, but not terribly interested*)

Oh? *Is* it.

CHARLIE (*Nods; quite happy*)

Instinct.

SARAH

Well, this isn't the sort of situation we run into every day, *and* . . . creatures do tend to be devious; you don't know what's going to happen from one minute to the next . . .

NANCY

Certainly, certainly. Will he be all right? I mean . . .

SARAH

Oh, certainly. He's kind and he's a good mate, and when he tells me what we're going to do, I find I can live with it quite nicely. And you?

NANCY

Uh . . . well, we manage rather like that I guess.

SARAH (*Rapt*)

Oh, my goodness; *see* them up there! How they go!

CHARLIE

Seagulls.

SARAH

Sea . . . gulls.

(*Still absorbed*)

The wonder of it! What holds them up?

CHARLIE (*Shy, but helpful*)

Aerodynamics.

SARAH (*Still enraptured*)

Indeed.

NANCY

Oh really, Charlie.

CHARLIE *(Feelings hurt)*

Well, it *is*.

SARAH *(To* HIM*)*

Oh, I wasn't *doubting* it.
   (Attention back to the birds)
See them swim!

CHARLIE

(More sure of himself now)
Fly, they fly; birds fly.

SARAH *(Watching the birds)*

The rays are rather like that: swimming about; what do you call it—flying.
Funny creatures; shy, really; don't give that impression, though; stand-
offish, rather curt.

NANCY

Rays. Yes; well, we know them.

SARAH *(Pleased)*

Do you!

CHARLIE

Nancy means we've *seen* them; photographs.

SARAH

What is *that*?

CHARLIE

Photographs? It's a . . . no, I'd better not try.

SARAH *(Coquettish)*

Something I shouldn't know? Something you could tell Leslie but not me?

NANCY *(Laughs)*

Heavens, no!

SARAH

I mean, I *am* a married woman.

CHARLIE *(Surprised)*

Do you *do* that? I mean, do you . . . ? I don't know what I mean.

NANCY

Charlie! Just think what we can tell our children and our grandchildren:
that we were here when Sarah saw it all!

CHARLIE

Sure! And if you think they'd have us put away for all that other—for living on the beach . . .

NANCY *(Nodding along)*

... "from beach to beach, seaside nomads . . ."

CHARLIE

. . . yes, then *what* do you *think* they'd *say* about *this!*

(*Mimics her*)

"Charlie and I were sitting around, you see, when all at once, lo and behold, these two great green lizards . . ." How do you think they'd take to *that?!* Put it in one of your postcards, Nancy, and mail it out.

NANCY

Ohhhhh, Charlie! You give me the pip, you know that?

SARAH *(Calling to* LESLIE*)*

Leslie, Leslie.

LESLIE

(LESLIE *cautiously starts down the dune*)

Are you all right?

SARAH

Oh, Leslie, I've had an absolutely fascinating time. Leslie . . .

(*Points to the sky*)

. . . up there.

LESLIE

What *are* they?

SARAH *(Bubbling with it)*

They're called *birds,* and they don't swim, they fly, and they stay up by something called aerodynamics . . .

LESLIE

What is *that?*

SARAH *(Rushing on)*

I'm sure I don't know, and *I* said they looked like rays, and *they* said they knew rays through something called photographs, though they wouldn't tell me what that *was,* and Charlie gives Nancy the pip.

LESLIE

There, I was right! You can't trust somebody like that! How can you trust somebody like that? You can't trust somebody like that!

NANCY

(*With a desperate attempt to save the situation*)

Well, what does it matter? We're all *dead.*

SARAH

Dead? Who's dead?

NANCY

We are.

SARAH *(Disbelief)*

No.

NANCY

According to Charlie here.

CHARLIE *(Without humor)*

It's not to be joked about.

SARAH

All of us?

NANCY *(Chuckles)*

Well, I'm not certain about that; he and I, apparently. It all has to do with liver paste. The fatal sandwich.

CHARLIE

Explain it right! Leave it alone if you're not going to give it the dignity it deserves.

NANCY

(To LESLIE *and* SARAH; *a trifle patronizing)*

I mean, we *have* to be dead, because Charlie has decided that the wonders do not occur; that what we have not known does not exist; that what we cannot fathom cannot be; that the miracles, if you will, are bedtime stories; he has taken the leap of faith, from agnostic to atheist; the world is flat; the sun and the planets revolve about it, and don't row out too far or you'll fall off.

CHARLIE *(Sad; embarrassed)*

I couldn't live with you again; I'm glad it doesn't matter.

NANCY *(To* CHARLIE; *nicely)*

Oh, Charlie.

LESLIE

(To CHARLIE, *not believing any of it)*

When did you die?

CHARLIE

Pardon?

SARAH *(To* NANCY; *whispering)*

He's not dead.

NANCY *(To* SARAH*)*

I know.

LESLIE

Did we frighten you to death, or was it before we met you?

CHARLIE

Oh, *before* we met you; after lunch.

LESLIE

Then I take it *we* don't *exist*.

CHARLIE *(Apologetic)*

Probably not; I'm sorry.

LESLIE *(To* NANCY*)*

That's quite a mind he's got there.

NANCY

(Grudgingly defending CHARLIE*)*

Well . . . he thinks things through.

(Very cheerful)

As for *me*, I couldn't care less: I'm having far too interesting a time.

SARAH

Oh, I'm so glad!

LESLIE *(Puzzled)*

I *think* I exist.

CHARLIE *(Shrugs)*

Well, *that's* all that matters; it's the same thing.

NANCY

(To SARAH*; considerable enthusiasm)*

Oh, a voice from the dead.

LESLIE *(To* CHARLIE*)*

You mean it's all an illusion?

CHARLIE

Could be.

LESLIE

The whole thing? Existence?

CHARLIE

Um-hum!

LESLIE

(Sitting down with CHARLIE*)*

I don't believe *that* at all.

CHARLIE

Well, it isn't *my* theory.

LESLIE

Whose theory *is* it, then?

CHARLIE (*Angry*)

What?!

LESLIE

Whose theory *is* it? Don't you yell at me.

CHARLIE

I am not *yelling* at you!

LESLIE

Yes, you are! You *did!*

CHARLIE

Well, then, I'm sorry.

LESLIE

Whose *theory* is it?

CHARLIE (*Weary*)

Descartes.

LESLIE (*Annoyed*)

What is *that?*

CHARLIE

What?

LESLIE

What you *said.*

CHARLIE (*Barely in control*)

DESCARTES!! DESCARTES!! I THINK: THEREFORE I AM!!
   (*Pause*)
COGITO! ERGO! SUM! I THINK: THEREFORE I AM!!
   (*Pause. Pleading*)
Now you're going to ask me what *think* means.

NANCY

(*Comforting, moving to him, genuine*)
No, he's *not;* he wouldn't *do* that.

CHARLIE

I haven't got it *in* me.

NANCY

It's all right.

LESLIE (*To* SARAH)

I know what think means.

SARAH

Of course you do!

LESLIE (*Agreeing*)

Well!

CHARLIE

I couldn't take it.

NANCY

It's not going to happen.

CHARLIE

It's more than I could . . . Death is release, if you've lived all right, and *I*
have.

> (NANCY *hugs him, but he goes on*)

As well as most, easily; when it comes time, and I put down my fork on the
plate, line it up with the knife, take a last sip of wine, or water, touch my
lips and fold the napkin, push back the chair . . .

NANCY

> (*Shakes him by the shoulders, looks him in the eye*)

Charlie!

> (*Kisses him on the mouth, her tongue entering, for quite a little;
> he is passive, then slowly responds, taking comfort, and sharing;
> they come apart, finally; he shrugs, chuckles timidly, smiles,
> chucks her under the chin*)

CHARLIE (*Shy*)

Well.

NANCY

It is all *right;* and you're alive. It's all right and, if it isn't . . . well, it will just
have to do. No matter what.

CHARLIE (*Irony*)

This will have to do.

NANCY

Yes, this will have to do.

SARAH

Is he all right?

NANCY

Well . . . he's been through life, you see and . . . yes, I suppose he's all right.

> (*The sound of the jet plane again from stage left to stage right,
> growing, becoming deafeningly loud, diminishing.*
> CHARLIE *and* NANCY *follow its course;* LESLIE *and* SARAH *are terri-
> fied; they rush half out of sight over the dune*)

NANCY
(In the silence following the plane)
Such *noise* they make.

CHARLIE
They'll crash into the dunes one day; I don't know what good they do.

NANCY
(Seeing LESLIE *and* SARAH, *pointing to them)*
Oh, Charlie! Look! Look at them!

CHARLIE
Hm? What?
(Sees them)
Oh!

NANCY
Oh, Charlie; they're frightened. They're so frightened!

CHARLIE *(Awe)*
They are.

LESLIE
(From where he is; calling)
What *was* that?!

NANCY *(Calling; a light tone)*
It was an aeroplane.

LESLIE
Well, what *is* it?!

CHARLIE
It's a machine that . . . it's a method of . . .

LESLIE
What?

CHARLIE *(Shouting)*
It's a machine that . . . it's a method of . . .
*(*LESLIE *and* SARAH *begin to move back, paw in paw, glancing back at the plane as they move)*
It's a . . . it's like a bird, except that we make them—we put them together, and we get inside them, and that's how we fly . . . sort of.

SARAH *(Some awe)*
It's terrifying!

NANCY
Well, you get used to it.

LESLIE

(To CHARLIE; *to get it straight)*

You . . . fly.

CHARLIE

Yes. Well, some do. *I* have. Yes! *I* fly. We do all sorts of things up here.

LESLIE

I'll bet you do.

CHARLIE

Sure; give us a machine and there isn't anywhere we won't go. Why, we even have a machine that will . . . go down there; under water.

LESLIE *(Brow furrowed)*

Then . . . you've *been*—what do you call it: under water?

CHARLIE

Well, not in one of the machines, no. And nowhere near as deep as . . .

NANCY

Charlie *used* to go under—near the shore, of course; not very deep.

CHARLIE

Oh, God . . . years ago.

NANCY

Yes, and Charlie has missed it. He was telling me how much he used to love to go down under, settle on the bottom, wait for the fish to come . . .

CHARLIE

(Embarrassed; indicating LESLIE *and* SARAH)

It was a *long* time ago.

(To NANCY)

Nancy, not now! Please!

LESLIE *(Very interested)*

Really.

CHARLIE

It didn't *amount* to much.

NANCY

Oh, it *did;* it *did* amount, and to a great deal.

CHARLIE *(Embarrassed and angry)*

Lay off, Nancy!

NANCY

(Turns on CHARLIE, *impatient and angry)*

It used to make you *happy,* and you used to be *proud* of what made you happy!

CHARLIE

LEAVE OFF!!
(Subsides)
Just . . . leave off.
(A silence. Now, to LESLIE *and* SARAH; *quietly)*
It was just a game; it was enough for a twelve-year-old, maybe, but it wasn't
. . . finding out, you know; it wasn't *real.* It wasn't enough for a memory.
(Pause; shakes his head)

CHARLIE

(Barely controlled rage; to LESLIE)
Why did you come up here in the first place?

LESLIE *(Too matter-of-fact)*

I don't know.

CHARLIE *(Thunder)*

COME! ON!

LESLIE

I don't know!
(To SARAH; *too offhand)*
Do I know?

SARAH *(Yes and no)*

Well . . .

LESLIE *(Final)*

No, I don't know.

SARAH

We had a sense of not belonging any more.

LESLIE

Don't, Sarah.

SARAH

I should, Leslie. It was a growing thing, nothing abrupt, nor that anything
was different, for that matter.

LESLIE *(Helpless)*

Don't go on, Sarah.

SARAH

. . . in the sense of having changed; but . . . *we* had changed . . .
(Looks about her)
. . . all of a sudden, everything . . . down there . . . was terribly . . . interesting, I suppose; but what did it have to do with *us* any more?

LESLIE

Don't, Sarah.

SARAH

And it wasn't . . . comfortable any more. I mean, after all, you make your nest, and accept a whole . . . array . . . of things . . . and . . . we didn't feel we *belonged* there any more. And . . . what were we going to do?!

CHARLIE *(After a little; shy)*

And that's why you came up.

LESLIE *(Nods, glumly)*

We talked about it.

SARAH

Yes. We did, for a long time. Considered the pros and the cons. Making do down there or trying something else. But what?

CHARLIE

And so you came up.

LESLIE

Is that what we did? Is that what we were doing? I don't know.

CHARLIE

(He has hardly been listening; speaks to himself more than to any-one else)

All that time; the eons.

LESLIE

Hm?

NANCY

What was that, Charlie?

CHARLIE

The eons. How long is an eon?

NANCY *(Encouraging him)*

A very long time.

CHARLIE

A hundred million years? Ten times that? Well, a distance certainly. What do they call it . . . the primordial soup? the glop? That heart-breaking second when it all got together, the sugars and the acids and the ultraviolets, and the next thing you knew there were tangerines and string quartets.

LESLIE

What are *they*?

CHARLIE

(Smiles, a little sadly, shrugs)

It doesn't matter. But somewhere in all that time, halfway, probably, halfway between the aminos and the treble clef—

(Directed to SARAH *and* LESLIE*)*

listen to this—there was a time when we *all* were down there, crawling around, and swimming and carrying on—remember how we read about it, Nancy . . .

NANCY

Yes . . . crawling around, and swimming . . . rather like it is now, but very different.

CHARLIE

Yes; very.

(To LESLIE *and* SARAH*)*

Are you interested in any of this?

SARAH *(Genuine, and pert)*

Oh! Fascinated!

CHARLIE

And you understand it; I mean, you follow it.

LESLIE

(Hurt, if not quite sure of himself)

Of *course* we follow it.

SARAH *(Wavering a little)*

Of . . . of course.

NANCY

Of *course* they do.

LESLIE *(A kind of bluff)*

"Rather like it is now, but very different" . . .

(Shrugs)

Whatever that means.

CHARLIE

(Enthusiastic didacticism)

It means that once upon a time you and I lived down there.

LESLIE

Oh, come on!

CHARLIE

Well, no, not literally, and *not* you and me, for that matter, but what we became.

LESLIE *(Feigning enthusiastic belief)*

Um-hum; um-hum.

SARAH

When were we all down there?

CHARLIE

Oh, a long time ago.

NANCY

Once upon a time, Sarah.

SARAH *(After a pause)*

Yes?

NANCY

(Laughs, realizing she is supposed to continue)

Oh my goodness. I feel silly.

CHARLIE

Why? All you're going to do is explain evolution to a couple of lizards.

NANCY *(Rising above it)*

Once upon a time, Sarah, a long, long time ago, long before you were born—even before Charlie here was born . . .

CHARLIE *(Feigning great boredom)*

Veeeerrry funny.

NANCY

Nothing was like it is at all today. There were fish, but they didn't look like any fish you've ever seen.

SARAH

My goodness!

LESLIE

What happened to them?

NANCY *(Trying to find it exactly)*

Well . . . they were dissatisfied, is what they were. So, they grew, or diminished, or . . . or sprouted things—tails, spots, fins, feathers.

SARAH

It sounds extremely busy.

NANCY

Well, it *was*. Of course, it didn't happen all at once.

SARAH *(Looks to LESLIE)*

Oh?

NANCY *(A pleased laugh)*

Oh, *heavens* no. Small changes; adding up. Like . . . well, there probably was a time when Leslie didn't have a tail.

SARAH *(Laughs)*

Oh, really!

LESLIE *(Quite dry)*

I've always had a tail.

NANCY *(Bright)*

Oh, no; there was a time, way back, you didn't. Before you needed it you didn't have one.

LESLIE *(Through his teeth)*

I have *always* had a *tail.*

SARAH

Leslie's very proud of his tail, Nancy . . .

CHARLIE

You like your tail, do you?

LESLIE

(Grim; gathers his tail in front of him)

I have *always* had a *tail.*

SARAH

Of course you have, Leslie; it's a lovely tail.

LESLIE

(Hugging his tail in front of him, anxiety on his face)

I have. I've always had one.

NANCY *(Trying again)*

Well, of course you have, and so did your father before you, and his, too, I have no doubt, and so on back, but maybe they had a smaller tail than you, or a larger.

LESLIE

Smaller!

SARAH

Leslie's extremely proud of his tail; it's very large and sturdy and . . .

NANCY

Well, I'm sure; yes.

LESLIE *(Eying CHARLIE)*

You don't have a tail.

CHARLIE *(Rather proud)*

No, I don't.

LESLIE

What happened to it?

CHARLIE

It fell off. Mutate or perish. Let your tail drop off, change your spots, or maybe just your point of view. The dinosaurs knew a thing or two, but that was about it . . . great, enormous creatures, big as a diesel engine—

(*To* LESLIE)

whatever that may be—leviathans! . . . with a brain the size of a lichee nut; couldn't cope; couldn't figure it all out; went down.

LESLIE (*Quite disgusted*)

What are you talking about?

CHARLIE

Just running on, and trying to make a point. And do you know what happened once? Kind of the crowning moment of it all for me? It was when some . . . slimy creature poked his head out of the muck, looked around, and decided to spend some time up here . . . Came up into the air and decided to stay? And as time went on, he split apart and evolved and became tigers and gazelles and porcupines and Nancy here . . .

LESLIE (*Annoyed*)

I don't believe a word of this!

CHARLIE

Oh, you'd better, for he went back under, too; part of what he became didn't fancy it up on land, and went back down there, and turned into porpoises and sharks, and manta rays, and whales . . . and you.

LESLIE

Come off it!

CHARLIE

It's called flux. And it's always going on; right now, to all of us.

SARAH (*Shy*)

Is it . . . is it for the better?

CHARLIE

Is it for the *better*? I don't *know*. Progress is a set of assumptions. It's very beautiful down there. It's all still, and the fish float by. It's very beautiful.

LESLIE

Don't get taken in.

CHARLIE

What are you going to tell me about? Slaughter and pointlessness? Come on *up* here. *Stay*. The optimists say you mustn't look just yet, that it's all going to work out fine, no matter *what* you've heard. The pessimists, on the other hand . . .

NANCY

It is. It all *is.*

CHARLIE *(Slightly mocking)*

Why?!

NANCY

Because I couldn't bear to think of it otherwise, that's why. I'm not one of these people says that I'm better than a . . . a rabbit; just that I'm more interesting: I use tools, I make art . . .

(Turning introspective)

. . . and I'm aware of my own mortality.

(Pause)

Very.

(Pouting; very much like a little girl)

All rabbits do is eat carrots.

SARAH

(To CHARLIE; *after a little pause; sotto voce)*

What are carrots?

CHARLIE

(Shrugs it off; not interested)

Oh . . . something you eat. They make noise.

LESLIE *(Curiously bitter)*

And tools; and art; and mortality? Do you eat *them?* And do *they* make a noise?

CHARLIE *(Staring hard at* LESLIE)

They make a noise.

NANCY *(She, too)*

What is it, Leslie?

LESLIE *(Intense and angry)*

What *are* these things?!

NANCY

Tools; art; mortality?

CHARLIE

They're what separate *us* from the brute beast.

NANCY *(Very quiet)*

No, Charlie; don't.

LESLIE *(Quiet, cold, and formal)*

You'll have to forgive me, but what is brute beast?

NANCY

Charlie; no!

CHARLIE *(Defiant)*

Brute beast?

LESLIE *(Grim)*

I don't like the sound of it.

CHARLIE *(Stares right at him)*

Brute beast? It's not even aware it's *alive,* much less that it's going to die!

LESLIE

(Pause; then, as if to memorize the words)

Brute. Beast. Yes?

CHARLIE

Right on.
   (Pause)

LESLIE

(Suddenly aware of all eyes on him)

Stop it! Stop it! What are you looking at? Why don't you mind your own business?

NANCY

What more do you want?

CHARLIE *(Intense)*

I don't *know* what more I want.
   (To LESLIE *and* SARAH*)*

I don't know what I want for *you.* I don't know what I feel toward you; it's either love or loathing. Take your pick; they're both emotions. And you're finding out about them, aren't you? About emotions? Well, I want you to know about *all* of it; I'm impatient for you. I want you to experience the whole thing! The full sweep! Maybe I envy you . . . down *there,* free from it all; down there with the *beasts?*
   (A pause)
What would you do, Sarah? . . . if Leslie went away . . . for a long time . . . what would you do then?

SARAH

If he didn't tell me where he was going?

CHARLIE

If he'd gone!
   (Under his breath)
For God's sake.

(Back)

If he'd taken off, and you hadn't seen him for the *longest* time.

SARAH

I'd go look for him.

LESLIE *(Suspicious)*

What are you *after?*

CHARLIE

(To SARAH; *ignoring* LESLIE*)*

You'd go look for him; fine. But what if you knew he was never coming back?

*(*SARAH *does a sharp intake of breath)*

What about that?

NANCY

You're heartless, Charlie; you're relentless and without heart.

CHARLIE *(Eyes narrowing)*

What would you do, Sarah?

(A pause, then she begins to sob)

SARAH

I'd . . . I'd . . .

CHARLIE

You'd cry; you'd cry your eyes out.

SARAH

I'd . . . cry; I'd . . . I'd cry! I'd . . . I'd cry my eyes out! Oh . . . Leslie!

LESLIE

(Trying to comfort SARAH*)*

It's all right, Sarah!

SARAH

I want to go back; I don't want to stay here any more.

(Wailing)

I want to go *back!*

(Trying to break away)

I want to go *back!*

NANCY

(Moves to SARAH, *to comfort her)*

Oh, now, Sarah! Please!

SARAH

Oh, Nancy!

(Bursts into new sobbing)
I want to go back!

NANCY

Sarah!

CHARLIE

I'm sorry; I'm . . . I'm sorry.

LESLIE

Hey! Mister!
(Hit)
You've made her cry; she's never done anything like that.
(Hit)
You made her cry!

CHARLIE

I'm sorry, I . . . stop that!
I'm sorry; I . . .
(Hit)
. . . stop that!

LESLIE

You made her cry!
(Hit)

CHARLIE

STOP IT!

LESLIE

I ought to tear you apart!

CHARLIE

Oh my God!
(LESLIE begins to choke CHARLIE, standing behind CHARLIE, his arm around CHARLIE's throat. It has the look of slow, massive inevitability, not fight and panic)

NANCY

Charlie!
(SARAH and NANCY rush to stop it)

SARAH

Leslie! Stop it!

CHARLIE

Stop . . . it . . .

LESLIE (*Straining with the effort*)

You . . . made . . . her . . . cry . . . mister.

NANCY

Stop! Please!

SARAH

Leslie!

CHARLIE (*Choking*)

Help . . . me . . .
(LESLIE *suddenly lets go;* CHARLIE *sinks to the sand*)

LESLIE

Don't you talk to me about brute beast.

SARAH (*To* LESLIE)

See to him.

LESLIE (*Cold*)

Are you all right?

CHARLIE

Yes; yes, I am.
(*Pause*)

LESLIE

(*Attempts a quiet half joke*)
It's . . . rather dangerous . . . up here.

CHARLIE (*Looks him in the eye*)

Everywhere.

LESLIE

Well. I think we'll go back down now.

NANCY

(*Hand out; a quiet, intense supplication*)
No!

LESLIE

Oh, yes. I think we must.

NANCY

No! You mustn't!

SARAH (*As a comfort*)

Leslie says we must.
(LESLIE *puts his paw out*)

NANCY

No!

(CHARLIE *takes it*)

LESLIE

This *is* how we do it, isn't it?

SARAH *(Watching; tentative)*

Such a wonderful thing to want to do.

LESLIE *(Tight; formal)*

Thank you very much.

NANCY

No!

CHARLIE *(Eyes averted)*

You're welcome.

NANCY

NO!

LESLIE *(Sighs)*

Well.

(LESLIE *and* SARAH *start moving up to the upstage dune to exit*)

NANCY *(In place)*

Please?

(NANCY *moves to follow them*)

SARAH

It's all right; it's all right.

NANCY

You'll have to come back . . . sooner or later. You don't have any choice.
Don't you know that? You'll have to come back up.

LESLIE *(Sad smile)*

Do we?

NANCY

Yes!

LESLIE

Do we have to?

NANCY

Yes!

LESLIE

Do we *have* to?

NANCY *(Timid)*

We could *help* you. Please?

LESLIE *(Anger and doubt)*

How?

CHARLIE *(Sad, shy)*

Take you by the hand? You've got to *do* it—sooner or later.

NANCY *(Shy)*

We *could* help you.

(LESLIE *pauses; descends a step down the dune; crouches; stares at them*)

LESLIE *(Straight)*

All right. Begin.

(NANCY *and* CHARLIE *look at each other.*)

CURTAIN

Listening

A CHAMBER PLAY

LISTENING was commissioned as a radio play, but it has been composed so that it may be performed on a stage without change.

LISTENING *was first performed on radio in 1976.*

IRENE WORTH *as* THE WOMAN

JAMES RAY *as* THE MAN

MAUREEN ANDERMAN *as* THE GIRL

Co-Directed by
JOHN TYDEMAN *and* EDWARD ALBEE

LISTENING *was first performed on stage at
The Hartford Stage Co., January 28, 1977.*

ANGELA LANSBURY *as* THE WOMAN

WILLIAM PRINCE *as* THE MAN

MAUREEN ANDERMAN *as* THE GIRL

Directed by EDWARD ALBEE

CHARACTERS

THE MAN   *Fifty, or so; a good head, good profile, longish grey hair, tall rather than short, body average to thin; dress, casual, but a bit flamboyant.*

THE WOMAN   *Fifty; plain, ample, tall, hair pulled back, little makeup, "sensible" clothes.*

THE GIRL   *Twenty-five, give or take; thin, fragile, pretty, dressed in a simple, lovely pastel.*

THE VOICE   *A recorded voice, not stagey.*

THE SCENE

A great, semi-circular wall. Maybe we see over the top of it—trees and sky behind, and maybe ivy hangs down, but the walls continue to the wings: a sort of cyclorama. Stone. In the center of the wall, coming out in a semi-circle (reverse to that of the wall) as many feet in diameter as will make a graceful design for the size of the stage, a fountain pool, raised two or three steps. Above it, a monster head in half relief, the spigot of the fountain emerging from the mouth. A green stain down the wall from the spigot to the pool basin. Two benches, one to either side of the pool, following the shape of the wall. Hot, white light.

THE MAN *sits on the edge of the fountain bowl; looks about; no haste; looks into the fountain bowl; looks off, back.*

THE VOICE

One.

THE MAN *(Nods to himself)*

Very much as promised. Great circular wall . . . *semi*circular wall; granite, probably. Or is it marble? Well, *I* don't know. *And* the formal fountain here in the center; French fountain; Italianate. Italianate: those Florentine curves! Pool . . . empty. Ever filled? Well, yes, sometime, of course; back *then.* Back when all this . . . overgrowth was a formal garden—clipped and trained and planned and . . . *then* it was full, I imagine. *Were* you? Were you full? Back when all this was . . . back before it had all become . . . impersonal?

(Pause. Nods)

Very much as stated. The marble pool . . . *that* I'm sure of now; very . . . marble. And look at *you!* What a spigot you are! Monster head? Satyr? Which are you? Monstre,* probably . . . or God. Where does the water come from . . . came . . . where did the water come? From your mouth! Of course, right there! The green stain down your chin. What a fountain! Very much as announced.

(Pause)

Very much as announced, indeed. All this was personal—long ago. Oh, turn of the century? Or brought over—stone by stone, numbered, lettered, *mis*numbered, *mis*lettered? No question of it: personal, once. Once. Once the walls were for the curious—to keep them *out,* when it was personal. And now they keep them *in,* do they not? The curious—the very curious, and the rest of us: the curious and the *less* curious. Once, someone who had all this would leave the structure— the Man . . . si . . . on— would leave the patio—God, what a sound it makes! You wouldn't think it would, outdoor and all, merely footfall; but what a sound, echoing out of doors like that!—would leave the patio, alone, or arm in arm, the sudden

*French pronunciation.

silence of the grass after all that echoing, pass through a bower and come on . . . all this, clipped, then, trained, planned . . . and at the end of it all . . . you: you monster, or God.

(*Pause*)

Very much as imagined . . . I would imagine. Would they come . . . *did* they come here, sit on the edge, trail a hand in, exchange empires? I fancy.

(*Pause*)

Very much as suggested, but . . .

(*Talks to the air around him; vaguely accusatory*)

All right, *I'm* here. Where are *you*? Where *are* you?

(*Back as before*)

Be here, she said; *I'll* show you something!

(*Chuckles. Pause. More sober*)

And many, I suppose, over all the years, many sentences like that. *Be* here! *I'll* show you something. Hands trailing, exchanging glances . . . empires, exchanging empires . . . or whatever.

(*Sees someone off*)

Ah! Finally!

(*Calls*)

Hel-*lo*-o!

THE VOICE

Two.

(*The* WOMAN *enters*)

THE MAN (*Rises; hearty*)

Be here, you said. *I'll* show you something.

THE WOMAN (*A big, deep laugh*)

Well, I *will*.

THE MAN (*Vaguely intimidated*)

You're *look*ing well.

THE WOMAN

I am? Well, it's a wonder.

(*Calls off*)

Hey! Come on, now!

(*Back*)

For my age, you mean?

THE MAN

(*Not entirely comfortable*)

Is *she* coming? Is *she* with you? No; for anything.

THE WOMAN (*Stretches*)

Well . . . I may have a few pounds now where ounces were, and . . . what did Houseman say . . . "A dewlap nestles in the chinfolds, now, where once . . . ?" Or something. *And* . . . once you're fifty . . .

THE MAN

Not a chance!

THE WOMAN (*Chuckles*)

Oh, go sit down!
(HE *does;* SHE *calls off*)

THE WOMAN (*Continued*)

Come on! Don't dawdle; you'll forget where you are!

THE MAN

I thought *I* was the only one past *that* mark.

THE WOMAN

Forgetting where you were, or fifty? It comes on little poet's feet, and clubs you in the back of the head. You've stayed thin . . . thinnish; not much, but thinnish. And that orator's profile; that Emperor! I *like* that.

THE MAN (*An actor's reading*)

Hold my hand!

THE WOMAN (*Laughs*)

Don't be silly.
(*Calls off*)
Come on, you!

THE MAN (*Considers it*)

Don't hold my hand.

THE WOMAN (*Calls off*)

Don't dawdle!

THE MAN

(*To himself, but so* SHE *will hear*)
You *did* hold my hand.

THE WOMAN (*Stretches*)

I've held everybody's hand.
(*Pause; a twinkle*)
And, *did* I? *Did* I hold your hand?
(*Looks off again*)

THE MAN

(*Pause; rational consideration*)
Did you hold my hand?

(Conversational)

Is she coming?

THE WOMAN

(Rises; sighs)

Oh, I'd better see. She may have tripped on a leaf, or become a butterfly. We're a fairy today, don't you know.

THE MAN

We *are!*

THE WOMAN *(None too pleased)*

Yes; we are.

(Moving off)

Don't dawdle, I said; where are you now, hunh?

(SHE *exits whence* SHE *entered)*

THE VOICE

Three.

THE MAN

(To himself; very reasonable, dispassionate, interested; a proposition)

Did we hold hands.

(Pause; another)

Did I hold your hand.

(Pause; another)

Did you hold my hand.

(Pause; conclusion)

We held hands.

THE VOICE

Four.

(The WOMAN *reenters, one hand around the* GIRL's *arm; businesslike)*

THE WOMAN

Here we are; I've got her.

THE MAN *(Slightly sad)*

Such a pretty little thing.

THE WOMAN

We weren't a fairy at all; nor had we become a butterfly.

THE MAN *("Really")*

No!

THE WOMAN

No; we were a statue, or a forest thing, one or the other—near a tree, fronds and dapple; very still; quite invisible if you pretended not to see.

(The GIRL *wrenches her arm away, sits on the steps of the pool. The* MAN *moves to one side; the* WOMAN *sits on one of the benches*)

THE MAN (*As before*)

Pretty thing.

THE WOMAN (*Arranging her skirt*)

Oh? You like that . . . tightness around the mouth, that . . . assumptive air? Matriarch at twenty-two, or whatever?

THE MAN (*Determined*)

Well, she looks pretty there by the fountain—sad; pretty.

(*Smiles*)

A resting butterfly, if I may.

THE WOMAN (*Scoffs*)

A butterfly! More like a . . . a praying mantis. *That's* it! A praying mantis; I've been looking for it! Watch her; she won't move now; she'll stay where she is, listening, planning, judging . . .

THE MAN

Judging?

THE WOMAN

. . . when it's safe—to move; to jump? She'll wait it out. *Us* out. She'll try to wait it out.

THE MAN

(*A little remote; a joke, nonetheless*)

Did she devour her husband? They do, you know—the mantis, the female. Has she had one?

THE WOMAN (*Her big laugh again*)

No! Her!? No!

THE MAN

She looks so . . . Shall I talk to her? Shall I go over?

THE WOMAN (*Snorts; laughs*)

You go right ahead.

THE MAN

And that means . . . ?

THE WOMAN

That means you go right ahead. I always say what I mean.

THE MAN

(A statement; a question)

She won't bite me.

THE WOMAN

Let you get close, your guard down, and then—crack!—right in the neck? Like that?

THE MAN

Something like that.

THE WOMAN *(Wrinkles her nose)*

Nothing like that.

THE MAN *(Dubious)*

Well . . .

THE WOMAN

Nothing *like* that! I *told* you! It's not actually the neck, is it.

THE MAN

No.

THE WOMAN

No; they chew the head right off, don't they—the mantis? During the act, as they say?

THE MAN *(Sad)*

As they say. Look at her!

THE WOMAN

(Turns her gaze languidly)

Mmmmmmmmm.

THE MAN

Why is she doing that? With her mouth?

THE WOMAN

(As the GIRL opens and shuts her mouth, a bit like a frog; calm and preoccupied)

Open and close; open and close. That it?

THE MAN

Is she . . . what? Gulping for air?

THE WOMAN *(Doctrinaire)*

No; she's opening and closing her mouth. Is that simple enough? She's breathing perfectly well; let her alone: she'll stop.

THE MAN

Well, hyperventilation is known to be . . .

THE WOMAN

(Through her teeth; curiously angry)

She is not hyperventilating! I hate that term!

THE MAN *(Retreating; defensive)*

Oh. Well. If you say.

THE WOMAN *(That laugh)*

She's . . . well, I *know* her; I know what she does.

(Smiles)

Go talk to her.

THE MAN

Hm?

THE WOMAN

Go *talk* to her. Sidle on over; sit down next to her—well, near; not on top, or she might bolt—mantis or no.

THE MAN *(Accusatory)*

Why don't *you* talk to her?

THE WOMAN

I've *talked* to her. *You* talk to her.

(Pleased with her idea)

Tell her something interesting; tell her something she can chew on.

(Laughs)

Tell her you do her food.

THE MAN *(Shy)*

Oh . . .

THE WOMAN *(Full of enthusiasm)*

Tell her! Tell her you do her food! God, she eats enough! What does she do with it?She must throw it up! Go tell her!

THE MAN

(Rises; moves toward the GIRL*)*

All right.

THE WOMAN

Gently, though; don't be abrupt.

THE MAN *(Approaching)*

She knows I'm coming; she senses it.

THE WOMAN

That's all right.

THE MAN
(Admiration; tenderness)
She *is* an animal, isn't she.

THE WOMAN *(Laughs)*
Oh *ho;* you've found it out. That's close enough; she knows you're there.
Say it. Say whatever you're going to. Softly.

THE MAN *(Softly; gently)*
Hello; I do your food.
(Pause)

THE VOICE
Five.

THE WOMAN *(Giggles)*
Say it again! I love it!

THE MAN
Shall I?

THE WOMAN
Oh, yes! Please! Please!

THE MAN *(Gently)*
Hello; I do your food.
(The WOMAN *giggles again)*
Nothing. Will she . . . can she . . . just not listen?

THE WOMAN
She listens. She may even speak to *you.*

THE MAN
I'll say it again. Shall I?

THE WOMAN *(Eyes closed; giggles)*
Good.

THE MAN *(Leans forward)*
Hello; I do your food.
(The WOMAN *giggles softly)*
She's turning toward me.
(Gasps)
Oh! The eyes! Such beautiful, beautiful eyes!

THE WOMAN
Mmmmmmmm.

THE MAN *(To the* GIRL; *a whisper)*
I do your food.

THE WOMAN

(Eyes closed until notice)
Anything?

THE MAN *(Still gentle)*
I say: I do your food.

THE WOMAN
Something?

THE MAN

(Shoots a silencing hand out)
SHHHH!

THE WOMAN
Oh? Is she going to?

THE MAN

(To the GIRL*; leaning in; urgent)*
Yes? Go on. Speak.

THE GIRL *(A little "away")*
You do . . . what?

THE MAN *(Patient)*
I do your food.

THE GIRL *(Face all screwed up)*
What?!

THE MAN *(Mortified, but persisting)*
I . . . I do your food.

THE WOMAN *("I told you so")*
You wanted to *talk* to her.

THE MAN *(Offended)*
Hush, you!
(To the GIRL*; a little too slow, too precise)*
I—do—your—food.

THE GIRL

(Nods slowly, knowingly; speaks softly)
I do *your* food.
(The WOMAN *laughs quietly)*

THE MAN *(Wheedling; disapproving)*
Oh . . . hush, I said.

(*To the* GIRL)
No; no, you don't.

THE GIRL (*Absolutely flat*)

I don't do your *food.*
(*The* WOMAN *laughs quietly*)
You do my . . . what?

THE MAN

Food.

THE GIRL

(*Considers; shakes her head*)
No.
(*The* WOMAN *laughs quietly*)

THE VOICE

Six.

THE WOMAN

Oh, that was splendid!

THE MAN (*Serious reproach*)
You don't *help.*

THE WOMAN (*Quietly pleased*)
Well . . . I didn't intend to.

THE MAN

(*Sees the* GIRL *has withdrawn into herself*)
She's gone back *into* herself.

THE WOMAN

(*Looks over at the* GIRL *who is staring into the pool again*)
Do it again: say your sentence.

THE MAN (*Will not be mortified*)
No-o!

THE WOMAN

Oh . . . *do!*

THE MAN

No; stop it; no.

THE WOMAN

You have no adventure.
(*Mocking tone*)
"You lack adventure."

THE MAN (*Rebuke*)

Oh!

THE WOMAN (*Pleased with a secret*)

You want her to *talk?*

THE MAN

Well, she *did.*

THE WOMAN

More, I mean. A whole . . . you want to hear a *lot?*

THE MAN (*Embarrassed*)

I don't care.

THE WOMAN

Are you embarrassed?
   (*Laughs*)
Are you embarrassed?

THE MAN (*Too loud*)

Yes! Have her talk!
   (*Under his breath*)
I don't care *what* you do.

THE WOMAN

Oh yes you do!

THE MAN (*Tight-lipped*)

All right; I *care* what you do.

THE WOMAN (*A smug smile*)

You bet you do!

THE MAN

   (*Shakes his head, devout in denial*)
No!

THE WOMAN

Watch me, now!
   (*Raises both arms for attention*)
I said: watch me!

THE MAN

   (*Looking away, at the* GIRL)
I am.

THE WOMAN

Not her! Who do you think I *am?* Me! Watch me!

THE MAN

(Weary; turns and looks at the WOMAN*)*
All right; I'm watching.

THE WOMAN

(Rather like a magician)
I will snap my fingers . . . and *she* will snap; she will snap to, or, "it up." *She*
. . . will snap.

THE MAN *(Annoyed and puzzled)*
What!?

THE WOMAN

Watch me!

THE MAN

All right!

THE WOMAN

Watch *me,* and then watch *her!* Watch *me!*
    *(*SHE *snaps her fingers, looking at the* GIRL*)*
And now . . . look *there.*

THE VOICE

Seven.
    (The GIRL *reacts to the finger-snap rather like a timid animal;* SHE
    tenses, senses her surroundings, then "humanizes" again, pre-
    pares for a conversation, considers something in the pool, laughs,
    none too cheerfully)

THE GIRL

You don't *listen.*

THE WOMAN

(As if the MAN *were not there)*
Well, that may *be.*

THE GIRL

Pay attention, rather, is what you don't do. Listen: oh, yes; carefully, to . . .
oh, the sound an idea makes . . .

THE WOMAN

. . . a *thought.*

THE GIRL

No; an idea.

THE WOMAN

As it does what?

THE GIRL

(Thinks about that for a split second)

Mmmmmmmm . . . as the chemical thing happens, and then the electric thing, and then the muscle; *that* progression. The response—that almost reflex thing, the movement, when an idea happens.

(A strange little smile)

That *is* the way the brain works, is it not? The way it functions? Chemical, then electric, then muscle?

(The WOMAN does an "et voilà!" gesture)

THE MAN *(Quiet awe)*

Where does it come from?

THE WOMAN

What?

THE MAN

The . . . all that. Where does it come from?

THE WOMAN

I haven't found out. It all begins right there: she says, "You don't listen." Every time, she says: "You don't listen."

THE MAN

To what!? You don't listen to what!?

THE WOMAN *(Sotto voce)*

I don't *know* what I don't listen to.

THE MAN *(Accusatory)*

Yes, and do you care?

THE WOMAN *(So reasonable)*

I don't *know.*

THE MAN *(Snorting)*

Of course not!

THE WOMAN *(Quite brusque)*

Defend the overdog once in a while, will you!? At least what you *think* it is. How do you know who's what!?

THE MAN

I don't!

THE WOMAN

All right!

THE MAN *(Shrugs; throws it away)*

Get behind that sentence, that's all you have to do. Find out what precedes.

(Shrugs again)

THE WOMAN
(Nods; smiles ruefully)
Thanks.

THE GIRL
Me! We're talking to me!

THE WOMAN *(To herself)*
I do pay attention. And I hear. I'm ready for a lot.

THE GIRL *(A dare)*
Are you? You!

THE WOMAN *(To the GIRL)*
Am I what?

THE GIRL
Do you pay attention? *Do* you hear? *Are* you ready for a lot?

THE WOMAN *(Puzzles; recalls)*
Oh! *I* see. Well . . . I'd *know.*

THE GIRL
What! If I were . . . to do what?

THE WOMAN *(Languidly)*
Oh . . . say there was glass in there, in the fountain there—sharp glass.
(Pause; interest)
Is there?

THE GIRL *(Looks)*
No; and no water, either—all dry. Leaves, a strand of . . . ivy, all dry; dead
ivy; a stone, and the basin is all set with pebbles; it's rough between them;
smooth pebbles. No sharp glass.

THE WOMAN
If there were, I'd know. Rather, I'd know if you saw it.

THE GIRL
That it was sharp glass?

THE WOMAN
No: that I should pay attention.

THE GIRL
I'm full of guile.

THE WOMAN
But I'd *know.*

THE GIRL
There are so *many* things I could do.

THE WOMAN

Yes? What?

THE GIRL

Say—for example—see how the marble has a waterline, and you'd never look; that's *one* way. Whine, and say I'm hot and don't want the sun anymore; scratch my leg.

THE WOMAN (*Claps her hands softly*)

Very *good*.

THE GIRL

Nothing unsubtle; nothing like reach and pull back, or hold my breath, or . . . start chattering—running on, as they say. Oh, I'd be subtle.

THE WOMAN

Of course; but I'd *know*.

THE GIRL

What!

THE WOMAN (*Calm*)

That you'd found glass . . . sharp glass.

THE GIRL

You *say* you would.

THE WOMAN

I told you: I pay attention. They all make sounds—your chemical thing and your electric thing. I can . . . I can hear your pupils widen.

THE GIRL (*Smiles*)

No you can't.

THE WOMAN

Sharp senses. And the decision *not* to hold the breath . . . that breaks a pattern, too.

THE GIRL (*Breaks in*)

I used to take sharp glass, when I was little and sunburned—brown, not burned—sunbrown, and scrape it along my leg, pretend it was a scalpel; take off the top scale; just that, leave an irregular white path, thin as a thread. The skin below my knees was . . . so glistening. In the summer.

THE WOMAN

Where would you find it?

THE GIRL

Hm?

THE WOMAN

You would *find* it.

THE GIRL

The sharp glass?

THE WOMAN

Mmmmmmmm.

THE GIRL (*Laughs*)

Oh . . . sitting somewhere, seeing the waterline on the marble, or a bottle on the beach, the bottom showing. Pick it up and always broken off just at the bottom. There's lots of sharp glass when you're little. Always. And . . . there's enough later.

THE WOMAN

You're *sure* there's none *there* . . . in the fountain.

THE GIRL

(*Looks back into the fountain*)

No. The skeleton of a mouse; half a blue egg; a feather.

THE WOMAN (*Pressing a little*)

And no glass.

THE GIRL

No.

(*Pause*)

Who built it?

THE WOMAN

What?

THE GIRL (*Impatient*)

Egg! Feather! Mouse! All this!

THE WOMAN (*Shrugs*)

Well, *I* don't know.

THE GIRL (*Puzzled*)

Don't you?

(*Pause; some pique*)

Yes you do!

THE WOMAN

I do?

THE GIRL (*Enraged*)

Yes! You do!

THE WOMAN (*Venomous*)

Subside!

(SHE *clicks her fingers*)

Subside.

(*The* GIRL *subsides*)

THE VOICE

Eight.

THE MAN

Subside?

THE WOMAN

Sure. *It* works: look at her.

THE MAN

Stop and start.

THE WOMAN

And caution.

(*Laughs*)

Oh, don't look at me with those eyes; one of you's enough . . . the "intensity."

THE MAN

How long have I known you?

THE WOMAN (*Cheerful; even coquettish*)

I don't know. Ever? Who knows a lady? Spaniel eyes; does 'ums have a problem?

THE MAN

(*Dismisses her with a gesture*)

I don't know. Go back to *her.*

THE WOMAN

All right. Watch me, now!

(SHE *snaps her fingers*)

THE VOICE

Nine.

THE GIRL (*Everything as before*)

You don't listen!

THE WOMAN (*Soft laugh*)

Well, that may be.

THE GIRL

Pay attention, rather, is what you don't do. Half a blue egg? Half a blue *egg?* I didn't say shell; I said egg.

THE WOMAN

Yes, I know, but it wasn't there . . . nor the mouse bones, nor the feather, so . . . it could be what you said, easily enough. *And* . . . I *thought* you meant shell: half a blue shell. But it doesn't matter, does it?

THE GIRL

Do they ever . . . is it ever filled up?

THE WOMAN

In rain.

THE GIRL

Not . . . not just filled?

THE WOMAN (*Two replies*)

No. I don't think so.

THE GIRL

Never?

THE WOMAN (*Getting peevish*)

Not *now!*

THE GIRL

(*Gazing at the fountainhead*)

Turned on? Neptune there?

THE MAN

Neptune! Of course!

THE WOMAN (*Unconvinced*)

Who?

THE GIRL

Neptune: Roman version of the Egyptian Hapyi, the Greek Poseidon. Isn't that who it is there? "Fountainhead?" Water dribbling off his chin, then coming down like a little boy, on the pebbles, peeing, then like in a tunnel—that hollow sound when there's water there? Don't they . . . don't you . . . isn't it ever filled?

THE WOMAN

I said: no.

THE GIRL

Reason?

THE WOMAN (*Daring contradiction*)

I don't know.

THE GIRL

I wish they . . . I wish it would.

THE WOMAN (*Pause; smile*)

Certainly.

(Pause)

What! Are you stopping? Nothing more to say?

THE GIRL

(Looking back down into the pool)

Well, you say the mouse is not there—the shell of *it*, the skeleton; the feather; the blue shell. It takes some thinking about . . . if they're not there.

THE WOMAN

Why? Do *you* see them?

THE GIRL

I said: it takes some thinking about. I didn't *say* I saw them.

(A smile; daring the WOMAN*)*

Nor that I did.

*(*SHE *looks back into the pool)*

THE WOMAN

(Turning away; slightly contemptuous)

Look away, Dixie*land*.

THE VOICE

Ten.

THE MAN

How do they say? "You're small of spirit."

THE WOMAN *(Unperturbed)*

Which one of us? Who?

THE MAN *(Apologetically)*

You, of course.

THE WOMAN *(Expansive)*

Why not her!?

THE MAN

I don't . . . *know* her.

THE WOMAN *(Mimicking)*

You don't . . . *know* me.

THE MAN

I *thought* so.

THE WOMAN *(Hoots)*

By what right? Holding a hand, or not? Holding whatever . . . or not? What did you hold? What did you *not* hold? Hunh?

THE MAN *(Weary)*

Never mind; leave off.

THE WOMAN

"Let me hold it! Please! Oh, God, I want to hold it!" And then they can't remember—eventually . . . A, if they did, and, B, if they did, what it was.

THE MAN *(Contemptuous)*

Or was not.

THE WOMAN

Go back to your pots.

THE MAN
(Reasonable, if rather pleased with the information)
You're just . . . not nice.

THE WOMAN *(Shrugs)*

Who's nice?

THE MAN

Lots of people.
(Points to the GIRL*)*
She is, probably.

THE WOMAN

Oh? Shall I show you? You want another example?

THE MAN *(Weary)*

Sure.
(Sad chuckle)
Are you going to disillusion me?

THE WOMAN

Oh, not deep down.
(Raises her hand)
Watch me, now.
(Snaps her fingers)

THE VOICE

Eleven.

THE GIRL
(Snaps to; overly enthusiastic)
You don't listen!

THE WOMAN

Well, that may be.

THE GIRL *(Correcting herself)*

Pay attention, rather, is what you don't do.

THE WOMAN

Now, about the girl yesterday . . .

THE GIRL *(Right in)*

What girl yesterday? She deserved it!

THE WOMAN *(To the* MAN*)*

Pay attention, you!

THE MAN

I'm here.

THE WOMAN *(To the* GIRL*)*

She deserved it?

THE GIRL

She deserved it!

THE WOMAN

But so *hard.* And why did you make a fist? Why not your open hand?

THE GIRL

I would have hurt it. Besides: she stole.

THE WOMAN

(A quiet, even correction)

Borrowed; she borrowed.

THE GIRL

Stole!

THE WOMAN *(Reasonable)*

No one would steal what she borrowed.

THE GIRL

Things are borrowed just because they're returned? Stolen things are returned, too.

THE WOMAN

Seldom willfully.

THE GIRL

(Sulking; tension underneath it)

My cardboard was returned? Willfully?

THE WOMAN

Yes!

THE MAN

Her what?

THE WOMAN *(Impatient)*

Her cardboard.

THE GIRL

My cardboard? You say she returned it!

THE WOMAN (*Abrupt*)

Yes! Returned! Willfully!

THE GIRL

After I *hit* her.

THE WOMAN

She hadn't had it long. It wasn't even off the table; her hand was just on it—feeling it, stroking it, not grasping. You made a decision.

THE GIRL

I did not!

THE WOMAN

That she had stolen.

THE GIRL

So did you! That she had borrowed.

THE WOMAN

She said, "Let me look at it." That's all she said to you, isn't it? Wasn't it? Did she say anything more? Did she indicate anything?

THE GIRL

Guile.

THE WOMAN

Indeed!

THE GIRL

Guile.

THE WOMAN (*Chiding*)

Not everything. Not . . . every*one*; not everything.

THE GIRL

She!

THE WOMAN

She, too, hunh?

THE GIRL

Hm?

THE WOMAN

"Such pretty cardboard," she said; "such pretty blue cardboard." And she touched it; just that; and you hit her . . . with a fist, not even open hand . . .

    (*Afterthought*)

ded; openhanded.

THE GIRL

(A general statement; an announcement)

There are things and things. Things to which rules apply—"the" rules—
and things to which . . . to which they do not. And that is that.

(To the MAN*)*

You! There are things and things, aren't there!?

THE MAN *(Startled)*

Me!

THE WOMAN *(Amused; vitalized)*

You! She's talking to you! It's your chance; don't botch it!

THE MAN

But . . .

THE GIRL *(To the* MAN*; again)*

There are things . . . and things. Did you *hear* me? Are *you* real?

THE WOMAN *(Head back; relaxing)*

Just listen; be nice; nod; smile once or twice; encourage her.

(The MAN *leans toward the* GIRL*)*

That's it; lean in.

THE MAN *(To the* GIRL*; private)*

There are things and things; yes.

THE GIRL

(Giggles a little; sharing a confidence)

Yes. Most cardboard is grey . . . or brown, heavier. But blue is . . . unusual. That would be enough, but if you see blue cardboard, tile blue, love it,
want . . . it, and have it . . . then it's special. But—don't interrupt me!

THE WOMAN *(Startled)*

I'm not!

THE MAN

Don't interrupt her!

THE WOMAN *(Annoyed)*

I'm not!

THE GIRL *(Exaggerated woe)*

Neither of you cares.

THE MAN

I *care.*

THE WOMAN

He cares!

(*Afterthought*)

And you *know* about *me*.

THE GIRL (*Snorts*)

You!

(*Back to the* MAN)

Well, if you want more value from it, from the experience, and take *grey* cardboard, mix your colors and paint it, carefully, blue, to the edges, smooth, then it's not *any* blue cardboard but very special: grey cardboard taken and made blue, self-made, self-made blue—better than grey, better than the other blue, because it's self-done. Very valuable, and even looking at it is a theft; touching it, even to take it to a window to see the smooth lovely color, all blue, is a theft. Even the knowledge of it is a theft . . . of sorts.

THE WOMAN

(*To the* MAN; *smiling unpleasantly*)

So, take care!

THE GIRL

Ignore her. Very special.

THE WOMAN (*Leans toward the* GIRL)

But had you *done* that?

THE GIRL (*Sharp*)

What!?

THE MAN (*Puzzled*)

What!?

THE GIRL (*Sharper*)

What!?

THE WOMAN (*Patient smile*)

Taken the grey and carefully made it blue?

THE GIRL

(*Imitates the* WOMAN's *tone and smile*)

It was what I would do it from. It was the model; it was the blue from which I would have made my own. It was the model.

THE WOMAN

So you *didn't* . . . *do* all that.

THE GIRL

It was the model! I would have done it *from* it!

THE WOMAN

Not even *worth* taking.

THE GIRL
It was the *model!* It was worth *taking!*

THE WOMAN
Half, then—half what you said it was; half worth taking. Mitigation; always mitigation.

THE GIRL *(Chin raised)*
Half a theft is worse than none.
(Smiles; quite pleased)

THE WOMAN *(At no one)*
She's a sad girl.
   (Sees the MAN is about to react)
No, no; not this one; the other one; the one she struck at.

THE MAN *(Sad irony)*
Ah. Not this one.

THE WOMAN *(To the GIRL)*
She's a sad girl. You! She's a sad girl!

THE GIRL *(Not really interested)*
Yes? She is?

THE WOMAN *(A catalogue)*
Parents dead; baby dead; husband to the wild wind; catatonic sometimes; others . . . well, not pretty. You caught her at a *good* time. You're not the only one with a couple of problems. Learn to look around you.

THE GIRL
   (Laughs abruptly; leans toward the fountain)
Well, if I were to do *that* . . . I might find something useful—hyperbolic, but . . . useful.

THE WOMAN
I didn't mean to look around. By look around, I didn't mean to look around. I meant . . . look *around.*
   (Pause)
Is there anything there? In the fountain? Anything new?

THE GIRL
There's nothing—except what I said, and who knows about that? Look around me?
   (Sad)
There's nothing. What did the nice one say? You have a past; look for it.
   (Looks into the fountain; shakes her head)
Well, I'm looking. There's nothing.

THE WOMAN (*Gently*)

Well, you have the blue in a piece of cardboard.

(*Sees a refusal to react*)

No? Closing up again? All right.

THE MAN (*Quietly*)

Let her alone.

THE WOMAN (*Sarcastic*)

You see a tear? Is the lower lip a-tremble? The dimple puckered?

THE MAN (*Sad smile*)

No. Just . . . just nothing. Forget it.

THE WOMAN (*Patronizing*)

All right.

(*To the* GIRL; *brusque*)

You! You in the dress! Did I tell you she cried?

(*The* GIRL *shakes her head; pauses, shakes it again, longer*)

No? Well . . . yes. You hit her and she cried; cause and effect.

THE GIRL (*Shakes her head*)

No she didn't; I didn't see it, so it didn't happen: cause and effect.

THE WOMAN (*Grudging admiration*)

You *are* a *wonder!* Well, she did; she did cry. Does that make you feel anything?

THE GIRL

(*As if discovering it for the first time*)

Why is there no *water?*

THE WOMAN

And so much for *that,* hunh? Choose a subject out of the hat? Play pickatopic? Well, we'll come *back* to it, you can't go 'round striking people . . .

THE GIRL (*Strident*)

Why is there no *water!*

THE MAN (*After a pause*)

Tell her.

THE WOMAN

No; *I'll* pick a subject.

THE MAN (*Pleading a little*)

Tell her.

THE WOMAN

You tell her. Subject: *I* used to come here.

THE GIRL *(Hisses it)*

You never did!

THE WOMAN

He . . . and I did.

(*The* MAN *straightens up, startled*)

THE GIRL *(Quite offended)*

No!

THE MAN *(Correcting)*

No now, you and I, we never . . .

THE WOMAN *(Curt; contemptuous)*

I said *he; he!* Are you *he?* I said *he* and I. What are you assuming? Both
of you!

THE MAN

Well, I mean . . . anyone.

THE WOMAN

No; not anyone; I'm not your come into the garden, Maude; nor am I
Maude; but ooooohhhhh . . . yessssss, *I* used to come here.

THE GIRL

It was him! That one there! Wasn't it!

THE MAN

No; no; *listen.*

THE GIRL

WHO THEN!?

THE WOMAN *(Offhand; teasing)*

Oh . . . one of my beaux.

THE GIRL

Well . . . never mind about it! The cardboard! The blue! *I'm* talking about
that!

THE WOMAN *(Dreamy)*

Yes; I know.

THE GIRL *(Dogmatic)*

Blue. That is the subject.

THE WOMAN *(Ibid.)*

Yes; I know.

(*Recalling*)

We would come here, and I would begin to understand things, I think, or
. . . appreciate them, certainly . . . *like* them, at any rate.

Quite together, he not much older; but in *those* days . . .

. . . one was much younger than one *was*.

(*Sees the* GIRL *reaching for something*)

DON'T *DO* THAT!! GET YOUR HAND OUT OF THE POOL!

(*The* GIRL *stops; it has been nothing*)

I'm *not* a stupid woman . . . nor a slow one. Or, have you gathered?

(*Pause*)

THE MAN (*To fill the silence*)

You asking me?

THE WOMAN (*Smiles*)

No. Her. I'm not a stupid woman . . . or have you gathered?

THE GIRL (*Glum*)

You do all right.

THE WOMAN (*Pleased*)

I thought I did.

THE GIRL (*Grudging*)

Well enough.

THE WOMAN

Thank you. *Is* there something there all of a sudden, by the way? In the
pool? Or were you testing me, moving like that?

THE GIRL (*Defiant; quiet*)

Who are *you*?

THE WOMAN

(*Amused; pretends confusion*)

Who *am* I?

THE MAN

(*Not really expecting an answer*)

How many? And when? And was it?

THE WOMAN (*Answering him, in a way*)

Who am *I*?

THE GIRL

You *did* know, then.

THE WOMAN

What? What did I know then?

THE GIRL *(Mumbles)*

Whether it was filled up—a long time ago; whether it was filled up.

THE WOMAN

Speak up!

THE GIRL

Whether it was filled up! If it was filled up!

THE WOMAN

(Pretending not to have heard)

When!?

THE GIRL

You were here! When you were here!

THE WOMAN

(Thinks about it for a moment)

Well, I wouldn't necessarily have known, would I? I *did* . . . but I needn't have. How long ago *was* it?

THE GIRL *(Tentative; after a pause)*

How long ago was it?

THE WOMAN *(Eyes closed)*

Hmmmmmmmm?

THE GIRL *(Pleading)*

How long?

THE WOMAN

(A slow smile; spreads it out)

A long time ago.

THE VOICE

Twelve.

THE MAN

(As the WOMAN *hmmmmmmms and chuckles—closemouthed— throughout)*

Did you?

(Pause)

Did you know?

(Pause)

Did you come here with someone else, and did you know?

(Pause)

Was it full?

(Pause)

Was it *full?*

(Pause)

Did you come here with someone else?

(Pause)

Did you know?

(Pause)

Did you?

(Pause)

THE VOICE

Thirteen.

THE WOMAN *(Laughs)*

Nosey, aren't you.

THE MAN *(Shrugs)*

It's reasonable.

THE WOMAN *(Sighs)*

Nothing is reasonable.

(Raises a hand)

Watch me, now; snap the fingers.

(SHE does; The GIRL comes to attention as before)

THE GIRL *(High-handed accusation)*

You don't *listen.*

THE WOMAN

(Soft laugh; a look at the MAN)

Well, that may be.

THE GIRL

Pay attention, rather, is what you don't do. Cry? She cried!? The girl: she cried?

THE WOMAN *(After a moment)*

Oh, yes.

THE GIRL

Over sky blue!

THE MAN

Sky blue?

THE WOMAN

Cardboard. Can't you retain?

THE MAN *(Offended)*

Well, mostly; not . . . *some* things; the perverse, the obscure, the out of kilter. *I* can follow pretty well, most things.

THE GIRL *(A dare)*

Over sky blue!?

THE WOMAN

Over sky blue?

(Laughs gently)

Oh, my, yes; one of the most frequent. Sky blue? Very frequently; more even than rain—sadness in the face of beauty, day following night—relief: tears of relief; oh, my; or for no reason at all . . . merely how blue it is. Speech after long silence? Remember?

(Pause)

No?

(Pause; the GIRL *shakes her head stubbornly)*

Nothing subtle for you, hunh! Just the *hard* stuff to get *you* crying, eh?: blood?, or shadows on the wall?, or footsteps?

THE GIRL

(Very loud; clearly a new subject)

When did you come here?

THE WOMAN

Oh, you're up to that again.

THE GIRL

When did you *come* here?

THE WOMAN

Hmmmmmm?

THE GIRL

When!

THE MAN *(Quiet pleading)*

Tell her; please.

THE GIRL *(Close to hysteria)*

When!? When did you *come* here!?

THE WOMAN

(Too loud, too slow, too distinct)

A—very—long—time—ago.

(Then, an afterthought)

The benches were only *this high.*

(SHE *gestures and laughs)*

THE GIRL *(Puzzles; laughs)*

Silly!

THE WOMAN

What if *she* had hit *you? Back*, I mean?

THE GIRL

(Thinks a moment; chuckles)
Well, and I would have hit *her* back.
    (Louder, and triumphant)
That would have brought them running!
    (A loud laugh)

THE WOMAN

Yes, but what if it hadn't?
    (The GIRL doesn't respond; stares into the pool)
Don't look down all the time.
    (Pause; no response)
All right; *look* down all the time.

THE VOICE

Fourteen.

THE MAN *(Reaffirming)*

You're *not* nice.

THE WOMAN

    (Smiles; mimics her reply from before)
Who's *nice?*

THE MAN *(Rather vacant)*

Oh . . . *some* people are.

THE WOMAN

Well, *that* may be.

THE MAN *(Laughs brusquely)*

Ha! Don't start in with *me!* That phrase won't work with *me*. Don't try to
snap *me* to attention; I won't *follow* you.

THE WOMAN *(Snorts)*

Who follows *who!*

THE MAN

Whom.

THE WOMAN

I know: who follows who! Does *she* follow *me?* I don't *know* anymore; it's
so *long*.

THE MAN

How long?

THE WOMAN

I said: I don't *know* anymore.

THE MAN (*Curiously superior*)

Not even how long?

THE WOMAN

Not *even*. It's an old vaudeville act now . . . except not very funny, and . . .
thin of reason. Familiar? Familiar territory?

THE MAN (*Chuckles*)

Sort of.

THE WOMAN (*An exaggerated sigh*)

Oh . . . I should have gone into something else, I suppose.
   (*Bright*)
But, then again, so should you!

THE MAN (*Surprised; offended*)

Why!?

THE WOMAN

   (*Laughs; parodies him*)
"I do your food; I do your food." Is that a *life?*

THE MAN

I *repeat*.

THE WOMAN (*Quite light about it*)

I mean, we only go through it once. "I do your food." Is that *enough?*

THE MAN (*Tosses it off*)

Oh . . . go slit your throat.

THE WOMAN

(*Considers that; sucks the end of her forefinger. Matter-of-fact tone*)
I don't think you should say that.

THE MAN (*Quite pleased*)

Does it *bother* you? Does it *get to* you?

THE WOMAN

   (*Shakes her head; doesn't indicate the* GIRL)
You never know who's listening.

THE MAN

Who!?
   (*Realizes; looks quickly at the* GIRL)
Oh!

(To the WOMAN; *sotto voce)*

I'm sorry. Of course! She *does* listen, does she? Or, can? I mean, all the time?

THE WOMAN

Well, you never *know*. You know?

(Chuckles)

God, what a language!

THE MAN

(His attention on the GIRL *again)*

I assumed she . . . turns off. "Turns off" is how they say, isn't it? I assumed she did *that*. On and off.

THE WOMAN *(Bland)*

On and off; up and down; in and out . . . you mustn't be too sure of anything. We listen when we don't think we are, and sometimes when we think we are we haven't heard a thing. *I've* done it—*both* ways.

(Overly interested; overly articulated)

Haven't *you?*

THE MAN *(Tricked into a reply)*

Of course, but . . . oh, go slit your . . . go slit whatever you like.

THE WOMAN *(Shakes her head)*

We must have a *talk* about this; you don't *listen; nobody* listens anymore. Why does nobody *listen?* Hm? I told you not to say it and you say it.

(The MAN *dismisses her with a gesture)*

What! What does that gesture mean? You, too? Are you turning off, too? Well, what will I be left with? Hm?

(Exaggerated wringing of hands)

Oh my, oh my.

(Normal again)

Contemplation of . . . what? Contemplation of whether I should or should not slit my whatever. Take my own etcetera in my very hands. Well, it runs in the family—I suppose there's that. My *grand*mother did it—didn't slit her throat, but did herself in, quite nicely . . . and on purpose, too!

THE MAN

(Interested in spite of himself)

Really?

THE WOMAN

Really! Poisoned herself.

THE MAN

No!

THE WOMAN (*Feigning surprise*)

Oh, I thought she *did*.

THE GIRL (*A whine*)

Me!

THE WOMAN (*To the* GIRL)

Oh, be still, you!

(*The* GIRL *makes a quick, startled sound; withdraws into herself.
To the* MAN)

The event I am about to describe is the day her husband vanished—my grandfather that would be, the day he disappeared. *He* was over seventy—can you follow?

THE MAN (*Impatient; testy*)

Yes yes!

THE WOMAN (*Not to be rushed*)

He was over seventy, and I *think* they'd been happy—though it was a generation wouldn't let you know, you know?—and one fine day he simply disappeared, didn't pack a bag, or act funny beforehand, simply said he was going into town to get some snuff, my grandmother used to tell it—snuff, for God's sake!—and off he went, and do you think he came back? He did not! Never came back? The man at the tobacco store where they sold the snuff said no, he'd not come in, when they asked, and you can be sure they did; and *one* man said he'd seen him take a left at the library, and a policeman said no, *he'd* seen him go off down Willow past the hardware store; and Mrs. Remsen—the Lord rest her soul—said *that* wasn't true at all, that he'd said good day to *her* at the corner of Pocket and Dunder and sauntered off in the direction of the bank—to which, of course, it turned out he had not been. And so my grandmother made a map—being that way, you know: a methodical family—and found the locus where they all had seen him, some others, too, and determined from that, from all the information they'd put together, that from that *spot*, the *locus*, he had gone off in several directions at the same time. He had, in effect . . . dispersed.

THE MAN (*Puzzled*)

He didn't come back? Ever?

THE WOMAN (*Quite miffed*)

He did not!

THE MAN (*Not quite believing*)

And so your *grand*mother took *poison*.

THE WOMAN

O, ye of little faith! She waited for him—being a proper lady, and nearly seventy, herself, at that, she waited for him for seven years, which is the legal time—or was—and when he had not come back by then . . .

THE MAN

(*Finishing it for her; considerable disbelief*)

. . . she went upstairs and poisoned herself, having put a vial away some time before, to have for some such occasion, being a proper lady.

THE WOMAN

That is what we believe.

THE MAN (*Considers it; then*)

No.

THE WOMAN (*Eyes narrowing*)

How do you know she went upstairs?

THE MAN

What!?

THE WOMAN

How do you know she went upstairs? You said . . . and then she went upstairs and poisoned herself. How do you know she went upstairs? That's very suspicious.

THE MAN

(*Unable to believe the discussion*)

I *didn't* know! I assumed it! It's a phrase—she went upstairs and poisoned herself.

THE GIRL (*Plaintive*)

Me? Please?

THE WOMAN (*To the* GIRL)

No! Me! You wait your turn!

THE GIRL (*A whine*)

When?

THE WOMAN

Eventually.

THE VOICE

Fifteen.

THE WOMAN

(*The* GIRL *subsides as before. To the* MAN)

She said—my grandmother, and my mother would verify it if she were still alive, for she was there in the room with me, and I was very little—she said, my grandmother did—"It's seven years today, do you realize that? Seven years to the day. Clearly he's dead." She stood up then and went to the stair—and I remember her hand on the newel post, so well: delicate, withered hand, with liver spots—and she stood there by the stair, and she said, so evenly, so softly, "He's dead; clearly he's dead. I shouldn't think I'd enjoy it much without him, not after all this time." She turned then; she lifted her long skirt gently and went upstairs to her room—a light woman, all bones.

(Pause)

When we called her for dinner and she didn't come, we went up to her, my mother and I—she holding on to me, my hand, I was so little—we went in her room, calling first, then knocking, and there she was, on her bed, quite properly, long dress neat, fingers twined. She was dead.

(Simply; to explain dogma)

He died; so did she.

THE MAN *(Dry)*

One assumption, one fact.

THE WOMAN (SHE, *too*)

Be that as it may.

THE MAN *(A tinge of disrespect)*

Very touching.

THE WOMAN *(Nailing it down)*

He died; and so did she.

THE MAN *(Considerable disbelief)*

By poisoning herself.

THE WOMAN *(Above it)*

That is what we believe.

THE MAN

I dare say.

THE WOMAN *(Smiles, remembers)*

She said to me once, not long before she died, when I was just old enough to make sense of what I heard, she said, "We don't have to live, you know, unless we wish to; the greatest sin, no matter what they *tell* you, the greatest sin in living is doing it badly—stupidly, or as if you weren't really alive, *or* wickedly; taking it in your own hands, taking your life in your own two hands may be the one thing you'll ever do in the whole stretch that matters."

THE MAN

(Shakes his head in mock amazement)

You remember all that, every comma; and you so little.

THE WOMAN

(Opens her mouth, shuts it; opens it again)

You're not very nice.

THE MAN *(An imitation)*

Who's *nice?*

(THEY BOTH *chuckle ruefully*)

THE GIRL *(Very plaintive; a child)*

Me? Me, now? Please?

THE WOMAN *(Sing-song; to a baby)*

No, no; not now.

THE GIRL

Please? Me?

THE WOMAN *(Sighs heavily)*

All right. You.

THE GIRL *(Shy, tentative)*

Start me? Please?

THE WOMAN

With a snap? Like this?

(SHE *snaps her finders*)

THE VOICE

Sixteen.

THE GIRL

(More tentative, stumbling than usual)

You . . . you don't listen.

THE WOMAN

Well, that may *be*.

THE GIRL

Pay, pay . . . pay attention, rather, is what you don't do. Cry: you say she cried!

THE WOMAN *(Her mind elsewhere)*

Who? The girl you hit?

THE GIRL *(Shrill)*

Certainly!

THE WOMAN *(Not too involved)*

Yes; she cried.

THE GIRL

(Great, quiet intensity; a hissing quality)

What do *you* know about crying? Did you ever see *me* cry? Has *he* ever cried? How do you *know* she was crying?

THE WOMAN *(An abrupt laugh)*

That's quite a list.

(A barker)

The answers, ladies and gentlemen, are . . . plenty . . . yes, I *think* so . . .

yes, he has ... *and* ... tears were coming from her eyes, there were sounds in her throat, and there was no joy in her heart.

THE MAN *(Sadly ironic)*

Have you? Within memory? *Have* you cried?

THE WOMAN

Well, I'm not a blubberer, like *some.*

THE GIRL

(High-pitched; close to hysteria)

There was no joy in her heart?

THE MAN

(Answering the WOMAN; *a sad, quiet truth)*

The only people who can show it are those who have it.

THE WOMAN *(Smiles)*

No cod piece for the psyche, eh?

THE GIRL *(Even more insistent)*

There was no joy in her heart?

THE WOMAN

(Swings on the GIRL; *cold)*

No; no joy! Do you know why she was sitting there beside you that day? Hm? Do you know why she was *there?!*

THE GIRL

(Knowingly inventing a wrong answer)

Of course: to steal!

THE WOMAN

Or to be hit? *You* know better.

THE GIRL *(Transparent)*

No.

THE WOMAN *(Thinks for a moment)*

Well, maybe conscious lies are an improvement; they'll be interested in that. I must bring it *up.*

(Harsh)

Do you *want* to know why she was there?!

THE GIRL *(Totally ambiguous)*

Don't be silly.

THE WOMAN *(Pressing)*

She was there because she was at home one day—her sister tells it— around three in the afternoon, a September day, the weekend before them, her husband coming in on the train, when she folded her hands, pursed her lips and said, "Reality is too *little* for me."

   (Pause)

THE MAN *(Quietly)*

Well, *that's* a switch.

THE WOMAN *(To the* GIRL*)*

And so there she was, there beside *you,* things taking their course, and what did *you* do? You *hit* her.

THE GIRL *(Mild and unconcerned)*

I hit her because she deserved it.

   (Strangely curious)

She had *those* things? All *those* things?

THE WOMAN

What; which?

THE GIRL *(Shrugs)*

Weekends . . . September . . . reality.

THE WOMAN

Um-hum.

THE GIRL *(Dismissing it)*

Well, we've *all* had that.

THE WOMAN *(Playing her along)*

Oh, yes. *And* a husband, *and* a baby.

THE GIRL *(Knits her brow)*

Well, not all of us that.

THE MAN

I don't think of myself as a blubberer.

THE WOMAN

Oh, was it *you!?* Was I talking about *you?*

THE GIRL

It was three? It was in the afternoon?

THE WOMAN

   (Still gauging the MAN*'s reactions)*

Around three; I have it from the sister; September.

THE GIRL *(So reasonable)*

Well, she could have said she wanted it—the cardboard—that she needed it; she could have had it.

THE WOMAN

And you would have given it to her: "Here you are, sweetie." Now you're a liar on top of everything else.

THE GIRL *(Sudden)*

What else!?

THE WOMAN

Everything! You're a common liar.

THE GIRL *(Blasé)*

I don't *remember* much, that's all.

THE MAN *(Accusatory)*

Kiss the boys and make them cry? *All* of them? How *many?*

THE WOMAN *(Dismissing him)*

Oh, choose a number.

(*Back to the* GIRL)

No; common or garden variety liar. I thought I *knew* you.

THE GIRL

She had September, did she?

THE WOMAN

(*Looking her straight in the eye*)

A good month, September.

THE GIRL *(Shrugs)*

They *all* have something . . . *I* don't care; have it whatever way you want; these people cry or they don't cry; you don't have to *do* anything most of the time. They just cry.

(*Bright*)

Wasn't that good? They just cry.

THE WOMAN *(Following; tolerating)*

And she didn't cry because you *hit* her.

THE GIRL *(Contemptuous)*

No; she cried *when* I hit her; it took her that long; the tears were over what I had, not what I did.

THE WOMAN

(*Head-shaking, grudging admiration*)

Wow!

THE GIRL *(Quietly superior)*

Everything figures out; you just have to look; pay attention; listen. You *do* do that, don't you?

THE WOMAN (*Steel*)

I try. She was just a little slow, is that it?

THE GIRL (*Pleased*)

Just a little; that's it.

THE WOMAN (*Nailing it down*)

Not *you*, though: quick, if anything, hunh?

THE GIRL

No; yes.

THE WOMAN (*Airy*)

Well, I'll take it up at the next meeting.

THE GIRL (*Challenging*)

You do that.

THE WOMAN

All logical and well thought out; *that* deserves a session by itself; no telling *what* it means; step forward?, step back?

THE GIRL (*Head high*)

Have fun!

(*Becomes private, settles her gaze on the pool. Pause*)

THE MAN

What happened to the baby? You said she had a baby.

THE WOMAN

Who? The September girl? The one this one hit?

THE MAN

Yes.

THE WOMAN (*Quite matter-of-fact*)

September afternoon; she climbed the stair.

(*Laughs*)

Oh, God! "She climbed the stair." She climbed the stair; she took the baby from the crib, she took it by the ankles . . .

THE MAN

No! Please!

THE WOMAN

Took it by its ankles and bashed its head against the wall. I suppose that gained a *little* more reality; *I* don't know.

(*Pause*)

She's a sad girl.

THE GIRL

(Not looking up; quietly; a pout)

She took my cardboard, or would have. How can you trust someone climbs the stairs?

THE WOMAN *(Weary)*

Oh, hush!

(Pause)

THE VOICE

Seventeen.

THE MAN

(Shakes his head; determined, if sad)

I'm *not* a blubberer. I may have been once, and I may well be again . . . but I'm not *now*.

THE WOMAN *(Bright interest)*

Oh?

THE MAN *(A quiet dig)*

How *can* you trust someone climbs the stairs?

THE GIRL *(From "far off")*

Yes.

THE WOMAN

(Pointing the MAN *toward the subject)*

"Blubbering."

THE MAN

The baby by its ankles? Well, that might start me again, or turn me off for good. I think ankles is the word.

THE WOMAN

Oh?

THE MAN

Mmmm. It's the leverage—swung by the ankles, all that centrifugal on the way to it, to the wall. It's horrible!

THE WOMAN

Ohhhhhh . . .

THE MAN

Why are people so *inventive!?*

THE WOMAN

Grow up, will you! You romantics! If I'd told you she put the baby on the floor and stepped on its head you'd say the same thing—or pushed it in the toilet. You're a romantic: wars don't get you; you'd probably *come* in an earthquake. . . .

THE MAN

Be fair!

THE WOMAN (*Cruel*)

Who's fair!?
    (*Subsiding*)
Who's nice? Who's anything?

THE MAN (*After a moment; shy*)

I hate that laugh of yours, but in spite of it . . . *you* were fair; *you* were nice; *you* were something.

THE WOMAN

HA!
    (*Now a rueful chuckle*)
Well . . . I dare say I *must* have been—something or other. Maybe not fair; maybe not nice; but *something*.

THE MAN (*Nods*)

Um'hum.

THE WOMAN

Was I one-of-those-three-take-your-choice?

THE MAN

Um-hum.

THE WOMAN (*Almost coquettish*)

I wonder which one.

THE GIRL (*Stentorian—for her*)

A set of principles. One: you cannot trust someone climbs the stairs.

THE WOMAN

Ignore her.

THE MAN

Is that safe?

THE WOMAN (*Laughs*)

No; nor is paying attention, I begin to think. Don't answer is what I mean. Don't answer *her.* Answer me.

THE MAN

Oh?

THE WOMAN

Yes. Which one?

THE MAN

All three. I *said.*

THE WOMAN *(Very matter-of-fact)*

I don't *believe* it.

THE MAN

Well, that tells you less about how you were than how you are.

THE WOMAN

You never knew me. It was someone else; it was lots of *other* people.

THE MAN *(Smiles)*

I knew things *about* you; I knew *parts* of you.

THE WOMAN *(A sad sneer)*

You're a cook. It was lots of other people.

THE MAN

What were they?

THE WOMAN

You're a cook.

THE MAN *(A rather triste listing)*

I knew the things you liked—and I knew the things you pretended not to like, a longer list, by the way. Physical things, *and* ideas. I knew the phases of you.

THE WOMAN *(Precise distaste)*

An "institutional cook."

THE MAN

I knew your losses—even *then;* your prides and your losses. You told me *lots* of things.

THE WOMAN

It was lots of *other* people told you things; I told things to *other* people. I never knew *you.*

THE MAN

I knew which flowers you preferred; you told me all about your father's whip, and all about the day you were strong enough to take it from him, and how you beat him for an hour. , . .

THE WOMAN *(Curiously unconcerned)*

No, I never told you any of that; it was someone else.

THE MAN

Do you *still* not shave beneath your arms?

THE WOMAN (*After a pause*)

Who *are* you?

THE MAN

You saw me *cry;* remember? You *made* me cry; remember that?

THE WOMAN (*As if denying everything*)

You're a *cook.*

THE MAN

I knew the things you liked, I knew which flowers you preferred, I knew your thighs.

THE WOMAN (*Distressed, almost shocked*)

Please!

THE MAN

The . . . hot moist suffocating center of your temporal being? How's that?!

THE GIRL

Two: you cannot trust a woman's thighs.

THE MAN

(*To the* GIRL, *but looking straight at the* WOMAN)

Wrong; it's one of the few things you can trust.

THE WOMAN (*A harsh laugh*)

. . . suffocating center of my *what!?*

THE MAN

Temporal being; your temporal being.

THE WOMAN

Goodness! I'd forgotten I *had* one.

THE MAN

A suffocating center?

THE WOMAN (*Laughs nicely*)

No; a temporal being! It's not a *way* you think of things. "I have a temporal being." I think I recognize you; I saw you cry once. Once?

THE MAN

Once. How much do you want?

THE WOMAN

I don't remember.

THE MAN

(*Indicates the surrounding area*)

Is any of this familiar?

THE WOMAN (*Laughs*)

What! This!? Where we are!?

THE MAN

Well, as it was—as it may have been, back when it was . . . what? . . . personal, is that it? Back when it was clipped and trained and planned and . . . back *then*.

THE WOMAN (*Shakes her head*)

No.

THE MAN

Did we leave the patio? Remember the sound the footfall made on the stone, even outdoors?

THE WOMAN

No.

THE MAN

And the sudden silence of the grass after all that echoing, through a bower . . .

THE WOMAN

A what?

THE MAN

A bower.

THE WOMAN

No.

THE MAN

It was *full* then.

THE WOMAN

   (*Apprehensive; on guard, at least*)

What was!?

THE GIRL (*Echoing the* WOMAN)

What was!?

THE MAN (*At the air*)

Nothing.

   (*To the* WOMAN *again*)

You don't remember it.

THE WOMAN

No.

THE MAN

All this—clipped, then, trained, planned . . . and at the end of it all . . . you: God, or monster? No?

THE WOMAN

No.

THE MAN

"*I'll* show you something," you said.

THE WOMAN

No; I think you're mistaken. You look familiar, though.

THE GIRL

Three: the past is unreliable, as well.

THE WOMAN

No argument there. You *cried.*

THE MAN *(Rue; a slight smile)*

Oh *yes.*

THE WOMAN *(Getting it straight)*

I made you *cry.*

THE GIRL *(Quite bright)*

You made *me* cry.

THE WOMAN

Nah, *you* made *you* cry. You're special.

THE GIRL

Four: no; never mind.

THE MAN *(Triste)*

Do you *want* to know?

THE WOMAN *(A smile)*

How will I know until I know?

THE GIRL

Four: no; never mind.

THE MAN *(Sad smile)*

How do we know what we had until we lose it? How can we know pain without pleasure, and so on?

THE WOMAN

How did I make you cry? No nonsense now; *how* did I make you cry?

THE MAN

I rose.

(*Stops*)

THE WOMAN *(Waits a moment; then)*

You rose.

THE MAN

Sorry; I rose . . . I rose from the hot moist suffocating center of your etcetera . . . I rose—to be exact—I rose my *face* from the hot moist etcetera of your whatchamacallit, and brought my face to your face—my hot and moist face—and I opened my mouth to say to you, but you must have thought I was going to kiss you, my mouth from your cunt become a cunt, a cunt descending on your mouth, *yours* on your mouth, you must have thought I was going to kiss you . . . for you turned your face away.

(*Long silence*)

THE WOMAN

Well . . . I'm sorry.

THE GIRL

Four: . . . I'm sorry is never enough.

THE WOMAN (*Cuts in; huge*)

BE STILL!! THIS IS NOT THE TIME FOR YOU!!

(*To the* MAN, *though not looking at him*)

I'm sorry . . . I suppose. I don't *know*—whether or not I *am*, but I'll say it.

THE MAN

(*Curiously dispassionate*)

Odd, in retrospect: it's such a thing we all want—though we seldom admit it, and when we *do*, only part; we all wish to devour ourselves, enter ourselves, be the subject and object all at once; we all love ourselves and wish we could. I'm surprised you turned away; many don't.

THE WOMAN (*Slightly unpleasant*)

I said I assumed I was sorry.

THE MAN

Well, it mattered to me then. You turned away—*was* it the metaphor?, the sudden confrontation with yourself ?—and . . .

(*Laughs*)

and *I* said . . . oh, poor me! . . . what a sad puppy! . . . "I take it," I said, "I take it this is not destined to be one of the great romances."

THE WOMAN

You didn't!

(THEY BOTH *begin to laugh*)

THE MAN

I did; I swear I did!

THE WOMAN

You *take* it?

(*Their laughter grows*)

THE MAN

Yes! I swear!

THE WOMAN

You *take* it?

THE MAN

Yes!
(*Their laughter swells*)

THE GIRL
(*Loud, shrill, over their laughter*)
Five: mistrust laughter!

THE WOMAN (*Laughing fully*)
Oh my God!

THE GIRL
Five: mistrust laughter! Mistrust it!

THE WOMAN (*Subsiding*)
Oh, God.

THE MAN (*Subsiding*)
Ah me.
(THEY *subside, with brief bursts*)

THE GIRL
(*When it is quiet; precise, gently*)
Mistrust laughter.

THE WOMAN
(*Chuckles; dismisses her*)
Yes; we heard you.

THE MAN (*To the* GIRL)
Not always; not all laughter; some.

THE GIRL
(*Looking into the pool again*)
Yes; all; always.

THE WOMAN (*To the* GIRL; *lazy*)
Well . . . as you like.
(*To the* MAN; *bright*)
And did you cry right then?

THE MAN

With my mouth hanging over your neck, a drop on it? No, not then; later;
by myself; masturbating. Oh, God, I was young!

THE WOMAN (*After a moment*)

Then, I *didn't* see you cry.

THE MAN

Well, not literally—at least I hope not! But you said to me later, "I'm sorry I made you cry."

THE WOMAN (*Interested; amused*)

Did I? Are you sure? Was it you?

(*Pause*)

THE GIRL

Six.

THE VOICE

Eighteen.

THE WOMAN (*To the* GIRL)

Eighteen, you see? Not six.

THE GIRL (*Confused; tense*)

What!?

THE WOMAN

Eighteen; not six. You don't listen.

THE GIRL

Well, that may be.

THE WOMAN (*Smiling*)

Pay attention, rather, is what you don't do. Listen; oh, yes.

THE GIRL (*Shrill*)

Don't twist me! I'm . . . me!

THE WOMAN

Yes you are.

THE MAN (*Concluding the subject*)

So . . . you saw me cry. She's *right,* you know:

(*Referring to the* GIRL)

about time—effect comes *after* act, and you knew what I would do. She's *right.* You saw I would cry; therefore.

(*Shrugs*)

THE GIRL

(*To the* WOMAN; *strained smile*)

You saw *me* cry, too?

THE WOMAN (*Snorts*)

Hunh! The phases of the moon!

THE GIRL

It's important!
  (Louder)
It's important!!

THE WOMAN *(Some distaste)*

Nobody else; only you!

THE MAN

What!?

THE WOMAN

She bleeds; once a month she bleeds, and she cries: the phases of the
moon. God, every woman from the dawn of time . . .

THE GIRL *(Teeth clenched; intense)*

I am the only one.

THE WOMAN *(Ridiculing her)*

Oh, really.

THE GIRL *(More private)*

The only one.
  (Sudden; like a snake)
When did you see me?

THE WOMAN *(Laughs abruptly)*

Hah! Who *doesn't* know! It's down there on the report: she cries at the
sight of her own blood.

THE MAN

Like *that?* A condemnation?

THE WOMAN

Well, no; that's *me.*

THE MAN

I mean, who doesn't?

THE WOMAN *(A savoring pause)*

I don't.

THE GIRL

*Every*one does.

THE WOMAN

I don't.
  (Looks at them)
Goodness, there's so much disbelief in the world.

THE GIRL
(Quiet dignity; playacting version)
I had asked you a question.

THE WOMAN *(Very calm)*
(Pause)
What was it you wanted to know?

THE GIRL
(Sad; retreating within herself)
You don't listen.

THE WOMAN
Well, that may be.

THE GIRL
Why am I the only *one?*

THE WOMAN
(Briefest sardonic pause)
Is that the question?

THE MAN
Be nice.

THE WOMAN
Who's *nice?*
(To the GIRL)
Is that the question?

THE GIRL
Yes.

THE WOMAN
(Stating it as a subject)
Why are you the only one.

THE GIRL
Yes!

THE WOMAN
Because *every*one is the only one.

THE GIRL
No! *I* am the only one!

THE WOMAN *(Overly patient)*
Yes; you are the only one; everyone is the only one. Nothing happened
before you? Yes? Well, very true. What you see for the first time is invented
by your seeing it? Yes? Well, very true. *You* are the only one. *He* is the only
one. *I* am the only one. All right?

THE GIRL (*Shy*)

Will I be the last?

THE WOMAN

Since you were the first, you'll be the last; it *follows*.

THE GIRL (*Simple*)

I don't think I can accept that.

THE WOMAN (*Soothing*)

Well . . . you accept so *little*.
　(*To the* MAN; *laughs*)
I remember once, when I was in the park . . .

THE GIRL (*More insistent*)

I don't *think* . . . I can *accept* that.

THE WOMAN (*Through her teeth*)

I'm not *interested*.

THE MAN

Be nice.

THE WOMAN

Who's *nice*?

THE GIRL (*Vaguely disoriented*)

What . . . what *would* interest you?

THE WOMAN (*Perverse; smiling*)

Remembering once, when I was in the park.

THE GIRL (*Almost a mumble*)

About me; I mean, about me.

THE MAN

Be nice.

THE WOMAN (*To the* GIRL)

Who's *nice*?

THE GIRL (*Louder*)

About me! What about me!

THE WOMAN (*Almost daring*)

What *about* you!

THE GIRL (*Pouting*)

Nothing; never mind.

THE WOMAN (*Sighs*)

You want to know when I saw you *cry*? Is *that* it?

THE GIRL (*Great, inflated dignity*)

Nothing . . . is *it*.

THE WOMAN

Do you want to *know?*

THE GIRL (*Indifference*)

I don't *care*.

THE WOMAN

Of course not.

THE GIRL

(*Accusatory and speculative at the same time*)

What would it *take!?*

THE WOMAN (*Smiles*)

Search me.

(*Tiny pause*)

You're good at *not* crying; I've watched *that* a lot.

THE GIRL (*Shakes her head*)

I don't *want* this.

THE WOMAN (*To the* MAN)

Catatonia—as they said in training—is *not* a small country in Europe.

THE·GIRL

(*Agitated head movements—searching for something*)

I don't *want* this!

THE WOMAN

(*To the* MAN; *excessively sweet*)

One of the jokes.

(*To the* GIRL)

Oh, yes you are! *Very* good at it!

THE GIRL

(*Perched on the lip of the fountain pool, shoulders turning every which way*)

I said: I don't *want* any of *this!*

THE WOMAN

(*Eyes closed, a gesturing finger up*)

I saw you . . . *almost* cry—which is as close as we can *come*—one afternoon; now, when *was* it?

THE GIRL (*An adder*)

Piss on you!

THE WOMAN *(Pause)*

Tut.

THE GIRL

Piss on you!
  (Giggles)

THE WOMAN *(Shrugs)*

Tut.

THE GIRL

Piss piss piss piss!
  (Giggles)

THE WOMAN

  (Will not be drawn in)
When *was* it?

THE GIRL *(Venomous)*

On you.

THE WOMAN

  (Laughs; intentionally not looking at the GIRL)
Of course! It was that afternoon your family . . . *and* your friends . . . and
your *dog,* as I recall . . . your grandmother, your mother and your father,
your sister and your dog, and a nice boy, and some older lady . . . and they
all came parading up, in . . . *three* cars, I think, with one bouquet and two
cakes, and ladies magazines . . . do you remember it? Visiting time?

THE GIRL

  (Considerable equilibrium)
Nothing has happened . . . of any sort . . . to any *one* . . . which you *say.*

THE WOMAN

And wishing will make it so, eh? Trooping up, *all* of 'em . . .
  (Recites, very exaggerated)
"Somber of countenance, bright of dress . . ."—all save the dog, of course,
which yapped a lot and wagged its tail with a great ferocity—all of 'em
come to see the praying mantis here.

THE GIRL

Nor ever *will.*

THE WOMAN

  (To the MAN; *matter-of-fact, but a little sad)*
And she sent them off; wouldn't see them; sent them back.

THE GIRL *(A question in a test)*

What can happen if I won't admit it?

THE WOMAN *(Shrugs)*

Nothing, of course.

(To the MAN*)*

Sent them all packing—yapper, Mademoiselle, ga'ma—whole bunch of 'em. Who *was* that nice boy?

THE GIRL *(Caught off guard)*

He was . . .

(Puzzles)

I don't *know.*

(Bright, in a cheerless way)

Besides, it never happened.

THE WOMAN *(Agreeing)*

No. *Such* a nice boy.

THE GIRL *(Remembering)*

Yes; he was.

THE WOMAN *(Very off-hand)*

Did he *betray* you?

THE GIRL *(Shrugs; a little sad)*

Of course.

THE WOMAN *(Gentle, but smiling)*

Good it never happened.

THE GIRL

Yes.

(Sudden animation, venom)

Piss on you!

THE WOMAN

She wouldn't see anybody; ever.

THE GIRL

(Stands abruptly on the rim of the fountain)

No; nor *will* I.

*(*SHE *jumps into the fountain bowl, sits;* SHE *looks rather like someone in a bathtub)*

THE MAN

(To the WOMAN, *who is gazing at her hands)*

Pardon me.

THE WOMAN (*Still gazing*)

Ever. Hm?

THE MAN

Pardon me; she's jumped into the fountain.

THE WOMAN (*Before looking; laughs*)

She has!? You've jumped into the fountain!
   (*Looks, laughs again*)
You look like someone sitting in a tub; well, you look like *you* sitting in a tub.

THE GIRL

Piss on you!
   (*Giggles*)

THE WOMAN

Is it comfortable?
   (*No response*)
Do you feel . . . conspicuous?
   (*No reply*)
Well, if you find soap, do your neck.

THE GIRL

Piss on you.
   (*Does not giggle*)

THE WOMAN

(*To the* GIRL; *great concern*)
Is there anything in there with you?

THE GIRL

You mean, besides the half blue egg, the mouse bones, the feather and a strand of ivy?

THE WOMAN

Whatever it was.

THE GIRL

That was it; that was all; and . . . was it, or wasn't it; I can't remember.

THE WOMAN (*Shrugs*)

*Which*ever it was.

THE GIRL (*Exact imitation*)

*Which*ever it was. So, it either *is* there, or is not . . . as am *I*.

THE WOMAN

Oh?

THE GIRL

Certainly!

THE WOMAN (Weary)

All right.

   (To the MAN)

And after the silence came—after she'd stopped them all . . . though they
phone now and again, some of them, not the dog, nor the nice boy—after
she'd stopped them all, and the silence came down, I saw her . . . *al*most cry.

THE GIRL (Enraged)

On *you!* On *you!!*

   (SHE holds on to the edge of the bowl)

THE WOMAN

   (Closes her eyes momentarily, reopens them; goes on, to the MAN)

She sat in the silence, puzzled it, and finally figured what it was—that
she'd *done* it, *finally;* she'd rid herself of it all; she'd made it . . . to that
awful plateau.

THE GIRL (Less intense)

On *you.*

THE MAN

   (Holds his hand up to quiet the GIRL)

Sh!

   (SHE makes a hurt sound)

I'm sorry, but . . . sh!

THE WOMAN

   (Clicks the side of her mouth)

Well, when I've got 'em, I've got 'em. No one would come anymore. And
that's when she almost cried, almost let it out—whatever it was: relief?
pain? what? I don't *know.* She puffed up; her eyes brimmed; her lips were
all aquiver; she turned two shades red, but she held it in, by God!

   (Snorts)

Hunh!

   (Softer; a trifle sad)

Well, without a soul to hear . . . why shouldn't she?

THE MAN (Feels dumb saying it)

You were there.

THE WOMAN

   (Soft, ridiculing laugh)

Well. That's close enough; *I* don't exist, you know.

THE GIRL

(Hands still on the rim; fingers pressed hard; speaks in a loud whisper)

I don't exist. How can *you* not?

THE WOMAN *(Pause)*

Well . . . *that* may be.

THE GIRL *(A whimpering tone)*

I *do* exist.

THE WOMAN

Well, that may *be*.

THE GIRL *(A tearful child)*

Which is it?

(No reply)

Which is it?

(No reply)

I didn't *hear* you!

THE WOMAN *(Quite empty)*

I didn't answer you.

(Pause)

THE VOICE

Nineteen.

THE MAN

You cry.

THE WOMAN

Hm?

THE MAN

You: you've cried, too.

THE WOMAN

(Coming back into it; a little too offhand)

Oh; yes, certainly!

THE MAN *(Clinical)*

When? Over what?

THE WOMAN *(Bravado)*

Oh . . . all the things.

THE MAN *(Waits; then)*

Yes?

THE WOMAN

(Disappointment, and a degree of self-loathing emerge during the speech)

I said: all the *things:* I cried when my parents died; I cried when my cats died; I cried when I was fourteen and someone told me I wouldn't live forever, and I cried when I was forty and I *believed* it; you see? all the *things;* I cried the first time I realized someone had lied to me; I cried the first time I realized someone was trying very hard to be very truthful; I cried the first time I had an orgasm, and I *didn't* cry the last time; you see? I told you: all the *things;* I cried when my parents died; I cried when my cats died; I cried when *I* . . . died.

(Silence)

THE MAN *(Offended urging)*

Go on!

THE WOMAN *(Furious)*

I told you!

THE MAN (HE, *too)*

There's more!

THE WOMAN

No! There isn't!

THE MAN

Reveal yourself!

THE WOMAN *(Weary intensity)*

There is no revelation *in* me.

THE MAN *(Great intensity)*

I've kept you as an *object.*

THE WOMAN *(Very tired)*

Well . . . stop it. There are no secrets; everything is exactly what you would expect; leave me alone: there's nothing even . . . unusual.

THE MAN *(Sad)*

Why did you turn your face away from me?

THE WOMAN *(Offhand)*

Was it *you?*

THE MAN

Was it because I had no blood on my mouth?

THE WOMAN

(Thinks about that; chuckles sadly, shaking her head)

Oh . . . you're not nice.
    (A hand up)
I *know:* who's *nice?* Hm?

THE VOICE

Twenty.

THE MAN

You like blood? Is it more than . . . *is* there something?

THE WOMAN
    (Laughs, a little uncomfortably)
No! Of course not!
Blood is another superstition.

THE MAN *(Snorts)*

Really!

THE WOMAN

The sight of blood and we think our insides are coming out; every pin prick
is an avalanche; we're carefully put together, you see, with tape—and if we
spring a leak the ball game's over, or however they say. Or, is red the color
of the soul?

THE MAN

No! Blood is the color of pain!

THE WOMAN

Nonsense!

THE GIRL *(Softly)*

Oh, it is; it really is.

THE MAN

Pain, you see.

THE WOMAN

Yes, but I take pain as a warning, not a punishment; it's information; what's
wrong with all you people?

THE MAN *(Quiet irony)*

Much, I dare say.

THE WOMAN

Everything scares us—prolapse, blood, the heartbeat . . . Why live!?

THE MAN *(Shrugs, smiles)*

Indeed.

THE GIRL *(Softly)*

Indeed.

THE WOMAN (*To the* MAN)

I turned my face away for reasons I no longer remember.

THE MAN (*Overly patient*)

All right.

THE WOMAN

But I'm sure it was neither blood nor hygiene. Most probably . . .

THE MAN

All right!

THE GIRL

All right!

THE WOMAN

(*Closes her eyes for a moment, opens them*)

Most probably . . . well, no; I won't speculate. Not blood, though, certainly. Blood doesn't bother me much. It did once, though! Remember, I was telling you—once in the park, one afternoon when I was in the park, early Spring, a humid day burning off, surprisingly hot and muggy.

THE GIRL (*Acquiescing to something*)

All right.

THE WOMAN

I'd come in with a book—it was many years ago—in the city—and I'd found a slope I liked—or didn't mind—and I'd lit myself a cigarette— you see? I even smoked!—and I'd set myself to the book, which was . . . I can't recall, the one thing of it all I can't recall, but I'd set myself to it, and was fifteen minutes in when all at once I had a sense of someone —near me, and standing. Nothing unusual in that—nothing for apprehension . . .

THE MAN (*Smiles*)

Not *then*.

THE WOMAN (*Smiles, too*)

No. So I looked up, and there was a girl standing, and being what I am is something like a detective, I knew what to look for, and it was natural to take it all in . . . more than someone else would.

THE MAN

Yes, of course.

THE WOMAN

Something was evidently wrong. Her face was shiny and not too clean, and I saw she had no stockings—which was unusual then—and her hair was pulled back but uncertain, and there was a tightness to the mouth and that . . . wideness of the eyes, and—most extraordinary, in all the mugginess and unseasonable heat—she had on a huge, oversize, ratty, matted fur coat, pulled tight around her, her hands jammed into deep pockets— fur arms going into fur pockets. Well . . . I knew there was something wrong. "Hello," she said, in that . . . detached voice I have come to know so well, so often. "Hello," I said; "Aren't you warm, in all that?" "What are you doing?" she asked me. The nonsequential is probably the most difficult to adjust to.

THE MAN

Oh?

THE WOMAN

Jigsaw *puzzle* time, *all* the time. "What am I doing? Reading a book and smoking a cigarette. Do you want to know the title . . . or the brand?" "Do you want me to *show* you something?" she said. Well, I knew very well I didn't, and while I can't say for certain that I knew what it was going to be—*exactly*, that is, for a gun was possible, or a dead baby, who knows?— I knew I wasn't going to be surprised—startled, perhaps, but not surprised. "All right; what is it?" And then she slowly drew her hands from the deep fur pockets, palms forward, like this.

(Demonstrates, very slowly)

And her hands were all blood, up through the wrists where she'd cut them, and she'd drawn her hands from pockets filled with her blood. "See?" she said.

THE MAN

(Pause; dismay and disgust equally)

Oh, God!

THE WOMAN

"See?" she said.

(Pause. The GIRL, *who has been preparing the event behind the lip of the fountain, offers her hands over the edge, in the manner of the girl described above. Her hands are covered with blood)*

THE GIRL

Like this?

(No one notices)

Please? Like this?

THE MAN

(Looks over; greater dismay; greater disgust)

OH! GOD!

THE GIRL *(A small smile)*

Please? Like this?

THE MAN

Oh, my God! Her wrists! She's cut her . . . Oh, God!
  (Pathetic)
Do something?

THE GIRL *(Shows her palms again)*

Like this? Please?

THE WOMAN *(Pause; level)*

Is the blood all over the bottom of the pool now? Are you sitting in it?

THE GIRL

  (Looks, without moving her hands, looks back, small smile)
Yes; all over the pool.

THE WOMAN

Well; you've been at it a while.

THE GIRL

It only stings. I feel *light*headed.

THE MAN *(Helpless; not loud)*

Do something?

THE WOMAN

Well, you should by now.
  (To the MAN; *calm)*
What is there to do? Lock the barn door after the horses are gone?

THE MAN *(Outraged)*

Something!

THE WOMAN *(To the* GIRL)

Very lightheaded?

THE GIRL

Very. Done well?

THE WOMAN *(Gently)*

Done beautifully. There *was* something, then.

THE GIRL *(A little faint)*

Pardon?

THE WOMAN

In the pool; there *was* something; or you brought it *with* you.

THE GIRL

Well, one or the other. *You* said you could hear my *pupils* widen; *you* said they *all* make sounds—the chemical thing, the electric thing.

THE WOMAN

Did I?

THE GIRL

Yes, you did.

THE WOMAN

Then it must be so.

THE GIRL *(Fainter)*

You said you could hear my pupils widen.

THE WOMAN *(Pause)*

Well . . . I can.

THE GIRL *(Pause)*

Then . . . you don't *listen.*

THE WOMAN *(Long pause)*

I listen.

THE VOICE *(Long pause)*

End.

CURTAIN

Counting the Ways

A VAUDEVILLE

THE SCENE

I see a fairly short rear wall, and two side walls angling from it to the proscenium. In each of the side walls I see an archway cut, for entrances and exits. Beyond these archways we see black. On stage, there should be a round, or oval table, three feet diameter, dining-table height. To either side of the table there should be a straight back armless chair. The walls bare: on the table: a magazine, a pipe, and whatever else may be needed. No clutter, though!

LIGHTS

Clear, white light; the only shift is the fade at the end of the play. (See: BLACKOUTS *for further notes)*

COSTUMES AND MAKEUP

Both of these simple and naturalistic.

BLACKOUTS

This is more a term than a method, though I would like the lights to go out at once, and come on as suddenly, when called for. If need be, a curtain could be swiftly drawn and as swiftly opened.

THE SIGNS

Exactly as described. If coming from above is a problem, they may appear on a signboard, far stage right, in the old vaudeville manner—placed there by a disembodied hand.

COUNTING THE WAYS *received its first American performance at The Hartford Stage Co., January 28, 1977*

ANGELA LANSBURY *as* SHE

WILLIAM PRINCE *as* HE

Directed by EDWARD ALBEE

AVANT SCENE

The stage empty.

A sign drops:

COUNTING THE WAYS.

Stays four seconds, rises.

BLACKOUT

SCENE ONE

The TWO *reading.*

SHE

(Puts her magazine down, looks at him for a little while, HE *reads, smokes his pipe. Objective curiosity)*

Do you *love* me?

HE

(Takes a while to register that HE *has been asked a question)*

Hm? Pardon?

SHE

(Even more emphasis on the word "love")

Do you *love* me?

HE

(Considers it for quite a while; suspicious)

Why do you ask?

SHE *(Considers that)*

Well: because I want to know.

HE *(Pause; puzzled)*

Right *now?*

SHE (*Suddenly uncertain*)

Well . . . *yes.* Or . . . no, no, not really.
  (*Short pause*)
Yes.

HE
  (*Considers it, finds the question silly, shows it*)
Of course.

SHE (*"Good for you!"*)

Well . . . good.
  (SHE *smiles, goes back to her book.* HE *looks at her for a moment, goes back to his*)

BLACKOUT

SCENE TWO

THEY *both have moved to standing positions, each to one side of the stage, near their exitways.*

SHE (*Bright, but not idiotic*)

Walnuts!
  (*This is a list; small expectant pauses*)
Parsley!
Bone marrow!
Celery root!
Crème brulée!
  (*Pause; enthusiastic*)
Do you love me?!

HE (*Hungry and delighted*)

Of course!

SHE (*"Right on!"*)

I *knew* you did!
  (THEY *both exit*)

BLACKOUT

SCENE THREE

Stage empty; SHE *reappears, bitter and resentful;* SHE *crosses toward his exitway, talks toward it.*

SHE

Do you suppose stuffing it in me for you fat and flabby is something I enjoy? Do you? Putting it in me like a wad of dough . . . hoping it'll "rise" to the occasion? Do you think that fills me with a sense of . . . what? Fills me with anything but itself? There are deserts, you know! And think about hence!!

(Pause)

There are two things: cease and corruption. And that's all there is to say about hence!

(Pause)

Except, perhaps, that predetermination is even more awful than . . . what do they call it?—"the sudden void"? There's that, too.

(Pause; grim assurance)

One day . . . one day stuffing it in me for you—fat and flabby, yes, fat and flabby—it will *not,* in its own good time, "rise" to the occasion, and never-more, as the bird said. When *that* day comes . . . well, that day comes.

(Short pause)

And knowing all that, what do you call it now!?

(Short pause)

You call it love!

(Longer pause; more determined)

You call it love! Remember it!

*(*SHE *exits, her exitway)*

BLACKOUT

SCENE FOUR

Stage empty; HE *enters, holding a newspaper open to where* HE *has been reading;* HE *has his reading glasses on;* HE *assumes* SHE *is in the room.*

HE *(Reads from his paper)*

"Love in the afternoon."

(Sees HE *is alone; calls)*

"Love in the afternoon." What does that *mean?*

(Pause)

Where *are* you?

SHE

(Enters, carrying a plate and dishcloth)

What? Love in the what?

HE

"Love in the afternoon," it says; that's a title. What does it mean?

SHE *(Considers it)*

"Love in the afternoon"? It means *sex* in the afternoon, I should imagine.

HE *(Mildly incredulous)*

Really? That's what they *mean? Sex* in the afternoon? Love means sex? I mean, to *them?*

SHE

Sure: love means sex; eyes are thighs; lips means hips. I kiss your lips means . . .

HE *(The incredulity less mild)*

. . . I kiss your *hips?* I kiss your lips means I kiss your hips?

SHE

Sure.

HE

No.

SHE *(Shrugs)*

I don't care.

HE *(More emphasis)*

I kiss your *hips!?* Nobody ever said that: "Hello, I want to kiss your hips."

SHE *(Laughs)*

I rather like it!

HE *(Dogmatic)*

Nobody ever *said* that.

SHE

Still . . . it's what it means.

HE

And the limpid pools of your eyes? Is that meant to be thighs? The limpid pools of your thighs?

SHE *(Some distaste)*

Don't be literal.

HE

The limpid pools of your thighs.
  (*Offhand*)
I don't believe it.

SHE (*Also*)

Call 'em up; find out.

HE (*Taking the dare*)

I will! "Love in the afternoon." I'll just *do* that.

SHE (*A chuckle*)

Good! You do that!
  (THEY *both exit*)

BLACKOUT

SCENE FIVE

Stage empty. SHE *enters, still carrying her plate and towel.* SHE *comes center stage, looks at the audience.*

SHE

(*Objective; maybe a bit too bright*)
Here's a thought; I think it was my grandmother's: *love* doesn't die; we pass *through* it.
  (SHE *stares at the audience for a little, without emotion, looks at the plate in her hand, exits*)

BLACKOUT

SCENE SIX

SHE *is center, putting a rose in a vase;* HE *enters.*

HE

You're right.

SHE

Hm? Pardon?

HE

You're right. I went there and I asked them. "Love in the afternoon" means sex. Sex in the afternoon.

SHE

Well, of course; I told you.

HE (*A little hurt*)

I was surprised.

SHE (*Busy*)

Did you ask about eyes and thighs and lips and hips?

HE

No; I was embarrassed.

(*Pause*)

Love in the morning means sex in the morning, too.

SHE

Oh, you asked about that.

HE

Yes; they smiled; smirked.

SHE (*A trifle tart*)

And love at night?

HE

I didn't ask.

SHE (*Starts slow, offhand, builds*)

Love at night? After all the drinks? And too much food? The old arguments hashed over for the guests? The car? That week in Bermuda? The nursing home? All that? The bile and the regrets and half numb and better off straight to sleep but no, fumbling and a little hatred with each thrust—both ways?

(*Laughs*)

Oh my; love in the afternoon may be one thing, and love in the morning very much the same, they may both be dirty games, but love at night . . . oh, that has to be love.

(*Long pause*)

HE (*Embarrassed*)

They smirked.

SHE (*Right at him*)

Did they.

(*Pause; a little too offhand*)

What time is it?

BLACKOUT

SCENE SEVEN

SHE *has exited;* HE *is alone with the rose in the vase.* HE *circles it, looks to see if* SHE *is coming, looks at the rose, takes it from the vase and begins to depetal it.*

HE

She loves me.
She loves me not.

(*Etc., for maybe 10 petals, varying in speed, varying in mood, but with no imposed psychological progression*)

She loves me.
She loves me not.

(HE *becomes aware of the audience and cups the remainder of the rose from view; now* HE *feels conspicuous*)

She loves me.
She loves me not.

(HE *peers into his hand at the cupped rose, looks very seriously at the audience, and then suddenly pops the remainder of the flower into his mouth, chews, pretends to swallow.* HE *holds up the stem;* HE *smiles*)

BLACKOUT

SCENE EIGHT

HE *is sitting; the stem is in the vase;* SHE *enters.*

SHE

(*Comes to the table for something, sees the stem*)
What's this!?

(SHE *picks up the stem*)

HE (*Looking up*)

What?

SHE

This. What happened?

HE

I ate it.

SHE

The rose?

HE

The flower.

SHE

What for?

HE *(Calm; a trifle confused)*

Well . . . I took the rose and I was doing the petals for she-loves-me-she-loves-me-not . . .

SHE *(Points to the table top)*

Yes, I can see.

HE *(Looks)*

Oh; there they *are*. And I was counting away—very interested—and I was nearing a decision—she-loves-me-she-loves-me-not . . .

SHE

Who?

HE

You, of course. And I was near a verdict . . .

SHE *(None too friendly)*

Why didn't you just *ask* me?

HE *(Slow and determined)*

Well, I had already begun with the *rose,* and it was here and you were not . . .

SHE *(Sniffs)*

You should have asked *me*.

HE

. . . and it was going along quite nicely . . .

SHE

I would have told you.

HE

. . . one way, then the other, when all at once I saw I was being watched . . .

    (Waits to see if SHE *will react;* SHE *doesn't)*

. . . out *there.*

    (Ibid.)

. . . out *there!*

    (Points; SHE *looks, accepts, turns back to him, nods)*

HE *(cont'd)*

. . . and so . . .

SHE

. . . so?

HE *(Deflated)*

. . . and so I ate it—what was left.

SHE *(Triumphant)*

You just didn't want to know!

HE *(Holding his own)*

They were *watching!*

SHE

Ask *me! I'll* tell you!

HE *(Pause; moves to exit)*

I'll get another rose.

SHE

Ask *me!* I'll *tell* you!

HE

I'll get another one.
 (Exits)

SHE *(Pause; calls after him)*

You'll get *sick*. You can't eat *roses!* You'll get *sick!*

BLACKOUT

SCENE NINE

SHE *is alone on stage.* SHE *looks at the stem in her hand, looks down at the petals on the table, looks toward his exit, back. Taking the opportunity of being alone—but still furtively—*SHE *picks up the petals one by one and relates them to the stem.*

SHE

He loves me?
He loves me not?
No; that's not right; that's when you take them off.
Not me loves he?
Me loves he?

Not me loves he?
Me loves he? (Etc.)

> (SHE *does this for not more than 30 seconds, as little as 10, at the discretion of the director.* SHE *will vary in mood and intensity— enthusiasm, dismay, surety, uncertainty, anger, pleasure—but by the end of the mood will be some confusion and bitterness*)

Not me loves he?
Me loves he?

> (HE *enters, carrying a new rose, the other hand behind his back*)

HE

(Puzzled and faintly superior)
What are you doing? Aren't you silly! Here's a new one. What were you doing?

> (SHE *looks at him, then at his rose, then at her stem.*
> SHE *puts her stem down on the table, takes his rose with a swipe of her hand, exits.*
> HE *stands for a moment, looking after her*)

BLACKOUT

SCENE TEN

> *As at the end of the previous scene.* HE *turns toward the audience, brings his hand from behind his back;* HE *is holding another rose.* HE *smiles gently, looks at it, smells it.*

HE *(To himself, more or less)*

Maybe it was the daisies.

(Now to the audience)
Maybe it was daisies.

(Pause)

After all, I mean. Maybe you can't *do* it with roses. Well . . . maybe you can't do it with daisies, either. Daisies tell? Daisies do *what?* What did we do with dandelions? In the fall, when we were young, when the yellow was gone and they were ready to blow . . . so . . . fragile, regular showoffs. Dandelion?° Lion's tooth? For all that fluff? Must have been the leaves. All that fluff. One blew them for a reason. What was it? In the fall, when we were young. Was it for love? I mean, was it a way of telling?

(Pause)

———
°French pronunciation.

I could look it up. I *could;* I probably *will,* but not knowing anymore—having known, of course, *aware* of that, and longer—there's a kind of shivery thing there. There's something thrilling to the mind going. *As* with deafness—all the encroachments. Or can less encroach?

(*Small pause*)

Slow falling apart; it's interesting. Well, it had better be!

(*Pause*)

What did we use them for? We blew them for a reason when we were young. What was it? Was it for love?

(*Louder, so* SHE *will hear, offstage*)

Was it for love?

SHE (*Offstage*)

Hm? Pardon?

HE

(*A little louder; over his shoulder*)

Was it for love? Did we blow them for love?

(HE *sees her stick her head in; softer*)

Was it for love?

SHE

I'm sorry I grabbed it like that.

(*Hands it*)

Do you want it back?

HE (*Doesn't take it*)

I mean dandelions, after all, I think; not roses.

SHE

What?

HE

Not roses any longer; probably never; dandelions. I don't *mean* roses anymore.

SHE (*Pause; thinks for a bit*)

We shouldn't each have a rose like this; they should be together; one of us should have both of them.

HE

(*Pause; a slight, superior laugh*)

What will you do, make an arrangement?

SHE

(*Pauses momentarily; snaps*)

Never mind.

(*Exits with her rose*)

HE *(Looks after her; pause)*

I *think* it was for love; it was a long time ago.

(HE *looks at his rose, holds it at stiff arm's length toward her exit, closes his eyes tight)*

Here.

BLACKOUT

SCENE ELEVEN

As at the end of the previous scene. Eyes still closed, HE *makes a grimace, extends, shakes his flower-held arm even further.*

HE *(Between-the-teeth tone)*

HERE!

(Nothing happens)

BLACKOUT

SCENE TWELVE

As before.

HE

Here!

(SHE *enters, with rose, pauses, sighs, takes the rose)*

I mean! . . . really!

(HE *exits)*

SHE *(After him)*

Well, you see . . .

(Stops, considers the roses; speaks to the audience now; begins brightly)

There was another time I had them like this—two of them; two flowers! Not in my hand, though, but two. I was what!? I was seventeen and seventeen was younger, then.

(A confidence)

Some of us—believe it; try to believe it—some of us at seventeen were, oh, shame, I suppose, to present eyes, still maidens, still maidens, head and hood.

(Considers that)

Hm! And I was at a dance, and we all wore satin then and looked very much alike—not from the satin, not only that, but our hair was of a style, and our skin—what was it? Was it something we used, or was it seventeen?—our skin was glistening and palest pink—save when we blushed, which was deep and often—the palest pink, and we all had a bit of . . . pudge. That's a nice way to put it, I think: a bit of pudge. I had come, I think, with the boy my mother said I should, and that didn't matter, for one was like another. I think I was *sixteen.* One was like another: one bit his nails; one wore brown shoes, dirty brown shoes with his tux; another . . . these roses will wilt. Ah, well.

One was like another and it didn't matter. The music was . . . well, it was a prom.

The boy had bought me a gardenia, a flower I have always, perhaps irrationally, loathed—nowadays their scent makes me faintly ill; the gardenia; a corsage; not a wristlet, alas, for I could have kept it some distance *from* me, but a corsage which, he asked, could he *place* on me.

Well, it was a chance for a feel, though God knows what they got, those bras our mothers had us wear, but the boys *I* knew weren't too adventurous—lots of blowing in the ear, nibbles, a creeping hand in the dark once or twice; nothing much. I *must* have been sixteen.

HE *(Appearing stage right)*

Where are my shirts?

SHE

(Hears, pays no attention; still to the audience)

Well, he put it on me—placed, as he said—above my left breast, and a little low, sort of . . . *on* it rather than above it.

(Demonstrates with the flower in her left hand; keeps it in place)

HE *(Moving right of center)*

I want my shirts!

SHE *(As before)*

I kept my head to the right a lot, but there's no avoiding a gardenia once it gets the body heat. Suddenly . . . suddenly there was another boy at our table, standing there, looking down at me with a sort of . . . puzzled hurt.

HE

(Moving left of center; a whine)

Where are my shirts?

SHE *(As before)*

I couldn't place him at once. He was from school; I couldn't place *that,* and then the water cooler sprang to my mind!

HE *(Left of center; louder)*

I want my shirts!

SHE

(Vague intimation of having heard him but still to the audience; some wonder)

The water cooler, and the image of *that* boy . . . he was a loner, or new, or no one liked him: a cabal, perhaps—a week or so previous, I had stopped by the cooler—though tepid as often as not—and coming back up from my drink, I *sensed* him . . . or, who he proved to be, rather as I suddenly sensed him at our table. I remember, he said . . .

HE

Why don't I have any shirts?

SHE *(Right on)*

. . . are you going to the prom? Not inviting me, it is important to remember, but . . . asking. Sure, I said, nodding my head, swallowing; quiet smile; you? He nodded. I walked away. See you! I said. Maybe *that* was it! "See you!" Could he have? . . . he *must* have!

HE

Everyone has *shirts*. Why don't *I* have any?

SHE *(Pays no attention)*

Does "See you" mean something more? Does "See you" mean "I suspect you're inviting me, subtly, of course, and naturally I accept."? Does "See you" mean *that*? It *must!*

HE

I must have *shirts*. Where are my *shirts?*

SHE *(As just before)*

He was so shy. "I'm late," he said; "here." And from behind his back he brought a gardenia corsage, twin to the one I already had. Everyone sensed the error, the gaffe, the poor boy's . . . misunderstanding. There was no need for my date, whoever he was, to be so rude, so . . . cruel and . . . "Well, hey, can I pin 'er?" "Sure; sure! Pin 'er. Pin 'er and scram!"

HE

Thousands have lived without love, but none without shirts.

SHE *(Teacherlike)*

The numbing inevitability of dream!

(Back to chatty tone)

There was only one breast left, of course, and the right one at that, and he sought it out! He stood off, measured the mark, and pinned me on the right, twin to the left.

(Let her demonstrate this)

"Now, scram!" And scram he did, if one can do it slowly; well, he went, with a little smile and a wink which touches me deeply as I think of it now. It did not, then, for there I was, both breasts aflower and no direction to turn my head.

    (*Pause;* SHE *gazes at the roses*)

These will wilt!

    (*An afterthought; a smile*)

No, I didn't marry him—the shy boy—either one, for that matter.

    (*Offhand*)

I never saw the shy boy again. I have thought about him, though, from time to time, during love.

BLACKOUT

SCENE THIRTEEN

HE *alone on stage, holding the flowers.*

                HE *(Chuckling)*

Did you hear what I said? I thought it was rather good. "Thousands have lived without love . . .

                SHE

    (*Swats him with the roses; urgently, vaguely accusatory*)

These will wilt!

    (SHE *exits*)

                HE

    (*Looks at the flowers; accepting but uninvolved*)

Wilt they will.

    (*Puts his arm down; the heads of the flowers face the floor. To the audience*)

I thought that was rather good, there, before, what I said: "Thousands have lived without love, but none without shirts." I did; I thought it was quite good.

    (*Tosses it off*)

What does *she* know?

    (*As before*)

It's a parody, of course. You *knew* that; *some* of you knew that. It's W. H. Auden. "Thousands have lived without love, but none without water" . . . is the line. What's it from? . . . "In Praise of Limestone"? Probably.

Something in the middle there. You can do it with most anything:
Walnuts.
Parsley.
Bone marrow.
Celery root.
Crème Brulée.
"Thousands have lived without love, but none without Crème Brulée."
You see? It works.
It lacks . . . well, it doesn't . . . there's not as much *resonance* that way . . .
Crème Brulée for water, or *shirts* for water, for that matter, but if parody
isn't a diminishment . . . well, then, was it worth it in the first place?

    (*Thinks*)

Auden was one of the ones I cried when he died. Did I *cry?* Well, something. Something . . . *left* me, at any rate. If you can get *away*, if you can
watch your emotions, you know that pain is a misunderstanding: it's really
loss; loss is what it's *really* about.

    (*Looks at the flowers; objective tone*)

When will they wilt?

    (*Lowers them again; to the audience again*)

Oh . . . there *is* the breathtaker, that sudden sharp sense, but that's the *brain*
. . . panicking, sending out contradictory impulses: not enough oxygen, and
the host can faint, you know? And that heart attack at shocking news? It's just
the head saying, "That's enough! I've had enough; I don't want any more; let's
quit all this . . . what do you call it? Life?" But most of it's not that *way*. Most
of it's slow and after the fact and has to do with going on *without* something,
something we thought was necessary—essential—but then discovered it
merely made all the difference: one *could* go on if one really *wanted* to.

    (*Considers*)

Three times, I think, in long pants; crying: Auden; a cat, a very old cat; and
something to do with civilization.

    (*Pause*)

I suppose one selects.

    (*Pause*)

SHE

    (*Pokes her head in; curiously excited*)

They're going to wilt!
They're going to wilt!

HE (*Preoccupied; at a loss*)

Yes; well, bring a vase.

SHE (*Eager*)

No, they should be on the table . . . between our beds!

    (SHE *exits whence* SHE *entered*)

HE

(Long pause as that sinks in. Exits after her, bewildered)

When did *that* happen?

When did *that* happen!?

(Exits)

BLACKOUT

SCENE FOURTEEN

Stage empty; THEY *re-enter,* SHE *first,* HE *urgently following after.*

SHE

I don't want to discuss it!

HE *(Persisting)*

When did it happen!?

SHE

I do *not* wish to *discuss* it!

HE

Well, I *do.*

SHE

(Smiles a small, superior smile)

Then, we are at an impasse.°

HE

No, we are not; we will discuss it.

SHE *(Didactic)*

If I will not, and only you will, that is not a discussion.

HE (HE, *too)*

Silence is a reply.

SHE *(Snorts)*

Of sorts. For some, I suppose. Martyrs in the desert? Old people at the post office?

HE *(Stern)*

When did it happen?

SHE *(Transparent)*

What? I have no idea what.

———

°Fr. pronunciation

HE

Two beds.

SHE *(Ibid.)*

So?

HE *(Voice rising)*

There are two beds!

SHE *(Straining to remain calm)*

Yes; there are two beds.

HE *(Suddenly; loud, hysterical)*

WHY!!??

SHE *(Overly calm)*

Well; let us sit down and discuss it.

   (SHE sits)

With calm and reason.

HE

   (Bolts down into the other chair; urgent if softer)

O.K.! Right! O.K.!

SHE

Greater calm.

HE *(Softer, but still urgent)*

O.K. Right. O.K.

SHE

And reason.

HE

   (Some reason, but still aquiver)

Reason? Sure! All of a sudden there are two beds. Once upon a time there was one.

SHE *(Grudging)*

I . . . I *noticed* that.

HE

I wake up this morning . . . in our king-size bed . . .

SHE

You've moved into the historical present, I hope you realize.

HE

   (Tries to ignore her; voice tenser)

I wake up this morning in our king-size bed . . .

SHE *(To the audience)*

It's an odd tense, isn't it—sort of common, if you know what I mean. It's useful, I know, but . . . *still.*

HE

I won't be put *off.*

SHE

(Back to him, reassuring, not patronizing)

No, no; of course not!

HE

I wake up this morning in our king-size bed, the one I've waked in every day for all our marriage . . .

SHE

I know.

HE

. . . and so have you—save trips and hospitals—the bed I can reach across and touch you in the dark . . . in the night . . .

SHE

(The slightest tinge of impatience)

I know the *bed.*

HE

I wake up there; I find you gone.

SHE

To the kitchen; for your tea, for my coffee.

HE

It's the same as every day.

(Tiny pause)

Is it *not?*

SHE

Yes; yes it is.

HE

This morning I wake in the king-size bed; I find you gone; I find you in the kitchen; I find nothing amiss.

SHE

No; nothing. I understand you.

HE

It's a day like every other day.

SHE

And I sympathize with you. I understand you, and I sympathize with you.

HE

We are each other's rod?

SHE *(Agreeing after a pause)*

So to speak.

HE

Nothing is amiss—except perhaps the coffee.

SHE *(Patient)*

Now, now.
    (Afterthought)
You should taste the *tea.*

HE

It's a day like every other day—*except!*

SHE *(Vaguely embarrassed)*

Yes; I know.

HE

Except!

SHE

I said: I know.

HE

This afternoon you come to me and say you want the flowers for a vase
between our *beds.*

SHE *(Sort of sad)*

Yes.

HE

Between . . . our *beds.*

SHE *(Glum and impatient)*

Yes; yes!

HE *(Overly calm)*

When did it happen?

SHE

    (Pretending not to comprehend)
Hm?

HE

When did it happen? When did our lovely bed . . . split and become two?
When did a table appear where there had been no space, in the center of
our lovely bed?

SHE *(Very reasonable)*

Well, I suspect it's been coming.

HE

Pardon?

SHE

(Closes her eyes momentarily)

I suspect it's been coming.

HE

And those *beds!* They're not wide, those beds; they're single; they're for a solitary, or for a corpse!

SHE

These things sneak up on you.

HE

Did you have someone in? Hm?

(SHE *shakes her head*)

Did the bed people come and take our lovely bed away and leave these . . . these pallets? Hm?

SHE *(Apologetic)*

No one came: these things happen. We've been lucky.

HE *(Quietly authoritarian)*

I want an *answer* for this!

(SHE *sighs, smiles, shrugs*)

I want an *ANSWER* for this!!

SHE *(A trifle strident)*

Well, it happens sooner or later; look around you; look at our friends. Sooner or later it happens. Maybe we'll be lucky and it won't go any further.

HE *(After a second)*

Further? *Further!?*

SHE *(Quietly; shrugs)*

Of course: separate rooms.

HE *(Pause; quietly)*

Separate . . . oh, *God.*

(Pause)

BLACKOUT

ENTRE SCENE

As at the end of the previous scene.

HE (*As before*)

Oh *God.*

SHE (*Tentative*)

Yes; well.

(*A voice is heard, or a sign descends:* IDENTIFY YOURSELVES. THEY *notice it simultaneously*)

HE

Oh. Of course; yes, of course. You want to go first?

SHE

No; you go.

HE (*Smiles*)

Ladies first.

SHE (*Smiles*)

All right.

(SHE *stands. Improvisation:* SHE *tells a bit about herself [the actress], her career—training, roles, etc., then a bit about herself [kids, husband, etc.; finishes with:]*)

There's more there in the program; you can read it—*after* the play. I think the author would rather.

(*To him*)

Now you; you go.

(*Sits*)

HE

All right.

(*Stands. Similar improvisation. Finishes with:*)

Well, I think that's most of it.

(*Sits.*

The sign rises, disappears)

HE (*As before*)

Separate rooms . . . oh, *God.*

(SHE *begins exiting*)

Where are you going?

SHE

Off.

(SHE *exits, leaving him sitting. Pause*)

BLACKOUT

SCENE FIFTEEN

At the end of the previous entre scene.

HE *alone on stage, except standing.*

HE

(*Clears his throat, speaks to the audience*)

Which brings us, then, to a discussion of this thing called . . . "premature grief."

(SHE *rushes in*)

SHE *(To* HE*)*

Not yet!
Not yet!

HE

I beg your pardon.

SHE

(*To the audience; friendly*)

"Premature grief!" Well, yes; but not yet! I wish to discuss protocol.

(*To* HIM, *privately*)

Do you want to . . . you know, go off?

(*To the audience; very chatty*)

Look here! This is the problem! My sister and her husband are giving a dinner party—to which we are invited, of course, it being a close-knit family . . . closely knitted?—and she has presented me with a dilemma, not the *first* she has set in my lap, by a long shot, but the first in ages which I've found intellectually stimulating.

Two of the guests are dying—well, we all are, but these two are *closer* to it—and both are of equal importance, rank, one would have said at one time, both men and both fit to sit to my sister's right. The question is: which to put there.

The tricky part is this: One of the men knows he is dying; the other man does *not*—*as* far as can be gathered, or, *has* been gathered.

You would think—*one* would think, *might* think—the man who knows he is dying must be put to my sister's right, since everyone knows that he is dying, and he knows that everyone knows. The honor is both deserved and transparent. Protocol is served.

On the *other* hand, everyone also knows that the *other* man is dying, while we suspect that he does not, and isn't there, then, an honor due him based on the sympathy stemming from our special knowledge, plus the fact that he is of equal rank?

Were he, however, to be placed to my sister's right, might he not, assuming he did not, after all, know already, *sense* the reason he had been placed there . . . in place of the other? *Might* he, conceivably, gain his first inkling of his approaching death or, perhaps as unfortunate, might he not reason that the other man had been misdiagnosed, was not dying at all, and propose a toast in celebration of the faulty diagnosis?

And think of the *other* man—the one who *knows* he is dying: might *he* not succumb to the theory of misdiagnosis him*self*, and go so far as to propose a toast in his own behalf? Or, more likely, might he not think we no longer care, and have dropped him in rank in our cruelty—in our haste to have him gone?

I have begged my sister to consider alternatives: cancel the party; dis-invite both gentlemen; make it a *buffet!* This last being a stroke of near genius, I thought—and still *do!* But, no: it cannot be cancelled, for it is important to her husband, as are the two gentlemen, for a while, at any rate; and she does not like buffets—will not *have* one in her *house!*

I come to the conclusion that she is fond of the dilemma, which is not a kind conclusion, I grant; she, on the other hand, insists that protocol will give us the answer. And since protocol is—as she puts it—my "bag," it is for *me* to supply *her* with the solution.

I think what my sister has done—unintentionally, I will say, out of great sibling generosity—is: to fashion a test for protocol, so willful that pro-tocol's function as the coding of order will be put into question. Civilization, in other words, will collapse.

That is an unsisterly thing to do, an unfriendly one, and it brings up once again all those old questions about the veneer we call civilization.

BLACKOUT

SCENE SIXTEEN

Same as the end of Scene 15; clearly a different scene, though.

HE *enters, comes a step or two in from an exitway.*

HE

(Mildly curious tone; offhand)

How many children do we have?

SHE *(Smiles; cheerful)*

Three.

*(*HE *just stands there. Her voice takes on a tiny edge)*

Three!

*(*HE *just stands there. Not believing it)*

Four?

*(*HE *just stands there. Reassuring herself)*

Three!

*(*HE *just stands there. Quite incredulous)*

Four!?

*(*SHE *exits.* HE *just stands there)*

BLACKOUT

SCENE SEVENTEEN

As at the end of Scene 16.

HE *(Standing; smiles)*

Which brings us, then, to a discussion of this thing called . . . "premature grief."

(Imitates her tone, but softer)

"Not yet!
Not yet!"

(His own voice again; nods)

Yes; yet.

And premature to what? To the incident properly to be grieved over, I believe. Properly? Incident? I grieve every day—a little bit—over my *own* death; no time to, for *me,* when it *happens* to me; and I grieve over *her* death, a little, every day, assuming it may happen before mine. *I'll* have enough grief left when—*if!*—the time comes.

Are those afraid of it who have so little? Afraid they might exhaust the supply—those old theories about semen, or "spunk" as we used to call it?

    (Flat, midwestern accent)

"Ya only got a coupla thousand in ya; don't waste it in ya hand!"

    (His own voice again; scoffs)

Premature grief? I don't believe it for a minute! *Auden* used to say—you see? I come back to him—Auden is *reputed* to have said that he would imagine a lover's death, to see how it felt—for the sake of poetry, I wager.

    (Shrugs)

Maybe he didn't deeply care; I imagine he did. It's good to get in touch with the mind now and again. No harm.

    (Begins to exit; reconsiders)

Do you believe . . . do you believe the mind and the brain are separate entities? Some scientists are beginning to come back to that view. Scientists!

    (Pause)

Really!

    (Exits)

BLACKOUT

SCENE EIGHTEEN

Stage empty; SHE *enters.*

SHE

    (Nodding, smiling, relieved)

Three!

    *(*SHE *sees* HE *is not there; exits.* HE *enters)*

HE

Pardon?

    *(*HE *sees* SHE *is not there; stays. Pause.)*

SHE *(Enters)*

Three!

HE

(Pause; no great enthusiasm; accepting a fact)
Aha!
(Pause; SHE *exits; blank expression)*

BLACKOUT

SCENE NINETEEN

As at the end of Scene 18, except HE *is sitting.*
SHE *enters, sucking a finger, a dishrag over one arm.*

SHE

(Quite businesslike, if a trifle preoccupied)
Walnuts.
Parsley.
Bone marrow.
Celery root.
  (Suspicious)
Do you *love* me?

HE

(Pause; HE, *too, suspicious)*
Crème Brulée. What happened to the Crème Brulée?

SHE *(Flat)*
There's no Crème Brulée.

HE

What do you mean there's no Crème Brulée?

SHE *(As before)*
There's no Crème Brulée.

HE *(Pause)*
There's *always* Crème Brulée.

SHE

Not today.
  (Pause; uncertain)
Do you love me?

HE

(Pause; shrugs; some distaste)

Sure.

(Pause; not too friendly)

What happened?

SHE *(Sits; dispirited)*

You know that lovely caramel that coats the Crème Brulée.

HE

Yes! Yum-yum!

SHE

You *know* it. You know how it's *done:* the sugar, the maple sugar is sprinkled over the lovely custards—remember the lovely custards?

HE

Yes! Yum-yum!

SHE

And popped into the oven, so to caramelize.

HE

Yum-yum!

SHE

And then, at the end, into the broiler; under the broiler for a little, so the sugar crusts—that lovely crust you love.

HE

Yes!

SHE

Under the broiler for just a moment, just enough. It is *not* the time to straighten up, look out the window, unfocus your eyes on some distant spot and daydream—ruminate; think.

HE

Certainly not!

SHE

For if you *do* that, your caramel will scorch, or worse: will blacken, become hard, burned and *awful!*

HE

Ugh!

SHE

There is nothing for it then but to throw it all away . . .

HE

I should think so!

SHE

The pan as well.

HE *(Long pause; quiet tone)*

I see. Well. Indeed.

SHE *(Sighs heavily)*

So *that* is why . . .

HE *(A sad, soft truth)*

. . . there is no Crème Brulée.

SHE *(Suspicious)*

Do you love me?

HE *(Very grudging; coarse tone)*

Yeah.

SHE *(Apologetic)*

I can make you something else.

HE *(Rather cool)*

Yeah? What?

SHE *(Straining for forgiveness)*

What would you like?

HE *(Heavy)*

We got any pans left?

SHE *(Soft)*

Be nice.

HE

How about . . . how about that *other* thing you make . . . that, uh . . . whatever you call it, Idiot's Delight?

SHE

(Pause, 'til it comes to her)

Raspberry *Fool!!* Oh! Yes; well, all right!

HE *(Brightening)*

I *like that.*

SHE *(Stands; brightens)*

Raspberry Fool it is!

(SHE starts toward the exit, pauses; tentative again)

Will you *love* me?

HE *(Looks up; big smile)*

You bet!

(Exits)

BLACKOUT

SCENE TWENTY

(SHE *enters;* HE *as before*)

SHE

There aren't any raspberries!

BLACKOUT

SCENE TWENTY-ONE

Both sitting; HE *reading; some silence.*

SHE *(Quite straightforward)*

If you *love* me . . . how do you *know* you love me?

HE *(Not looking up)*

"How do I love thee?
Let me count the ways?"

SHE

Be serious.

HE

I thought she *was.*

SHE

You be.

HE *(Looks up at her)*

I thought *I* was.

SHE

How *do* you know?

HE *(Speculates a little)*

Not enough I *do?*

SHE

Most of the time; not just now.

HE

What's with now?

SHE
(Putting his question aside)
I don't *know*. How *do* you know you *love* me?

HE
Right now? Seriously?
(Indicates the audience)

SHE *(No matter)*
Yes; right now; seriously.

HE *(Tries to make light of it)*
You mean: some fella with a machete comes at us, breaks into the house, all mad-eyed and frothing, what would I do? Would I protect you or try to save *myself*? Something like *that*?

SHE
Don't be silly; what would anyone be doing with a *machete*? Be *reasonable*.
(Pause; eyes narrowing a little)
What *would* you do?

HE *(Quite open about it)*
Damned if *I* know! Protect you, probably—if the old animal instinct was working; give it a split-second of civilized thought, of course, and who's to say!?
(More serious)
I do *love* you, you know. I mean, I'm young enough to make a change if I wanted—start again, fully, without it being substitutive, or anything. I could *do* all that, but I'm not *going* to; I don't even *want* to.

SHE
(Bitter and hopeful simultaneously)
Do you cheat on me a lot?

HE *(Pause)*
No; I don't. Good phrasing.

SHE *(Noncommital)*
Hmmm.

HE
I *do* love you. Let well enough alone. If it's well enough . . . let it alone.

SHE *(Noncommital)*
Hmmm.

HE *(Closing the subject)*
I *do* . . . *love* you.
(Long pause; a half-amused afterthought)
Do *you* love *me*?

            SHE *(Pause; very open, rather wistful)*
I don't *know.*

    (Pause; his mouth opens a little. SHE *speaks as gently as the subject will allow;* SHE *smiles to reassure him)*
I *think* I do.

    (Pause. Slow fade. A voice announces: THE END.)

CURTAIN

The Lady from Dubuque

For
Stephani Hunzinger
—From the beginning

FIRST PERFORMANCE
January 31, 1980, The Morosco Theater, New York City

CELIA WESTON *as* LUCINDA

DAVID LEARY *as* EDGAR

TONY MUSANTE *as* SAM

MAUREEN ANDERMAN *as* CAROL

FRANCES CONROY *as* JO

EARLE HYMAN *as* OSCAR

BAXTER HARRIS *as* FRED

IRENE WORTH *as* ELIZABETH

Directed by ALAN SCHNEIDER

Setting ROUBEN TER-ARUTUNIAN

Costumes JOHN FALABELLA

Lighting RICHARD NELSON

Stage Manager JULIA GILLETT

CHARACTERS

The characters in order of speaking are:

SAM *a good-looking, thinnish man; 40*

JO *a frail, lovely, dark-haired girl; early 30's*

FRED *a blond ex-athlete going to fat; 40*

LUCINDA *your average blonde housewife; 35*

EDGAR *balding perhaps; average; 40*

CAROL *brunette; ripe; 30*

OSCAR *an elegant, thin black man; 50 or so*

ELIZABETH *a stylish, elegant, handsome woman; splendid for whatever her age.*

THE SCENE

A living room with stairs to the second floor and a balcony; a bay window; an all-purpose entrance hall.

I see the environment as uncluttered, perhaps with a Bauhaus feeling. No decorator has been at work; what we see is the taste of the occupants. I think the predominant color should be light grey.

PERFORMANCE NOTE

With some regularity throughout this play the characters address the audience—usually in brief asides, but occasionally at greater length. This is done without self-consciousness, quite openly, and without interrupting the flow of the play. In other words, the characters are aware of the presence of the audience, and since the audience has always been there, the characters are not upset by it, even though there are times they wish it would go away.

It is of utmost importance that the actors make it clear that it is not they, but the characters, who are aware of the presence of the audience.

Speeches to the audience (asides, etc.) are clearly marked, as is their termination.

ACT ONE

SAM, JO, FRED, CAROL, EDGAR, *and* LUCINDA *Onstage.* EDGAR *Center, his back to the audience;* FRED *at the bar;* SAM *at the window seat; the* OTHERS *seated or sprawled. It is midnight;* THEY *are tired and* THEY *have been drinking a little.*

The GROUP *applauds* EDGAR *as the curtain rises;* HE *bows to them, exaggerated, mocking.* THEY *are playing Twenty Questions, and* EDGAR *has finished his turn.*

LUCINDA

Good for Edgar! Good for you, Edgar!

SAM

(Rises, moves Center, as EDGAR *moves to sit)*
O.K., now; my turn.
(As the OTHERS *mumble to each other)*
All right, now; silence! It's my turn! Who am I?

JO

Well, if you don't know who you are, I don't see . . .

FRED

Who's talking?

SAM

C'mon, Fred!

FRED

Who's *talking!?*

EDGAR

O.K., give the man some silence.

JO

The man asked for silence; give it to him.

SAM

From the wives, too?

JO *(Deep voice)*

From the wives, too.

FRED

Who's *talking?*

LUCINDA

You are, for one, Fred.

CAROL

Leave Fred alone.

SAM

From the wives? Please? The girl friends and the wives?

JO

The man asked for silence; give it to him; he doesn't know who he is.

FRED *(Clapping)*

O.K.! O.K.! Let's have a little silence for the man.

SAM

Come on, gang; you've all had a turn, and now it's mine.

FRED

Carol didn't have a turn. Why is it your turn?

SAM

Carol didn't *want* a turn. Besides, it's my house, and you're drinking my liquor, and it's my turn.

FRED *(Shrugs; sits)*

You can't argue with logic.

EDGAR *(To create order)*

O.K. one more time; Sam's turn; Sam goes.

LUCINDA

Remember! Edgar's winning! You all took twelve to get Edgar.

FRED *(Bored)*

Good old Edgar.

EDGAR

(Hand in champ pose, but weary)

Yea for me.

SAM

Let me have silence; *please!* Who *am* I?

JO

The man asked for silence; give it to him. Poor man: he doesn't know who he is.

LUCINDA

Let there be silence!

(*There is silence*)

SAM

Well; at last! Thank you! Twenty questions . . . who *am* I?

JO

(*Leans forward; to the audience*)

Don't you just hate party games? Don't you just hate them?

(*Turns her attention back*)

SAM

(*To* JO, *commenting on her involving the audience*)

Come on! Don't do that!

(*To the* OTHERS)

Twenty questions! Who *am* I?

FRED (*Bored*)

Your name is *Sam;* this is your *house* . . .

CAROL

Stop it, Fred; I don't want any help.

FRED

I'm not giving you any!

CAROL

So *you* say.

FRED

Jesus!

SAM

Who am I! Come on! Who am I!?

JO (*Rote*)

Your name is Sam; this is your house; they're drinking your liquor . . .

SAM

Awwww, Jo . . .

JO

Your name is Sam, and this is your house, and I am your wife, and I am dying . . .

SAM (*Private*)

Don't, Jo.

(*To the* OTHERS)

Come on, gang. Who am I?

EDGAR *(Sighs)*

O.K. one more time

LUCINDA

Let's play!

JO *(Shrugs)*

O.K. let's play.
        (To the audience)
What can you do? He's a nice man.
        (Her attention back to the OTHERS*)*

EDGAR

Are you a man?

SAM

No.

JO

Coulda fooled *me.*

CAROL *(To* FRED*)*

Then he's a woman.

FRED

Of course he's a woman! What the fuck do you think he is!?

CAROL *(Getting angry)*

He could be a dog, or a horse, or something!

FRED

A horse!? What do you mean, a horse? Nobody's ever been a horse! You're
always embarrassing me!

CAROL

I'm trying to learn the game! You want me to fit in, don't you? Well?
Besides, what's embarrassing about a horse?

JO

        (As if the question were to be answered)
What's embarrassing about a horse? Well, let's see . . .
        (To the audience)
They're certainly no brighter than you'd want them to be.

SAM

Aw, come on! Hunh? Jo? Please?
        *(*JO *shrugs, turns her attention back in)*

EDGAR *(Bored)*

Play the game; play the game.

CAROL

(To SAM, *very unsure of herself)*
You a horse, or something?

SAM *(Smiles)*

Nope; nothing like that.

JO *(To the* GUESTS*)*
And . . . they're said to bear grudges, but with their tiny brains, I wonder.

LUCINDA *(An announcement)*
Neither a man nor a horse. That's two.

CAROL *(To* FRED; *not pleasant)*
So he's a woman, hunh?

FRED

Ask him!

CAROL

What!? Ask him if he's a woman? I just asked him if he was a horse.

FRED *(Enjoying it finally)*
Yeah; ask him; ask him if he's a woman.

CAROL *(Tiny pause)*
You a woman?

SAM *(Smiles)*

No, I'm not a woman; that's three.

CAROL

(To FRED: *enraged with embarrassment)*
You see!?

FRED

Whadda you mean you're not a woman!? You're not a man, you gotta be a woman! What are you: one of those sex changes, or something?

SAM *(Laughs)*
No, I am not one of *those.* That's four down.

EDGAR

Hey, hey, wait! Are you more than one person?

SAM *(Pleased)*

Right!

FRED

Ah, for Christ's . . .

EDGAR

How many people are you? You two people?

SAM

Right; two people; that's six questions.

EDGAR

He's two people, gang. Uh . . . men?

SAM

Right.

LUCINDA

Living!

SAM

Wrong; that's eight.

EDGAR

O.K. Two dead people; both men.

FRED

Probably a couple of queers! Famous queers!

JO

You *would* think of that, Fred.

EDGAR

O.K. Let's see . . . Marx and Engels.

LUCINDA *(A loud whisper)*

Were they queer?

EDGAR

Of course not!

CAROL *(To* FRED*)*

Marx and who?

FRED

Engels! Marx and Engels!

JO *(To* CAROL*; helpful)*

The Kaufman and Hart of their day.

SAM *(Rueful laugh)*

Oh ho, you just wait!

LUCINDA *(Bright)*

Gilbert and Sullivan, Rimbaud and Verlaine . . .

CAROL *(General)*

Who *are* these people!?

JO

They're foreign, Carol.

SAM

That makes eleven.

JO

They're not foreign?

SAM

No! They're not who she said!

FRED

Lum and Abner, Abbott and Costello, Sacco and Vanzetti, uh . . .

SAM

Nope, nope, nope; fourteen.

EDGAR

Hey, you're not playing it right, guessing wild like that. You gotta be scientific.

JO

Old people, Sam? Very old people?
 (*To the audience*)
I know who it is.
 (*Her attention back to the* GROUP)

CAROL

They're dead!

FRED (*Trying to remain pleasant*)
She means a long time ago, Carol.

CAROL (*Not convinced*)
Oh.

SAM (*Still enthusiastic*)
Yes, old people; long time ago; long, long time ago.

JO

Were they brothers, Sam?
 (*To the audience*)
I know who it *is*.
 (*Her attention back to the* GROUP)

SAM

Were they . . .
 (HE *realizes* JO *knows the answer*)
Aw, that's not fair, Jo.

LUCINDA *(Happy)*

What's not fair!?

EDGAR *(Brows knitted)*

Yeah. What's not fair?

SAM

Jo knows who it is; that's not fair.

FRED *(The edge of anger)*

What do you mean it's not fair!? It's a game, isn't it? She knows, she knows.

SAM

Wives shouldn't be allowed to play.

FRED *(Stern)*

Wives play; girlfriends play; husbands play; everybody plays. Who the fuck is it, Jo?

JO *(Smiles)*

Brothers, Sam? A long time ago? And these brothers, by the faintest of possibilities did they happen to be suckled by a wolf, and did they happen to found the city of Rome?

SAM *(Real down)*

Yes, yes. Fifteen, sixteen, something; I win.

LUCINDA

Oh, *what's* their name!? Remus and something.

EDGAR *(Overly clear)*

Romulus and Remus.

CAROL *(To* FRED*)*

I don't *know* any of these people!

JO

Don't worry, Carol; you wouldn't have liked them.

SAM

I win. Big deal. It's no fair—really.
    (To the audience)
Really; it's no fair.
    (Back to the OTHERS*)*

EDGAR

Sore winner.

SAM

She knew who it was; she could figure it out!

(To the audience)
She knew all along.
(Back to the OTHERS*)*

EDGAR

Awwwwwwwwww!

CAROL *(To* JO*)*

How'd you know?

JO

Weeeellll . . .

SAM

Aw, come on, Jo!

JO *(To quiet* SAM*)*
No, I think it's nice, shows we . . . I think it's nice.
(To the OTHERS*)*
Sam and I were in bed a couple of nights ago—talking and sort of lying
around—and he was stroking me—which is about it, now; hey, gang?

EDGAR *(Profound sadness)*
Aw, Jo.

JO
(To the audience; a little rueful herself)
Death's door, and all. *And* . . . he had one of my breasts, and he was sort
of bouncing it around a little bit . . .

FRED *(To* SAM*)*
You debbil!

JO *(Still to the audience)*
. . . and he started nibbling, and then he started sucking . . .
(To SAM*)*
. . . which breast was it, Sam?

SAM
(Embarrassed, therefore cold)
I don't recall: I was occupied.
(Refers to the audience)
For God's sake, Jo!

JO *(To* SAM*; kind)*
It's all right.
(To the audience)
You don't mind if I talk about my breasts, do you? Humor the lady a little?

(To SAM*)*

They don't mind.

(To the GUESTS*)*

Which breast *was* it—left, I think. And . . . he said—all of a sudden—he said he was Romulus, and I was the she-wolf, and I asked where his broth-er Remus was, and he told me not to be greedy . . .

SAM

O.K.! Big deal!

(A mocking chorus of "Awwwww, poor Sam; Aw, what's the mat-ter, Sam?; he's embarrassed!" etc.)

O.K.! O.K.!

LUCINDA

("Isn't he too cute for words?")

Aww . . .

SAM *(To the audience)*

Now, if you want to know the real and true reason I wouldn't tell her where my brother Remus was . . .

JO

Was that you'd killed him!

(To the audience)

He'd built the city—Rome—and he was standing around looking at the fortifications—very proud of himself—and Remus came up, took one look, and said, "Wow! Are those ever lousy fortifications."

(To SAM, *now)*

And you killed him. Right on the spot.

LUCINDA

What an unpleasant thing to do!

FRED

(Leans forward in his chair)

Oh, *I* don't know; a man's proud of his fortifications.

JO *(A trifle glum)*

Anyhow, that's how it was. Sam wins. I guess it, and Sam wins.

EDGAR *(Not much enthusiasm)*

Anyhow, Sam wins; Sam's the champ. Game's over; hurray!

SAM

(Playing Romulus; speculative)

I was always jealous of Remus; I never knew why.

JO

What was it, did he hog the nipples? How many do wolves *have,* for God's
sake.

SAM

Oh, there were enough . . . but he took my favorites.

FRED *(Laughing)*

The four or five you liked the most.

SAM

Something like that.

JO *(Glum)*

At least you had a *mother.*

SAM *(Curiously annoyed)*

Oh, come on, Jo!

JO *(Undaunted)*

WELL . . .

SAM

You've got a perfectly good mother!

JO

(Clearly this is a private argument)

Yeah? Where is she? Where the hell is she?

SAM *(Spits it out)*

"In the hour of your need?"

JO *(Hard)*

YEAH! IN THE HOUR OF MY GODDAMN NEED!!

EDGAR

Come on, Sam.

JO

Yeah? Big deal!

LUCINDA

(Bright; maybe just to help)

I've never met your mother!

JO

Big deal!

LUCINDA *(Offended)*

Well. I'm sorry.

JO *(Ugly mimicking)*

"Well. I'm sorry."

LUCINDA

I mean, I know she lives in New Jersey . . .

JO

Fuck New Jersey!

SAM

Jo . . .

LUCINDA *(Grim)*

With her sister, is it?

JO

Fuck Jo's mother's sister!

SAM

Jo . . .

LUCINDA *(Persisting)*

And you don't see her? Is that it?

EDGAR

Leave it alone, Lu.

LUCINDA *(To* EDGAR*; sotto voce)*

I was merely trying . . .

JO

Fuck merely trying.

SAM

C'mon, Jo.

JO *(Perversely casual)*

O.K. O.K. by *me.*

SAM *(To the audience)*

Jo's mother . . .

JO *(Cheerful)*

Ah, fuck Jo's mother.

SAM *(Still to the audience)*

The lady leaves something to be desired. She's tiny, thin as a rail, blue eyes—darting furtive blue eyes—

JO

Fuck furtive blue eyes.

SAM *(Ibid.)*

—pale hair, tinted pink, balding a little; you know; the way women do, when they do. We don't see her much. We don't like her; I don't like her.

LUCINDA

Still; a mother is a mother!

FRED

Jesus!

EDGAR

You just can't leave well enough alone, can you?

JO

"A mother is a mother." I like that!

SAM *(To the* OTHERS*)*

Anyhow, game is over; *I* win: suckled by a wolf, fratricidal but victorious.

EDGAR *(Claps his hands)*

Game's over, kids; game's over.

JO *(Sarcastically enthusiastic)*

Yes, and wasn't it boring? Wasn't it all . . . empty, ultimately? Didn't we waste our time?

(To the audience; without emotion)

Especially if you're dying, as I am.

SAM *(So sad and weary)*

Come on, Jo. Please?

JO

(Shrugs; to SAM, *and generally to the* GUESTS*)*

I merely wondered; it doesn't matter; I thought I'd ask; forget I said it.

SAM

Please, Jo?

FRED

(Rises, empty glass in hand; moves toward the bar)

Boring? I don't know. I thought it was like every other night around here; I thought it was fine.

SAM *(To* JO*)*

I mean, are you tired?

JO *(Waves* SAM *off; to* FRED*)*

Is this the beginning of your hostility, Fred, or are you still pretending to be pleasant? I can never quite catch the moment when you turn.

(To the audience)

Fred turns. ·

(Snaps her fingers)

Just like that.
(Back to the GROUP *now)*

CAROL *(Generally)*

What did Fred do?
(To the audience)
What did Fred do?
(Back to the GROUP *now)*

FRED

(Ponders, with a small smile)
I'm still pretending to be pleasant, I think. Get anyone a drink?

CAROL *(To no one in particular)*
Leave Fred alone; he's bad enough when he's awful.

FRED
I don't think I understand that, Carol. Who can I make a drink?

JO

(Holding her empty glass out)
Me.

SAM *(Concerned)*
You all . . . you O.K.?

JO *(Bravura)*
Sure.

FRED

(Moves to JO, *takes her glass)*
A little night crap?

JO
A little what? A little night crap? Fred, you aren't vulgar, you're just plain
dirt common.

FRED
You be careful now; I'm still pretending to be pleasant, but these social
events are wearing on a man.

JO
Mmmmmmm; what a pity they're compulsory.

SAM *(Guardedly pleased)*
Hey, come on; I'll think you two like each other.

FRED *(Muses)*
Ooooh, I wouldn't worry, Sam; I like Jo a lot bettern'n Jo likes me.

(To JO; *twang)*
But ah'll make it up to ya, honey; you just see.
(Normal tone again)
Lucinda? Is Edgar having another drink?
*(*JO *laughs)*

LUCINDA
Well, ask *him.* Who do you think I *am?*

FRED
Carol? Edgar, what about it? Lucinda says ask *you.*

CAROL
None for me; it's hard enough to follow as it is.

EDGAR
Well . . . what does everyone think?

SAM
About what?

EDGAR
About having a *drink.* Should I have *another?*

SAM *(A tiny pause)*
Most of us don't care, Edgar.

EDGAR *(Curiously hurt)*
Oh. I see.

SAM *(Mildly patronizing)*
I mean, it's the sort of thing a man's just got to decide for himself.

FRED *(A drawl)*
Sam isn't being unfriendly, Edgar, just laying it on the line, as they say.

LUCINDA
You leave Edgar alone.

EDGAR *(Grim)*
Gee, am I glad I asked.

SAM
(Overly serious and solicitous)
I think you ought to do what you want to, Edgar.

JO *(A toast)*
Drink 'til you puke!

LUCINDA *(Nervous distaste)*
Jo! That's not *like* you!

JO

I wasn't *talking* about *me;* I was talking about Edgar. If I were Edgar, I would drink 'til I puked.

(*Small smile*)

No offense.

LUCINDA (*An hysterical little laugh*)

Well! And none taken!

FRED

(*Friendly; an arm around* EDGAR)

I'd think twice about having another drink if I were you, Edgar. My God, all the things that could happen? They coulda put poison in the ice cubes; it's three blocks home . . . in the *dark;* the sky might fall? *And* . . . if Doomsday comes, mushroom Doomsday . . .

EDGAR

(*Quiet and as dignified as the situation allows*)

I think I will have a drink, Fred; I just think I will.

(HE *goes to the bar, pushing* FRED *aside*)

SAM (*Laughs, nicely*)

Oh, Edgar! Poor, sweet Edgar!

JO (*Shy little girl imitation*)

The sky might fall? And Doomsday come?

(*A long, hollow sound*)

Doooooooooooomsday!

EDGAR (*A little put off*)

Don't you worry about me, Sam; I'm all right.

SAM

(*Looking at the bar; a small pause*)

Oh. Well. Well, in that case I'll get some more soda; we're out of soda.

(HE *begins to exit*)

FRED (*As* SAM *exits; broad*)

You're a good man, Sam!

JO

Dooooooomsday!

(*To the audience*)

Doomsday. It follows Thursday . . . if you're lucky.

EDGAR

You all right, Jo?

FRED *(Sitting, heavily)*

Good man, Sam. You have a good husband, Jo.

JO

(Back to the OTHERS, *now; to* FRED; *deep voice)*

Thanks, Fred.

(To EDGAR; *nice)*

Sure thing, Edgar; I'm O.K.

FRED

No, I mean it; he's O.K.

LUCINDA *(Cheerful)*

Everybody likes Sam. Well, *I* like Sam, too.

FRED *(None too pleasant)*

Hey, that's swell, Lucinda.

(To the audience)

We *do* like Sam; Sam's really O.K. We like Sam a lot.

EDGAR *(To the audience)*

Oh, we do; we *like* Sam.

JO

God! What are you planning to *do—knife* him, or something?

*(*FRED *and* EDGAR *turn their attention back to* JO*)*

FRED *(Angry)*

We *like* him, for Christ's sake!

EDGAR

Come on, Jo!

JO

We *all* like Sam! Great! Big deal!

(Ruminative)

We all like Sam, and that should make it Samsday. Samsday precedeth Doomsday: Samsday, Thurmsday, Doomsday. Isn't that how it goes, Fred?

FRED *(Casual)*

I don't give a shit, Jo, *how* it goes; just *stop* it!

JO

O.K.

FRED

All I care about right now is my drink.

JO *(A mock aside, to* CAROL)

Fred really doesn't deserve Sam's friendship; Sam's too good for Fred; Sam knows it, but . . . well, you know.

FRED *(Much too casual)*

Knock it off, Jo.

JO *(To the audience)*

Sam's a real egalitarian; Sam pretends to like everyone equally.
(*Looks to* FRED *for his reaction;* HE *gives her the finger*)

CAROL *(Looking at her nails)*

Sounds sort of indiscriminate to me.

JO

(*As* FRED *chuckles; briefly taken aback; to* CAROL)

Well, yes, it *is* that. But Sam is a man of facets. Who *are* you, Carol?

CAROL *(Stretches)*

Ooooooh, I'm a lady of parts; I got facets, too, you know.

FRED

She's a lady of parts.

CAROL

By which I mean I'm not all bimbo; I'm not your dumb brunette for nothing. I'm gonna go pee.

FRED

You, uh . . . you know where it is?

CAROL

(*Hand on hip; feigns puzzling it out*)

Well, let's see; it's either outdoors or inside, and since this is the sort of neighborhood's probably got zoning regulations I bet I'll find it somewhere here on the ground floor.

FRED *(Sorry* HE *brought it up)*

O.K. O.K.

CAROL *(Relentless)*

And if I don't find it, I'll just squat on the rug. O.K.? O.K., lover?

FRED

O.K.! O.K.!

CAROL

(*To the audience, as* SHE *exits*)

God! These people!

JO *(Looks after* CAROL*)*

She's not bad; she's got a good mouth.

FRED

Carol's gonna marry me one day.

JO

(In reaction to FRED*'s remark)*

Not a very good brain, maybe . . .

FRED

I'm a three-time winner; might as well make it four.

EDGAR

Have you asked her?

FRED

Hm?

EDGAR

Have you asked her to marry you!?

FRED

Have I *asked* her!? I ask her every night before we go to sleep; I ask her
when we get up; I ask her when I'm in the saddle . . .

LUCINDA *(Smiles at the memory)*

I made Edgar propose to me three times.

JO *(After a slight pause)*

You take big chances, girl.

FRED *(Intensely serious)*

Edgar, if I'd known that, I sure woulda been nicer to you all these years.
I'll make it up to you, fella!

JO *(Imitating)*

I'll make it up to you, fella! Big pal; big fella!

EDGAR *(Weary)*

Lay off, Jo.

FRED

No, no, it's all right.

(Histrionic)

Where else can you come in this cold world, week after week, as regular
as patchwork, and be guaranteed ridicule and contempt? Where else, I ask
you, in this cold world?

(To the audience)

There is nowhere else, in this cold world, where you can come, week
after—

JO (*Level*)

Oh, there must be lots of other places, Fred. *You* have friends; this can't be the only place.

EDGAR

Is the pain bad, Jo?

JO (*Offhand*)

Pretty bad.

LUCINDA (*A little dreamy*)

We love you, Fred; we all love each other.

JO

Speak for yourself, Lu.

FRED (*Not to the audience*)

Name one; name one other place; name one other place where I can come and be *sure* of it, where I can *count* on it.

EDGAR (*Bland*)

Well, you could come to *our* place, Fred; we got as much ridicule and contempt as the next house.

LUCINDA (*Snapped out of her revery*)

We have not!
    (*To the audience*)
That is not true!
    (*To* EDGAR)
Really, Edgar!

EDGAR (*Dogmatic*)

Well, we *should*. *If* you are managing the house as you're supposed to, *if* you are keeping the larder full, then we should have just as much ridicule and contempt as the next . . .

FRED (*Ruminative*)

I used to have *lots* of it—*closets* full; open a cupboard, and the ridicule and contempt'd just . . . fall out all over the place! I don't know what happened.

JO (*Soothing*)

Well, maybe when you and Carol get married everything'll get back to normal.

FRED (*Overly concerned*)

Gee; I sure hope so.
    (*A rumpus Offstage; the sound of* CAROL *and* SAM *arguing.* CAROL *catapults Onstage, followed by* SAM *with his soda bottles*)

CAROL (*At* SAM)

Just keep your fucking hands off me, that's all!!

SAM

Will you shut up!? Will you just—

CAROL

Goddamn creep! Goddamn son of a bitch! Jesus, you can't even go take a leak around here!

SAM

I said, shut up about it!

CAROL

Just keep your fucking hands off me!

FRED

(*Realizing what is happening*)
Hey hey hey hey!

CAROL (*To* JO; *quivering*)
You better put locks on your bathroom doors, lady, or handcuffs on this one!

FRED

Hey! What the hell *is* this!?

LUCINDA (*Thrilled*)
What's going on!? What's going on!?

EDGAR

What *is* this?

SAM

(*Making weapons out of the soda bottles*)
Will you just shut up about it!?

CAROL

You dirty, dirty old man!

FRED

(*Getting to his feet; belligerent*)
O.K. now, just what the fuck's going—

CAROL

(*A sudden imitation of a violated maiden; falsetto*)
Fred? Would you take me home, please? I've been vastly insulted!

FRED (*Ready for battle now*)
You're fuckin-A right I will! Jesus Christ, Sam!
(*But* CAROL *and* SAM *have dissolved into laughter, are hanging on to each other for support*)

SAM

Oh, boy; oh, boy!

CAROL

Christ! Oh, Jesus!

EDGAR

Hey, what *is* this? Another game?

CAROL

Oh, Jesus! Oh, sweet Jesus!

SAM

Oh, hey! Wow!

FRED

What the fuck's going on!?

SAM (*Hugging* CAROL)

Oh, boy! Hey, we ought to work up an act!

CAROL

Oh, God, that was fun!
   (SHE *sees that* FRED *is not amused*)
Fred! Hey, Fred!
   (SHE *goes to him, hugs him*)
Hey, Fred!

FRED (HE *flings her arm away*)

It's all *right!* Just . . . it's all right. Let go of me!

LUCINDA (*Rather sour*)

That was a *joke.* Is that it?
   (*To the audience*)
Is that what everybody's laughing about? That it was a joke?

SAM

   (*Very pleased with himself*)
Yes, Lu; that was a joke.

LUCINDA

   (*Ugly little smile; to* SAM)
I just want to keep up. I don't want to fall behind all you bright types.

EDGAR (*Hugs her*)

Luuuuuuuuu!

FRED

   (*Trying to recover his dignity*)
That was very funny; you got a big rise out of me, and it was very funny;

(Indicates the audience)
everybody had a good laugh.

SAM

Awwwww, Fred!

JO *(Challenging)*

Including you, Fred?

FRED *(Bluff)*

Sure! Sure!
(The OTHERS *are silent)*
No! To be truthful, *no.*

CAROL *(Sincere)*

Aw, Fred.

FRED

No! I rose to the bait, I took it, and I was hauled in. I was humiliated!

EDGAR

No! You weren't!

CAROL

Awwww, Fred!

SAM

You just showed you cared, Fred.

FRED *(Heavily sarcastic)*

Yeah? Is that it?

CAROL

Yeah! That's it!

FRED *(Shrugs)*

O.K. that's it. You saw me with all my clothes off.

JO *(A half-smile)*

How come you don't hit somebody, Fred? This isn't like you.

FRED

Yeah; I know.

LUCINDA *(Bright)*

Oh, that's interesting!

EDGAR *(Really fed up)*

Why don't you just shut up, Lu?
*(*SHE *glares at him for quite a while;* HE *ignores her)*

FRED *(Ingenuous)*

Maybe I'm getting soft; maybe I like you guys.

SAM

Maybe you're in love.

FRED *(Shrugs)*

Maybe I'm in love.
   (To the audience)
Maybe I'm in love.

JO *(Into her glass)*

I wouldn't count on it.

SAM

Aw, come on, Jo.

FRED *(To CAROL)*

You gonna marry me, Carol?
   (To the audience)
Carol's gonna marry me one day.

JO

You gonna marry Fred one day, Carol?

CAROL

   (Appraises FRED; to the OTHERS)
I don't know. How many of us end up marrying Fred?

FRED *(To the GROUP)*

Three, so far; I'm a three-time winner. You wanna marry me, Carol?
Christ, now I'm asking her in public! Three-time winner, Carol; you wanna
make it four?

CAROL

   (Very true, if nose-wrinkling)
I don't *know.*
   (To the audience)
Really. I don't know.

SAM *(To JO)*

Four of a kind isn't bad.

JO *(Shrugs)*

Beats a full house.

EDGAR

You gonna marry Fred, Carol?

CAROL *(Quite pestered)*

I don't know, I don't know, I don't know! I know it's late and I got the itch, but beyond that I'm not sure.

FRED

I should drink up?

CAROL

Suit yourself; I've done it solo.

FRED *(Sighing, rising)*

Maybe we ought to go, host and hostess.

LUCINDA *(Rises, nudges EDGAR)*

Well, we certainly are. Come on, Edgar.

FRED *(Sits again)*

Oh, well, then, we'll stay.

SAM

(To LUCINDA and EDGAR; only mildly protesting)

Oh? You . . . taking off?

EDGAR *(Reluctantly rising)*

Apparently.

JO *(Moody; to the audience)*

Hardly anyone stays up late anymore. Why do you think that is?

LUCINDA *(To JO; a schoolmarm)*

It's because we all get tired earlier than we used to.

JO

(Still to the audience; sags her shoulders; great, mock defeat)

Oh, God! Do you think it's that!?

EDGAR

Thank you, Sam—especially for the games, all of 'em.

(To JO; a concerned tone; light, though)

You take it easy, Jo.

JO *(To EDGAR; toasts him)*

Alley-oop!

EDGAR

(An arm around SAM's shoulder now)

Night, you two; you suffer fools so gladly; it's a gift.

JO *(Salutes EDGAR)*

Help yourself, if there's any left.

EDGAR

Remember the alimony, Fred; remember the itch, but remember the alimony.

(FRED *waves*)

LUCINDA *(Generally)*

Good night, now; good night.

(No one reacts.

To the audience; quite peeved)

No one says good night to me, you may have noticed.

JO

Nobody says good night to you? Not even Edgar?

LUCINDA *(To* JO*)*

Well, of course *Edgar* says good night to me!

JO *(Deep chest tone)*

Well, then!

LUCINDA *(Sort of hysterical)*

Of course, Edgar more or less *has* to say good night to me!

JO

Still! Count your blessings!

LUCINDA *(Beady-eyed and tough)*

My cup runneth over, hunh?

JO

Right! But watch the rug.

EDGAR

Come on, Lu, let's get you out of here in one piece. Be good to one another.

JO

Any particular order we should do that in?

EDGAR

Nah; touch one, touch all.

LUCINDA *(Eyes narrowing; to* JO*)*

Just what did you mean by "count your blessings"? Just what did you mean by that?

EDGAR *(Eyes to heaven)*

Oh, Christ!

SAM

What are you two going to do now, have a fight, or something?

LUCINDA *(Clearly spoiling)*

No, we're not going to have a fight; I merely want to know what Miss Smartypants here means by "count your blessings," that's all.

EDGAR

Oh, Christ!

JO *(Rising to it)*

All I meant *was*—my *dear* Lucinda—that you are lucky . . . that *any*one . . . says good night to you, by which I sus*pect* I meant . . .

SAM

Oh, God.

JO *(Louder)*

By which I sus*pect* I meant you're lucky you've got anybody living in the same *house* with you, much less merely *talk*ing to you.

LUCINDA *(Stiff; cold)*

I see.

JO

Is that *clear?*

LUCINDA *(Nose out of joint)*

I think *so;* thank you very *much.*

JO *(Drawl)*

Ooooooh, you're welcome; my goodness, you're welcome.

EDGAR

Come on, Lu.

SAM *(Quietly cajoling)*

Be *nice*, Jo.

LUCINDA *(Grand, if stern)*

I'm going to forgive you, Jo.

JO *(Deep tone again)*

Thanks, Lu.

SAM

Jo . . .

LUCINDA *(None too kind)*

I'm going to forgive you because I assume the pain is very bad.

(*A general silence*)

JO *(Sighs, stares at the ceiling)*

Well, nothing compared to the one you give me, Lu.

(*Snarls*)

Get out of here, will you!?

LUCINDA

(A brave smile; to the audience)

Jo used to have at me this way when we were at college—making fun of me all the time.

(To the OTHERS, *now)*

It's become a habit; we don't even know we're doing it anymore.

JO *(Pretending consternation)*

Gee, I thought *I* knew.

EDGAR *(Pulls at* LUCINDA*)*

Come on; get out of here before you're plucked clean.

LUCINDA *(To* FRED *and* CAROL*)*

She really doesn't know she's doing it.

EDGAR *(Impatient with her)*

O.K.; O.K.!

(To SAM *and* JO; *drawled)*

Thank you, you two; it was your nice, average, desperate evening; we had fun.

SAM

So did we; so did we!

FRED

So did we!

CAROL

Yeah!

JO

(Still pretending to be puzzled)

I thought I *knew* I was having at her; I could *swear* I *knew.*

LUCINDA *(Close to tears)*

Come on, Edgar; Jo's "tired."

JO *(Mocking)*

"Jo's tired." Fuck off.

EDGAR *(Gentle)*

Take it easy, Jo. Night, Sam.

SAM

(Goes to the hall with them)

Let me come with you.

EDGAR

No, no; come on!

JO

"Let me come with you." "No, no; come on."

(Calls after, too bouyant)

Night! Thanks for coming!

(To FRED *and* CAROL*)*

Wanna keep me alive? Wanna cause a remission?

FRED *(Smiles nicely)*

What do I have to do—kill Lucinda?

JO

That'd sure help.

(To herself, mostly)

Wouldn't do any good, but it'd sure help.

CAROL *(Trying to help)*

I lost a sister.

JO

What'd you do, leave her in the parking lot, or something?

CAROL *(Tiny pause)*

Skip it.

(A silence; SAM *reenters)*

JO

Night? Thanks for coming?

SAM

Is it? *Is* it very bad?

JO *(Transparent)*

What? Is what?

SAM

The pain. Is it very bad?

JO *(A harsh laugh)*

It could be worse . . . they keep telling me.

(Shrugs)

Nah; I just don't like her.

SAM *(Gentle correction)*

C'mon; I know you.

JO *(Dismissive)*

Change the record.

SAM

Look, I'm not one to complain . . .

JO

Good! Pull up a drink and sit down; join us.

FRED

Clear a space somewhere; c'mon in; the Scotch and water's fine.

SAM *(Views the room; sighs)*

I don't know how six people can make such a mess of a perfectly good . . .

JO

Leave it. Let it pile up.
    (SAM *laughs, shrugs)*
Tired, baby?

SAM

Lots of things. Why do we ask them over, Jo?

JO

(A child giving the correct answer)
Because they're our friends, tha's why.

SAM

God, you're awful to Lucinda.

FRED *(Feigned surprise)*

Jo? Awful? To Lucinda?

JO *(By way of apology)*

Everybody's awful to Lucinda, except Edgar, maybe, and who knows?

SAM

No; everybody makes *fun* of Lucinda, but you're *awful* to her.

JO *(Languid)*

Well, maybe we ought to even it out more. You want to be awful to her
next time? How about you, Fred?

FRED *(Helpful)*

Sure, I'll do it.

SAM *(To JO)*

Be careful; you may need Lucinda one day.

JO *(Laughs)*

Who? Me?
    (Detached)
Well, I dare say the day will come I'll need you all. Then, of course, the
day will come I won't need a soul. And then, of course, the day won't come.

SAM *(Little-boy sad)*

Oh, Jo.

JO *(To the audience, as above)*

That's what they tell us, isn't it—that growing pile of books on how to die? That somewhere along the line you stop needing those you . . . need the most? You loose your ties? God, what do you need then?

(To SAM; *some energy)*

Hey! Rub my shoulders.

SAM *(Moves to her; begins)*

Why *do* we have them over, Jo?

JO

Why do we have *anyone* over? Less on the neck when I'm trying to talk, or is that the idea? Why do we have them over? Did I say because we love them?

SAM *(Rubbing her shoulders)*

Nope; you said because they were our friends.

JO *(Offhand)*

Oh. Well, add because we love them, but secretly mean because we need a surface to bounce it all off of . . .

SAM

I'm moving back toward the neck.

JO

I'm almost done. Because! Because it's too much trouble to change it all, and because we probably do love them in spite of everything . . .

SAM *(Examining her neck)*

There's meant to be a pressure point, a nerve right about here on the neck . . .

JO

O.K.! O.K.! If you're going to ask me broody-type questions, don't expect me to be . . .

SAM

Lucinda isn't all that bad.

JO

Yes, she *is*.

FRED

She *is*, Sam.

CAROL

Oh, yes; she really is.

SAM *(To the* THREE *of them)*

She's no worse than Edgar for putting up with it—with *her.*

JO

What she's no worse than is your friend Fred, the floozy-bopper; that one over there.

SAM

What's the matter with Fred?

CAROL (*Eyes narrowing*)

The what?

FRED

What's the matter with me?

JO

You're a pain; that's what's the matter with you.

CAROL

(*Assimilating it, with interest*)

The floozy-bopper?

SAM

What's Fred ever done to you?

FRED

Yeah. What've I ever done to you?
(*Wiggles his eyebrows*)
'Cept in my mind, maybe?

CAROL

Floozy-bopper?
(*Grudging admiration*)
That's pretty good.

JO (*Swings around to* FRED)

What have you done to me? You have subjected me to three—count 'em, three!—of what I assume is to be an endless parade of wives, each of whom is further from the mark than the previous one.

SAM (*The peacemaker*)

Well, now he's got Carol.

FRED

And Carol's different.

SAM

And, besides, it's his business.

JO

Shut up! I'm being irrational! It is *not* his business; we have to put up with it. Besides, he's a reactionary, Bush-loving fag baiter; he's . . .

FRED

Nobody's a Bush-lover; nobody ever *was* a Bush-lover; nobody even voted for him; ever! Don't you keep up?

JO *(Grudging)*

Well, that's true. Still! I don't like you, Fred, when you get right down to it.

FRED *(No help at all)*

I like *you*.

JO *(Head back; Bernhardt)*

Oh, God! Oh, God! The burdens!

(Wriggles free)

What are you doing? Fiddling with me? God!

SAM *(Mild)*

The lady don't want to be coddled no more?

JO

Coddle me not.

(Afterthought)

On the lone prairie.

(SHE rises, stretches, begins to move about; suddenly SHE is bent double with pain; SHE falls back on her footstool, her hands clutching her belly. SHE howls; it is a sound of intense agony and protest at the same time. It is not very loud, but profound. SAM stands where HE is, watches. A silence; then SHE howls again; same nonreaction from SAM, though CAROL covers her ears and leans in toward FRED, who cuddles her.

EDGAR has come back in during this last. HE is framed in the doorway)

EDGAR *(Into the silence)*

Please?

(Pause)

Hello?

SAM *(Great weariness; sighs)*

Hello, Edgar.

FRED

What did you forget, Edgar? Your youth? Your dignity, your—

EDGAR *(Cutting FRED off)*

Neither; both; take your pick. Jo?

(HE walks over to JO; SHE looks up at him with pleading and pain; no sound, though. Softly)

Jo, I came back because Lucinda is . . . because Lucinda is sitting out on the lawn, crying her heart out.

FRED *(Sotto voce)*

On the lawn?

(Now, and during the rest of EDGAR's *following speech,* JO *will howl from time to time, not very loud, but intense, as a counterpoint to his remarks)*

EDGAR

(A dismissing gesture to FRED; *then)*

We get outside, Jo, and we start across the lawn, and she plops right down and she starts crying, right there. She says she can't take it anymore, Jo, the way you go at her; the way you make such terrible fun of her in front of everybody! She says it was all right until you got sick but now you're sick you mean it in a different way, and it's breaking her heart.

*(*SHE *howls)*

Don't do that, Jo; I'm trying to *tell* you. Lucinda's down there on the lawn, and she's pulling up tufts of grass and throwing 'em around, and she's got dirt all over her, and I don't think it's any crap: she means it; she's not going to get up from that fucking lawn 'til you say you're sorry. So I think you better get down there and help her—apologize, or what—in spite of your pain, because she's in pain down there, too, and she didn't cause yours.

(A silence)

JO *(To the audience)*

Well, I don't suppose there's any answer to that 'cept get up and go down there with her—"sit upon the ground and tell sad stories"?

(To the OTHERS *now)*

Tear up a few mutual tufts, hold on to each other, rock, console? I guess I'd better.

SAM

No, Jo!

JO

Edgar's right: Lucinda's in pain.

*(*JO *rises, clearly still in some pain herself)*

OWWW! And pain is less fun than a few other things. Can I have a hand?

*(*SHE *puts her hands out;* SAM *helps her up)*

CAROL

You want your shoes?

JO

Nah, it's bedtime; besides, the grass tickles; I like it. Edgar? I'll set it right as best I can; no promises; your wife ain't easy; she can turn a kindly phrase sour in the best of mouths, but I'll try.

EDGAR *(Sincere)*

Thank you, Jo.

JO *(To* SAM)

Give Edgar a drink; give him some comfort; tell him some lies.

SAM

(As THEY *move toward the hallway)*

Easy. You're so light.

JO

I weigh nothing; I'm air. Off to the lawn.

FRED

We better go, too. C'mon, toots.

SAM

Be careful, Jo; it may be damp.

CAROL *(Not too enthusiastic)*

O.K.

JO

You mean I may get a cold to go with the rest?

FRED

(Moving to JO, *taking her from* SAM)

One strong arm.

JO

What's the matter with the other one?

FRED

Take it easy, lady.

JO *(A laugh)*

What is all this—in case I fall? In case I become dust on the threshold?

FRED

Take her other arm, Carol.

CAROL

She can make it; she's a good girl.

JO *(To* SAM)

I'm a good girl.

SAM

Come back, Jo.

JO

I'm a good girl. Who are you?

(JO *exits, with* FRED *and* CAROL)

SAM (*To the empty hallway*)

You're a good girl; come back.

(EDGAR *stays standing;* SAM *doesn't look at him, but picks up a few glasses*)

EDGAR (*Finally*)

Do you want to talk?

SAM

Nope.

EDGAR

You want to make me a drink?

SAM

Nope.

EDGAR

Uh . . . you want to give me some comfort? You want to tell me some lies?

SAM (*Almost laughing*)

Oh . . . go make your own drink.

EDGAR

(*An imitation: what? a girl?*)

Gee, I thought you'd never ask.

SAM (*Sitting*)

You *want* some comfort? You *want* some lies?

EDGAR (*Looking*)

I want some bourbon.

SAM

Right in front of you. O.K., let's see: *you're* looking well; *Lucinda's* looking well; *Fred's* looking well; *Carol's* looking well . . .

EDGAR

(*Concentrating on his drink*)

Very funny.

SAM

Jo's looking well; *I'm* looking well . . .

EDGAR (*Abrupt, but not loud*)

Can't you control her? Even a little? You let Jo just run wild these days, these nights?

SAM *(Looks away; sighs)*

Yeah, I pretty much let her do what she wants to do.

EDGAR *(Cool)*

You figure that's best?

SAM *(Unintimidated)*

I figure that's best.

EDGAR *(Pause; rather arch)*

Well, I suppose that's the way it ought to be. I mean, I suppose you should know.

SAM *(Closing the subject)*

I suppose I should know.

EDGAR *(Muted)*

I suppose you should.

(Pause; HE *slams his drink down)*

JESUS CHRIST, WHAT KIND OF A HOUSE DO YOU RUN AROUND HERE!?

SAM *(Too calm, if anything)*

Hm? Pardon me?

EDGAR

YOUR FUCKING GUESTS END UP CRYING!?

SAM *(Still calm)*

They love us: they cry. Look to your own house, buddy.

EDGAR

(Intense, but less loud than before)

People don't cry at *our* house! People don't come over and visit *us* and go away sobbing!

SAM *(Harsh)*

No! They go away laughing! Behind your back, of course, but laughing!

EDGAR *(Clearly an old subject)*

Oh, Christ, not that again, hunh!? I am not you; Lucinda is not Jo; black is not white, and when the fuck are you going to get it all straight?

SAM

(Shakes his head; mock consternation)

I keep *trying;* I keep *trying.*

EDGAR

I *know* you don't like the way I run my marriage . . .

SAM

I didn't know you ran it.

EDGAR

What? I know you don't even *like* Lucinda, for that matter; *any* of you!

SAM *(Mock shock)*

Oh! How did you ever figure that out!? We've kept it so . . . so . . .

EDGAR *(Serene; even superior)*

But I don't *care.*

SAM

Oh, that's clear.

EDGAR

I decided a long time ago that the fact I love Lucinda gives her all the virtue she needs—if there's any lack to begin with. It's a common enough thing; we all do it; I just admit it.

SAM *(Almost a sneer)*

Well, I dare say you'd have to.

EDGAR *(Furious)*

You're no different!

SAM *(Cool)*

Edgar, you're my only friend whose every virtue embarrasses me. You're the only man I know does something good and I want to hit him.

EDGAR *(So reasonable)*

Well, I guess you *need* me, Sam.

SAM

I'm not into M and S.

EDGAR

S and M.

SAM

What?

EDGAR *(Turning a little nasty)*

Yeah, I guess you need me. I mean, shit!, what's a martyr for 'less there's someone 'round the corner to do him in? Fred'd never turn on me: he's too straightforward; Carol hasn't been around long enough to learn the game.

SAM

Any game.

EDGAR

What? Jo has her own problems, and so that just leaves you, ol' buddy. I don't need to take my shirt off, do I? You got a whip goes right through cloth, don't you? You say you're not into it?

SAM (*Smiles; to the audience*)

It's the self-indulgence of these martyrs gets me most.

EDGAR (*Smiles; to* SAM)

Is it? Does it? Glad you got it pinpointed.

(*Pause; gentle*)

Can I help?

SAM

(*To* EDGAR; *pause; shakes his head*)

Nobody can help.

EDGAR

Can *any* of us help?

SAM

Nobody can help.

EDGAR (*Acknowledgment*)

Not even the village martyr.

SAM

Move *over.*

EDGAR (*As above*)

Yeah; sure thing.

SAM

(*Looks up; tears, but no outburst*)

It's a death house I'm keeping here, old friend . . . to answer your question.

EDGAR (*A silence*)

I know; and nobody can help.

SAM

No; nobody.

EDGAR (*Helpless shrug*)

Right!

(*Pause*)

I'll go see how they're doing.

SAM

You do that.

EDGAR (*By the hallway*)

I'll even put the divots back. How's that for friendship? Hunh?

SAM

Pretty good. Not bad.

(EDGAR *moves to exit, but stops, listens as* SAM *begins.*

To the audience/to himself/to anyone)

Each day, each night, each moment, she becomes less and less. My arms go around . . . bone? She . . . diminishes. She moves away from me in ways I . . . The thing we must do about loss is, hold on to the object we're losing. There's time later for . . . ourselves. Hold on! . . . but, to what? To bone? To air? To dust?

(JO *enters as* SAM *begins to weep.* HE *lets his weeping develop, slowly, softly, toward a full expression of misery. His shoulders shake;* HE *sobs;* HE *lets it spend naturally. As* HE *weeps,* JO *replaces* EDGAR *in the archway,* EDGAR *exiting.* JO *leans against the hall, observing* SAM. HE *becomes aware of her presence;* SHE *becomes aware of this.* HE *finishes his weeping notwithstanding)*

JO

(When HE *is about done; seemingly offhand)*

Don't *cry;* don't *cry.*

SAM

You cry.

JO

(Begins to move about the room)

Ah. Well.

(Afterthought)

Women cry.

SAM

Men cry.

JO (A *smile; apologetic)*

Yes, but if *you* cry, I will, *too,* and haven't I enough? I mean, if I started crying for myself, what would hold me together?

(SHE *goes to him; strokes his head)*

Help me not to cry? Please?

(HE *buries his head in her crotch, his hands on her buttocks;* HE *shakes his head slowly)*

Now; now; now.

SAM (Releases her; turns away)

None of this is easy, you know.

JO (Small, sardonic smile)

Your pain's as bad as mine, eh?

SAM

(Angry at being misunderstood)

I didn't *say* that!

JO *(SHE too, angry)*

I didn't *say* you said that!

SAM

Of *course* it's not as bad as yours; it's not even like yours! What do you take
me for?

JO

Husband?

SAM

But I *share* it.

JO *(Strokes his cheek)*

No, you don't, and I'm glad. Yours is almost all in your head—in your
mind, I mean—and mine isn't, thank you, ma'am!

(To the audience)

God! I wish it *was*—all in my head, in my mind.

SAM *(To JO, for her attention)*

You can't measure pain! I'm in pain! I love you!

JO *(To SAM; comforting)*

I *know* you are; and I love *you*.

(To the audience again, with a harsh, abrupt laugh)

Jesus, that would be funny!—if you could measure pain?

SAM *(Crying again)*

Dear God, stop it! Please?

JO

(Very gentle; almost lyrical; to SAM)

All right. See? Stopped.

(To the audience; shrugs)

Stopped.

(A silence. JO takes a small pill vial from a pocket)

SAM *(Sees it)*

How many today? How often are you . . . ?

JO *(Ironic again)*

Popping the old pills? Oh, ten, twelve a day. Guess I better get myself
down to ol' Doc Wheeler for a new prescription—or a stronger one.

SAM *(Hollow)*

Ten or twelve?

JO *(Laughter in the dark)*

Sure; why not!

SAM

A day?

JO *(Deflated)*

Oh, come on.

SAM

God, Jo.

JO *(A heavy sigh)*

Look, Sambo, you better get used to it. It's not going to get any less and it's not going to get any better. I'm up; I'm moving about; I'm engaged in what they refer to as social intercourse; I don't scream more than seven or eight times a day, on a good day . . .

(SAM *covers his ears, hunches over*)

Don't cover up like that! It's *me* we're talking about!

(SHE *pulls his hands from his ears*)

I say it's *me* we're talking about! Christ, if you can't take it now, what will you be like when I *need* you? *Really* need you!?

(*Afterthought*)

Or something?

SAM *(A truthful answer)*

I don't know.

JO *(Far away)*

No. And I don't know what I'll need.

SAM

No.

(THEY BOTH *seem huddled and sort of lost*)

JO

Well, give it some thought: the day *is* going to come. What did ol' Doc Wheeler say? Don't plan great distances ahead? Like, don't try getting your master's or anything.

SAM *(Softly)*

You have your master's?

JO

Hm?

SAM

You *have* your master's?

JO

I don't think he knows that; . . . what I think he *meant* was: wind it up; you're winding down, so . . . wind it up.

SAM *(Glum; dogmatic)*

Everything is reversible.

JO *(A vulnerable smile)*

Spontaneous combustion, or whatever they call it?

SAM

Mmm-hmmmm.

JO

But that's the localized ones, or the ones in the blood sometimes . . .

SAM *(Exploding)*

DON'T GIVE ME YOUR FACTS! YOU'RE SO PROUD OF YOUR FUCKING FACTS!!

JO

(Calm and steady, to counter his outburst)

I have a right to know what's going on, 'specially if it's going on in *me*.

SAM

Let it *go!*

JO

(Leans in toward him; so dispassionate)

Some day, when *you're* dying, when *that* day comes, when the day comes you're *told,* or the day comes you realize you've known but haven't admitted it, I would dearly love to be around.

SAM *(Hurt)*

Jo . . .

JO

(Winces a little: to the audience)

That isn't *kind, is* it.

SAM

No.

JO *(To SAM)*

No. There are two *theories* on that, you know—on being the first to go, or not.

SAM

Oh?

JO

Well, there are two theories on *everything*. One theory is that dying first is kinder—showing the way, and all, I suppose; none of this "after you" stuff. The other theory is that "staying on alone," is the gentlemanly thing to do—or the gentlewomanly, as the case may be.

SAM

Or . . . not doing it at all.

JO

Or . . . not doing it at all.
    (Pause)
Well, yes; *that* has something to be said for it.

SAM *(Absurd and sincere)*

Please? Don't do it at all?

JO

(A tiny pause; to the audience; for the sake of not letting a silence happen)
In the *olden* days, in *some* societies, they would do it together—a hubby and wife, when one or the other was "going"—and in *Egypt*, now, they used to take the servants, and bury *them* along with . . . .

SAM *(Shocked wonder)*

Can't you stop?

JO

(Looks at SAM, *rather surprised to see him; speaks to him)*
I say, they used to bury the servants with their masters. 'Course, with the way help is today . . . I'm sorry, Sam; I'm really sorry.

SAM *(Disgust?)*

What kind of pills are you *taking*, for Christ's sake?

JO

Pain and sleep; pain and sleep. Got any *other* suggestions? No?
    (Harsh laugh)
They'll have me on heroin eventually.
    *(*SAM *moves behind her)*
Bet you never knew you were marrying an incipient dopie, did you; bet you never knew one day you'd have to—
    *(*HE *claps his hand over her mouth, pulls her head to his body.* SHE *resists momentarily, then turns, puts her arms around his legs/hips. It is a reversal of the previous embrace. A silence)*

SAM *(So gentle)*

We just can't talk about it, it's that simple.

JO *(Finally; subdued)*

There are two theories on that, too. Bet you don't want to hear them.

　　(SAM *shakes his head.* JO *rises, moves off a little;* SAM *stays where*
　　HE *is)*

What was it? You do, or you don't?

SAM

No. No, I don't want to hear them.

JO *(Shrugs)*

*Some*one's got to listen; *some*one's got to humor me.

SAM

I listen; I humor you.

JO

Not enough!

SAM *(Sad and weary)*

Jo, you warn me not to humor you, and then you tell me I'm not . . .

JO *(Doesn't want to hear it)*

I know!

SAM

You tell me to ignore you when you get like this, and then you yell at me
for . . .

JO

I know! I know!! Don't . . . don't . . . just don't . . .

　　(Calms down)

I've got to have it both ways. Don't pay any attention. Pay attention?
Please?

SAM *(Defeated)*

Whatever you want.

　　(A silence)

JO

(Clearly whistling in the dark)

Do you think you'll marry again, Sam? Who'll you marry?

SAM

Jo, I . . .

JO

Come on! Play!

SAM

Jo . . .

JO

Come on! Humor me! Who you gonna marry?

SAM *(Hard)*

Carol; naturally.

JO *(Chuckles a little)*

That'd upset old Fred.

SAM

Why? Does old Fred want to marry me?

JO

I can't speak for Fred, but if *I* were Fred, *I'd* marry you.
  (Instinctively, THEY *run to each other and embrace)*
Oh, my Sam, my Sam! I'd marry you in a minute!

SAM *(Picks her up in his arms)*

Shhhh, shhhh, shhhh, shhhh.

JO

In a minute.
  (Cuddled; protected; content)
Am I heavy? No, of course I'm not heavy. What am I thinking of?

SAM

Shhhh, shhhh, shhhh.

JO

I think my sleepy pills are working. Shall I go to sleep right here? Can you
stand there all night?

SAM

You're not *that* light. I'll take you up.
  *(*HE *doesn't move, beyond kissing her neck)*
I'll take you to bed.

JO

  *(Giggles contentedly, interrupted by a sudden spasm of pain, a
  sharp intake of breath)*
Giddyap!

SAM

Hm?

JO

Gidd*yap!* I think you'd better get me upstairs right now. I need a couple
of more pills.

SAM
(Standing still, cuddling her)
Not sleepy enough?

JO
Oh, I'm plenty sleepy, but if I start in screaming . . .

SAM *(Galvanized)*
O.K.! O.K.! Right!
(HE *starts with her toward the stairs)*

JO *(Clearly in pain)*
Don't jiggle me! I think I'm all coming apart! Aaaaaaaaaaahhhhh-
HHHHHHH!!
(This is a cry of beginning and rapidly growing sudden pain)

SAM
(HE *starts up the stairs with her)*
O.K.! O.K.!
(JO *grabs at the banister, leaves* SAM's *arms.* HE *hovers above her)*

JO
AaaaaaahhhhHHHH!! Sweet Jesus!! AaaaaaaaHHHHHHHHH!!

SAM *(Helpless)*
Let me help you.

JO
AaaaaaannnnnnNNHHH!
(SHE *waves him off)*
In a minute.
(Very heavy breathing)
AAAAARRRRrrrrrrrrrrrrgggggggHHHHHH! God! God! God! Try to lift
me!
(SAM *tries)*
Haaannnnh!
(HE *has her on her feet again. This next through heavy breathing
and gulping)*
It's . . . been . . . easier to . . . get me . . . to bed . . . before.

SAM
(Gently taking her to the top of the stairs; soothing, crooning)
I'll take care of you now; I'll make you better; you'll see; I'll put you right
to bed, and take a cold cloth to your . . .

JO

(*A harsh laugh that is also a jolt of pain*)

Just . . . get me up there and lay me down. Haaaannhhh!

SAM

Sh, sh, sh. Easy, now; easy.

(THEY *vanish from the landing. Silence for a moment.*
JO *howls Offstage; then again, louder; then again, pathetic.
Silence again.*
ELIZABETH *and* OSCAR *enter the set from one side, from without
the set, in that order.* OSCAR *is dressed in a suit and tie;* ELIZA-
BETH *is dressed elegantly.* ELIZABETH *sees the audience, puts her
finger to her lips, lest* THEY *start commenting, or applauding, or
whatever*)

OSCAR

(*Looking about, with some distaste*)

You say this is the place?

ELIZABETH

(*To the audience, not urgent, not languid, but no nonsense*)

Is she alive? Are we here in time?

(*The sound of* JO'*s scream from upstairs; a brief silence, then
another scream*)

ELIZABETH

(*Still in the audience, her eyes acknowledging the sound with a
brief, upward movement of her head*)

Ah yes! Well, then; we *are* in time.

(*Turns her head slightly toward* OSCAR)

Yes; this is the place.

CURTAIN

ACT TWO

Morning. ELIZABETH *alone Onstage, looking out the bay window, maybe.* SAM *comes down the stairs, just awake, still in his sleeping gown;* HE *does not see* ELIZABETH; HE *sees the remains of the party's mess;* HE *takes a few more glasses, etc. As* HE *does this,* ELIZABETH *hears him, turns, sees him.* HE *sees her.*

ELIZABETH *(A smile; steady)*

Good morning.

SAM

(A long silence. Finally, not loud)

Who are *you?*

ELIZABETH

It was *late* last night; you'd already gone upstairs; there seemed no point in . . .

SAM

(Still not loud, but more persistent)

Who *are* you?

ELIZABETH

There seemed no point in calling you back down don't interrupt me, *please;* there seemed no point, from the . . . sound of it, so to speak. So, I did not, or, *we* did not, to be more accurate.

SAM

W-we!?

(Looks about swiftly, sees no one)

Who *are* you!?

ELIZABETH

Do you always leave your lights on? Glasses about? I straightened up for you a bit. If you have a fire going, do you . . . abandon it, and hope for the best? Civilizations have gone down that way, you know.

SAM *(Teeth clenched now)*

Who *are* you!?

ELIZABETH

Look at Russia! Carelessness; putting off; no other reason for the Bolsheviks. If the Czar and his boys had been a little quicker, a little more precise, Lenin wouldn't have had a chance. He'd have stayed in Zurich and taken a job teaching at some university.

SAM (Overly polite)

Who *are* you?

ELIZABETH

Probably would have gotten tenure—if they had tenure in those days. Don't you think it's ironic Karl Marx was a Jew?—the Soviets being so anti-Semitic, and all?

SAM

I don't believe he had Russia in mind. WHO ARE YOU!?

ELIZABETH

You don't believe he had . . . ! Is that so!
  (To the audience)
Of course! It was probably Germany he had in mind all along, and if it had worked out the way Marx and Engels had it planned we would have been spared both Hitler and Stalin. Good old Marx! Good old Engels!
  (Back to SAM*)*
Or, do you think we would have had Hitler and Stalin anyway, in some other guise—the "we-get-what-we-deserve-no-matter-what" theory? I'm of two minds.

SAM

  (Losing patience, but still understated)
Who are you?

ELIZABETH

Which is an odd phrase, is it not: "I'm of two minds."
  (A shift of tone to more serious, concerned)
It sounded pretty awful up there last night. The pain, I mean. It sounded . . . well, relentless.

SAM (Rage coming)

Who *are* you!?
  (To the audience)
Who *is* this woman?

ELIZABETH

You'll be on injections soon—*she* will be, rather. I hope you're prepared for all that—man into nurse; overseer; the diminishment. I hope you're prepared for all that.

SAM

  (To ELIZABETH*; threat deep in the throat)*
Who AAARRRRE you!?

ELIZABETH

(This speech to both SAM *and the audience)*

I remember someone, a lady who had been good to me, a lady much older than I, older than I am now and I was young; I remember there was no one else to do it all; it was on *me;* I didn't like any of it: injecting, swabbing, bathing, changing, holding close, holding her close to crush the pain out of her; picking her up—my God, no weight at all, a sack of dust—picking her up to take her to the window, so the roses and trees could get a look at her, I guess; and taking her back. "Where are you taking me," she said. "Where did you take me to, and where are you putting me?" Her eyes were open; she'd gone blind with it and I hadn't known. She hadn't said—or noticed.

(To SAM *alone now)*

I wonder who she was? Was she my mother? I hope you're prepared for it.

SAM *(Finally)*

WHO ARE YOU!!!???

ELIZABETH *(So calm)*

You're shouting. Who *am* I?

(To the audience)

The gentleman wants to know who I am.

(To SAM*)*

Well . . . who are *you?*

SAM

I'm Jo's husband; this is my house . . .

ELIZABETH

You'll wake her with your shouting. Is she still asleep? You'll wake her.

SAM

(A quick glance above; intense, whispered)

Dear, great God, woman, who are you!?

ELIZABETH

(Quietly amused by SAM's *phrasing)*

Dear, great God, woman, who am I?

*(*OSCAR *enters from the library)*

Oscar? Who am I?

(To SAM*)*

This is Oscar; Oscar and I are . . . together.

*(*SAM *swings around to face* OSCAR, *who bows his head slightly, smiles.* SAM *stiffens, takes a few steps back, to have* BOTH *of them in view)*

OSCAR *(To* SAM*)*

Good morning, young man.

(To ELIZABETH*)*

Who *are* you? Well, ooze my widda wubby cupcake, is what'ums *ooze* is.

ELIZABETH *(Laughs)*

Widda *wubby* cupcake? What's a wubby?

OSCAR *(Great dignity)*

A wubby? A wubby is an adjective.

(To SAM*)*

I said: Good morning, young man.

ELIZABETH *(Some disbelief)*

An adjective?

OSCAR *(To* SAM*)*

It was late last night; you'd already gone upstairs; there seemed no point in calling you back down.

(To ELIZABETH*)*

Yes; an adjective, as is widda; widda and wubby are both adjectives.

ELIZABETH

It *seems* . . . excessive.

SAM *(Quiet threat)*

I want you both out of here—whoever you are.

OSCAR *(To* SAM*; unintimidated)*

Do you always leave your lights on? Glasses about? If you have a fire going, do you . . . abandon it, and hope for the best?

ELIZABETH

We've *done* that. He pointed out, by the way, that Marx and Engels didn't have Russia in mind at all.

OSCAR *(Broad, to the audience)*

Well, everyone knows that.

ELIZABETH *(Quarrelsome)*

Not *every*one. I'm sure there are perfectly good people, walking upright and all, who have never heard of Marx and Engels—Engels certainly.

OSCAR *(To* ELIZABETH*)*

Impossible! A ridiculous idea!

SAM *(Flat)*

Carol.

OSCAR

Hm? Pardon?

SAM
Carol; she didn't know who Marx and Engels were.

ELIZABETH
There! You see!? A perfectly good person.

OSCAR
Who says!
(To the audience)
Who is this *Carol,* and what do we know of her? Is she to be trusted?
Would she *pretend* not to know who Marx and Engels were?
*(SAM is moving toward the telephone slowly, keeping his eyes on
them BOTH.
To ELIZABETH)*
Is she the sort of person who would get *pleasure* from appearing stupid?

ELIZABETH
Not Carol. Not if I know Carol.

OSCAR
Do you know Carol?

ELIZABETH *(Shrugs, giggles)*
I don't know. Show me Carol, and I'll tell you.
(SAM moves to the phone, begins dialing)

OSCAR *(To SAM)*
Who are you calling? The police? What will you tell them? What will you
tell them we are? Thieves? Murderers? Relatives come to call? House
inspectors? What?
(SAM hesitates, hangs up)

ELIZABETH
House inspectors?

SAM *(Curiously close to tears)*
Will you *please* leave?

OSCAR
You don't even know who we *are* and you want us to leave.
(To ELIZABETH)
House inspectors: that's the people who inspect houses.
(To SAM again)
Don't you want to know who we are?

SAM *(Explodes)*
No! No, I don't want to know who you are! I want you out of here! I want
you out of here now!

(Looks toward the ceiling, points)
Damn it! My wife is very ill . . .

OSCAR *(To* SAM*)*
Well, why else are we here?
(To the audience)
Oh, I suppose there could be other reasons: a ride in the car; a breath of
fresh air; a look at how the neighborhood's changed; the thrill of expecta-
tion—all that.

SAM *(Suspicious)*
You know Jo?

OSCAR *(To* SAM*)*
Why would we come here if we didn't *know* someone? What do you think
we are?

SAM *(Not to be put off)*
You know her? Tell me how you know her.

OSCAR *(To* SAM*)*
Look here; do you think we're house inspectors? Do we *look* like house
inspectors?
(No reply)
Well, maybe you don't know what house inspectors look like. They wear
hats; they carry cigars; they tend toward overweight; you can turn
their heads with a twenty, or a kiss. Why are you wearing that strange
garment?
*(*SAM *becomes aware of how* HE *is dressed)*

ELIZABETH
I rather like it.

SAM *(Iron)*
It's how I dress; it's how I dress for bed.

OSCAR
Ah, then you're going to bed.

SAM
I've *been* to bed.

OSCAR
Ahhhh. Then you've just gotten *up?*

SAM *(Irritated)*
Yes!

OSCAR *(To the audience)*
I've been up for hours; I rarely sleep.

ELIZABETH *(To the audience)*

I dozed; I watched the night die.

(Pause)

SAM *(Fairly assertive)*

Leave!

OSCAR *(To* SAM*)*

What did *you* do?

ELIZABETH *(To* SAM*)*

Did *you* sit up? We heard the cries, and then the silence. Did you sit up, and hold her hand until the drugs had done their work? Did you lie down beside her then, put off the light, and stare up into the dark? Where did you fall asleep? Where did you wake up? Hm?

SAM *(Softly)*

Please? Leave?

ELIZABETH *(As softly; comforting)*

No.

OSCAR *(Bright; after a pause)*

Since we are not house inspectors, nor have ever been, and, for that matter—though I speak for myself—cannot imagine being, then we are thieves, murderers, or . . . relatives come to call.

SAM

Please!

ELIZABETH

Be gentle, Oscar.

OSCAR

Are you very wealthy? If we are thieves, after all . . .

(Looks about. To the audience; wrinkles his nose)

"Comfortable," I should think, as the definitions go. Not much ostentation, but *still* . . . a little too obvious for "old money," wouldn't you say? No battered greatness.

(Back to SAM *now)*

Where are your animals? Very rich people always have livestock. No, you're comfortable, nothing more.

SAM *(Heavily sarcastic)*

Sorry!

OSCAR *(Spies a print on the wall)*

What is that!?

(Goes to it. To the audience)

My goodness; a Jaspar Johns!

    (To SAM *again)*

None of that Warhol shit for you, eh? Good taste! A nice print.

SAM

Take it!

OSCAR

What! A print!? Don't be silly.

SAM

Take whatever you want. Take the stereo; take the television; there are *three* of them, take 'em all!

ELIZABETH

Why?

SAM

Pardon?

ELIZABETH

Why are there three TVs? There aren't enough programs for one. What happened, did they just . . . accumulate?

SAM *(Shrill)*

I'm not going to apologize for having three TV sets! Get out of my house!

OSCAR *(To* SAM*)*

She wasn't suggesting you should; be calm. We don't *want* your gadgets; next you'll offer us a microwave oven, or a Cuisinart. Your stereo and all that stuff are for junkies and for punks. *Look* at us; we don't even want your nice little Jaspar Johns. We're not *thieves.* Are you relieved?

SAM

    (Very unpleasant; an edge of threat)

No!

ELIZABETH

Nobody would offer a Cuisinart to a pair of thieves—punks *or* junkies; you're being outré.

OSCAR *(To* ELIZABETH*)*

Well, if I were a *thief,* that would be something I would *know.*

    (To SAM*)*

Which proves what I said—that we are not . . . thieves.

SAM

WHAT *ARE YOU!?*

OSCAR

Well, from the original list that leaves murderers and relatives come to call.

ELIZABETH

Not necessarily a happy choice—though I don't know your circle.

SAM

WHAT THE FUCK DO I HAVE TO DO TO GET YOU OUT OF HERE!!??

(*A silence*)

OSCAR (*Quietly*)

Guess who we are, for beginners. And you're so close.

SAM (*Sits; rather defeated*)

All right; who *are* you? Who *are* you?

OSCAR (*Going to him; gentle*)

We are not murderers, nor are we thieves . . .

ELIZABETH

Nor are we house inspectors . . .

OSCAR (*The end of a fairy tale*)

Then we are relatives, come to call.

SAM (*Weary*)

You're relatives; good. You're . . .

(*Looks at* OSCAR)

. . . no, you're not! You're not a relative at all!

OSCAR

Oh?

SAM (*Gestures*)

Well . . . *look* at you.

(ELIZABETH *chuckles throughout*)

OSCAR

Look at me? Am I dressed oddly? Do my clothes offend?

SAM

(*Knows what's being done, but can't fight it*)

No.

OSCAR

Am I too tall?

SAM

No.

OSCAR

Too *short*.

SAM

No; no.

OSCAR

Am I too old?

SAM

No.

OSCAR (*Feigning confusion*)

Too young?

SAM

No, of course not.

OSCAR

Too thin, then.

SAM

No!

OSCAR

Too fat?

SAM

NO!

OSCAR

Is it my way of speaking? Am I too . . . refined?

SAM

NO!

OSCAR

Am I . . . too rich?

SAM

How would I know?

OSCAR

Too poor?

SAM

How would I *know!*?

OSCAR

Well, it *is* a puzzle. What could it *be?* Could it . . . oh, my goodness, I think I have it! Is it . . .

 (HE *leans over and whispers in* SAM's *ear*)

SAM (*Listens, nods*)

Yup; that's it; you got it.

OSCAR

(To ELIZABETH; *mock distress)*

It's that I'm . . .

(Stage whisper)

Too black.

ELIZABETH *(Absurd!)*

Too what! Too black!?

OSCAR

It would appear so.

SAM

No offense.

OSCAR

Given or taken?

(To ELIZABETH*)*

It would appear so. Too black. What did Mister Blake say? . . . But I am black, as if bereav'd of light."

(Hamming)

"And, I am black, but, oh, my soul is white!" Some shit like that.

SAM

I said: no offense.

OSCAR *(Suddenly friendly)*

And none taken, white boy; none taken. Well, now, if I am too black to be a relative—though there's a nigger in many a woodpile, and don't you forget it!—then *I* must be a *friend*. Perhaps Elizabeth here is a relative.

SAM *(Almost a mumble)*

Well, I'm sure Jo will be very happy to see you.

ELIZABETH *(To* SAM; *arch)*

Was that sarcasm?

(To OSCAR*)*

Oscar, did that sound like sarcasm to you, to your black ears?

SAM *(Weary)*

It was not sarcasm.

OSCAR

It sounded like it to me.

(Smiles unpleasantly. To the audience)

But then, so much does.

SAM *(Frustration, fatigue)*

It was *not* sarcasm; I'm very *tired*; I sat *up*; I'm sure Jo will be very happy to *see* you. God! Let it *go!*

OSCAR *(Rather cheerful; to* SAM*)*

Be nice to this lady; she has come a distance.

SAM

(Trying to be conversational)

What, uh . . . what kind of relative . . . uh, *are* you?

ELIZABETH

(Surprised, but gracious)

Why . . . I'm Jo's mother.

(Considerable pause)

SAM

(As if HE *hadn't heard properly)*

Pardon?

ELIZABETH *(Patient)*

I'm Jo's mother.

OSCAR

(To SAM*, when* HE *fails to respond)*

Her *mother!* Jo's *mother!*

*(*SAM *begins to laugh, quietly, shaking his head; the laughter is close to crying.*

To SAM*)*

Is that the laughter to keep from crying?

(To ELIZABETH*; chipper)*

Do you think that's the laughter to keep from crying?

SAM *(A heavy sigh)*

O.K., gang; out! Whoever you are . . . get out.

ELIZABETH *(Rather harsh)*

I'm Jo's mother, come from Dubuque!

OSCAR

The Lady from Dubuque; this is the lady from Dubuque; Jo's mother!

ELIZABETH *(A hand up)*

Never mind, Oscar.

OSCAR *(To* SAM*)*

Jo's mother; from Dubuque. What's the *matter* with you!? *Kiss* her!

SAM *(Anger through the fatigue)*

You are *not* Jo's mother.

(To the audience)

She is *not* Jo's mother.

(*To* ELIZABETH *and* OSCAR)
JESUS CHRIST, HAVE SOME COMPASSION, WILL YOU!?

OSCAR

(*Very offhand; to the audience*)
I wonder why he's resisting?

ELIZABETH (*Sighs; rises*)
I wonder why we're *talking?* Clearly it's no use. It's time I went upstairs.

SAM

(*Frightened, but standing his ground*)
You're both crazy; both of you, you're crazy.

ELIZABETH

(*Dismissing him with a little gesture*)
Oh . . . fiddlesticks! Oscar, will you stay down here with this young man?

SAM

YOU STAY AWAY FROM JO!!

ELIZABETH (*Amused*)
Stay away from her? Not let her hug me? Where do you think she learned
it all? Do you think she put her arms around nobody before *you?* What
gall! We all have antecedents, and we all can be replaced. Keep that in
mind.

SAM

You stay away from her!

ELIZABETH

Why don't you be a good boy and go in the kitchen now and make us all a
hearty breakfast?

OSCAR

(*Wringing his hands; smacking his lips*)
Corn pone, grits . . .

ELIZABETH

A Sunday breakfast! Steaming pots of coffee, rolls, and eggs, and slabs of
ham. Jo used to love that, back on the farm.

SAM (*Contemptuous*)
You were never on a farm in your life.

OSCAR (*Almost to himself*)
Iowa *is* farm country.

SAM

(*To the audience; desperate*)
Jo's mother lives in New Jersey!

ELIZABETH

(After SHE *and* OSCAR BOTH *hoot)*

New Jersey!? Do you mean this person you're trying to pass off as Jo's mother comes from . . . New Jersey?

SAM

What are *you* . . . some kind of *comic?*

ELIZABETH *(Suddenly very sober)*

No; very serious, and very concerned. Will I find the bedroom to the right?

*(*SHE *starts toward the stairs;* SAM *moves to a blocking position)*

SAM

You stay where you are.

ELIZABETH *(Stone)*

I have come home for my daughter's dying. Get out of my way.

SAM *(An almost-whispered litany)*

You are not Jo's mother, you have never been on a farm, Jo was not raised on a farm, you are not from Dubuque; you are not a relative and this black man is not a friend.

ELIZABETH

This black man here, who is probably very rapidly becoming what you say—*not* a friend—is wise and quick and shockingly strong.

OSCAR *(Smiles)*

Imperial Japanese Army; World War Two.

ELIZABETH

I think he will help me if I need him.

OSCAR *(Mock ecstatic)*

Oh, Elizabeth! Anything!

SAM *(Kind of punchy)*

You were *not* in the Japanese Army in World War Two.

OSCAR *(To the audience)*

I wonder where I learned my love for uncooked fish?

ELIZABETH

Not to mention your command of the martial arts.

(To SAM, *with a charming smile)*

He'll have you unconscious just like that.

OSCAR

(Bows in the Japanese manner; to SAM*)*

Ohayoo gozaimasu. Ogenki desuka?

(SAM *doesn't respond*)

Do shimashita ka?

(*To* ELIZABETH)

What's the matter with *him*?

ELIZABETH (*Shrugs*)

He doesn't know Japanese; he's lost face.

(*To* SAM)

Don't fret; it's not a required language yet. Just like that! Unconscious, flat on your back. *So*-o, if you will let me pass . . .

(SAM *blocks the stairway;* OSCAR *moves slightly;* SAM *includes him in his defense posture—arms angled in front, hands as barriers, eyes flickering from* ONE *to the* OTHER)

SAM (*Steel*)

Stay away from me, you crazy people!

OSCAR

(*Karate pose; to* SAM)

HIIIIIIIIIYYYYYEEEEAAAAAHHH!!!

SAM

Oh, my *God!*

ELIZABETH (*Purring*)

Would you care to negotiate, young man?

SAM

(*Not taking his eyes off* OSCAR)

Would I care to . . . would I *what?*

ELIZABETH

You have a woman upstairs. You *say* she is your wife; *I* say she is my daughter. Surely we can negotiate this.

OSCAR (*A sinister echo*)

Surely you can negotiate this.

SAM (*Quietly; to* ELIZABETH)

Who *are* you? *Really?*

ELIZABETH (*Gentle*)

Who are *you? Really?*

(*A long silence;* SAM *looks at them* BOTH)

SAM (*Finally; very calm*)

I'll go upstairs, and I'll talk to Jo. I'll wake her if she's asleep, and I'll tell her what's been happening; she won't believe me, but I'll tell her.

ELIZABETH

Bring her down.

SAM *(Adamant)*

I'll *tell* her.

ELIZABETH *(Harder)*

You'll bring her down; that's our negotiation. Negotiation's over; I'll call off
the dogs.

(SHE *turns her back on* SAM)

OSCAR *(Quite amused)*

You'll call off the *what?*

ELIZABETH *(Laughs)*

Oh, hush!

SAM

If she says she'll come—if she believes what I tell her and she says she'll
come—maybe you'll be gone. You aren't really here, are you? I'll come
back down and you'll be gone?

OSCAR

Gone?

ELIZABETH *(A harsh laugh)*

Oh, *we* exist. Worry about your*self.*

SAM

(Starts backing up the stairs)

I exist; *you* don't.

ELIZABETH *(Lazy)*

Well, we'll see.

(Amused)

Oh! While you're up there . . . *do* change out of that silly getup.

SAM *(Near tears)*

It's how I dress; it's how I dress for bed!

(HE *hesitates, then rushes up the stairs and Offstage)*

ELIZABETH *(Convulsed)*

It's how I dress!

(To the audience)

It's how I dress for bed!

(THEY BOTH *laugh greatly;* ELIZABETH *holds her hands out, palms
upward;* OSCAR *slaps them in an exaggerated imitation of street
blacks. Their backs are to the entry hallway)*

OSCAR *(To* ELIZABETH*; sober)*

He doubts you.
   (To the audience)
He doubts her.

ELIZABETH *(To* OSCAR*; to herself)*

I know.
   (To the audience)
How can he doubt me? How can he doubt me?
   (LUCINDA *and* EDGAR *enter from the hallway,* LUCINDA *leading the way)*

LUCINDA *(With enthusiasm)*

Surprise! Surprise! Sur . . .
   (SHE *sees* ELIZABETH *and* OSCAR, *finishes it, deflated and cautious)*
. . . prise; surprise.

EDGAR

Well . . .

LUCINDA *(To* ELIZABETH*)*

Good . . . good morning.

ELIZABETH *(A grand hostess)*

Good morning; I'm Jo's mother . . . and you must be . . . ?

LUCINDA

   (Nonplussed; self-conscious)
Jo's . . . what? Jo's mother?
   (Fairly faint)
I'm Lucinda and this is Edgar.

OSCAR *(Uncomfortable)*

Hi.

ELIZABETH *(Grand)*

How do you do? This is Oscar.
   (OSCAR *bows)*
Oscar is black.

LUCINDA

I noticed.

EDGAR

Yes; so did I.
   (More formal)
Where's Sam? Where's Jo?

ELIZABETH
(Rather offhand, if final)
They are . . . upstairs.

EDGAR *(Puzzled)*
Thank you.

LUCINDA
(Nervously, to fill the gap)
So. You're Jo's mother.

ELIZABETH
Yes; I am.

LUCINDA
I never would have guessed! I mean . . . you're not at all what I imagined.

ELIZABETH
Oh?

LUCINDA
We've never had the pleasure, of course—you're something of a recluse; a famous name in these parts, but nothing more.

ELIZABETH
Oh?

LUCINDA
(Not helped by ELIZABETH*)*
You . . . you live with your *sister* now.

ELIZABETH
I . . . move about all the time.

LUCINDA *(Confused)*
Oh?

ELIZABETH *(A short laugh)*
Well! One may *be* from Dubuque . . .

OSCAR
Iowa; Dubuque, Iowa.

LUCINDA
Du . . . buque?

ELIZABETH
But certainly one *roams:* Dubuque is not everything.

LUCINDA *(Puzzled)*
Sam says you live with your sister, couple of hours from here.

(With an uncomfortable look at OSCAR*)*
With your older sister; you two sort of . . . look out for one another.

ELIZABETH *(Laughs)*
Sam says that?
(To OSCAR*)*
What can Sam mean?

LUCINDA *(To* EDGAR; *uncertainly)*
I'm sure that's what we've been told?

OSCAR
Sam's a joker all right.

LUCINDA *(Quite puzzled)*
You never go out; you stay in.
(Nudges EDGAR*)*
Edgar! Help me!
(A nervous laugh)
And you're very tiny, and terribly thin.

ELIZABETH *(Crystal laughter)*
You must have me confused with someone else—a great aunt, perhaps. I have my Christmas in Switzerland, though, to be completely candid with you, I spent *one* December in Peru.

LUCINDA
Pe . . . ru?

OSCAR *(Helpful)*
The country.

LUCINDA
And . . . and you have pink hair.

ELIZABETH *(Greatly amused)*
Pink hair!? On purpose?!
(To the audience)
Pink hair!?

OSCAR
Clearly you have Elizabeth confused in your mind with someone else—some defective or eccentric somewhere, some embarrassment your friends are taking care to see is . . .

LUCINDA *(Close to hysteria)*
Well, I must be mistaken! Edgar? Jo's mother is clearly not a recluse; I mean . . . *look* at her: she does not have pink hair, nor is she tiny.

EDGAR

No.

OSCAR (*Mollifying*)

She's not . . . gigantic, of course.

LUCINDA

No! We can *see* that!

OSCAR

She is what you might refer to as a normal-size mother.

LUCINDA

Yes! Yes! Still . . .

EDGAR

Oh, come on, Lucinda! For Christ's sake!

LUCINDA

(*Making ineffectual little slaps at* EDGAR)

Don't *be* that way to me! Give me one good reason why Sam, or *Jo—Jo*, for heaven's sake—give me one good reason why Jo would pretend her mother is a tiny, pink-haired recluse, living—

ELIZABETH

BECAUSE!!

(*Silence; attention is paid. Quietly; to end the matter*)

Because . . . there are things you would not be expected to understand.

(*A long silence*)

EDGAR (*Finally*)

Right.

LUCINDA

Oh.

(*Pause*)

All right; if you say so.

(*To save it*)

Besides, I knew it wasn't true from the beginning—New Jersey, pink hair, and all!

EDGAR

(*To* LUCINDA*; humoring her*)

You get everything so mixed up! Can't put one over on you, eh Lu?

(LUCINDA *starts to reply, but* FRED *and* CAROL *appear in the hall-way*)

FRED

(Just as HE *comes into view,* CAROL *following)*
Hey? Anybody up?

OSCAR *(To the audience)*
My gracious! It *is* a party!

FRED
Anybody . . .

EDGAR
Fred! For Christ's sake!

FRED *(Takes it all in)*
. . . hey, what's all this!

ELIZABETH
(Still the grand hostess)
Good morning! I'm Jo's mother, and you must be . . . ?

FRED *(Some urgency; to* EDGAR*)*
Where's Sam? Where's Jo?

EDGAR
It's O.K. They're upstairs.

FRED *(To* LUCINDA *and* EDGAR*)*
What the hell are you two doing here?

CAROL
(Peering at ELIZABETH *and* OSCAR*)*
We in the right house, Fred?

FRED
(Not really unpleasant; preoccupied)
Shut up, Carol.

ELIZABETH
How do you do!—whoever you may be.

CAROL
I don't think we're in the right house, Fred.

FRED *(To* EDGAR*)*
What the hell are you two *doing* here?

EDGAR
Lucinda wanted to make it up with Jo . . . for last night . . . out on the lawn.

FRED
Oh.

ELIZABETH

And you?

(*To the audience*)

Don't these people answer questions?

FRED

Hunh?

ELIZABETH (*Too precise; to* FRED)

And . . . you! To what do we owe the pleasure? Are you friends of my daughter as well?

CAROL (*To* FRED; *sotto voce*)

Is that Jo's *mother?*

FRED

Shut up, Carol.

(*To* ELIZABETH)

Well, Carol here and I, we decided to get married—you know, what the hell!—and so we wanted to tell Sam and Jo, and . . .

ELIZABETH

Well, well; congratulations.

EDGAR

How *about* that! Hey!

CAROL (*Shrugging twice*)

You know: what the hell!

LUCINDA

(*Badly disguised distaste*)

Oh; you two are getting married; how wonderful.

FRED

Ah, fuck off, Lucinda.

LUCINDA (*Defend me!*)

Edgar?

EDGAR

Do what Fred says, hunh?

(*To* FRED *and* CAROL)

That's swell, kids; that is just swell.

OSCAR (*To the audience*)

I haven't heard "swell" in a very long time. Can you remember when you last heard "swell"?

ELIZABETH (*To* FRED *and* CAROL)
This is Oscar. Oscar is black.

FRED (*None too pleasant*)
I noticed. How come your friend is black?

ELIZABETH
How come he's what?

FRED
Black.

ELIZABETH
Black!?
(*To* OSCAR)
How come you're black?

OSCAR
Because my mammy and my pappy was black.

CAROL (*A smile*)
Fred's a redneck.

ELIZABETH (*To* CAROL)
Isn't that nice?
(*To* FRED)
Have you been one long?

FRED (*A cold smile*)
It comes and goes.

OSCAR
(*To the audience; quite chummy*)
I met a foreign lady once—Belgian, I think—nice lady, very solicitous, kept asking me questions about something she insisted was called the Ku-Ku-Klan. Nice lady.
(*To* FRED; *very pleasant*)
Are you a member of the Ku-Ku-Klan?

FRED (*Tight smile*)
What do you want to bet?

CAROL
Aw, come on! Fred's a pussycat.
(OSCAR *laughs, unpleasantly.*
A silence)

LUCINDA
Jo's mother here has come all the way from Dubuque to pay Jo a visit, Jo being sick and all . . .

FRED

Dubuque?

ELIZABETH

I am from Dubuque; I am the lady from Dubuque.
(Specifically to EDGAR*)*
Though I have not just come from there. I was in . . . uh . . .
(Clearly SHE*'s improvising)*
St. Paul de Vence, on my way from Paris down to . . .

OSCAR *(Right in)*

Rome; Rome, Italy.

ELIZABETH

Thank you.
(To the OTHERS*)*
I do not . . . summer in Dubuque.

CAROL *(An aside, to* FRED*)*

Who is this *person?*

LUCINDA *(Effusive)*

Jo's mother is not at all what we had been led to believe.

ELIZABETH *(To* FRED *and* CAROL*)*

Tiny, pink-haired, reclusive, living on the dole somewhere with a sister.

LUCINDA

No; well; you *see!* Not at all what we'd imagined. The idea of Sam leading us on like that . . .

CAROL *(Merely curious)*

Are those pearls real?

ELIZABETH

Real what?

CAROL *(Hostile)*

Real pearl!

FRED

Shut up, Carol.

CAROL

(Quite angry, but not loud)
Don't tell me to shut up all the time. You want me to marry you? Just come off it about shut up all the time. We aren't married *yet,* so *watch* it!

ELIZABETH *(Gracious)*

I don't know; they were given me; but I've no reason to assume they're other than that which they pretend to be.

(SAM *has appeared at the top of the stairs;* HE *has changed into a shirt and trousers)*

SAM

Unlike some people I could mention.

FRED

Hey! Sam!

(SAM *slowly descends the stairs)*

LUCINDA *(Nervous; sing-song)*

You're having a *party*! You may not have *known* it, but you're having a *party*! Fred and Carol are getting—

FRED

Hey, Sam, you hear about Carol and me? We're getting married.

EDGAR

Morning, Sam.

ELIZABETH

I've been entertaining your friends; they're charming, absolutely charming. Oscar and I have been enthralled.

CAROL *(Sheepish)*

Hi, Sam.

LUCINDA

We've gotten to know Jo's mother here. We were so surprised; we came in, more or less on tiptoe, and . . .

FRED

Carol and I are getting married, Sam.

(SAM *is at the bottom of the stairs now.* HE *has not taken his eyes off* ELIZABETH *the entire journey down.* HE *stops in front of her)*

OSCAR *(To* ELIZABETH; *cooing)*

See how he loves you already; he can't take his eye off of you.

FRED

Sam? You O.K.?

EDGAR

Sam?

OSCAR *(To the audience)*

See how he stares at her! See the intensity of his gaze! *This* is passion!

FRED *(Concerned)*

Sam?

SAM

(Waves them off; to ELIZABETH, *precise, quiet, formal, controlled)*
I spoke to Jo; I told her . . . you two had arrived; I told her who you said
you were.

ELIZABETH

And?

SAM

She's getting up; she's coming down; and that will be the end of it.

LUCINDA *(To* EDGAR *and* CAROL*)*
I don't understand what's going on!

EDGAR

Sam? You O.K.?

SAM

It's . . .
(Bravura; slightly hysterical)
. . . it's all right, folks, it's . . . all . . . just wonderful. This . . . this lady here
and her—and this one—the two of them were waiting for me when
I came downstairs this morning. *This* one—this lady here—says she's
Jo's *mother.* I don't know who *this* one thinks *he* is. *I* say she's *not* Jo's
mother.

FRED *(Laughs)*

Oh, come on, now!

SAM

No, now! Don't laugh!

FRED *(Harsh laugh)*
Nobody pretends to be somebody's *mother!*

SAM

(Contained, but the hysteria is underneath)
I know! Nobody pretends to be somebody's mother!
(Still the hysteria underneath; to FRED, CAROL, EDGAR, LUCINDA,
and the audience)
THIS IS NOT JO'S MOTHER!

FRED *(To* SAM; *sighs)*
O.K., Sam, what are you doing—playing some kind of game? Didn't you
have enough last night? What kind of game are you *playing?*

SAM

(*To* FRED; *sputtering; exploding*)
Am *I* playing! What kind of game am *I* playing!?

FRED

You got a sick wife upstairs, her mother comes home—with a friend, or
something—and all you can do is make jokes?

SAM (*Beside himself*)
All I can do is . . . ? THIS IS NOT JO'S *MOTHER!!*

FRED

Of course it's Jo's mother! Who the hell else is it!?

SAM (*About to burst*)
I don't know! I don't *know* who it is!

FRED

(*Weary of it, dismissing* SAM)
Oh, for God's sake!

SAM

I DON'T KNOW WHO IT *IS!*
(*A silence*)

LUCINDA (*Brisk; slaps her knees*)
Well! Who's for a good pot of coffee?

FRED

Fuck that! Let's open the bar.
(HE *moves toward the bar*)

SAM (*Fury*)

NOBODY!!
(*Pause*)
NOBODY!!

OSCAR

(*Into a silence; to the audience*)
Well, I suppose that's natural—a man who would deny his wife's own
mother could not be expected to provide his friends with a cup of coffee
or a drink.

SAM

(*Turns to* OSCAR, *fist cocked*)
Look, you fucker!

OSCAR

(*To* SAM; *loud, authoritative*)
I warn you!

(SAM *hesitates;* OSCAR *assumes a karate pose)*
I warn you; I have my black belt.

(*An aside, to* ELIZABETH)
Which should come as no surprise.

(OSCAR *holds out his palm;* ELIZABETH *slaps it, in an exaggerated imitation of street blacks)*

SAM

(*Turns away in disgust and defeat)*
Ah, for Christ's sake!

CAROL (*To* SAM)
Your mother-in-law's quite a card; so's her friend there.

(*To* ELIZABETH *and* OSCAR)
You're quite a pair.

ELIZABETH (*Queen Elizabeth)*
Thank you, *thank* you.

SAM (*Weary; ironic)*
You're quite a pair, too, Carol, but she isn't my mother-in-law.

LUCINDA (*Dismissing him)*
Oh, really, Sam.

SAM (*Hopeless)*
She's *not.*

FRED

Bullshit!

SAM (*To* CAROL)
You really gonna marry that sonofabitch?

CAROL

(*Argumentative, if not enthusiastic)*
He'll *do!*

SAM

Which says as much about you as it does about him! Congratulations to you both!

FRED (*Quietly; to* SAM)
Fuck yourself; and no kidding. Just go fuck yourself.

ELIZABETH (*Amused; above it all)*
Bicker, bicker! This is not the *time* for it.

SAM (*To* ELIZABETH; *enraged)*
You! You shut up!

FRED *(Disgust)*

Look, this is a nice lady you're talking to.

SAM

(Loud; looking down at the floor)

SHUT UP! SHUT UP! SHUT UP!

(JO appears at the top of the stairs. Suddenly shaken and in tears, pathetic)

Please! Please! All of you! Shut . . . up! Just . . . shut . . . up. Please!

(A silence)

OSCAR *(To the audience)*

The view from above, to the pit below.

ELIZABETH *(Gentle, deferential)*

The man has asked for silence; give it to him.

OSCAR

(Hands out, fingers wide; still to the audience)

Let there be silence; shhhhhhhhhhh.

JO *(Tentative)*

Sam?

SAM *(A whisper)*

Jo?

(All eyes go to JO. ELIZABETH moves slightly so that SHE is near the foot of the stairs)

JO

(As SAM makes to move toward her)

No; I'll make it down; don't anyone move.

(SHE begins her descent, her eyes on ELIZABETH. Halfway down SHE gasps in pain, nearly crumbles)

SAM

JO!

JO *(Straightening again; smiling)*

No one *help* me.

(JO completes her descent, save two steps; her eyes are still on ELIZABETH; SHE stops where SHE is)

ELIZABETH *(Gentle; a smile)*

Good morning.

JO

(After a pause; quiet, noncommittal)

Good morning.

OSCAR

(To ELIZABETH, *his eyes on* JO)

You never told me how lovely she was—so pure, so fragile: scented air.

SAM

These are the two who have come, Jo This is the woman claims to be your mother. Tell her, Jo tell her you don't know her.

ELIZABETH *(Gentle)*

Good morning.

SAM

Tell her she has no right to come into our house and pretend to be what she is not.

(JO *has a spasm of pain;* SHE *moans)*

LUCINDA *(True grief)*

Oh, Jo!

OSCAR

Take her in your arms, Elizabeth; ease her; hold her close.

SAM *(To* OSCAR)

YOU STAY OUT OF THIS!!

(JO *grimaces; a cry escapes her)*

ELIZABETH

Come to me.

SAM *(Through his teeth)*

You stay away from her!

JO *(Looks at* SAM; *quietly)*

Sam?

SAM *(Begging)*

Tell her, Jo. Tell her we don't know her.

(JO's *eyes return to* ELIZABETH)

ELIZABETH

Come to me, now. It's time to hold you close, to rock you in my arms.

JO *(Timid)*

Rock me?

ELIZABETH *(Soothing)*

Hold you, rock you, take you to my breast.

SAM

NO!

ELIZABETH *(A litany)*

Come, let me stroke your forehead, comb your hair, wash you, lay you down and tell you stories . . .

SAM

JO! NO!

ELIZABETH

Protect you from the dark and from the thunder?

JO *(A little girl)*

Protect me?

SAM

NO!

ELIZABETH *(Smiles)*

From the dark and from the thunder.

JO

Make it better?

SAM *(Agony)*

Oh, Jo!

ELIZABETH *(So tender, gentle)*

Make it better? What have I come for? Come to me.

SAM *(A howl of pain)*

NOOOOOoooooooOOOOOO!

(Finally, with tears and a great helpless smile, JO *rushes into* ELIZABETH's *arms; their embrace is almost a tableau, so involved is it with pressing together)*

ELIZABETH *(To the audience)*

And they wonder who I am.

SAM *(To his* FRIENDS*)*

No! NO! That is not Jo's mother! Believe me! BELIEVE ME!!

(But THEY *have either turned away, are looking away in embarrassment, or are regarding* SAM *with sadness)*

NO! NO!

*(*HE *looks about and sees it is hopeless, but* HE *persists, in rage and tears)*

NO!

(Pause)

NO!

(Pause)

NO!

OSCAR *(Quietly; gently)*

Oh, yes. Yesyesyesyes. Oh, yes.

SAM

(Fully in tears; quietly, desperate; to the audience)

Believe me; this is not Jo's mother.

OSCAR

(Quiet victory statement, to SAM*)*

Oh yes she is.

SAM

(In a final attempt to reverse the situation; to ELIZABETH*)*

NO!!

> *(*SAM *lunges at* ELIZABETH, *to wrest* JO *from her. As quick as lightning,* OSCAR *intercedes)*

OSCAR *(Grappling with* SAM*)*

I said . . . YES!

> *(To* FRED *and* EDGAR*)*

Help me with him!

> *(*JO *cries out in pain.*
>
> FRED *and* EDGAR *come to help.*
>
> SAM *and* OSCAR: *overlapping)*

SAM

No! No!

OSCAR

Yes, I said!

SAM

No! Jo!

OSCAR

Hold him for me. Hold him.

> *(*FRED *and* EDGAR *each grab one of* SAM's *arms.* OSCAR *touches* SAM *on the neck and* HE *is instantly unconscious)*

OSCAR

Ease him down.

> *(*SAM, *unconscious, slips to the floor)*

EDGAR

How did you do that?

> *(*FRED *ties* SAM's *hands behind him with his belt)*

OSCAR

There is a nerve there, in the neck; a little pressure in the proper spot . . .
and all the woes are gone, the troubles slip away . . . and peace descends.
Off you go, to the dreap and deemless.

EDGAR

Will he be all right?

OSCAR

He'll be all right. I can wake him . . .
(Finger snap)
. . . just like that.

FRED *(Having tied* SAM *up)*

I tied him up.

OSCAR

You did!? So you did. Those are splendid knots. Really first rate. He must
be *very* grateful to you.

FRED

Bastard hates me.

OSCAR *(Mollifying)*

Weeeellll, you've tied him up very nicely, nonetheless. A regular package.

FRED *(None too pleasant)*

That's not a bad idea: *mail* him somewhere.

OSCAR *(Bright idea!)*

We could send him to New Jersey! He could visit those mysterious ladies.

LUCINDA *(Amused)*

It would serve him right—hitting away like that!

EDGAR

(To ELIZABETH; *truly puzzled)*
God, the way he just . . . went at you.

LUCINDA

I've never seen such a thing! Really!
(To ELIZABETH)
Weren't you scared?

ELIZABETH *(Rather startled)*

Scared!? Why, no.

FRED

He was afraid to go after . . .
(Gestures)
. . . this one here.

EDGAR

Well, with good reason!
(*To* OSCAR)
Where did you learn all that . . .
(*Imitates* OSCAR's *judo*)
. . . all that . . . ?

OSCAR

Foreign Legion.

EDGAR

You were in the Foreign . . . ? No.

OSCAR (*Shrugs*)

All right.
(*To the audience*)
Then I *wasn't* in the Foreign Legion. *I* don't care.

JO (*A spasm alerts her*)

What's happening? What's . . .

ELIZABETH (*Soothes*)

Shhhhhh; shhhhhhhh; nothing.
(JO *becomes comatose again*)

FRED (*Regards* SAM)

I think he looks good this way. Perfect packaging.

CAROL (*Snorts; shakes her head*)

Hunh!

FRED

What's the matter with *you?*

CAROL

Sooner or later you're going to have to untie him, you know.

FRED

Yeah? So?

CAROL (*Shrugs*)

Sooner or later you're going to have to untie him; or Jo's going to get with
it, and you're going to have to let him go.

FRED

SO!?

CAROL

So . . . *then* you're going to have to explain why you tied him up!

FRED *(Exasperated)*
I tied him up . . . you saw why I tied him up!

LUCINDA *(After a crystal laugh)*
Really, Carol!

EDGAR *(Puzzled)*
Who should we have tied up, Jo's mother here?

CAROL *(A small smile)*
Who?

JO *(An echo)*
Who?

ELIZABETH *(A bit loud)*
Tied *me* up!? Why me?
(To the audience)
Why would anyone tie *me* up?

OSCAR *(Generally)*
Perhaps she meant *me*.
(To the audience)
People are always tying coons up for one reason or another, though less
these days than . . .
(smiles)
. . . times of yore?

CAROL
(Speculative; not giving an inch)
Well, it *could* be because I'm crazy . . .

FRED
Yeah! It could be because you're crazy!

CAROL *(Dubious)*
Yeah; could be; or it could be because I'm an outsider . . .

FRED
So why don't you shut up?!

CAROL *(Pursuing her logic)*
Or maybe it isn't either one; maybe it's just a feeling. Why are you all in
such a rush? Why doesn't anybody believe *Sam?*

LUCINDA *(Laughs)*
Oh, really, Carol!

FRED *(Furious)*
For Christ's sake, why don't you just . . . go into the kitchen and make some
coffee, or something!? Why don't you do something useful around here?

CAROL

What am *I!?* Some sort of a colored maid, or something?
(*To* OSCAR)
No offense.

OSCAR (*To* CAROL; *smooth*)

Oh, none taken!

FRED (*As* CAROL *doesn't move*)

Will you get your ass in there!?

CAROL

O.K.! O.K.! For Christ's sake!
(SHE *sweeps out, muttering*)

FRED

Good girl, Carol; just gotta goose her a little bit.

OSCAR (*To the audience*)

And I haven't heard *that* word, *either,* in a coon's age.

FRED (*Eyes narrowing a little*)

What word? Girl?

LUCINDA (*Slaps her knees, rises*)

I'll make toast; I'll make buttered toast.

ELIZABETH (*To* LUCINDA)

That will be heaven.
(LUCINDA *smiles, exits*)
Won't that be heaven, Oscar?

OSCAR

(*Considers it; to* ELIZABETH)
Well, it will be *toast.*

FRED (*At the bar again*)

You drinking, Edgar?

EDGAR

No thanks, Fred; not this early.

FRED

(*Pretending to be offended*)
Oh, I see; well; pardon *me.*

EDGAR

(*For fear of having offended*)
Of course. I'm not getting married.

FRED

Oh? Why not?

EDGAR

Because I'm already . . . I just don't want a drink, Fred.

FRED (*To* ELIZABETH *and* OSCAR)

I don't suppose either of you drinks in the morning, either.

OSCAR

No, no.

ELIZABETH

Certainly not.

FRED

(*Moves over to* SAM, *contemplates him*)

You want a drink, Sambo? A little Scotch with a straw? Sniff it, maybe?
    (*To* EDGAR)
Sambo doesn't seem to answer.

EDGAR (*Glum*)

Well, maybe *he's* not getting married, *either.*

FRED (*Cheerful*)

Well, *I* am. Fuck ya all!
    (*Toasts*)

JO (*Dreamy*)

Who's getting married?

ELIZABETH

Fred is; Fred's getting married.

FRED (*Loud*)

I'm marrying Carol, Jo.

JO (*Thinks, shakes her head*)

Terrible idea.
    (*Subsides.*
    LUCINDA *appears in the hallway, spoons in hand*)

LUCINDA

Edgar! Come help with the tray! Don't be a bump!
    (SHE *revanishes*)

EDGAR (*Fairly weary; rises*)

O.K. O.K.

ELIZABETH

A what? A bump?

EDGAR *(Exiting)*

As in on a log; a bump on a log; I shouldn't be a bump on a log.

OSCAR

(In the small silence as EDGAR *exits; to the audience)*

Quaint.

JO

(To ELIZABETH; *in confidence)*

I've told Fred a dozen times; I've been subtle, but I've told him—"Don't marry Carol."

ELIZABETH

Shhhh, shhh, shhh.

JO

And I've told Carol—"Don't marry Fred." Maybe nobody ever heard me; maybe nobody listens. I hurt.

ELIZABETH

Let me hold you.

JO

Fred is a terrible person.

ELIZABETH

(Smiles, to FRED, *shrugs)*

Shhh; let me hold you.

JO

He is . . .

*(*SHE *smiles at her phrasing)*

. . . unworthy of human solicitude.

(Gasps)

I really *hurt.*

FRED *(Slams his drink down)*

I gotta go take a dump!

*(*HE *starts out)*

ELIZABETH *(Calm)*

Do you say that to offend us?

FRED *(Daring her)*

What!?

ELIZABETH
(Will not be drawn in; smiles)
Or is it anger? Has Jo made you angry, and are you going to punish us all?
Are you a showoff, or a boor, or is Jo right on the mark, and are you . . .
"unworthy of human solicitude"?

FRED
I'm just plain dirt common; ask Jo.
(HE exits)

OSCAR
Well, he is nothing if not honest, eh?
(OSCAR wanders)
Are you happy with the decor?

ELIZABETH *(Casual)*
I would do something else about the carpet, I think, or put rugs down.
How's the library?

OSCAR
Very masculine—heavy leather, dark woods. What would you expect? Oh!
The TV set has doors, which close; they match the other wood.

ELIZABETH *(Delighted; giggles)*
It doesn't! They don't!
(To JO)
Oh, Jo! You are a *good* girl!

JO *(Vague)*
What have I *done?*

ELIZABETH
You're a good wife. You make a beautiful home.
(CAROL enters)

OSCAR
Very good, "Mother," very good.

ELIZABETH
Do be a help.

OSCAR
What more can I *do?* I am civil to people I cannot abide, I function as an
encyclopedia . . .

CAROL
You knock people out.

OSCAR *(Recovering nicely)*

I knock people out.

ELIZABETH *(Bright)*

My goodness, aren't you quick! Coffee all made?

CAROL

Too many cooks. Where's Fred?

ELIZABETH

(Hesitates just a split second)
I can't bring myself to tell you.

CAROL *(Shrugs)*

He can't be far: I'm still here.

OSCAR *(HE smiles, too)*

You hold yourself in high regard.

CAROL *(Matter-of-fact)*

No: accurate regard. I'm not your dumb brunette for nothing.
(Laughs)
Do you know I'm a natural blonde? I dye it brunette 'cause I look cheap as a blonde? I look cheap natural?

ELIZABETH *(Delighted)*

You don't! Are you really!?
(To the audience)
Isn't that extraordinary!?

CAROL *(To get JO's attention)*

Jo!?

ELIZABETH *(Protective; to CAROL)*

Hsshhh! Don't bother her!

CAROL

JO!?

JO

(Stirs, looks vaguely about to see who's calling her)
Hm? What?

CAROL *(Louder)*

JO!?

JO *(Focusing on CAROL)*

What . . . what's happened?

CAROL *(Points at* SAM*)*

Take a look over there; take a look at Sam.

JO

(Looks over at SAM *for quite a long time; turns to* ELIZABETH; *sort of dreamy)*

Why is . . . why is Sambo all . . . asleep?

ELIZABETH *(Sweet)*

So he'll be nice; he wasn't being nice.

JO

(Almost interested; sort of sad)

What happened?

ELIZABETH

(A look at CAROL; *to* JO, *a secret)*

He wasn't happy with the way things are. He wanted everything back the way it never was.

JO

That's not nice.

ELIZABETH

No; it isn't.

CAROL *(Eyes to heaven)*

Jesus!

JO *(Sort of lost)*

I don't understand.

ELIZABETH

(Pulls JO *to her, head to lap)*

You rest now.

CAROL *(Matter-of-fact)*

Sooner or later you're going to have to wake him up.

ELIZABETH *(Laughs)*

Well, of course!

OSCAR

Certainly you don't imagine we've thought of this as a . . . final solution.

CAROL *(No nonsense)*

Who *are* you?

ELIZABETH *(Grand)*

I beg your pardon?

CAROL

You can come off it for me; I don't count; I'm an outsider. Who are you, *really?*

ELIZABETH

(Observing CAROL carefully)

Oscar, the natural blonde is suspicious.

OSCAR

I noticed.

CAROL

Sam says . . .

ELIZABETH

Sam says! Sam says!

OSCAR

What does Sam know?

(To the audience)

What does Sam know? Sam only knows what *Sam* needs.

CAROL

Sam has rights, you know.

OSCAR (To CAROL)

And what about what Jo needs? What does what Sam needs have to do with that?

CAROL (Dogmatic, if uncertain)

Things are either true or they're not.

OSCAR

Oh? Really?

(To the audience)

Really?

(FRED enters)

FRED (To CAROL)

What'd they do: throw you outta the kitchen?

CAROL (Curiously angered)

Where the fuck have you been?

FRED

(Prissy and overarticulating)

Powdering my nose.

CAROL

Whyn't ya untie Sam?

FRED (*To* OSCAR)

You gonna keep him like this all day? Whyn't you wake him up?

OSCAR

Really?
  (*To* ELIZABETH)
Shall I?

ELIZABETH

Try. See what happens.

OSCAR (*Shrugs*)

All right.
  (HE *wakes* SAM *up*)
Voilà!

SAM

  (*At once; as loud as possible*)
HELP!? HELP!? HELP!? HELP!?
  (*Etc., until* OSCAR's *slaps—below—stop him*)

FRED

Jesus!

OSCAR

  (*To* FRED)
You see? I told you.
  (*To* SAM, *slapping*)
Now! . . . you! . . . stop! . . . that!
  (SAM *gasps, sobs a bit, subsides*)

FRED (*Shakes his head*)

Jesus!

SAM

Help me? Someone?

OSCAR

Behave yourself!

SAM (*Softly; in his throat*)

Someone? Help me?

JO (*An echo*)

Help me; help me.

SAM

Carol, can you . . . ?

FRED (*Unpleasant*)

Carol isn't here to *help you.* Keep your hands off him, Carol.

JO (*As above*)

Help me; help me.

SAM

Fred? Please?

CAROL (*To* SAM; *kind*)

Fred isn't here to help you either. I don't think *any*one is.

(LUCINDA *and* EDGAR *reenter,* LUCINDA *leading the way;* THEY *have trays—cups, plates, coffee, toast, marmalade, etc.*)

LUCINDA

My gracious, what yelling! What's going *on*?!

EDGAR (*Slightly embarrassed*)

Coffee; coffee, everyone.

LUCINDA

What's going on!!?

SAM (*Softly*)

Help me? Help me, please?

EDGAR (*Puts his tray down*)

Hey, Sam; hey, boy!

SAM

God, Edgar, help me?

LUCINDA (*To the audience*)

What's going *on*!?

EDGAR

(*To* OSCAR; *to* FRED; *to them* ALL)

You gonna untie him now?

OSCAR

We woke him and how did he repay us: he shrieked to raise the very dead.

ELIZABETH (*Softly*)

The very dead; who hear nothing; who remember nothing; who are nothing.

EDGAR

Was that Sam?

LUCINDA

(*Still to the audience; delighted*)

Was that Sam? Was all that yelling Sam?

CAROL

Getting off on it, Lu?

LUCINDA *(To* CAROL*)*

Pardon?

SAM

Edgar!? Help me!

LUCINDA

Leave Edgar alone; *you* don't love Edgar; you don't love anyone.

EDGAR *(More sad than sarcastic)*

Oh, he loves me, Lu: I'm the only man he knows does something good and he wants to hit; I am his only friend whose every virtue embarrasses him.

SAM

Oh, God, Edgar!

LUCINDA

We don't forget, Sam; we forgive, but we don't forget.

OSCAR *(To* SAM; *cheerful)*

I like your friends.
    (To the audience)
I like his friends.

CAROL *(Matter-of-fact)*

I'll untie him; I don't know him; I'm not his friend; I'll untie him.

FRED

Keep your fucking hands off him.

CAROL

'Cause I'm not his friend?

LUCINDA

It's getting cold. Who will have what? I know about you, Edgar.

EDGAR *(Offhand)*

I don't want any.

LUCINDA *(Pours for him)*

Don't be silly.

FRED

I'm a lush, Lu; don't give *me* any coffee.

LUCINDA *(Furious)*

You *asked* for coffee! You yelled at Carol!

FRED
(Waving LUCINDA *off; dismissing her)*
I wanted her out of the room; I wanted her to shut up; fuck your coffee.
(Afterthought)
Fuck *you,* for that matter.

LUCINDA *(Defend me!)*
Edgar?

ELIZABETH
(Half to break into the argument)
I will have mine with white sugar and real cream; and if that stuff is instant
take it all back into the kitchen and pour it down the drain.

SAM *(Intense; a supplication)*
The coffee is not instant, the sugar is white and the cream is real, I have
no friends, please let me go.

CAROL
If you're a lush, why should I marry you?

FRED *(Another dismissing wave)*
You'll marry worse. I'm not so bad.

OSCAR
(To ELIZABETH *and generally; taking* ELIZABETH *her coffee and toast)*
"The coffee is not instant, the sugar is white and the cream is real." Here
you are, my dear. "I have no friends, please let me go." Really!

ELIZABETH
Thank you. You spilled! You sloppy man!

OSCAR *(Indicates* LUCINDA*)*
She spilled; I wouldn't spill.

LUCINDA *(Enraged)*
I didn't spill! I *never* spill! *You* spilled!

OSCAR *(A calming tone)*
Very *well;* you didn't spill; no one spilled; there has been no . . . spillage.
Spillage?

ELIZABETH *(Shrugs)*
Why not?

SAM
Please? Untie me? Let me go?

LUCINDA
Carol? Cream and sugar?

CAROL *(Her attention on* SAM, *etc.)*

Nah; I don't want your coffee.

LUCINDA *(A little laugh)*

It is not . . . *my coffee.*

EDGAR *(An edge to his voice)*

No one *wants* it, Lu!

OSCAR *(Dusts his palms)*

I'm going up.

(HE *moves toward the stairway)*

SAM *(Helpless suspicion)*

Where are you going!?

OSCAR

Up.

SAM

Don't *go* up there!

OSCAR

There's no one upstairs. What can you possibly mind?

SAM

(Enraged by both the constraint and the action)

DON'T GO UP THERE!!

EDGAR *(Mild; rational)*

Why are you going up there?

OSCAR

(Considers it as HE *takes a few more steps up; smiles)*

Because I've never *been.*

SAM *(Trying to break loose)*

YOU HAVE NO RIGHT!!

JO *(Vague)*

Who? Who has no what?

CAROL *(Softly; to* OSCAR)

You *don't* have any right, you know.

OSCAR *(To* ELIZABETH; *laughs)*

Tell them. Tell them all. Give them a reading about rights.

(Starts up again; to audience)

Christ, these people!

(HE *disappears into the upstairs hallway)*

CAROL *(Shrugs)*

No right at all.

FRED

What are *you* going to be, a troublemaker?

CAROL *(A gentle dismissal)*

Annnnh, go back to your boozing; don't worry about me; I'll fit in; it'll just take a while.

SAM

(To himself; head down, shaking it)

No right; no right at all.

ELIZABETH

(Putting down her cup; to SAM; *rational)*

These . . . these rights; these rights people do not have.

SAM *(Slowly meeting her eyes)*

Yes?

LUCINDA *(An aside, to* EDGAR)

Did he really say that to you? That he wanted to hit you?

EDGAR

Shhhhhhh.

ELIZABETH

(Pleased that SAM *is meeting her eyes)*

Are these rights rights *no* one has . . . or, merely some?

LUCINDA *(As above)*

What's she talking about?

EDGAR

SHHHHHHH! Jesus!

SAM

Merely some.

ELIZABETH

Aha! Then, there are rights which *you* possess . . .

SAM

In this *house!*

ELIZABETH

. . . which are yours alone!

SAM

In this house!

ELIZABETH *(Smooth)*

Good; then we are not talking about the rights we pretend we give ourselves in this bewildered land of ours—life, liberty, and the pursuit of the
unattainable—though we *may* be learning our limits—finally—here in the
. . . last of the democracies. Or just about.

LUCINDA *(Offended)*

The *last!*

ELIZABETH

Oh . . . probably; we're too moral to survive. A *real* Bush will come along
one day, if the Russians don't.

LUCINDA *(Disgusted)*

You're a cynic!

ELIZABETH *(Truly bewildered)*

Am I!? Dear God!

SAM

I have my *own* rights! My own personal rights! Jo! Pay attention to me!

ELIZABETH

Have you? What—this house? Jo? Surely you don't mean property—noth-
ing as crass as that. Is it dignity you have in mind?
   (To the audience)
I had a dog named Dignity once—or, that was her name when I got her; I
changed it; I called her Jane. She's dead.
   (To SAM*)*
Is it Jane you have in mind? Is it dignity?

SAM

Jo!? Please!

ELIZABETH

It is *not* Jane you have in mind; it is Jo.

JO *(Vague)*

Me?

ELIZABETH

Back on the farm, when I was growing up, back on the farm in the outskirts of Dubuque . . .

SAM *(So weary)*

You did not grow up on a farm; you did not grow up on the outskirts of—

ELIZABETH

Will you let me finish the story!?

FRED
(Pointing at him with his glass; not nice)
Sam, you shut up and let her talk.

SAM

Get out of my house.

EDGAR

Take it easy, Sam.

SAM

Get out of my house! *Both* of you! *All* of you! *All* of you get out!

JO *(Far away)*
Did you want something, Sam?

ELIZABETH *(Patient)*
Back on the farm, in the outskirts of Dubuque . . .

SAM *(At the top of his lungs)*
OUT?! OUT?! OUT?! OUT?!
(Etc. During this, FRED puts his drink down, walks over to SAM, punches him hard in the stomach; SAM doubles over as best HE can; gasps)

FRED *(To SAM)*
You don't throw people out of *any*where, you superior bastard. We'll leave when we're finished.
(Pause; generally)
I'm finished.
(HE turns to go; to CAROL)
You coming?

CAROL *(A sneer)*
Why'n't you wait around and see if you killed him?

EDGAR

Christ, Fred.

FRED
(Of SAM; to CAROL; oddly enraged)
Look at him! *He's* alive! *Look* at him!
(Indeed, SAM is gasping)

EDGAR

Sam?

FRED
YOU COMING!? I SAID I'M GOING. YOU COMING!?

CAROL *(Pause; calm)*

I think I'll have a cup of coffee before I go. Lucinda, I think I'll have a cup of coffee after all.

(FRED *moves to the coffee service, sweeps it to the floor*)

JO *(Faint; at the sound)*

Oh; oh.

FRED

There's no more coffee.

(Between his teeth)

You coming?

CAROL

I'll stay for a little; I'll help clean up the mess.

FRED *(Pause; cold)*

I'll wait for you in the car.

CAROL *(Nods)*

O.K. And if you're not there when I come out I'll go on over to the apartment; and if you're not there . . .

(Shrugs)

. . . well, I'll just marry somebody else.

FRED *(Pause; equivocal)*

I'll wait in the car.

(HE *turns; exits.*

A pause. LUCINDA *goes to the floor, begins to clean up*)

EDGAR

(To CAROL*; gentle with disbelief)*

You gonna marry that man?

CAROL

(Looks at him; no emotion)

You think of any reason why I shouldn't?

EDGAR

(As CAROL *moves to help* LUCINDA*; thinks)*

No, no, I guess not.

LUCINDA *(Loss)*

All the pretty cups and saucers.

CAROL *(To* EDGAR*)*

I didn't think so.

(*To* LUCINDA)

Hey, here's one isn't broken . . . Yes, it is.

EDGAR

You O.K., Sam?

SAM

Sure, Edgar. My wife is dying; I am invaded; I am abandoned by my friends. But you really don't care how I am, Edgar; you didn't raise a finger.

LUCINDA

Don't you have at Edgar that way!

EDGAR (*Quietly raging*)

I *asked* if I could help. Remember? You said no, no one could help. Remember?

SAM (*Mocking*)

Sure, sure, Edgar.

EDGAR (*Awe and disgust*)

My God, Sam; you don't *want* any help.

SAM

Well, not from you, Edgar; not from you.

EDGAR

(*Rises abruptly, moves to the window seat for his coat*)

Come on, Lu.

LUCINDA

(*Still with her broken crockery*)

But, Edgar, I'm just . . .

EDGAR

COME *ON*! If you think I'm going to stay and go through this!

CAROL

You two going? Did we hit an iceberg?

EDGAR (*Quivering with rage*)

You staying? You wanna watch? O.K. You stay!

CAROL (*Shrugs*)

G'by, rats.

LUCINDA

Don't you talk to Edgar that way!

CAROL *(Moves away from them)*

I was talking to *both* of you.

EDGAR *(To* SAM*)*

We came over here to *forgive* you!

SAM *(Shakes his head; gently)*

It doesn't matter, Edgar.

EDGAR *(Quivering with rage)*

How *dare* you let this happen to you!

LUCINDA *(Realizing it)*

That's right! We came to forgive you!

SAM *(To stop the exchange)*

It's all right; it doesn't matter.

EDGAR

How *dare* you let this happen! I'm not *here* anymore, Sam.

LUCINDA *(Suddenly in tears)*

I never want to come here again! I never want to come to this house again!
　(She runs out)

EDGAR

I'm not *here* anymore, Sam.

SAM *(Pause; accepting)*

O.K., Edgar.

EDGAR *(Sudden contained emotion)*

I'm not here, God damn you!
　*(*EDGAR *backs into the hall, turns, exits)*

CAROL

Three down and only me to go.

ELIZABETH

Aren't you bright! Why are you marrying that awful man?

CAROL

It's the *least* I can do.

ELIZABETH

You don't have to.

CAROL

I don't? Why don't I? He's on his way downhill; he's a barrel of laughs; he's a lush; he's a great fuck; I'm not doing anything else this week; I'm not twenty-two anymore, and I'm scared? Take your choice; they're all true.

ELIZABETH

(This and the following both to the audience and generally to SAM *and* CAROL)

In the outskirts of Dubuque, on the farm, when I was growing up—back there, back then—I learned, with all the pigs and chickens and the endless sameness everywhere you looked, or thought, back there I learned— though I doubt I knew I was learning it—that all of the values were rela- tive save one . . . "Who am I?" All the rest is semantics— liberty, dignity, possession.

(SHE *leans forward; only to* SAM *now)*

There's only one that matters: "Who *am* I?"

SAM *(Simple)*

I don't *know* who I am.

ELIZABETH

Then how can you possibly know who I am?

(OSCAR *appears on the balcony, dressed in* SAM's *nightshirt, noth- ing else.* HE *poses)*

OSCAR *(To the* GROUP)

Do I look well? Does it suit me?

(CAROL *giggles)*

ELIZABETH

(Claps HER *hands together in delight)*

Oscar! You are a dream!

JO *(Looks up)*

Sam? Is that you?

SAM *(Pain)*

Oh, Jo! Don't!

OSCAR *(To* CAROL)

Don't you think I make a splendid Sam?

JO

Sam? Is that you?

SAM

Jo? Please don't?

OSCAR *(Arms wide; beatific)*

Am I not . . . am I, indeed, not Sam?

(To the audience)

Am I not Sam?

CAROL

I'm going to untie him.

OSCAR

It's on your shoulders, pretty lady; you open the package, you take the present.

CAROL

That's O.K. by me; I'm not a friend.
   (SHE *unties* SAM)
Who the fuck tied these knots?

OSCAR

Duh menfolk; dey tied him up; dem's duh ones.

SAM

Jo?

JO

Sam?

CAROL

You *wanna* be untied, don't you?

SAM

Sure.

CAROL

It's the least I can do.

SAM

Don't go.

CAROL

Everyone else has gone.

SAM

Yes!

CAROL *(Shrugs)*

What do you want me to do?

SAM *(Lost little boy)*

Make Jo better? Make them go away?
   (OSCAR *shakes his head;* ELIZABETH *laughs gently)*

CAROL *(To* SAM; *gentle)*

Jo thinks she's better. They make her think so.

SAM *(Chilling knowledge)*

Is that what matters?

CAROL

Ask Jo.

SAM

(One final time; but soft, lost)
Please? That's not Jo's mother?

CAROL

(After a long pause; totally noncommittal)
Right. I mean . . . who's to say?
(To the audience)
Who's to say?

ELIZABETH

(Rises, moves toward CAROL*)*
You're a very special lady.

CAROL *(A rueful laugh)*

You're pretty special yourself.
(Looks up at OSCAR*; ironic)*
You're not so bad, either.
*(*SHE *looks once more at* SAM*; exits)*

OSCAR *(Waves)*

Bye-bye; bye-bye.

SAM *(Soft)*

Don't go.

JO *(An echo)*

Bye-bye; bye-bye.
(A silence. Finally, SAM *rushes from his chair, over to* JO. ELIZABETH *gestures* OSCAR *not to interrupt.* SAM *kneels by* JO*, grabs her by the shoulders, shakes her. We see that* SHE *is rubber.* OSCAR *watches from his position on the stairs.* ELIZABETH *stays where* SHE *was standing with* CAROL*)*

SAM

(Tears; choking; loss; fury; tenderness)
Do you want this? Hunh?
(Shakes her)
Is this what you want!? Yes!?

ELIZABETH *(Level; gentle)*

Of course she wants it. Just . . . let her go.

SAM (*Shakes her*)

Because if this is what you want, I'm not any part of it; you've locked me out. I . . . I don't exist. I . . . I don't exist. Just . . . just *tell* me.

(JO *manages to look at him, puts her hands to his face, cups it*)

JO (*Explaining; gently*)

Please . . . just let me die?

(SAM *pulls away, stares at her, wracked with sobs. To the audience; explaining*)

Just let me die . . . please?

(*Here her explanation begins to become pain*)

PLEASE? . . .

(*This time the word is prolonged as long as possible; it is urged out by pain; it is filled with gasps; to no one, to everyone. Now* SHE *grasps her belly in short spasms of pain*)

Anhhh! Anhhh! ANHHHHH!

(OSCAR *comes down the stairs to her*)

OSCAR

All right; all right, now.

(SAM *watches the following without moving from his position; his sobs continue, though*)

JO

Aaaaaaaaaaaannnnnnnhhhh! Sweet Jesus! Aaaaaaaaaaaannnnnnnhhhhhhhh!

OSCAR

(*Scooping her into his arms*)

Let me help you.

SAM

Jo!

JO

(*Through her gasps; to* OSCAR)

Just . . . get . . . me . . . up . . . stairs.

SAM

Jo?

OSCAR

(*As* HE *carries her upstairs; soothing, crooning*)

I'll take care of you now; I'll make you better; you'll see; I'll put you right to bed; I'll make you better . . .

JO

Just get me . . . AAAANNNNHHHHHHH!

OSCAR

(As HE *carries her Offstage*)

Shhhh, shhhh, shhhh; easy, now; easy.

(*A howl from Offstage; another*)

ELIZABETH

(*Moves to a chair; gently*)

She's dying, you see.

SAM (*Sobs under; shivering*)

I'm dying.

ELIZABETH

Oh, no; not yet. You don't know what it *is*.

(*A softer howl from upstairs;* ELIZABETH *laughs abruptly; then smiles*)

I had a dream once about dying. Shall I tell it to you?

SAM (*Shivering*)

No.

ELIZABETH

All right: I dreamt I was on a beach at sunset—with friends; we had a driftwood fire, I believe.

SAM

I don't want to know.

ELIZABETH

(*Begins to share this with the audience, too*)

There were seagulls in the distance, and there was the sound of the surf—but muted, for it was sunset.

SAM

I don't want to know.

ELIZABETH

And all at once . . . it became incredibly quiet; the waves stopped, and the gulls hung there in the air.

SAM

No? Please?

ELIZABETH

Such silence. And then it began; the eastern horizon was lighted by an explosion, hundreds of miles away—no sound! And then another, to the west—no sound! And within seconds they were everywhere, always at a great distance—the flash of light, and silence.

SAM

Please?

ELIZABETH

We knew what we were watching, and there was no time to be afraid. The silence was . . . beautiful as the silent bombs went off. Perhaps we were already dead; perhaps that was why there was no sound.

(*A silence*)

SAM (*A shivering little boy*)

That was . . . that was the end of the world.

ELIZABETH

(*A pause; comforting; to* SAM, *now*)

I thought that's what we were talking about.

(*To the audience*)

Isn't that what we were talking about?

(OSCAR *appears in the upstairs hallway, dressed in his own clothes. To* OSCAR)

Is it all right?

OSCAR (*Looks down at them*)

Yes; it's all right.

(*Indicates*)

And that one?

ELIZABETH

He's better; calmer.

SAM (*Still the little boy*)

It *is* true, isn't it? What you told me?

ELIZABETH (*Dreamy*)

No sound? No time to be afraid? Everything done before you know it?

SAM

Yes. It is true?

ELIZABETH

Everything is true.

OSCAR

(*Descending. Quietly; to* ELIZABETH; *to* SAM)

Therefore, nothing is true.

ELIZABETH *(Looks up at him)*

Therefore, everything is true.
(SHE *smiles*)

OSCAR

(Descending. HE *smiles; an endearment)*
Oh, Elizabeth.
(A silence)

SAM

And Jo?

ELIZABETH *(Tiny pause)*

Don't worry about Jo.

OSCAR

We can go now.

ELIZABETH

(Vaguely, momentarily surprised)
What? Yes, of course we can.
(SHE *stands*)

SAM

No time to be afraid?

ELIZABETH

No! No time!

SAM *(More insistent)*

No time to be afraid!?

ELIZABETH

No! No time! Everything done before you know it.

SAM

. . . Before I know it.

ELIZABETH

Everything done.

OSCAR

(Faintly contemptuous, to the audience)
Nothing is retained; nothing. Come.

ELIZABETH

All right.

SAM

(Finally; timid; to ELIZABETH*)*
Who are you? Really?

ELIZABETH

(Looks at him for a moment)

Why, I'm the lady from Dubuque. I thought you knew.

(To the audience)

I thought he knew.

CURTAIN

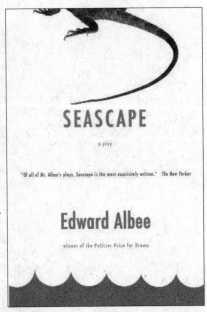

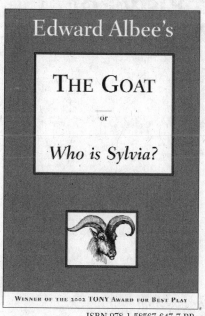

Edward Albee's

THE GOAT

or

Who is Sylvia?

WINNER OF THE 2002 TONY AWARD FOR BEST PLAY

ISBN 978-1-58567-647-7 PB

"Unquestionably one of the wittiest and funniest plays Albee has ever written . . . a truly fascinating play . . . enthralling."
—CLIVE BARNES, *New York Post*

"Endlessly disturbing and surprising . . . Albee's play, revealed here to be among his very finest, proves the point: It is a deeply painful experience, but like all great art, it leaves you feeling more alive."
—CHARLES ISHERWOOD, *Variety*

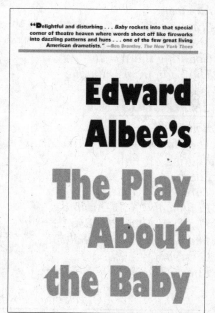

"Delightful and disturbing . . . *Baby* rockets into that special corner of theatre heaven where words shoot off like fireworks into dazzling patterns and hues . . . one of the few great living American dramatists." —Ben Brantley, *The New York Times*

Edward Albee's The Play About the Baby

ISBN 978-1-58567-511-1 PB